THE CAR
BOOK

THE CAR BOOK

THE DEFINITIVE VISUAL HISTORY

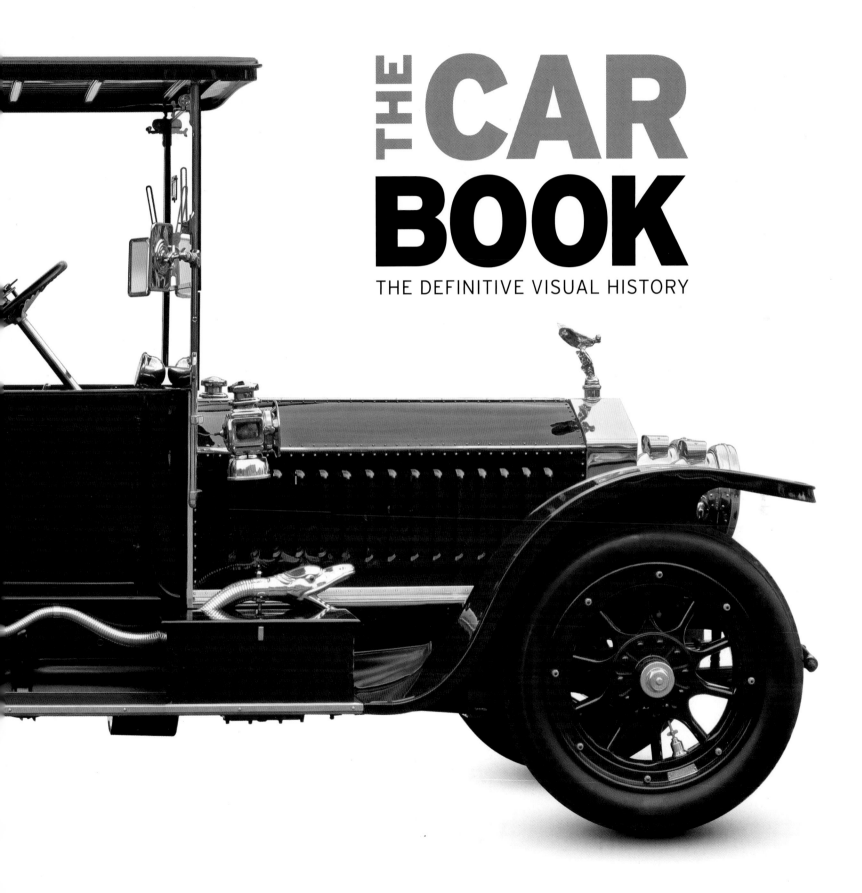

LONDON, NEW YORK, MELBOURNE, MUNICH, AND DELHI

DORLING KINDERSLEY

Senior Project Editor Kathryn Hennessy

Senior Art Editor Helen Spencer

Editors Steve Setford, Andrew Szudek, Manisha Majithia, Scarlett O'Hara

Designers Mark Lloyd, Anna Hall, Amy Orsborne, Paul Drislane, Richard Horsford, Philip Fitzgerald

Photographers James Mann Gary Ombler, Paul Self, Deepak Aggarwal

Picture Researchers Ria Jones, Julia Harris-Voss, Jenny Faithfull, Nic Dean, Myriam Mégharbi

DK Picture Library Claire Bowers, Emma Shepherd, Laura Evans

Database Peter Cook, David Roberts

Jacket Designer Mark Cavanagh

Production Editors Ben Marcus, Jamie McNeill

Production Controller Linda Dare

Managing Editor Camilla Hallinan

Managing Art Editor Karen Self

Art Director Phil Ormerod

Associate Publisher Liz Wheeler

Reference Publisher Jonathan Metcalf

DK INDIA

Editorial Manager Rohan Sinha

Senior Editor Ankush Saikia

Editor Sreshtha Bhattacharya

Assistant Editor Megha Gupta

Design Manager Arunesh Talapatra

Senior Designers Tannishtha Chakraborty, Sudakshina Basu

Designers Shomik Chakraborty, Devan Das, Arijit Ganguly, Niyati Gosain, Payal Rosalind Malik, Nidhi Mehra, Anjana Nair, Pallavi Narain, Neha Sharma, Shruti Singh Soharia

Production Manager Pankaj Sharma

DTP Manager Balwant Singh

Senior DTP Designers Dheeraj Arora, Jagtar Singh

DTP Designers Nand Kishor Acharya, Neeraj Bhatia, Jaypal Singh Chauhan, Arjinder Singh, Bimlesh Tiwary, Mohd. Usman, Tanveer Abbas Zaidi

Editor-in-chief Giles Chapman

Contributors Charles Armstrong-Wilson, Richard Heseltine, Keith Howard, Phil Hunt, Malcolm McKay, Andrew Noakes, Jon Presnell

This edition published in 2012
First published in Great Britain in 2011 by
Dorling Kindersley Limited,
80 Strand, London WC2R 0RL
Penguin Group (UK)

Discover more at
www.dk.com

Contents

FIRST AUTOMOBILES UP TO 1920

The concept of personal transport with its own mobile power source took off with Karl Benz's motorwagen in 1885. Within a generation, the car had arrived and could take you anywhere. When Henry Ford took his "Tin Lizzie" to the masses in 1908, America's automobile industry had come of age.

THE 1920s

This was a golden age for the car industry. The ritziest automobiles became status symbols for Hollywood stars, while smaller cars brought reliable, affordable motoring to their public for the very first time. Meanwhile, sports cars turned driving into an exhilarating pursuit, on roads and race tracks alike.

THE 1930s

In the shadow of the Great Depression, thrifty models and the advent of the "people's car" made motoring ever more egalitarian. Streamlining and teardrops were all the rage, newspapers hailed the superheroes who smashed speed records, and sports and luxury cars reached new peaks of power and style.

THE 1940s

World War II brought car production to a halt, but when peacetime returned and factories were rebuilt, the legacy of military technologies resulted in an explosion of excellent new engines, practical, no-frills pick-ups, and economical small cars that sold in their thousands.

THE 1950s

In the postwar boom US carmakers highlighted speed, luxury, and power by harnessing aerospace lines and chrome-plated decoration, with breathtaking (and sometimes absurd) results. In Europe fabulous sports cars and racing machines stirred the soul, and bubble cars bounced on to city streets.

THE 1960s

This was the age of anything goes. With new engines and body shapes, and a galaxy of all-time greats, from E-type to Elan, and Mini Cooper to Corvette Sting Ray, it was excitement all the way.

THE 1970s

If the 60s was the car party, the 70s was its morning after, with the fuel crisis and the first inklings that soaring car use required tighter controls. But cars also became better to drive: mid-mounted engines boosted responsiveness, turbochargers added bite, and automatic seatbelts and airbags gave assurance.

THE 1980s

With the rise of the Japanese car industry, this decade saw three car-making continents compete head to head. Cars became safer, more comfortable, and better equipped with improved electronic systems. There was still plenty of excitement too, as designers – led by the Italians – transformed family cars and supercars.

THE 1990s

Consumers demanded safety, luxury, performance, and perfect build – and got them all. Excellence in manufacture was satisfied; now imaginative design could shine. A new epoch in sports cars and executive saloons was matched by rapidly evolving and increasingly user-friendly genres such as the SUV and MPVs.

2000 ONWARDS

Crossover cars have blurred traditional genres by combining off-road ability, passenger accommodation, and performance. Hybrids are helping save fuel and cut emissions, while the latest supercars make 200mph (322km/h) seem ordinary. What next? Enthusiasts are hoping driving will still be the one thing it has always been – fun.

Car dates: The date given for each catalogue entry refers to the year that the model was first released. In some cases the accompanying photograph shows a later edition of the model, in these cases the year of the later edition is mentioned in the caption. **Engines:** A single engine size has been given for each catalogue entry. For models that have a range of engine sizes, the most powerful engine is given for fast cars, and the most common engine for family cars. Engine sizes can be converted to cubic inches (cu in) by multiplying the cubic centimetres (cc) figure by 0.061.

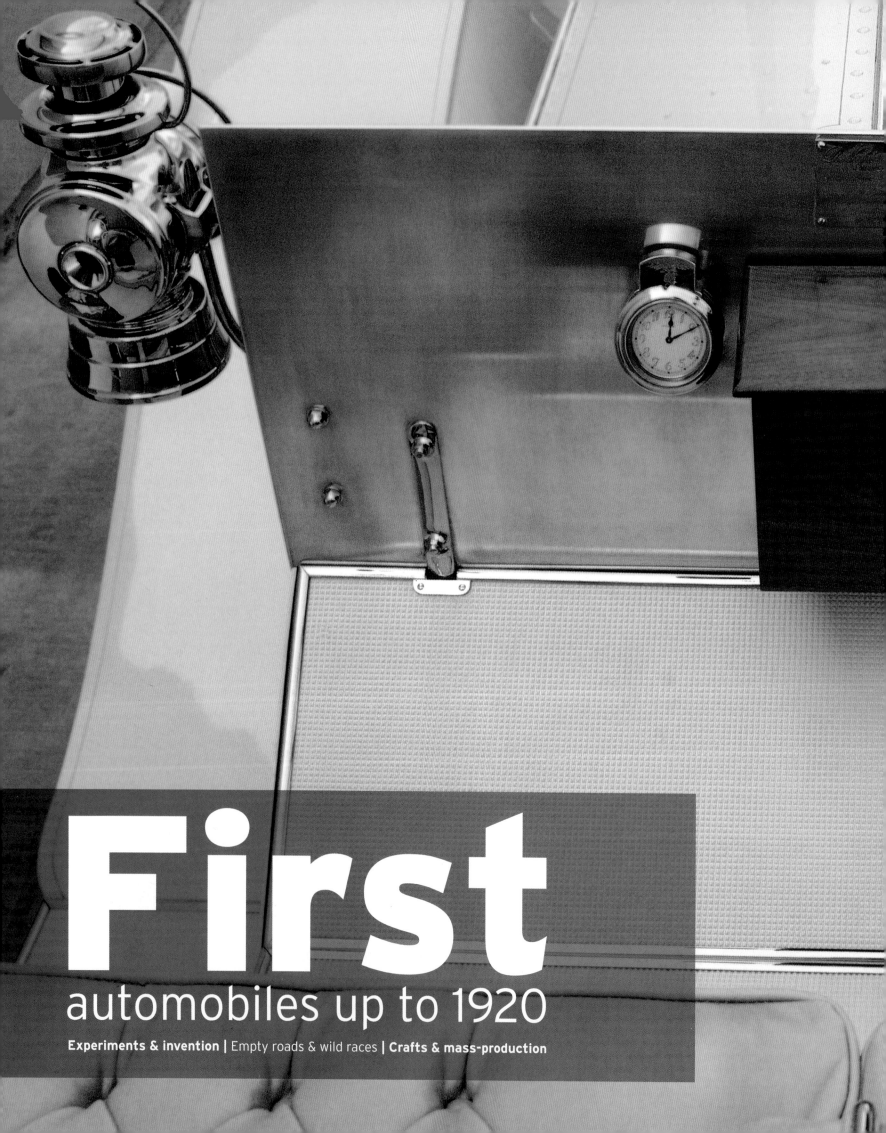

First
automobiles up to 1920

Experiments & invention | Empty roads & wild races | **Crafts & mass-production**

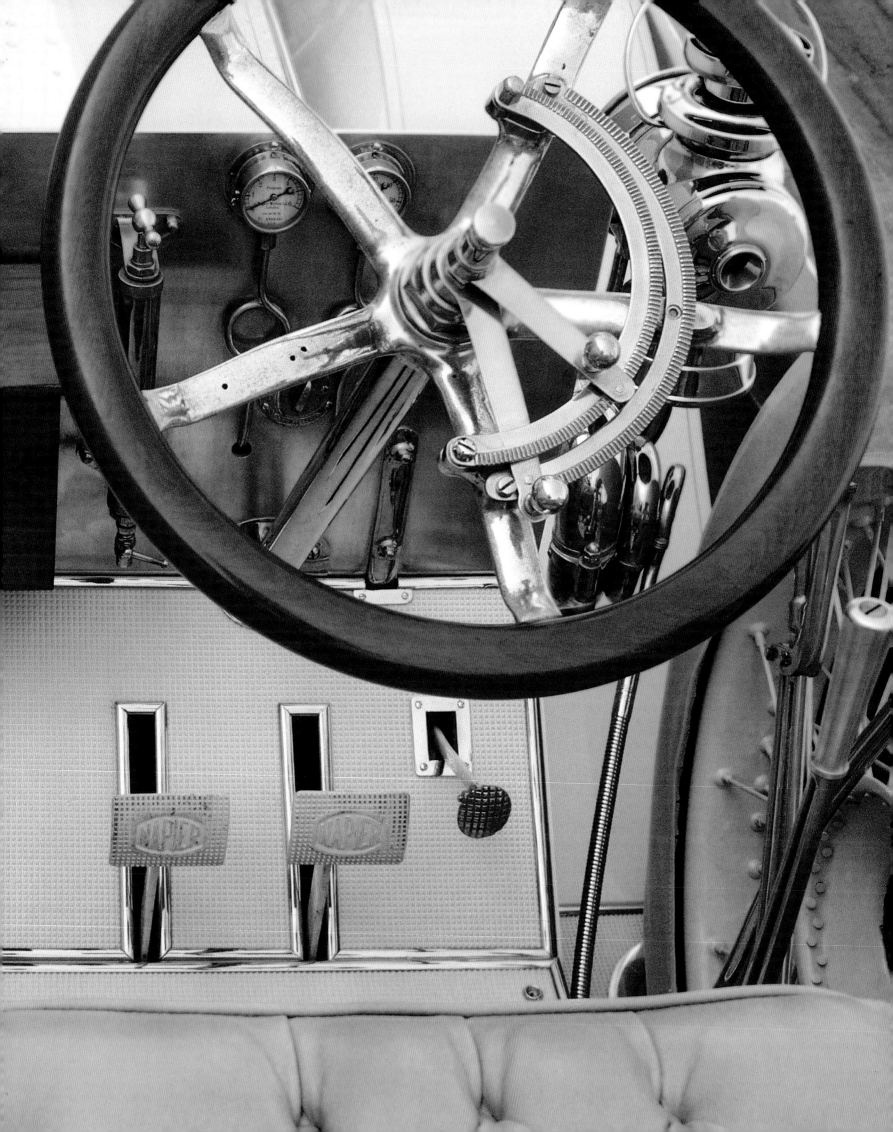

Pioneer Vehicles

The 19th century saw tremendous advances in engineering, as mechanisation transformed production in factories. Inventors turned their attention to replacing the horse with something that could go faster and further. Steam, electricity, gas, and petrol were all tried, and in this early period it was hard to say which would win; speed records went first to electric, then to steam.

◁ Grenville Steam Carriage c.1880

Origin UK

Engine vertical steam boiler

Top speed 20 mph (32 km/h)

Railway engineer Robert Neville Grenville from Glastonbury, UK, was one of dozens of Victorian inventors to build a steam-powered road carriage. Grenville's vehicle has survived.

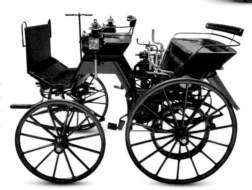

▷ Daimler 1886

Origin Germany

Engine 462 cc, one-cylinder

Top speed 10 mph (16 km/h)

Gottlieb Daimler and Wilhelm Maybach fitted their engine into a stagecoach in 1886, creating the first four-wheeled, petrol-engined vehicle to reach 10 mph.

▷ Stanley Runabout 1898

Origin USA

Engine 1,692 cc, straight-two steam

Top speed 35 mph (56 km/h)

Twins Francis and Freelan Stanley built over 200 of these inexpensive and reliable steam cars in 1898-99. In 1906 a more powerful model reached 127 mph (204 km/h).

▽ Daimler Cannstatt 4HP 1898

Origin Germany

Engine 1,525 cc, V2

Top speed 16 mph (26 km/h)

In June 1887 Daimler equipped a workshop for 23 employees in Cannstatt, Stuttgart, to build his engines. The engines were still fitted to modified stagecoaches.

◁ Franklin Model A 1902

Origin USA

Engine 1,760 cc, straight-four

Top speed 25 mph (40 km/h)

John Wilkinson designed the first four-cylinder car in the US for Herbert Franklin. The air-cooled engine had overhead valves and was mounted across the wooden chassis.

△ Benz (replica) 1885

Origin Germany

Engine 954 cc, single-cylinder

Top speed 6 mph (10 km/h)

Built in 1885 and patented in 1886, Karl Benz's Motorwagen had many clever features: it was lightweight and had a four-stroke petrol engine, rack steering, and steel spoke wheels.

◁ Lanchester 1897

Origin UK

Engine 3,459 cc, straight-two

Top speed 20 mph (32 km/h)

Brothers Frederick, George, and Frank Lanchester ran their first car in 1896 with a single-cylinder engine. The following year they built this car with a two-cylinder engine.

◁ Columbia Electric 1899

Origin USA

Engine single electric motor

Top speed 15 mph (24 km/h)

At the start of the 20th century, when most petrol-car makers were producing a handful of models a year, Columbia was building hundreds of smooth, silent electric cars.

△ Sunbeam-Mabley 1901

Origin UK

Engine 230 cc, one-cylinder

Top speed 20 mph (32 km/h)

John Marston's Sunbeam bicycle factory, along with Maxwell Maberley-Smith, developed this unusual vehicle with a seat either side of a central belt drive.

▷ Clément-Gladiator Voiturette 1899

Origin France

Engine 402 cc, one-cylinder

Top speed 20 mph (32 km/h)

Bicycle magnate Adolphe Clément saw the potential of the motor industry and promoted several marques. This simple voiturette had a 2.5 hp De Dion-type engine under the seat.

◁ Goddu Tandem 1897

Origin USA

Engine cc unknown, two-cylinder

Top speed 30 mph (48 km/h)

Inventor Louis Goddu made only a handful of cars, but pioneered features such as the overhead camshaft in a car that was exceptionally rapid for its time.

◁ Duryea Motor Wagon 1893

Origin USA

Engine 1,302 cc, one-cylinder

Top speed 12 mph (19 km/h)

Bicycle makers Frank and Charles Duryea made the first successful gasoline-powered automobile in the US in 1893. They also won the US's first motor race in 1895.

▷ Panhard et Levassor Phaeton 1891

Origin France

Engine 1,060 cc, straight-two

Top speed 12 mph (19 km/h)

René Panhard and Émile Levassor offered their first car in 1890, building a Daimler engine under licence. They pioneered sliding gear transmission and front engine with rear drive among other modern features.

◁ Arnold Benz 1897

Origin UK

Engine 1,190 cc, single-cylinder

Top speed 16 mph (26 km/h)

William Arnold & Sons built Benz-like cars with their own 1.5 hp engines. One was fitted with the first electric self-start dynamotor, which also assisted the engine on hills.

△ Bikkers Steam Car 1907

Origin Netherlands

Engine steam boiler

Top speed 10 mph (16 km/h)

Better known for its steam-driven fire engines, Bikkers also made steam vehicles, such as this one, for cleaning cesspits. This is the oldest commercial vehicle in the Netherlands.

First Cars for Customers

It was one amazing feat to build the first practical motor cars – it was another to start making more and selling them. Just convincing people of their benefits was often difficult. Entrepreneurs, engineers, and aristocrats all played their parts in the earliest faltering steps towards car manufacture. Germany was at the forefront of this development, followed by France, the UK, and the US.

◁ Adler 3.5HP Voiturette 1901
Origin Germany

Engine 510 cc, single-cylinder

Top speed 20 mph (32 km/h)

The typewriter and bicycle manufacturer Adler made components for Benz and De Dion cars before starting to make its own De Dion-engined vehicles in 1900.

△ Arrol-Johnston 10HP Dogcart 1897
Origin UK

Engine 3,230 cc, flat-two

Top speed 25 mph (40 km/h)

George Johnston conceived his rugged, simple Dogcart - the first British-built car - in Glasgow, Scotland. Powered by an underfloor opposed-piston engine, it remained in production for 10 years.

◁ US Long Distance 7HP 1901
Origin USA

Engine 2,245 cc, single-cylinder

Top speed 25 mph (40 km/h)

Ambitiously named for a runabout, this car had its horizontally mounted engine and two-speed epicyclic gearbox under the seat. It was renamed the Standard in 1903.

▷ Clément 7HP 1901
Origin France

Engine 7 hp, one-cylinder

Top speed 25 mph (40 km/h)

Adolphe Clément made a fortune from bicycles and pneumatic tyres, and then invested it in car manufacture. His cars were among the first models to feature front-mounted engines and drive shafts.

△ Rover 8HP 1904
Origin UK

Engine 1,327 cc, single-cylinder

Top speed 30 mph (48 km/h)

This was Rover Cycle Company's first four-wheeled car. The 8HP featured a tubular "backbone" chassis, column gearchange, and a camshaft brake. One 8HP successfully drove from London to Constantinople in 1906.

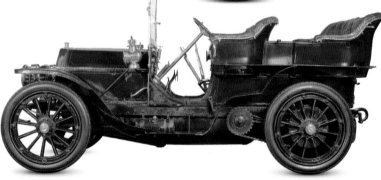

◁ Mercedes 60HP 1903
Origin Germany

Engine 9,293 cc, straight-four

Top speed 73 mph (117 km/h)

While other makes were building crude machines that were barely faster than a running man, Mercedes was manufacturing magnificent high-speed vehicles like the 60HP.

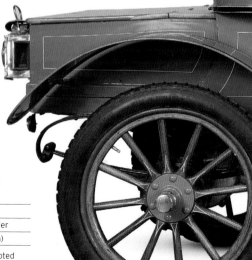

▷ De Dion-Bouton 3.5HP Voiturette 1899
Origin France

Engine 510 cc, single-cylinder

Top speed 25 mph (40 km/h)

Count Albert de Dion was one of France's motoring pioneers. His single-cylinder, water-cooled engines were used by dozens of early car makers around the world.

▷ De Dion-Bouton 8HP Type O 1902
Origin France

Engine 943 cc, single-cylinder

Top speed 28 mph (45 km/h)

In 1902 De Dion-Bouton adopted wheel steering and front, rather than underfloor, engine position for popular, light cars such as the Type O, which had a long production run.

◁ Renault Voiturette 1898
Origin France
Engine 400 cc, single-cylinder
Top speed 20 mph (32 km/h)

Louis Renault and his brothers started building cars in 1897, and their Voiturette quickly became popular in France thanks to its impressive performances in trials.

◁ Ford Model A 1903
Origin USA
Engine 1,668 cc, flat-two
Top speed 28 mph (45 km/h)

Henry Ford built his first car in 1896, but did not start production until 1903 with the underfloor-engined Model A. This was developed into the Model C of 1904.

▷ FN 3.5HP Victoria 1900
Origin Belgium
Engine 796 cc, straight-two
Top speed 23 mph (37 km/h)

The Belgian armaments manufacturer FN diversified into motorcycle and car making around the turn of the century. About 280 Victorias were made up until 1902.

△ Fiat 16/24HP 1903
Origin Italy
Engine 4,180 cc, straight-four
Top speed 44 mph (71 km/h)

With a front-mounted, water-cooled, four-cylinder engine driving the rear wheels via a four-speed gearbox, the 16/24HP was a thoroughly modern car.

△ Benz Ideal 4.5HP 1900
Origin Germany
Engine 1,140 cc, single-cylinder
Top speed 22 mph (35 km/h)

The maker of the first successful car in 1885. Benz's Ideal had tiller steering. In 1900, 603 cars were made - most car makers of the time produced only a handful each year.

△ Maxwell Model A Junior Runabout 1904
Origin USA
Engine 1,647 cc, flat-two
Top speed 35 mph (56 km/h)

Jonathan Maxwell and Benjamin Briscoe of New Jersey developed this simple and effective shaft-driven runabout, which sold for $750. It performed well in trials.

△ Holsman Model 3 Runabout 1903
Origin USA
Engine 1,000 cc, flat-two
Top speed 20 mph (32 km/h)

Harry K. Holsman built significant numbers of rope-drive "highwheelers" in Chicago for sale to mid-west pioneers: large wheels allowed them to drive over virgin prairie.

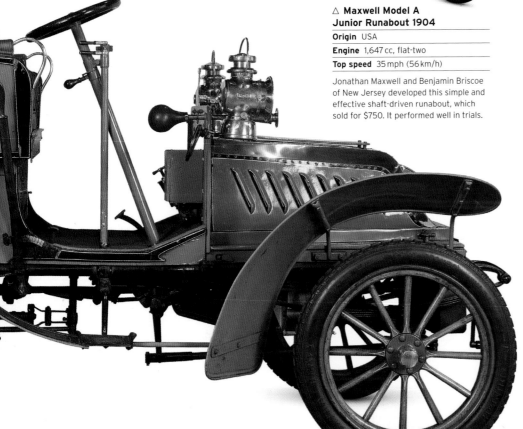

△ Rexette 1905
Origin UK
Engine 900 cc, one-cylinder
Top speed 28 mph (45 km/h)

One of many marques established in Coventry, Britain's "motor city", Rexette derived its 1904 three-wheeler from one if its motorcycles, adding wheel steering in 1905.

Karl Benz and daughter
Clara in the Viktoria, 1893

Great marques
The Mercedes story

The history of Mercedes is also the history of the car itself. The companies founded by the two German pioneers of the internal combustion engine and the automobile - Gottlieb Daimler and Karl Benz - came together to form a marque that now makes some of the world's most advanced and desirable cars.

MANY AUTOMOTIVE INNOVATORS can lay claim to the part they have played in shaping the modern car. But none can equal the contribution of Karl Benz, the man who invented the automobile. Benz patented his *Motorwagen* in January 1886, but his spindly three-wheeler – with its single-cylinder, four-stroke internal combustion engine running on coal gas – had spluttered into life on the roads of Mannheim, Germany, the previous year.

By coincidence, Gottlieb Daimler, an engineer based in Canstatt, had made a petrol-powered internal combustion engine in 1883. To demonstrate his engine, Daimler installed it into a primitive motorcycle, which made its first significant trip on 10 November 1885 when Daimler's son Paul took it for a ride. Daimler's

Mercedes-Benz badge
(introduced 1926)

The world's first motorcycle
Daimler's 1885 motorcycle had iron-banded front and rear wheels with wooden spokes, and a pair of spring-loaded "outrigger" wheels to stabilize the vehicle.

first car-like prototype was a four-wheeled vehicle made from an adapted horse-drawn coach in 1886.

No Daimler vehicles went on the market until 1892, but Benz worked hard to put a petrol-driven version of his tiller-steered *Motorwagen* on public sale; he delivered the first to Emile Roger of Paris in 1888. Benz's car possessed several features common to every automobile today, including an accelerator, a spark plug, a clutch, and a radiator for water-cooling. In 1893 Benz produced the Viktoria, a four-wheeled car with pivoting axles for better steering. The next year a development of the Viktoria, known as the Velo, became the world's first production car.

It was, however, the Daimler company that set the pace in this transport revolution – despite the death of its founder in 1900. Realizing that tall, compact automobiles – such as the 1898 Canstatt-Daimler racer – were inherently unstable, engineer Willhelm Maybach and Paul Daimler designed a new car for 1901. This 35HP model created the template followed by most car makers for decades to come.

Cradled by a chassis of pressed steel, the car's occupants sat behind the engine, rather than above it. The four-cylinder engine, which had an in-line aluminium

crankcase, was located under a bonnet and behind a honeycomb radiator. The car was also equipped with a gate gearchange, a foot throttle, and a steering wheel on a raked column. Furthermore, it had a lower centre of gravity than any previous vehicle, giving much-improved roadholding.

This 35 hp Daimler car also carried a new brand name – Mercedes. Emile Jellinek, an Austro-Hungarian entrepreneur, had ordered 36 cars from Daimler in return for exclusive marketing rights in several territories. He renamed them Mercedes cars,

Large and luxurious
The huge Grosser limousines of the 1930s were much loved by the rich and powerful. They were only made to order.

By this time they had become close rivals and forged parallel reputations for high-quality engineering. Benz, with Ferdinand Porsche overseeing design, produced the more exciting cars, including the Blitzen-Benz racer, which held the world land-speed record from 1909 to 1924. Mercedes, meanwhile, proved adept at building a range of models in several sizes. The recession that hit Germany in the 1920s created high levels of inflation and unemployment, and forced many

"**The name** ... has certain publicity characteristics. [It] is both **exotic** and **attractive**."
EMILE JELLINEK ON THE "MERCEDES" BRAND NAME, 1900

after his 11-year-old daughter, and the name quickly replaced that of Daimler. Sales of Mercedes cars soared, helped by the top-of-the-range 60 hp model of 1903, which featured overhead (instead of side) engine valves. It was the most advanced car on the market, and it immediately inspired imitators.

During World War I the Daimler-Mercedes and Benz companies made military vehicles for the German army.

firms into joint ventures. From being arch rivals, Daimler-Mercedes and Benz entered into limited cooperation over some elements of car production and marketing, and began to plan their future strategy together.

The two companies merged in 1926, becoming Daimler-Benz AG, and the cars were marketed under the brand Mercedes-Benz. The new emblem consisted of Benz's laurel-wreath logo encircling the three-pointed Mercedes

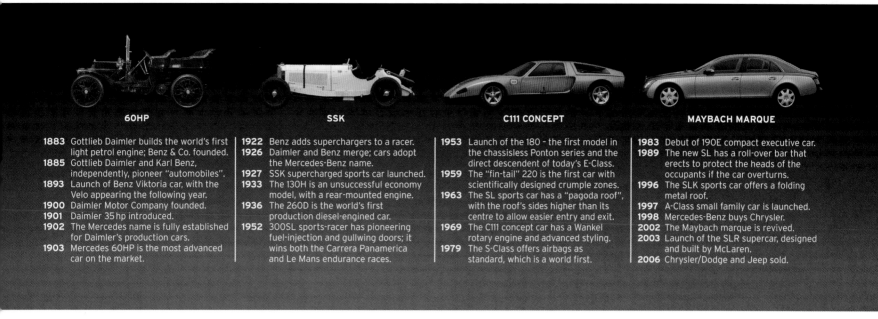

60HP

SSK

C111 CONCEPT

MAYBACH MARQUE

1883 Gottlieb Daimler builds the world's first light petrol engine; Benz & Co. founded.
1885 Gottlieb Daimler and Karl Benz, independently, pioneer "automobiles".
1893 Launch of Benz Viktoria car, with the Velo appearing the following year.
1900 Daimler Motor Company founded.
1901 Daimler 35 hp introduced.
1902 The Mercedes name is fully established for Daimler's production cars.
1903 Mercedes 60HP is the most advanced car on the market.

1922 Benz adds superchargers to a racer.
1926 Daimler and Benz merge; cars adopt the Mercedes-Benz name.
1927 SSK supercharged sports car launched.
1933 The 130H is an unsuccessful economy model, with a rear-mounted engine.
1936 The 260D is the world's first production diesel-engined car.
1952 300SL sports-racer has pioneering fuel-injection and gullwing doors; it wins both the Carrera Panamerica and Le Mans endurance races.

1953 Launch of the 180 - the first model in the chassisless Ponton series and the direct descendent of today's E-Class.
1959 The "fin-tail" 220 is the first car with scientifically designed crumple zones.
1963 The SL sports car has a "pagoda roof", with the roof's sides higher than its centre to allow easier entry and exit.
1969 The C111 concept car has a Wankel rotary engine and advanced styling.
1979 The S-Class offers airbags as standard, which is a world first.

1983 Debut of 190E compact executive car.
1989 The new SL has a roll-over bar that erects to protect the heads of the occupants if the car overturns.
1996 The SLK sports car offers a folding metal roof.
1997 A-Class small family car is launched.
1998 Mercedes-Benz buys Chrysler.
2002 The Maybach marque is revived.
2003 Launch of the SLR supercar, designed and built by McLaren.
2006 Chrysler/Dodge and Jeep sold.

star. After the merger, the Mannheim plant focused on trucks and buses, while car manufacture centred on the Unterturkheim and Sindelfingen factories in Stuttgart. Karl Benz lived long enough to see these changes; he died in 1929, at the age of 84.

The 1930s helped to consolidate the reputation of Mercedes-Benz cars for luxury and power. The German Third Reich adored the huge Grosser limousines, while playboys delighted in the supercharged 540K, and the W125 Grand Prix car dominated European motor racing. During World War II, when Daimler-Benz's resources were once again diverted to

military ends, around 80 per cent of the firm's manufacturing capacity was bombed. After the war, the occupying powers directed the company to build commercial vehicles to aid the reconstruction effort. Car production gradually resumed and by 1949 – when its first new post-war models made their debut – annual output was more than 17,000 cars; by 1958 this had climbed to 100,000 cars.

In motor sport, 1955 proved to be a watershed for Mercedes-Benz: the W154 gave Juan Fangio the World Championship for the second time, but tragedy struck at the Le Mans 24-hour race, where Pierre Levegh's

300SLR cartwheeled into the crowd, killing 83 spectators. The company abandoned all racing for 30 years, and only returned to Formula 1 in the mid-1990s as an engine supplier to McLaren. The McLaren-Mercedes team delivered championships for Mika Häkkinen in 1998 and 1999, and for Lewis Hamilton in 2008.

Traditionally, Mercedes-Benz preferred to expand its operations gradually. In one attempt to broaden its activities, it bought Auto Union/Audi in 1958, but sold it to Volkswagen in 1965. To move into the small-car

market, it backed the Smart city-car venture in 1994 and launched its own A-Class car in 1997 as an upmarket alternative to the Volkswagen Golf.

In a bolder move, Mercedes-Benz bought the Chrysler Corporation in 1998. After struggling for eight years to make a viable business out of the resulting multinational behemoth, it sold both the Chrysler/Dodge and Jeep divisions. The company was free once again to focus on Mercedes-Benz cars.

Reliable workhorse
Launched in 1953 and targeted at the middle classes, the 180 Ponton was Mercedes' first mid-size saloon. Being robust and reliable, diesel 180s were widely used as taxis in post-war Germany.

Early Production-Line Cars

By the end of the first decade of the 20th century, it was clear that the motor car was here to stay, and carmakers started looking at ways to increase production. De Dion-Bouton in France and Oldsmobile in the US both claimed sales of over 2,000 in 1902, but Henry Ford would eclipse them all, as he introduced the moving production line to motor car manufacture.

◁ **Vulcan 10HP 1904**
Origin UK
Engine 1,500 cc, straight-two
Top speed 35 mph (56 km/h)

Vulcan cars were exceptional value for money. The 1903 single-cylinder cost just £105 and the 1904 twin £200: consequently, sales rocketed during 1904–06.

△ **Wolseley 6HP 1901**
Origin UK
Engine 714 cc, single-cylinder
Top speed 25 mph (40 km/h)

Herbert Austin designed and oversaw manufacture of this Voiturette before setting up his own company. Its efficient design ensured successful production.

△ **Oldsmobile Curved Dash 1901**
Origin USA
Engine 1,564 cc, single-cylinder
Top speed 20 mph (32 km/h)

Ransom Eli Olds conceived the world's first mass-production car. It was light, simple, affordable, and reliable: 2,100 were sold in 1902 and 5,000 more in 1904.

◁ **Speedwell 6HP Dogcart 1904**
Origin UK
Engine 700 cc, single-cylinder
Top speed 25 mph (40 km/h)

Speedwell made a wide range of cars from 6 hp to 50 hp, though it only lasted from 1900 to 1907. The Dogcart used a De Dion-type engine.

▷ **L'Elegante 6HP 1903**
Origin France
Engine 942 cc, single-cylinder
Top speed 28 mph (45 km/h)

Like De Dion-Bouton, L'Elegante cars were built in Paris. They closely resembled De Dion-Boutons and used their engines; the L'Elegante only lasted four years.

▽ **Knox 8HP 1904**
Origin USA
Engine 2,253 cc, single-cylinder
Top speed 28 mph (45 km/h)

Knox sold hundreds of these simple cars, which were notable for full-length springs and an air-cooled, single-cylinder engine covered in screwed-in pins to increase cooling.

△ **Cadillac Model A 1903**
Origin USA
Engine 1,606 cc, single-cylinder
Top speed 35 mph (56 km/h)

Henry Leland set up Cadillac in 1902 after parting with Henry Ford; in 1903 he sold some 2,400 of these simple, well-engineered small cars for $750 each.

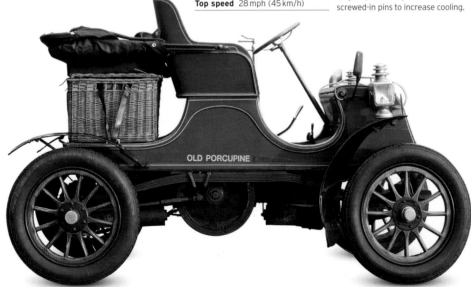

△ **De Dion-Bouton 10HP Type W 1904**
Origin France
Engine 1,728 cc, straight-two
Top speed 40 mph (64 km/h)

De Dion-Bouton claimed to be the world's largest car producer, selling 2,000 cars in 1902 alone, and offering a wide choice of popular, easy-to-drive vehicles.

◁ **Spyker 12/16HP Double Phaeton 1905**

Origin Netherlands

Engine 2,544 cc, square-four

Top speed 45 mph (72 km/h)

The Spijker brothers started selling other marques before producing their own from 1900. From 1904 they made a range of large, advanced cars, including a 4x4.

◁ **Ford Model T Tourer 1908**

Origin USA

Engine 2,896 cc, straight-four

Top speed 42 mph (68 km/h)

Henry Ford dreamt of bringing motoring to the wider public, and by using a moving assembly line he achieved it with the rugged, reliable, low-cost Model T.

△ **CID Baby 1910**

Origin France

Engine single-cylinder

Top speed 40 mph (64 km/h)

Cottereau of Dijon was renamed CID in 1910; its best-known product was the Baby, a light car with a Buchet engine driving through a four-speed friction transmission.

▷ **Renault AX 1908**

Origin France

Engine 1,060 cc, straight-two

Top speed 35 mph (56 km/h)

French manufacturers excelled at making lightweight, practical vehicles and the AX was a perfect example. It was in production for six years, and was popular with taxi drivers.

△ **Humber Humberette 1913**

Origin UK

Engine 998 cc, V2-cylinder

Top speed 25 mph (40 km/h)

This well-made economy model featured an air-cooled engine. It was classed as a "cyclecar" for tax purposes as it weighed under 320 kg (700 lb).

△ **Peugeot Bébé 1913**

Origin France

Engine 855 cc, straight-four

Top speed 37 mph (60 km/h)

Ettore Bugatti designed this car for Wanderer, but it was best known as a Peugeot; 3,095 were sold during 1913–16.

◁ **Twombly Model B 1914**

Origin USA

Engine 1,290 cc, straight-four

Top speed 50 mph (80 km/h)

Mounting the axles above the chassis gave the Twombly unusually low lines. It was very narrow, and its tandem seating was an uncommon feature that proved unpopular.

△ **Dodge Model 30 Touring Car 1914**

Origin USA

Engine 3,480 cc, four-cylinder

Top speed Unknown

The Dodge brothers were formerly subcontractors to Ford. Their own first car was twice as powerful as the Model T, and was supplied with an all-steel welded body.

◁ **Standard 9½ HP Model S 1913**

Origin UK

Engine 1,087 cc, straight-four

Top speed 45 mph (72 km/h)

Set up by Reginald Maudsley in 1903, Standard gained a reputation for making good engines, which were also used by other marques; its own cars sold well.

▷ **Stellite 9HP 1913**

Origin UK

Engine 1,098 cc, straight-four

Top speed 45 mph (72 km/h)

A subsidiary company of Wolseley, which later absorbed it, Stellite's advanced features included rack-and-pinion steering and overhead inlet valves.

Ford Model T

The Model T led an industrial and social revolution, introducing mass-production techniques to the manufacture of motor cars and motorizing the US. Thanks to Henry Ford's 1913 introduction of a moving assembly line, production hit 1,000 per day in 1914, and US output peaked in 1923 when two million "Tin Lizzies" were made. More than 15 million Model Ts were made from 1908 until 1927, a record-breaking figure that was overtaken only by Volkswagen's Beetle in 1972.

THE MODEL T introduced several innovations to the manufacture of motor cars. It had a monobloc engine and the transmission was directly attached to the power unit. With an unusual epicyclic (or "planetary") gearbox, it also offered near-automatic driving with no clashing of gears. Affectionately called the "Tin Lizzie", the car was known for its extreme robustness. Its ruggedness was due to Henry Ford's insistence on using strong materials; he pioneered the use of light but tough vanadium steel. Costs were controlled by keeping the specifications simple and squeezing dealer margins. From 1914 to 1926 black was the only colour offered: black enamel dried more quickly, enabling production-line speeds to be sustained. As sales went up, ever-increasing numbers of the Model T were made at ever-decreasing prices. Reliable and affordable, by 1918 the Model T accounted for half of all cars in the US.

SIDE VIEW WITH CLOSED TOP

Famous Ford script
The iconic Ford script was created by Childe Harold Wills – Henry Ford's chief engineering assistant – in 1903. Wills had trained as a commercial artist and the script was based on one he had previously used on visiting cards. The script is still in use today.

Acetylene powered lights standard until 1919, when replaced with electric lamps

Brass-framed windscreen needs struts for support

Rubber squeeze bulb for brass horn

Hood tensioned by long leather straps

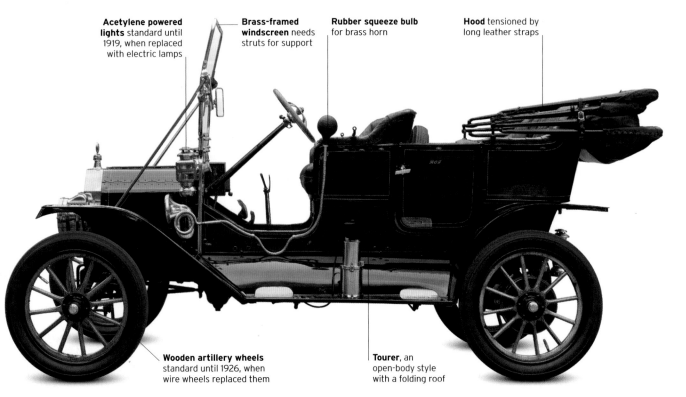

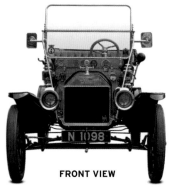

FRONT VIEW

REAR VIEW

Wooden artillery wheels standard until 1926, when wire wheels replaced them

Tourer, an open-body style with a folding roof

Built for American roads

With high ground clearance and simple transverse-leaf suspension, the Model T was tailor-made for the poor quality, often unsurfaced, US roads of the time. The absence of front brakes and of any dampers might be regarded as faults, but the engine's easy pulling power and the need for minimal gearchanging were virtues, as was its 25-30 mpg (11-13 km/l) fuel consumption.

SPECIFICATIONS

Model	Ford Model T, 1908-27
Assembly	Detroit, USA, and worldwide
Production	15,007,003
Construction	Separate chassis, steel body
Engine	2,896 cc, straight-four
Power output	20-22 hp at 1,800 rpm
Transmission	Two-speed epicyclic
Suspension	Rigid axles; transverse leaf springs
Brakes	Drum rear and drum on transmission
Maximum speed	40-45 mph (64-72 km/h)

THE EXTERIOR

The Model T underwent three fundamental styling changes. The brass radiator shell, as on this 1911 model, was replaced in 1917 with a painted shell and the mudguards became domed rather than flat. Then in 1923 a revised, more curvaceous bonnet-line gave the car a modern look. Finally, in 1926 the chassis height was reduced, and new lower bodies brought in, with the option of wire wheels.

1. "Ford" script   2. Boyce Motometer water-temperature gauge on top of radiator grille
3. Acetylene-powered headlamps   4. Starting handle needed to be cranked to get the Model T going   5. Additional lights mounted on the scuttle   6. Cogged drive on wheel hub operates speedometer   7. Wooden artillery wheels standard until 1926   8. Elaborate, scuttle-mounted bulb horn   9. Brass door handle   10. Cylinder stores acetylene to power lights
11. Branded footplate on running board   12. Tail and side lights are kerosene-powered

THE INTERIOR

The "T" has the simplest of interiors, but an odd pedal layout. Pressing the left-hand pedal fully engages first gear, releasing it halfway selects neutral, and fully releasing it gives top gear. The centre pedal operates reverse, the right-hand pedal works the transmission brake. The hand lever works the rear-wheel brakes.

13. Dashboard partly shields occupants from splashes of rain or road dirt   14. 0–50 mph speedometer reflects modest performance   15. Eccentric pedal layout   16. Spare wheel behind driver's seat   17. Buttoned leather upholstery   18. Brass "threshold" plate

UNDER THE BONNET

The 2,896 cc, side-valve, four-cylinder engine of the "T" was advanced in its day. It has four cylinders cast as one block. Lubricating oil is propelled around the engine by gravity rather than being circulated by a pump. The pistons are cast-iron. With small valves and a very low compression ratio, output is only 20–22 bhp and maximum crankshaft speed a mere 1,800 rpm.

19. Trembler coils for ignition housed in box on dashboard
20. Transmission housing under the floor **21.** Bonnet clip **22.** Bonnet handle **23.** Four-cylinder engine has a capacity of nearly 3 litres

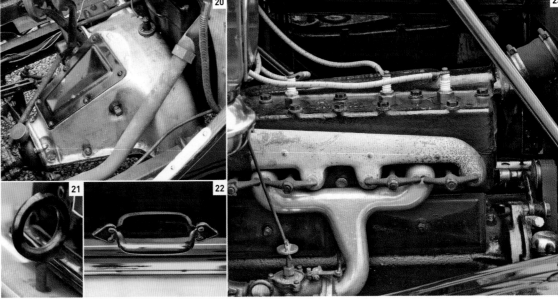

Ford Model T
straight-four

Henry Ford's iconic Model T – the car that would turn millions of Americans into motorists following its launch in 1908 – was remarkable for more than the efficient production-line methods used to build it. The "Tin Lizzie", as it became known, also boasted many novel engineering features, particularly in the design of its simple but rugged engine and transmission.

Running changes
The basics of the engine stayed the same throughout its lifetime, once the water pump of early models had been replaced by the Thermo Syphon system. Some adjustments were made to the compression ratio to account for changeable fuel quality. It peaked at 4.5:1, before being pegged at 3.98:1 from 1917.

KEEPING IT SIMPLE

Ford and his chief engineer, C. Harold Wills, were determined to make the Model T tough enough to endure America's unmade roads, but light enough to ensure adequate performance from its compact, low-power engine. The reliability of the engine and transmission were vital, so both were kept simple. Yet Ford and Wills did not shy away from incorporating innovations such as a removable one-piece cylinder head to ease servicing, and a Thermo Syphon cooling system that supposedly made a water pump unnecessary. However, water-pump kits were popular subsequent purchases among Model T owners.

ENGINE SPECIFICATIONS	
Dates produced	1908–1941
Cylinders	Straight-four
Configuration	Front-mounted, longitudinal
Engine capacities	176.7 cu in (2,896 cc)
Power output	20 hp
Type	Conventional four-stroke, water-cooled petrol engine with reciprocating pistons, magneto ignition, and a wet sump
Head	Side-valves actuated by short pushrods; two valves per cylinder
Fuel System	Single Holley carburettor, gravity-fed
Bore and Stroke	3.75 in x 4.00 in (95.3 mm x 101.6 mm)
Power	6.9 hp/litre
Compression Ratio	4.5:1, later reduced

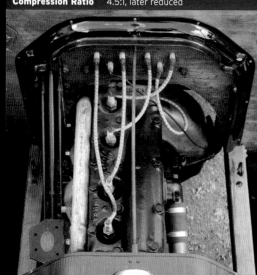

Brake pedal

Clutch pedal

Magneto
Together with static wire coils, magnets attached to the circumference of the flywheel form a magneto that generates high voltage for the spark plugs, eliminating the need for a battery and ignition coil.

Reverse pedal

Transmission
Hidden inside this casing is the transmission, comprising a two-speed epicyclic (planetary) gearset and a clutch built of 27 steel discs. The entire transmission operates in oil shared with the engine.

One-piece lower crankcase
(extended to include the transmission)

▷ **See pp.346-347** How an engine works

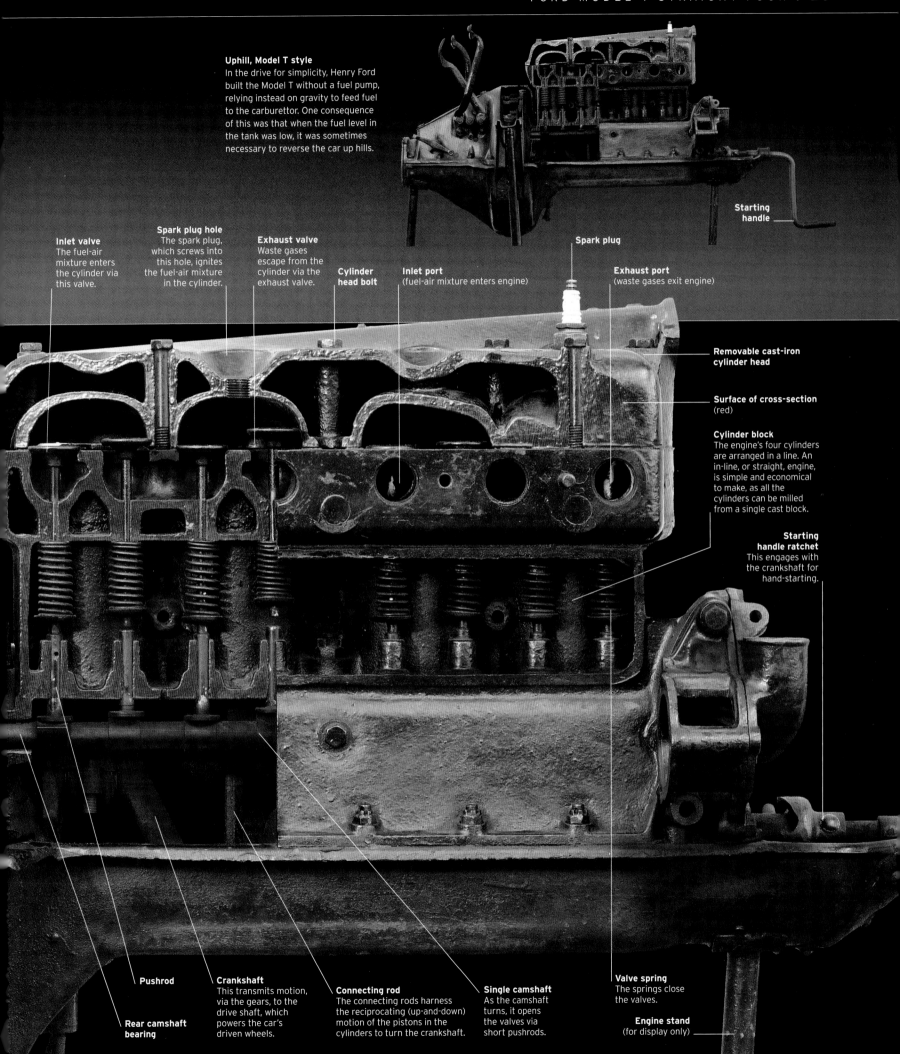

Uphill, Model T style
In the drive for simplicity, Henry Ford built the Model T without a fuel pump, relying instead on gravity to feed fuel to the carburettor. One consequence of this was that when the fuel level in the tank was low, it was sometimes necessary to reverse the car up hills.

Starting handle

Inlet valve
The fuel-air mixture enters the cylinder via this valve.

Spark plug hole
The spark plug, which screws into this hole, ignites the fuel-air mixture in the cylinder.

Exhaust valve
Waste gases escape from the cylinder via the exhaust valve.

Cylinder head bolt

Inlet port
(fuel-air mixture enters engine)

Spark plug

Exhaust port
(waste gases exit engine)

Removable cast-iron cylinder head

Surface of cross-section
(red)

Cylinder block
The engine's four cylinders are arranged in a line. An in-line, or straight, engine, is simple and economical to make, as all the cylinders can be milled from a single cast block.

Starting handle ratchet
This engages with the crankshaft for hand-starting.

Pushrod

Rear camshaft bearing

Crankshaft
This transmits motion, via the gears, to the drive shaft, which powers the car's driven wheels.

Connecting rod
The connecting rods harness the reciprocating (up-and-down) motion of the pistons in the cylinders to turn the crankshaft.

Single camshaft
As the camshaft turns, it opens the valves via short pushrods.

Valve spring
The springs close the valves.

Engine stand
(for display only)

Driving through Paris, 1908
Motoring at the turn of the century was for the
well-heeled few who could afford a car – and
a chauffeur to drive them about – as depicted
in *The Avenue Of The Acacias In The Bois De
Boulogne*, by Roger de la Fresnaye.

Birth of the Competition Car

The idea of proving the speed and durability of new cars by pitting them against each other in long-distance trials, hill climbs, or circuit races came early in the history of the motor car. By the end of the first decade of the 20th century motor sport was thriving throughout Europe and the US, with German, French, Italian, British, and American cars leading the field. In the absence of restrictions on engine capacity, many cars of this era had mammoth engines.

△ **Napier Gordon Bennett 1902**
Origin UK
Engine 6,435 cc, straight-four
Top speed 70 mph (113 km/h)

The sole British entrant in the 1902 Gordon Bennett Trial, this Napier driven by S.F. and Cecil Edge won. Its colour became known as British Racing Green.

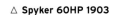

△ **Spyker 60HP 1903**
Origin Netherlands
Engine 8,821 cc, straight-six
Top speed 80 mph (129 km/h)

The Spijker brothers, Jacobus and Hendrik-Jan, pioneered magnificent cars, most notably this first production six-cylinder with permanent four-wheel drive and four-wheel brakes.

△ **Auburn Model 30L Roadster 1910**
Origin USA
Engine 3,300 cc, straight-four
Top speed 65 mph (105 km/h)

Auburn built 1,623 cars in 1912. The 30L was sold as a saloon, tourer, and roadster using a Rutenber engine with individually cast cylinders. The Roadster was the cheapest at $1,100.

△ **Darracq 12HP "Genevieve" 1904**
Origin France
Engine 1,886 cc, straight-two
Top speed 45 mph (72 km/h)

Darracqs were capable cars with light, pressed-steel chassis, but this one is most famous for its starring role in the 1953 comedy film *Genevieve*, which popularized veteran cars.

△ **Darracq 200HP 1905**
Origin France
Engine 25,400 cc, V8
Top speed 120 mph (193 km/h)

The world's oldest surviving V8, this car took the world land speed record in 1905 at 110 mph (177 km/h). In 1906 it exceeded 120 mph, and continued setting records up to 1909.

◁ **Vauxhall Prince Henry 1910**
Origin UK
Engine 3,054 cc, straight-four
Top speed 100 mph (161 km/h)

Vauxhall built three cars for the 1910 Prince Henry Trial in Germany. They went on to win many events, including the Russian Nine-day Trial and the Swedish Winter Cup.

△ Austro-Daimler Prince Henry 1910

Origin Austria

Engine 5,714 cc, straight-four

Top speed 85 mph (137 km/h)

Ferdinand Porsche led Austro-Daimler's split from its German parent. This car's overhead-camshaft engine helped it finish 1-2-3 in the 1910 Prince Henry Trial.

▷ Stutz Bearcat 1912

Origin USA

Engine 6,391 cc, straight-four

Top speed 75 mph (121 km/h)

A roadgoing racer with low build, no doors, and a monocle windscreen, the rakish Bearcat quickly became an icon of its era, winning 25 of the 30 races it entered.

△ Marquette-Buick 1909

Origin USA

Engine 4,800 cc, straight-four

Top speed 90 mph (145 km/h)

Louis Chevrolet drove one of these to victory in the first 5-mile (8-km) race on Indianapolis's "Brickyard" circuit in 1910. It was later disqualified for not meeting the criteria of a stock car.

△ Lancia Tipo 55 Corsa 1910

Origin Italy

Engine 4,700 cc, straight-four

Top speed 85 mph (137 km/h)

Lancia founder Vincenzo was passionate about motor sport and won the 1904 Coppa Florio in Italy. This car also won several races in the US, for the Vanderbilt family.

▷ Panhard et Levassor X-19 Labourdette Torpédo Skiff 1912

Origin France

Engine 2,100 cc, straight-four

Top speed 60 mph (97 km/h)

Coachbuilder Henri Labourdette built this skiff (rowing-boat) body without doors for driver Chevalier René de Knyff. Light and strong, its style appealed to French sportsmen. This is a replica of the 1912 original.

△ Bugatti Type 15 1910

Origin France

Engine 1,327 cc, straight-four

Top speed 55 mph (89 km/h)

Ettore Bugatti's first production car was the Type 13, also offered as the longer-wheelbase Type 15. Numerous giant-killing race performances boosted its sales.

▷ Mercer Type 35R Raceabout 1910

Origin USA

Engine 4,929 cc, straight-four

Top speed 80 mph (129 km/h)

Unusually low-slung with great handling for its time, the Raceabout won five of its first six races in 1911. A four-speed gearbox introduced in 1913 made it even faster.

◁ Fiat S61 Corsa 1908

Origin Italy

Engine 10,087 cc, straight-four

Top speed 97 mph (156 km/h)

A very successful race car derived from a Grand Touring model, the S61 Corsa won races in Europe and the US, including the 1912 American Grand Prix.

◁ Bugatti Type 18 "Garros" 1912

Origin France

Engine 5,027 cc, straight-four

Top speed 105 mph (169 km/h)

Ettore Bugatti himself won in this 100 bhp chain-drive, Grand Prix car with overhead camshaft and double inlet valves. Others were driven in the Indianapolis 500.

△ Fiat S74 1911

Origin Italy

Engine 14,137 cc, straight-four

Top speed 102 mph (164 km/h)

With a GP limit on engine bore, strokes grew: this OHC engine is so tall the driver has to look around it. David Bruce-Brown won the 1911 American Grand Prix in one.

Henry Leland
with his 1906
Model H

Great marques
The Cadillac story

Cadillac is one of America's oldest makes, and it has been mass-producing cars of quality ever since the company was founded in Detroit by Henry Leland in 1902. For more than 90 years Cadillac has been at the core of General Motors (GM), and it remains the aspirational, luxury brand within a GM that is reinventing itself.

HENRY MARTYN LELAND, born in Vermont in 1843, was a precision machinist who worked in the armaments industry. In 1890 he moved to Detroit, and with the backing of Englishman Robert Faulconer he set up a company to make components for the automotive industry, with the emphasis on precision and the standardization of parts. The Leland & Faulconer company designed a new single-cylinder engine for Ransom E. Olds of Oldsmobile, but Olds baulked at the expense of having to re-tool his company to produce the new engine.

Cadillac badge
(introduced 1905)

After being brought in to the Henry Ford Company in a consultancy role, Leland suggested combining his engine with the Ford chassis designs. To accomplish this, a new company, named Cadillac after Detroit's 18th-century French founder, was formed in 1902. The Cadillac Model A was unveiled at the 1903 New York Automobile Show. The car's high-quality construction was to become a Cadillac trademark. The four-cylinder, 30 hp Model D was added to the range in 1905, and it helped the company grow into the world's third-largest car maker,

behind Oldsmobile and Ford.
In 1909 Henry Leland sold Cadillac to William Durant in what was then the largest financial transaction the Detroit stock exchange had ever seen. Cadillac became part of Durant's General Motors organization, alongside the Oldsmobile and Buick marques. Under the slogan "Standard of the World", Cadillac became the first marque to routinely fit self-starters in its cars, and to mass-produce V8 engines. Leland remained president until 1917, when he left after falling out with Durant and went on to found the Lincoln Motor Company.

The Cadillac marque continued to prosper without Leland, issuing a series of V8-engined models in a wide range

of body styles that cemented the public perception of Cadillac as a luxurious, high-quality brand. In 1926 the lower-priced La Salle sub-brand was introduced, and soon both Cadillacs and La Salles were being styled by a young designer called Harley Earl. Over the coming decades Earl would become one of the world's great car designers.

In January 1930 Cadillac introduced a remarkable new engine – the 452 cu in (7,413 cc) V16, which offered 165 bhp with unrivalled smoothness and flexibility. A V12 followed later in

Tall tail
The fins on the 1959 Series 62 Cadillac – the tallest ever on a production car – featured the bullet-shaped tail lights that typify classic Cadillacs.

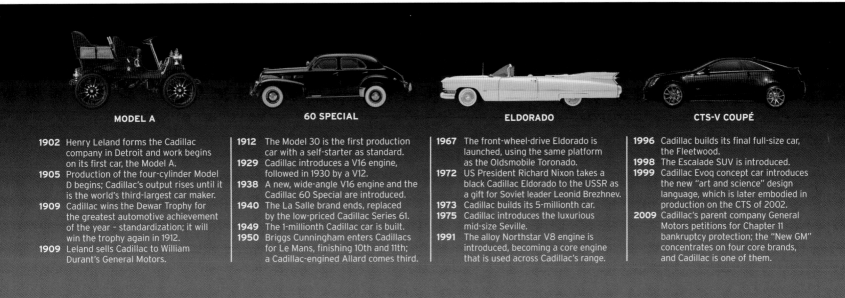

MODEL A

1902 Henry Leland forms the Cadillac company in Detroit and work begins on its first car, the Model A.
1905 Production of the four-cylinder Model D begins; Cadillac's output rises until it is the world's third-largest car maker.
1909 Cadillac wins the Dewar Trophy for the greatest automotive achievement of the year – standardization; it will win the trophy again in 1912.
1909 Leland sells Cadillac to William Durant's General Motors.

60 SPECIAL

1912 The Model 30 is the first production car with a self-starter as standard.
1929 Cadillac introduces a V16 engine, followed in 1930 by a V12.
1938 A new, wide-angle V16 engine and the Cadillac 60 Special are introduced.
1940 The La Salle brand ends, replaced by the low-priced Cadillac Series 61.
1949 The 1-millionth Cadillac car is built.
1950 Briggs Cunningham enters Cadillacs for Le Mans, finishing 10th and 11th; a Cadillac-engined Allard comes third.

ELDORADO

1967 The front-wheel-drive Eldorado is launched, using the same platform as the Oldsmobile Toronado.
1972 US President Richard Nixon takes a black Cadillac Eldorado to the USSR as a gift for Soviet leader Leonid Brezhnev.
1973 Cadillac builds its 5-millionth car.
1975 Cadillac introduces the luxurious mid-size Seville.
1991 The alloy Northstar V8 engine is introduced, becoming a core engine that is used across Cadillac's range.

CTS-V COUPÉ

1996 Cadillac builds its final full-size car, the Fleetwood.
1998 The Escalade SUV is introduced.
1999 Cadillac Evoq concept car introduces the new "art and science" design language, which is later embodied in production on the CTS of 2002.
2009 Cadillac's parent company General Motors petitions for Chapter 11 bankruptcy protection; the "New GM" concentrates on four core brands, and Cadillac is one of them.

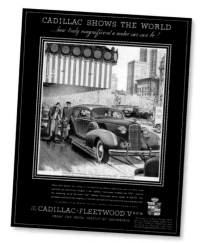

Showcasing luxury and style
High-quality Fleetwood styling was given to Cadillac's most expensive models, such as the Series 75 cars of the mid- to late 1930s.

1930, giving Cadillac a unique engine line-up of V8s, V12s, and V16s. During the 1930s the name Fleetwood (after a Pennsylvania coachbuilder) was used to denote top-of-the-range Cadillacs. A new, wide-angle V16 engine was introduced in 1938, and later the same year the 60 Special was launched. The 60 Special had strikingly modern styling by another young designer, Bill Mitchell, who later became head of the Cadillac styling studio.

Car production continued until 1942, when it was suspended so that Cadillac could assist the war effort by making tanks, staff cars, and aero-engine parts. Production of civilian cars resumed in 1945, but it was 1948 before the line-up received anything more than mild restyling. In that year Mitchell and Earl gave Cadillacs tail fins, starting a fad that swept through the US motor industry. The fin craze reached its zenith in 1959, with Cadillac fins being the tallest of all. By then American manufacturers were filling their cars with comfort and convenience devices, including air suspension, power-assisted steering and brakes, push-button automatic transmissions, and air conditioning – and Cadillac was leading the way.

The Cadillacs of the 1960s were less ostentatious in their styling, if no less luxurious. While there was ever greater commonality of parts between GM brands, Cadillac retained its own individual look. By the end of the 1960s Cadillac was using V8 engines

of up to 500 cu in (8.2-litres), but like other US automobile manufacturers, Cadillac soon had to scale back its engine sizes and power outputs to

meet the increasingly rigorous new emissions regulations. Its cars also had to adopt energy-absorbing bumpers to comply with safety rules.

The oil crisis of the late 1970s was bad news for Cadillac's range of large, petrol-guzzling luxury cars. Cadillac responded by initiating a downsizing programme for its larger models, and briefly offered an innovative "V8-6-4" engine management system for its V8 models, which could shut down engine cylinders in order to save fuel. Unfortunately, the system was unreliable and lasted only a year. Cadillac also introduced the compact Cimarron, although it was really little more than a luxuriously appointed Chevrolet Cavalier/Pontiac J2000. Cadillac's range was increasingly looking old-fashioned and out of tune with the times, especially compared with the best foreign models from Mercedes-Benz, BMW, Audi, Jaguar, and Lexus.

The renaissance for Cadillac began in 1998, by which time the full-size Fleetwood had finally been withdrawn and Cadillac had launched its first SUV, the Escalade. The new era was driven

by a fresh philosophy: "the power of art and science". It led to the sharply styled CTS compact saloon of 2002, which was both striking in appearance

> ## "My **high salary** for **one season** was **$46,000** and a **Cadillac**."
> "DUKE" SNIDER, MAJOR LEAGUE BASEBALL PLAYER, 1947–1964

and able to compete with models from rival marques in terms of quality and performance, and the Cien concept car (also 2002), whose looks were inspired by the F-22 Raptor jet.

The 2006 Cadillac BLS sold slowly in Europe, its intended market, but the STS mid-size saloon (2005), full-size DTS (2006), and second-generation CTS (2008) models all did well in the US. Cadillac boasted that its CTS-V performance model was the fastest V8-engined sports saloon in the world: on that score at least, Cadillac was once again the "Standard of the World".

The first mass-produced V8 engine
Cadillac's 1915 V8 regulated cooling-water temperature with an innovative thermostatic control. The engine, clutch, and gearbox were bolted together into a single unit.

Luxury and Power

Car makers saved their finest work for their richest customers. Such customers would not tolerate unreliability, and demanded cars that gave far greater performance than traditional horse-drawn carriages. They also demanded comfort – an important factor on the rough roads of the early 20th century – and luxuries such as preselect gearboxes and power steering.

◁ Nagant Type D 14/16HP Town Car 1909

Origin Belgium

Engine 2,600 cc, straight-four

Top speed 50 mph (80 km/h)

This Liège marque built its own high quality cars from 1907. The smaller 14/16 hp was remarkable for its efficient sidevalve engine, which was capable of revving to 3,000 rpm.

▷ HEDAG Electric Brougham 1905

Origin Germany

Engine Two electric motors

Top speed 15 mph (24 km/h)

A modified horse-taxi with an electric motor in each front wheel, the Brougham had power steering, four-wheel brakes, and electric indicators. It was built under licence from Kriéger of France.

▷ Panhard & Levassor 15HP Type X21 1905

Origin France

Engine 2,614 cc, straight-six

Top speed 50 mph (80 km/h)

In 1891 Panhard and Levassor laid the foundations of the modern motor car. By 1905 they were producing remarkably quiet and smooth-running cars, such as the X21.

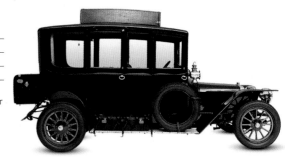

◁ Regal Model NC Colonial Coupé 1912

Origin USA

Engine 3,200 cc, straight-four

Top speed 50 mph (80 km/h)

Notable for its low, "underslung" build, which placed its axles above the chassis, the Regal was a light sporting car, though hardly aerodynamic with this body style.

▷ Rolls-Royce Silver Ghost 1906

Origin UK

Engine 7,036 cc, straight-six

Top speed 63 mph (101 km/h)

Charles Rolls and Henry Royce focused on making the finest car in the world, and succeeded with this 40/50 hp model. It was quiet, powerful, and superbly built.

△ Cadillac Model 51 1914

Origin USA

Engine 5,157 cc, V8

Top speed 55 mph (89 km/h)

Henry Leland stole a march on the opposition with the US's first mass-produced V8. With 70 bhp, it was powerful and reliable. Sales in the first year were over 13,000.

◁ Brooke 25/30HP Swan 1910

Origin UK

Engine 4,788 cc, straight-six

Top speed 37 mph (60 km/h)

The work of British engineer Robert Matthewson, of Calcutta, India, the Swan had a beak that sprayed water to clear a path through the crowded streets of Calcutta.

▷ Lanchester 28HP Landaulette 1906

Origin UK

Engine 3,654 cc, straight-six

Top speed 55 mph (89 km/h)

Frederick Lanchester was a brilliant engineer whose cars were innovative and original. This car has its original convertible bodywork, mid-mounted engine, and preselect gearbox.

▷ Peugeot Type 126 12/15HP Touring 1910

Origin France

Engine 2,200 cc, straight-four

Top speed 45 mph (72 km/h)

A family company founded in ironmongery, Peugeot was hugely successful in the early 20th century with a wide range of motor cars. Just 350 of this model were sold.

▽ Mors 14/19HP Landaulette Town Car 1904

Origin France

Engine 3,200 cc, straight-four

Top speed 40 mph (64 km/h)

Emile Mors was building 200 cars a year in 1898, so by 1904 his chassis were well developed. This luxury model carries a coachbuilt city-car body by Rothschild of Paris.

◁ Georges Roy 12HP 1909

Origin France

Engine 2,900 cc, straight-four

Top speed 45 mph (72 km/h)

Georges Roy, unusually, built its own car bodies. This model could be either a two- or a four-seater, the rear compartment ingeniously folding back when not required.

▷ Thomas Flyer Model 6/40M Touring 1910

Origin USA

Engine 7,679 cc, straight-six

Top speed 67 mph (108 km/h)

Thomas made increasingly rapid and large-engined cars, and won the New York to Paris race in 1908. From 1910 to 1919 it made more luxurious models, such as this Flyer.

▷ Argyll 15/30 1913

Origin UK

Engine 2,614 cc, straight-four

Top speed 47 mph (76 km/h)

Scotland's biggest car maker in the Edwardian era built splendid cars, such as this sleeve-valve-engined model. It was made in a magnificent, palace-like factory in Alexandria, on the banks of Loch Lomond, Scotland.

△ Fiat 24/40HP 1906

Origin Italy

Engine 7,363 cc, straight-four

Top speed 53 mph (85 km/h)

Fiat produced a broad range of large-engined cars for Italy's elite. These received weighty and luxurious bodies – though a light racer was also made for this chassis.

◁ Daimler 28/36 1905

Origin UK

Engine 5703 cc, straight-four

Top speed 50 mph (80 km/h)

The British Daimler company began by making replicas of German cars. By 1905, however, it had taken a strong lead in the market for quality cars with large engines and four gears, such as the 28/36.

▷ Lancia Alpha 1907

Origin Italy

Engine 2,543 cc, straight-four

Top speed 50 mph (80 km/h)

Vincenzo Lancia founded his company in 1906, after six years racing for the Fiat factory. With a four-speed gearbox, the Alpha was a modern, well-made car in its day.

▷ Pierce-Arrow Model 38 Park Phaeton 1913

Origin USA

Engine 6,796 cc, straight-six

Top speed 65 mph (105 km/h)

Pierce-Arrow made some of the US's finest cars. This model, which has an exclusive body by Studebaker, was started by pumping compressed air into its engine.

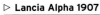

Rolls-Royce Silver Ghost

Strictly speaking, only one Rolls-Royce is named Silver Ghost: the unique, silver-painted, 40/50 hp open tourer with silver trim that was used in 1907 for a 15,000-mile (24,000-km) reliability trial. The title has, however, been retrospectively applied to all examples of the 40/50 hp made between 1906 and 1925 – the model that established Rolls-Royce as the maker of "The Best Car in the World". Beautifully engineered, it offered unparalleled smoothness and refinement for the era, together with effortless high performance.

ONE RESPECTED commentator described the 40/50 hp as being "a triumph of workmanship over design" – a cruel but not wholly inaccurate appreciation. The meticulous quality of engineering insisted upon by the perfectionist Henry Royce was what established the marque's reputation. Many items were created in-house, not least a Royce-designed distributor and carburettor. When electric starting was introduced in 1919, Royce also designed his own starter

and dynamo. But the engine was conservative in its construction, as was the chassis – which only gained front brakes in 1924. This was part of a servo-assisted mechanism that was notably efficient.

The 40/50 hp was sufficiently robust to have formed the basis for an armoured car during and after World War I. Its chassis was donated to the Phantom I that replaced it in 1925. This was in effect a "Silver Ghost" with a new overhead-valve engine.

FRONT VIEW

REAR VIEW

When Rolls met Royce
Pioneer motorist and automobile dealer Charles Rolls was highly impressed by the first cars built by electrical engineer Henry Royce. They decided, in 1904, to market the vehicles as Rolls-Royces. This arrangement continued after Rolls's death in a flying accident in 1910.

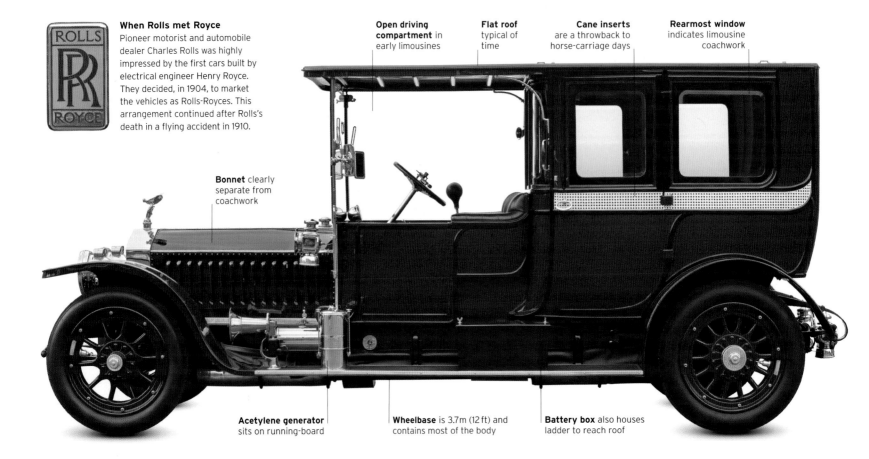

Open driving compartment in early limousines

Flat roof typical of time

Cane inserts are a throwback to horse-carriage days

Rearmost window indicates limousine coachwork

Bonnet clearly separate from coachwork

Acetylene generator sits on running-board

Wheelbase is 3.7m (12 ft) and contains most of the body

Battery box also houses ladder to reach roof

Classical grace

The front of the Silver Ghost is dominated by the "tombstone" radiator shell; this never received the Palladian vertical slats later associated with Rolls-Royces. The "letter-box" slot in the windscreen hinges open for visibility in stormy weather. The high roof accommodates gentlemen wearing top hats – and ladies with the generously sized headwear of Edwardian times.

THE EXTERIOR

The 40/50 hp's body was made to the customer's order by external coachbuilders. There was no such thing as a "standard" style, and coachwork ranged from sober open tourers to extravagant limousines made for various foreign potentates. From 1920 the Silver Ghost was also assembled with US-made bodies in Springfield, Massachussetts. This particular car dates from 1912, and it carries an accurate modern-day copy – created over 14 years – of a body by coachbuilder Rothschild.

1. "Spirit of Ecstasy" mascot features from 1911
2. Wooden "artillery" wheels have detachable rims
3. Acetylene lamps used until 1919 **4.** Fuel-pump settings are manually adjustable **5.** Exterior handle is throwback to horse-drawn era **6.** Wonderfully extravagant boa-constrictor horn **7.** Lamps display masterful tinsmithery

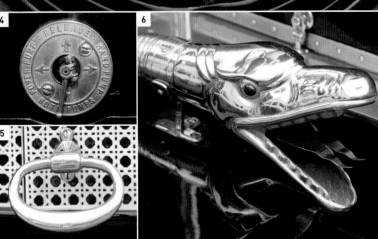

THE INTERIOR

The rear compartment is a magnificent reproduction of the Rothschild original. Flamboyant interiors were often found on the 40/50 hp. In 1921 an Indian maharajah commissioned two cars with interior fittings in gold, silver, and mother-of-pearl, and trimmed in mauve silk: the cost was £6,000 a car, at a time when a humble Morris started at £299.

8. West of England cloth trims at rear **9.** Jump seat
10. Overhead light **11.** Vanity box with clock **12.** Detailing around door pull worthy of an Edwardian drawing room
13. Intercom to chauffeur **14.** Fuel mixture, ignition timing, and engine speed controlled from steering wheel
15. Dashboard is spare and functional **16.** Mileage gauge **17.** Close-set gear lever and handbrake

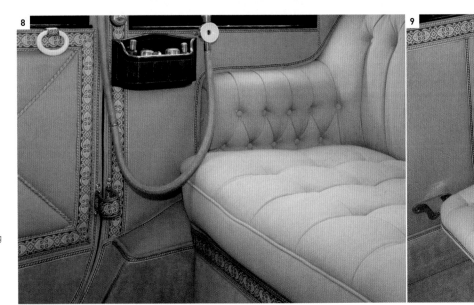

UNDER THE BONNET

The 40/50 hp engine mixes the conservative and the advanced. The use of two three-cylinder blocks was archaic (by post-WW I standards), as were the fixed cylinder heads and exposed valve gear. But the drilled and fully pressure-fed crankshaft – with seven main bearings – put Rolls-Royce ahead of the game. Initially 7,036 cc, engine capacity was increased to 7,410 cc in 1909. Output rose over the years from an estimated 48 bhp to approximately 75 bhp on later cars.

18. Located below the distributor, the governor maintains constant engine revs   **19.** Sidevalve six-cylinder engine has fixed cylinder heads, dual ignition

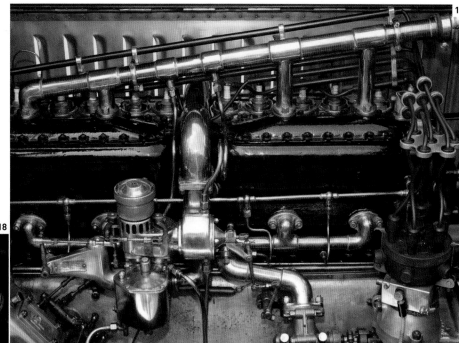

The
1920s

Speed & stamina | Racers & roadsters | **Flappers & flamboyance** | Nickel & whitewall

Competition Cars

The 1920s saw rapid technological progress in the world of competition cars, as the emphasis moved from proving road cars by racing them, to developing and testing advanced engineering in race cars, and then adapting it to road models. This decade saw innovations such as multiple valves and spark plugs per cylinder, double overhead camshafts, and front-wheel drive all proven in motor sport.

△ **Duesenberg 183 1921**
Origin USA
Engine 2,977 cc, straight-eight
Top speed 112 mph (180 km/h)

This was the only all-American car with a US driver – Jimmy Murphy – to win a European Grand Prix, at Le Mans in 1921. Murphy also won the Indianapolis 500 in it in 1921.

△ **OM 665 "Superba" 1925**
Origin Italy
Engine 1,990 cc, straight-six
Top speed 70 mph (113 km/h)

Founded in 1899, OM still exists, making forklifts within the Fiat Group. The 665 won its class at Le Mans in 1925 and 1926, and finished 1-2-3 in the first Mille Miglia in 1927.

▽ **AC Racing Special 1921**
Origin UK
Engine 1,991 cc, straight-six
Top speed 90 mph (145 km/h)

AC made only road cars until co-owner John Weller designed the Light Six engine. With a chain-driven overhead camshaft, it resulted in a series of fast sports cars, including the Special.

▷ **Mercedes-Benz Type S 36/220 1926**
Origin Germany
Engine 6,789 cc, straight-six
Top speed 106 mph (171 km/h)

Designed by Ferdinand Porsche, this was one of the best and most expensive vintage-era sports cars. It had a supercharger, which boosted power when the throttle was pushed right down.

◁ **Sunbeam 3-litre 1924**
Origin UK
Engine 2,916 cc, straight-six
Top speed 90 mph (145 km/h)

This big car was long and narrow for a racer, but a powerful, dry-sump, double-overhead-camshaft engine kept it competitive. A Sunbeam 3-litre came second at Le Mans in 1925.

▽ **Mercedes-Benz 710 SSK 1929**
Origin Germany
Engine 7,065 cc, straight-six
Top speed 117 mph (188 km/h)

With 170 bhp, boosted to 235 bhp by engaging the supercharger, the Ferdinand Porsche-designed SSK was an effective competition car, impressing in hillclimbs, Grands Prix, and road races.

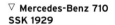

△ **Alfa Romeo P2 1924**
Origin Italy
Engine 1,987 cc, straight-eight
Top speed 123 mph (198 km/h)

Alfa Romeo poached the designer Vittorio Jano from Fiat to create the supercharged P2. Driven by Ascari and Campari, it won the first World Grand Prix Championship in 1925.

△ **Delage V12 1923**
Origin France
Engine 10,600 cc, V12
Top speed 143 mph (230 km/h)

In this car René Thomas set a World Land Speed Record of 143.31 mph (230.6 km/h) in 1924. At Brooklands John Cobb, Oliver Bertram, and Kay Petre all used it to set track records.

◁ **Riley 9 Brooklands 1929**
Origin UK
Engine 1,087 cc, straight-four
Top speed 80 mph (129 km/h)

Percy Riley's 9HP engine with hemispherical combustion chambers gave this sports car great performance for its size. The car's low build gave equally good road-handling.

◁ **Bugatti Type 39 1925**
Origin France
Engine 1,493 cc, straight eight
Top speed 100 mph (161 km/h)

Bugatti reduced the size of its Type 35 engine and used it to develop the Type 39, which was victorious in the 1,500 cc French Touring Grand Prix of 1925.

▷ **Bugatti Type 35C 1926**
Origin France
Engine 1,991 cc, straight-eight
Top speed 125 mph (201 km/h)

Bugatti's most successful racer, the Type 35 won more than 1,000 races in its career. The supercharged 35C triumphed in its debut race, the 1926 Gran Premio di Milano in Italy.

△ **Bugatti Type 35B 1927**
Origin France
Engine 2,262 cc, straight-eight
Top speed 127 mph (204 km/h)

The 35B was built to win Formula Libre races. Its supercharged engine employed a ball-bearing camshaft to help it rev to 6,000 rpm and produce up to 140 bhp.

▷ **Bentley 4½-litre 1927**
Origin UK
Engine 4,398 cc, straight-four
Top speed 92 mph (148 km/h)

One of the most famous British racing cars, the Bentley's advanced engine overcame the car's substantial weight to make it a successful long-distance racer.

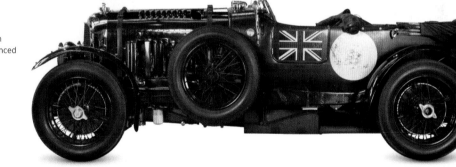

◁ **Fiat Mephistopheles 1923**
Origin Italy/UK
Engine 21,706 cc, straight-six
Top speed 146 mph (235 km/h)

English racing driver Ernest Eldridge fitted a World War I Fiat aero engine into a 1908 Fiat SB4 chassis to create this one-off car. In 1924 he used it to set a new World Land Speed Record of 146.01 mph (234.98 km/h).

▷ **Miller Boyle Valve Special 1930**
Origin USA
Engine 4,425 cc, straight-four
Top speed 140 mph (225 km/h)

Harry Miller was a brilliant engineer, and the race cars and engines he built were by far the most successful in US oval-track racing during the 1920s and 30s.

Bugatti Type 35B

The Type 35 Bugatti was emblematic of France's racing prowess in the 1920s. In motor sport, it was the French equivalent of the legendary British Bentley. The Bugatti was the product of an engineer born into a family of artists: for Ettore Bugatti, aesthetic perfection was as important as technical flair. The result was a car of extraordinary beauty in all its details, conservative in some aspects, but of proven effectiveness on the race circuit.

THE BUGATTI TYPE 35 was – and is – beautiful. But it also earned its keep: in its 1924 to 1931 lifespan, it claimed 2,000 racing successes. Many of these can be attributed to the supercharged 2,262 cc 35B. The car is instantly recognizable by its eight-spoke, cast-aluminium wheels. Lightweight and helping to boost brake cooling, these components made history because they were the first alloy wheels fitted as standard to a production car. The un-supercharged 1,991 cc Type 35 and the Type 35A came

with less elaborate 2-litre engines and wire wheels. For the Type 35 was a family of cars, and included an unblown 1,493 cc racer, a supercharged 1,100 cc racer, and various other sub-breeds. There was also a four-cylinder sister car, the Type 37, of which 290 were made. The Type 35 was, however, the more popular, with 336 produced. Of these, a healthy 139 were the more tame 35A, the so-called Técla model. But it is the blown T35B – with its tearing-calico engine note – that stirs the blood the most.

SPECIFICATIONS	
Model	Bugatti Type 35B, 1927-30
Assembly	Molsheim, France
Production	38
Construction	Separate chassis; aluminium panels
Engine	2,262 cc, ohc straight-eight
Power output	123 bhp at 5,500 rpm
Transmission	Four-speed manual, unsynchronized
Suspension	Semi-elliptic front; rear reversed-1/4
Brakes	Drums front and rear, cable-operated
Maximum speed	127 mph (204 km/h)

Artistry from Molsheim
The elliptical badge is found on all Bugattis from 1910 onwards and bears the initials of Ettore Bugatti. It was used until the end of Bugatti car production in the early 1950s, and revived when the marque resurfaced in the 1990s.

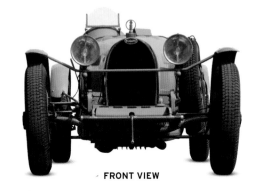

FRONT VIEW

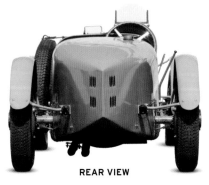

REAR VIEW

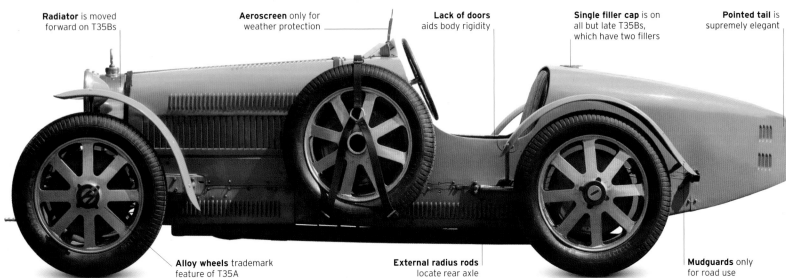

Radiator is moved forward on T35Bs

Aeroscreen only for weather protection

Lack of doors aids body rigidity

Single filler cap is on all but late T35Bs, which have two fillers

Pointed tail is supremely elegant

Alloy wheels trademark feature of T35A

External radius rods locate rear axle

Mudguards only for road use

True finesse

The Bugatti's lithe lines are hard to fault. The supercharged 35B and 35C have a wider radiator, moved further forward, as opposed to the more slender radiator of the Type 35, the roadgoing wire-wheeled Type 35A, and the four-cylinder Type 37. The tubular axle, through which the springs pass, is a Bugatti trademark, and the horseshoe-shaped grille is a reflection of Bugatti's love of all things equestrian.

THE EXTERIOR

The exquisitely detailed but stark bodywork of the Type 35 is all about function, but with a finesse that makes one recall Ettore Bugatti's supposed remark that the rival Bentley was a high-speed lorry. Arguably the four-cylinder Type 37 is even more pleasing, but it lacks the gutsy muscle of the Type 35. Bugatti had a sure eye for a car's lines, a gift he passed on to his son Jean, who styled future models.

1. Radiator-top water-temperature gauge 2. Free standing headlamps typical of 1920s French cars 3. Type 35 is larded with louvres 4. Only hand-starting on early T35s 5. Gear lever exits through slot in bodywork 6. Eared filler cap 7. Louvred tail 8. Securing wire 9. Tail lamps are later addition 10. Spare wheel

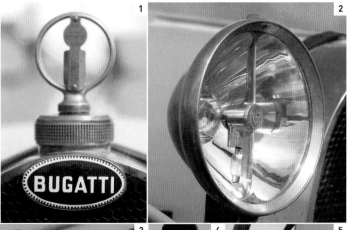

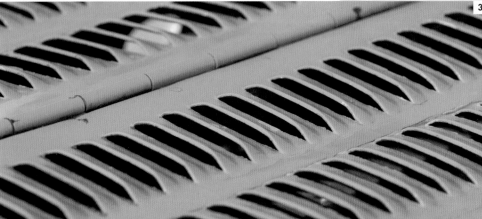

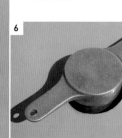

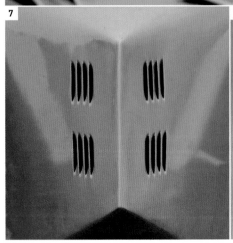

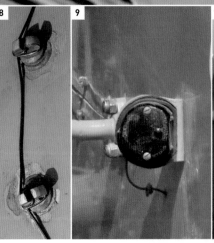

THE INTERIOR

This is the cockpit of a racing car, so creature comforts are absent while space is at a premium. The mechanicals are exposed in the car's footwells, leading to the presence of leaking oil, not surprising for a racing car where function and weight-saving is more important than comfort. The engine-turned aluminium dashboard is a typical finish of the time, used to good effect by Bugatti.

11. Wood-rim, four-spoke steering wheel is Bugatti trademark 12. Aeroscreen is the only weather protection 13. Rear-view mirror is cowled 14. Dashboard clock is typical Bugatti feature 15. Cockpit is basic, with dark tan leather seats

UNDER THE BONNET

Blistering performance – even by
today's standards – is a given with
the supercharged Bugatti. Helping to
achieve this is the overhead-camshaft
configuration and the use of three
valves (two inlet and one exhaust)
per cylinder. Free-revving reliability
is assured by the use of roller-bearing
and ball-bearing mains for the
five-bearing crankshaft; the big ends
also use roller bearings. Power is
transmitted via a multi-plate
clutch running in oil.

16. Sculptural straight-eight has single
overhead camshaft **17.** Magneto is driven off
end of camshaft **18.** Supercharger has
separate oil tank. **19.** Block is cast in two
four-cylinder units. **20.** Steering box known
for its robustness has worm and helical wheel

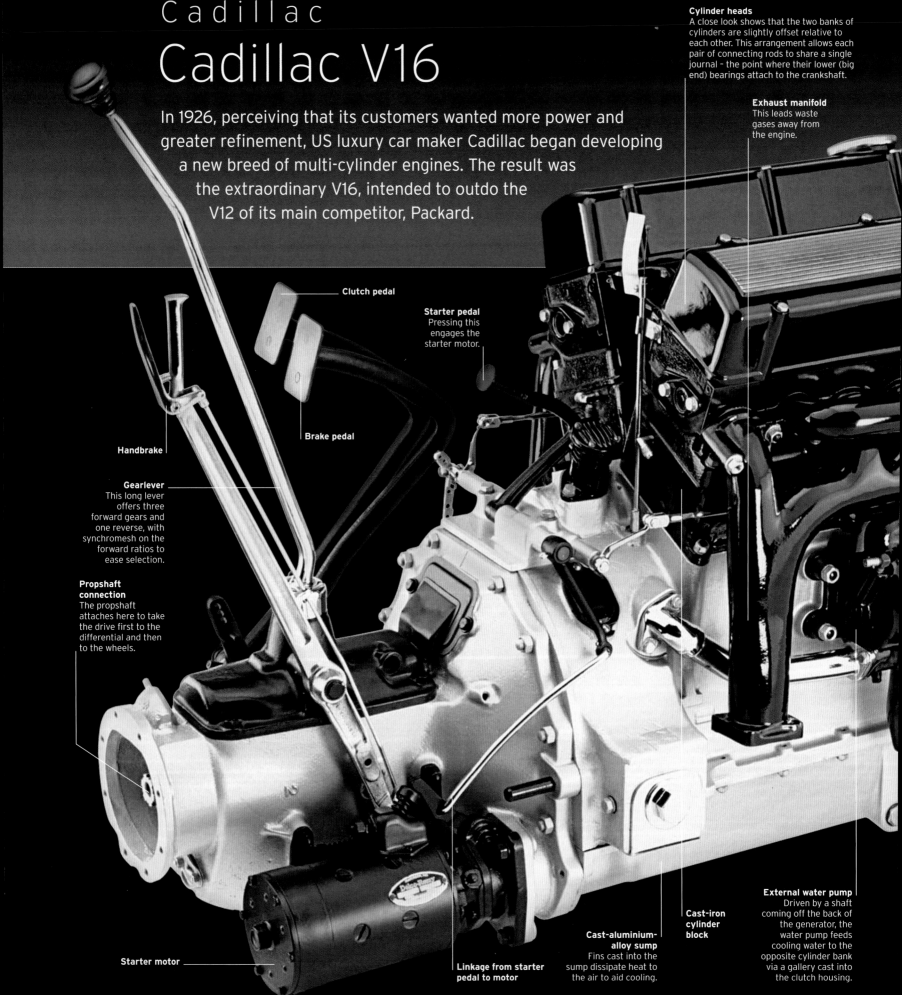

Cadillac V16

In 1926, perceiving that its customers wanted more power and greater refinement, US luxury car maker Cadillac began developing a new breed of multi-cylinder engines. The result was the extraordinary V16, intended to outdo the V12 of its main competitor, Packard.

Cylinder heads
A close look shows that the two banks of cylinders are slightly offset relative to each other. This arrangement allows each pair of connecting rods to share a single journal – the point where their lower (big end) bearings attach to the crankshaft.

Exhaust manifold
This leads waste gases away from the engine.

Clutch pedal

Starter pedal
Pressing this engages the starter motor.

Brake pedal

Handbrake

Gearlever
This long lever offers three forward gears and one reverse, with synchromesh on the forward ratios to ease selection.

Propshaft connection
The propshaft attaches here to take the drive first to the differential and then to the wheels.

Starter motor

Linkage from starter pedal to motor

Cast-aluminium-alloy sump
Fins cast into the sump dissipate heat to the air to aid cooling.

Cast-iron cylinder block

External water pump
Driven by a shaft coming off the back of the generator, the water pump feeds cooling water to the opposite cylinder bank via a gallery cast into the clutch housing.

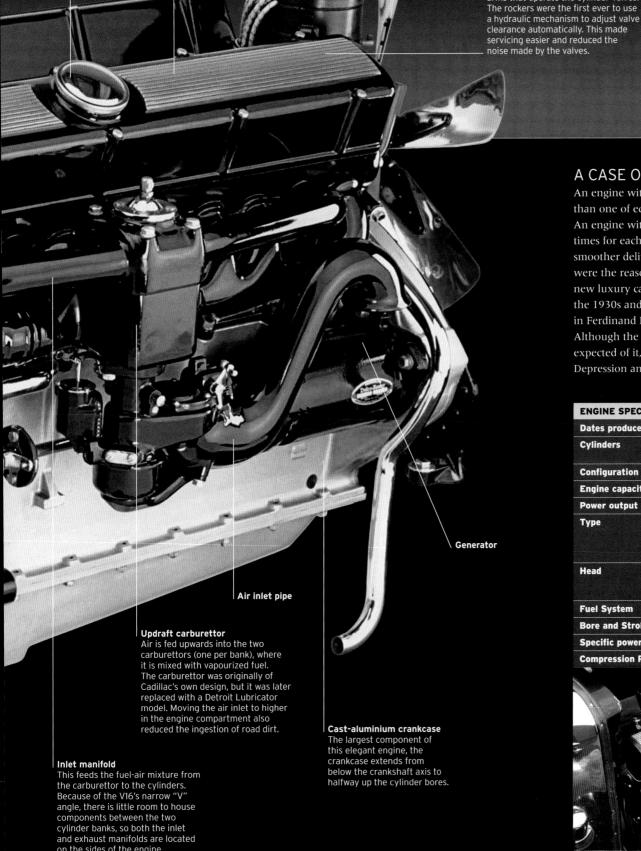

The rockers were the first ever to use a hydraulic mechanism to adjust valve clearance automatically. This made servicing easier and reduced the noise made by the valves.

retained the V16's 45-degree bank angle, instead of having the natural 60-degree "V" of a V12, cylinder firing was uneven, but the engine's smoothness remained acceptable.

A CASE OF BAD TIMING

An engine with more cylinders gives greater power than one of equivalent capacity but fewer cylinders. An engine with more cylinders also fires more times for each crankshaft revolution, giving a smoother delivery of torque (turning force). These were the reasons why Cadillac chose a V16 for its new luxury car – a configuration that, later in the 1930s and in supercharged form, would impress in Ferdinand Porsche's Auto Union racing cars. Although the Cadillac V16 delivered all that was expected of it, its success was limited by the Great Depression and the outbreak of World War II.

Generator

Air inlet pipe

Updraft carburettor
Air is fed upwards into the two carburettors (one per bank), where it is mixed with vapourized fuel. The carburettor was originally of Cadillac's own design, but it was later replaced with a Detroit Lubricator model. Moving the air inlet to higher in the engine compartment also reduced the ingestion of road dirt.

Cast-aluminium crankcase
The largest component of this elegant engine, the crankcase extends from below the crankshaft axis to halfway up the cylinder bores.

Inlet manifold
This feeds the fuel-air mixture from the carburettor to the cylinders. Because of the V16's narrow "V" angle, there is little room to house components between the two cylinder banks, so both the inlet and exhaust manifolds are located on the sides of the engine.

ENGINE SPECIFICATIONS	
Dates produced	1930–1940 (two versions)
Cylinders	Sixteen cylinders, 45-degree "V" (later 135-degree "V")
Configuration	Front-mounted, longitudinal
Engine capacity	452 cu in (7,413 cc)
Power output	165 bhp @ 3,400 rpm
Type	Conventional four-stroke, water-cooled petrol engine with reciprocating pistons, distributor ignition, and a wet sump
Head	ohv operated by pushrods and rockers; two valves per cylinder, hydraulic tappets
Fuel System	Single carburettor per bank
Bore and Stroke	3.0 in x 4.0 in (76.2 mm x 101.6 mm)
Specific power	22.3 bhp/litre
Compression Ratio	5.35:1

Luxury and Prestige

Despite the recession that hit much of the world in the aftermath of World War I, there were still plenty of wealthy customers in the 1920s looking for the latest and most opulent carriages to transport them across Europe or the US. Expensive cars were built as chassis complete with running gear, and were clad in the finest examples of the traditional coachbuilders' art.

▷ **Hispano-Suiza H6 1919**
Origin France
Engine 6,597 cc, straight-six
Top speed 85 mph (137 km/h)

Hispano-Suiza, a Spanish company based in France, made some of the finest cars of the 1920s. Designed by Swiss engineer Marc Birkigt, they featured the first servo brakes.

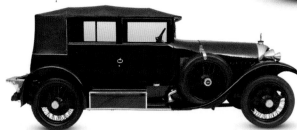

◁ **Spyker C4 All-weather Coupé 1921**
Origin Netherlands
Engine 5,741 cc, straight-six
Top speed 80 mph (129 km/h)

Despite royal patronage, and engines shared with Zeppelins, the expensive Spykers sold in very small numbers. The company stopped building cars in 1925.

△ **Pierce-Arrow 38HP Model 51 1919**
Origin USA
Engine 8,587 cc, straight-six
Top speed 75 mph (121 km/h)

This huge and powerful car had a four-valves-per-cylinder engine. US President Woodrow Wilson liked his official Model 51 so much that he kept it when he left the White House.

▷ **Lincoln L Sedan 1922**
Origin USA
Engine 6,306 cc, V8
Top speed 82 mph (132 km/h)

Ford rescued Lincoln from receivership in 1922 and produced this magnificent machine. Its luxuries include an electric clock, thermostatic radiator shutters, and a cigar lighter.

◁ **Hotchkiss AM 80 Veth Coupé 1929**
Origin France
Engine 3,015 cc, straight-six
Top speed 80 mph (129 km/h)

Hotchkiss built high-quality sporting cars. This example was bodied in Arnhem, the Netherlands, by Veth. It features a 29 mph (40 km/h) impact-absorbing front bumper by Overman.

▷ **Isotta-Fraschini Tipo 8A Van Rijswijk Dual-cowl Phaeton 1924**
Origin Italy
Engine 7,372 cc, straight-eight
Top speed 90 mph (145 km/h)

Italy's top car of the 1920s attracted some magnificent coachbuilt bodies, including this model from the Netherlands. Its 120 bhp engine was designed by Giustino Cattaneo.

△ **Lagonda 3-litre 1929**
Origin UK
Engine 2,931 cc, straight-six
Top speed 83 mph (134 km/h)

Lagonda produced sporting cars with seven-bearing engines that made them smooth-running and long-lasting. Some had sporting coachwork, other were saloons or limousines.

△ **Rolls-Royce 20HP 1922**
Origin UK
Engine 3,128 cc, straight-six
Top speed 65 mph (105 km/h)

Underpowered compared with the effortlessly potent larger Rolls-Royces, the 20 hp was a response to post-war austerity. It sold well, despite its limitations.

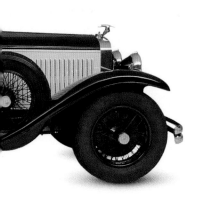

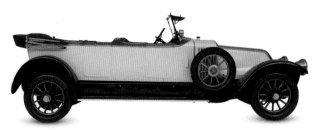

△ **Stutz Model K 1921**

Origin USA

Engine 5,899 cc, straight-four

Top speed 75 mph (120 km/h)

Alongside its highly successful Bearcat sports cars, Stutz built attractive touring cars with the same engines. From 1921 these had a detachable cylinder head.

△ **Renault 40CV 1921**

Origin France

Engine 9,123 cc, straight-six

Top speed 90 mph (145 km/h)

Renault's biggest luxury car of the 1920s had six cylinders, wooden wheels, and wheelbases of just over 3.6 m (12 ft) or 3.9 m (13 ft). A 40CV won the Monte Carlo Rally in 1925.

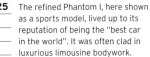

△ **Minerva 32HP AK Landaulette 1927**

Origin Belgium

Engine 5,954 cc, straight-six

Top speed 70 mph (113 km/h)

Belgium's premier car manufacturer made highly refined cars in the 1920s with Knight sleeve-valve engines. They attracted formal coachwork and multiple royal patronage.

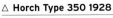

△ **Horch Type 350 1928**

Origin Germany

Engine 3,950 cc, straight-eight

Top speed 62 mph (100 km/h)

Horch was Germany's main rival to Mercedes-Benz in the luxury car market. Paul Daimler, son of Gottlieb Daimler, was employed to design this car's double-overhead-camshaft engine.

◁ **Packard 443 Custom Eight 1928**

Origin USA

Engine 6,318 cc, straight-eight

Top speed 85 mph (137 km/h)

One of the US's leading luxury marques of the 1920s, Packard built lavish cars on impressively long chassis – in this case with a wheelbase almost 3.6 m (12 ft) long.

△ **Bugatti Type 41 Royale 1927**

Origin France

Engine 12,760 cc, straight-eight

Top speed 120 mph (193 km/h)

With 24 valves and 300 bhp, the Royale was imposing in the extreme, and aimed at royalty worldwide. However, it was prohibitively expensive; just six were built.

▽ **Rolls-Royce Phantom I 1925**

Origin UK

Engine 7,668 cc, straight-six

Top speed 90 mph (145 km/h)

The refined Phantom I, here shown as a sports model, lived up to its reputation of being the "best car in the world". It was often clad in luxurious limousine bodywork.

Lancia Lambda, 1922
Screen legend Greta Garbo (at the wheel) epitomized the glamour and daring of the "flapper" era – as did the sporty Lancia Lambda, with its advanced construction and top speed of 70 mph (112 km/h).

Hollywood Coupés and Glorious Roadsters

The Roaring Twenties was a time of great style and decadence among the moneyed classes, where traditional wealthy families began to be outnumbered by newly rich film stars, business tycoons, and gangsters. The glamour and excitement of their lifestyle was reflected in the cars built for them, in Europe and the US, which displayed flamboyant bodies, shiny nickel or chrome plating, and bright colours.

△ **Cunningham touring car 1916**
Origin USA
Engine 7,200 cc, V8
Top speed 95 mph (153 km/h)

Exceptionally modern-looking at the time of its introduction, and boasting one of the first production V8 engines, the Cunningham attracted celebrity buyers, and was produced until 1933.

△ **Stanley Model 735 1920**
Origin USA
Engine 2,059 cc, straight-two steam
Top speed 60 mph (97 km/h)

At four times the price of a Ford Model T, and with limited power output, the Stanley steam car was an anachronism by the 1920s. Nevertheless, it stayed in production until 1924.

▷ **Bentley Speed Six 1928**
Origin UK
Engine 6,597 cc, straight-six
Top speed 100 mph (161 km/h)

Developed from the 1924 Standard Six, this two-times Le Mans winner was W.O. Bentley's most successful racing car. With its effortless performance, it also made a sensational road car.

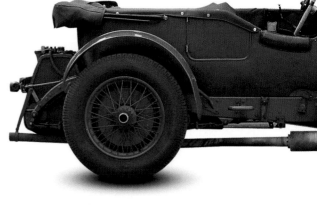

△ **Ford Model A 1927**
Origin USA
Engine 3,285 cc, straight-four
Top speed 60 mph (97 km/h)

The Model A was a mass-production car for middle America, but it still managed to exude gangster-movie style. It was given strong body colours and whitewall tyres.

▽ **Cord L-29 1929**
Origin USA
Engine 4,884 cc, straight-eight
Top speed 77 mph (124 km/h)

The remarkable L-29 used the Lycoming engine turned around to drive the front wheels. E.L. Cord's design was a long, low build without an intrusive transmission tunnel.

△ **Ford Model T roadster 1923**
Origin USA
Engine 2,878 cc, straight-four
Top speed 45 mph (72 km/h)

Ford began improving the Model T in 1923 in response to market challenge from Chevrolet. New styling touches included a raked windscreen and demountable wheels.

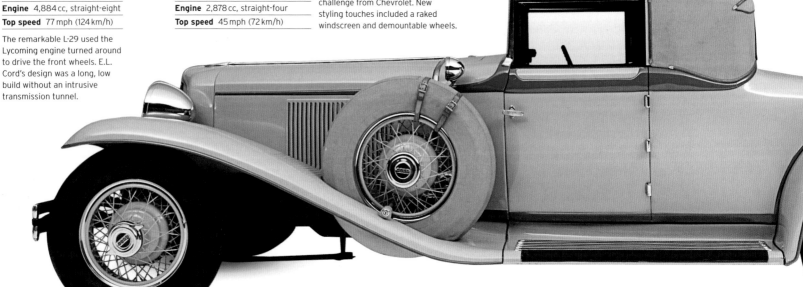

◁ Lincoln V8 1921
Origin USA
Engine 5,861 cc, V8
Top speed 88 mph (142 km/h)

Henry Leland left Cadillac to found Lincoln, named after his hero Abraham Lincoln. Henry Ford bought the company in 1922, inheriting this upmarket car that rivalled Cadillac.

△ Woods Dual Power 1917
Origin USA
Engine 1,560 cc, straight-four + electric motor
Top speed 35 mph (56 km/h)

The world's first petrol/electric hybrid used battery power up to 20 mph (32 km/h), then added its engine. It had no gearbox and utilized its engine and regenerative braking to charge its battery.

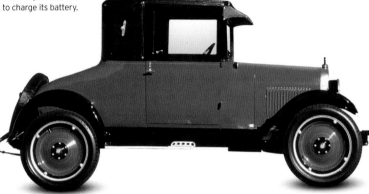

◁ Chevrolet Superior Coupé 1925
Origin USA
Engine 2,804 cc, straight-four
Top speed 56 mph (90 km/h)

William Durant wanted to beat the Model T Ford with this car. Though it could not compete on price, it was a fine car and increased Chevrolet sales by a handsome 70%.

▷ Plymouth Model U Coupé 1929
Origin USA
Engine 2,874 cc, straight-four
Top speed 60 mph (97 km/h)

Chrysler launched the Plymouth in 1928 as a budget-priced car, boasting special features that included hydraulic brakes. It was well timed, and kept Chrysler solvent through the Depression.

△ La Salle Model 303 1927
Origin USA
Engine 4,965 cc, V8
Top speed 80 mph (129 km/h)

General Motors introduced La Salle in 1927 as a way to sell more Cadillac-style cars without devaluing Cadillac's exclusivity. An instant hit, it was a fine car in its own right.

◁ Kissel straight-eight Speedster 1927
Origin USA
Engine 4,670 cc, straight-eight
Top speed 78 mph (125 km/h)

This Kissel was designed to race against the Stutz Bearcat and Mercer Raceabout. It stayed in production for four years.

▷ Lancia Lambda 1922
Origin Italy
Engine 2,120 cc, V4
Top speed 70 mph (113 km/h)

One of the most advanced cars of its day, the long, low Lambda boasted a monocoque body, overhead-camshaft V4 engine, and independent front suspension.

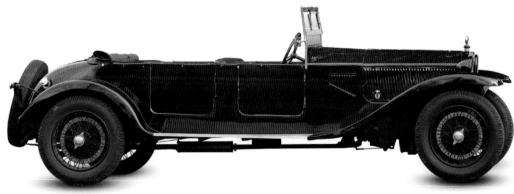

▷ Duesenberg Model J 1928
Origin USA
Engine 6,882 cc, straight-eight
Top speed 115 mph (185 km/h)

The Model J was bigger, faster, more elaborate, more refined, and more expensive than any other US car of the 1920s. It was powered by a double-overhead-camshaft engine.

Duesenberg Model J

In 1926 the ailing Duesenberg firm was bought by the businessman Errett Lobban Cord, who already owned the Auburn motor company and would go on to create a famous car marque under his own name. Cord briefed the Duesenberg brothers to design the ultimate high-speed luxury US car, and in 1928 they came up with the Model J. Powered by a superb straight-eight engine, it led to the popular phrase "It's a Duesy", meaning the very best.

AT THE HEART of the Model J was the magnificent power unit – built by aero-engine specialist Lycoming, a Cord-owned company. With its straight-eight engine, the Model J offered good acceleration despite its bulk, and was capable of cruising at 95–100 mph (153–161 km/h). From 1929 it also had hydraulic brakes with servo assistance, and light steering so the car was not demanding to drive. But the Model J, which carried bodies by top US coachbuilders, was expensive: the rolling chassis cost roughly 19 times the price of a Ford Model A. In the

lingering depression of 1930s America, this Duesenberg sold with difficulty and in the end only 471 were made. Of the total, an estimated 35 were the supercharged SJ models, with dramatic outside exhaust pipes that were also fitted to some later Model Js. Most SJs were built on a shorter-wheelbase chassis, but some had the regular-length frame. There were also two cars with a special ultra-short chassis called the SSJ; carrying rakish two-seat coachwork, these went to the Hollywood actors and Duesenberg marque loyalists Clark Gable and Gary Cooper.

SPECIFICATIONS	
Model	Duesenberg Model J, 1928-37
Assembly	Indianapolis, USA
Production	471, including Model SJ
Construction	Separate chassis
Engine	6,882 cc, dohc straight-eight
Power output	265 bhp at 4,250 rpm
Transmission	Three-speed manual
Suspension	Rigid axles, leaf springs
Brakes	Four-wheel drum, hydraulic
Maximum speed	115 mph (185 km/h)

Where eagles soar
Fred and August Duesenberg started making marine engines and racing cars in 1913, and introduced their first production car in 1920. The eagle in the badge epitomized American freedom. The company came to an end with the 1937 collapse of the Auburn-Cord-Duesenberg combine.

FRONT VIEW

REAR VIEW

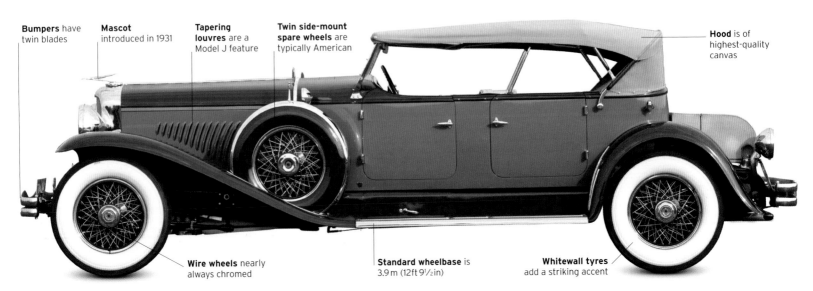

Bumpers have twin blades

Mascot introduced in 1931

Tapering louvres are a Model J feature

Twin side-mount spare wheels are typically American

Hood is of highest-quality canvas

Wire wheels nearly always chromed

Standard wheelbase is 3.9 m (12ft 9½in)

Whitewall tyres add a striking accent

Controlled exuberance
The Model J's lines were essentially conservative – at least for most examples. But occasional flourishes made a big difference, such as the sweeping dual-blade bumpers and the styling contours pressed into the mudguards. The car's frontage was a mass of gleaming chrome, with huge headlamps and a stylishly executed radiator grille; the round chromed objects seen under the front mudguards on this 1931 model are an early form of hydraulic damper, with a rotary action to absorb shocks.

THE EXTERIOR

The Model J's body was always built by outside coachbuilders, but often under the supervision of Duesenberg's head of styling Gordon Buehrig. This resulted in a certain shared look to many bodies. The most prolific builder of Model J bodies was Murphy of Pasadena, but this particular 1931 car is one of eight with "Tourster" open-touring coachwork by the respected Pennsylvania company Derham.

1. Mascot evokes winged flight **2.** Aperture for starting-handle has stylish cover **3.** Twin bumper bars **4.** Headlamps **5.** Generously-cut louvres aid engine cooling **6.** Opening vent in bodywork **7.** Spare wheel **8.** Ribbed running-board in chrome **9.** Chromed hinges **10.** T-shaped door handle **11.** Rear light has "STOP" sign **12.** Hood irons are wood-reinforced **13.** Trunk with drawers

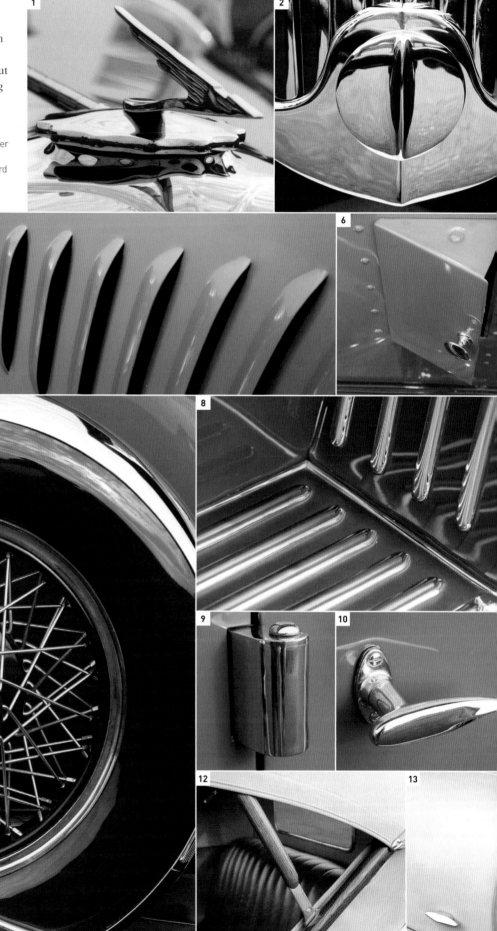

THE INTERIOR

Relative to luxury British cars of the time, their US counterparts were surprisingly sober. The Model J has a plain interior lifted only by the lustre of its engine-turned metal dashboard. The use of a right-hand accelerator is notable, as many European cars still had a central pedal at the time.

14. Minor controls on large steering wheel 15. Long gear lever typical of era; handbrake operates on transmission 16. Conventional dials with rolling drum rev counter and speedometer 17. Chrome highlights lift plain door trims 18. Rear side-window winder 19. Upholstery is plain, vertical-pleat leather

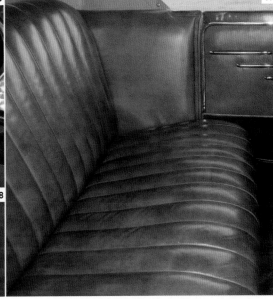

UNDER THE BONNET

In an era when plodding sidevalve engines were commonplace, the Model J's straight-eight engine, with four valves per cylinder, was extremely advanced. It featured overhead valves that were operated by double overhead camshafts. The 6,882 cc unit claimed to deliver 265 bhp, deliberately exaggerated, as Cadillac's V16 managed a genuine 165 bhp. The supercharged SJ of 1932–35 boasted a mighty 320 bhp.

20. Engine fed by a single carburettor 21. All Model J engines have green enamelled finish 22. Starter motor is also painted green

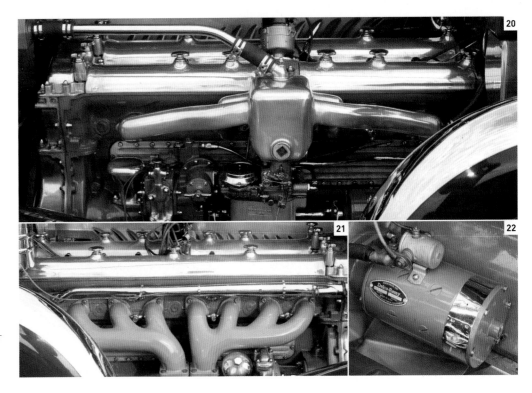

Cars for the Middle Classes

The 1920s saw huge changes in the motoring world, as high-volume production pushed down prices and it became the norm for the middle classes in Europe and the US to own cars. An Atlantic divide emerged, with European mainstream cars mostly being powered by four-cylinder engines of around 1500 cc, whereas US cars were substantially larger, housing six- or eight-cylinder engines of around 4,000 cc.

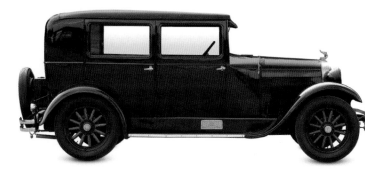

△ Dodge 4 1914
Origin USA
Engine 3,479 cc, straight-four
Top speed 50 mph (80 km/h)

In the 1920s Dodge was the second best-selling US marque, largely thanks to this rugged car, which had an all-steel body, sliding-gear transmission, and 12-volt electrics.

△ Citroën Type A 1919
Origin France
Engine 1,327 cc, straight-four
Top speed 40 mph (64 km/h)

André Citroën's first car was also Europe's first mass-produced model, with up to 100 being made a day. In all, 24,093 Type As were sold before production ceased in 1921.

△ Essex A 1919
Origin USA
Engine 2,930 cc, straight-four
Top speed 65 mph (105 km/h)

Linked with Hudson, the moderately priced Essex marque was an immediate success. More than 1.13 million Essex cars were sold up to 1932, after which the name was changed to Terraplane.

▷ Riley Nine Monaco 1926
Origin UK
Engine 1,087 cc, straight-four
Top speed 60 mph (97 km/h)

Percy and Stanley Riley designed an outstanding sporting car in 1926, which entered series production in 1928. The twin side-camshafts gave it exceptional performance.

△ Chrysler G70 1924
Origin USA
Engine 3,200 cc, straight-six
Top speed 70 mph (113 km/h)

Walter Chrysler's first car was a revelation, boasting impressive performance and four-wheel hydraulic brakes. It quickly took a significant slice of the US market.

▽ Willys-Knight Model 66 1927
Origin USA
Engine 4,179 cc, straight-six
Top speed 70 mph (113 km/h)

Willys-Knight built 50,000 cars a year during the 1920s, all with sleeve-valve engines. Its top-of-the-range 66 offered high comfort, good looks, and quality engineering – albeit at a high price.

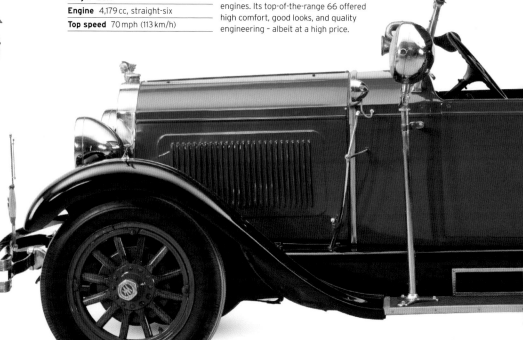

△ Morris Oxford 1919
Origin UK
Engine 1,548 cc, straight-four
Top speed 60 mph (97 km/h)

Part of the Morris "Bullnose" range, named after the rounded radiator, the Oxford's clean lines and consistent performance won it many fans among UK motorists.

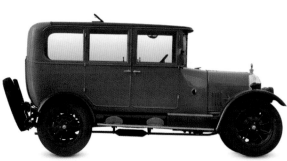

△ Morris Cowley 1927
Origin UK
Engine 1,548 cc, straight-four
Top speed 60 mph (97 km/h)

The Cowley, another Morris "Bullnose", was a cheaper version of the Oxford. The Bullnoses seemed dated by the late 1920s, but they continued to sell on their reputation for reliability.

△ Hupmobile Touring Series R 1921

Origin USA

Engine 2,990 cc, straight-four

Top speed 60 mph (97 km/h)

The strong sales of this simple, spacious, four-cylinder car made Hupmobile one of the success stories of the early 1920s. However, the company did not survive the Great Depression of the 1930s.

△ Ford Model A Tourer 1927

Origin USA

Engine 3,294 cc, straight-four

Top speed 65 mph (105 km/h)

This was the first Ford with conventional controls: clutch and brake pedals, throttle, and gearchange. Almost 5 million Model As took to the world's roads from 1927 to 1931.

△ Buick Model 24 1924

Origin USA

Engine 2,786 cc, straight-four

Top speed 55 mph (89 km/h)

Buick produced its last four-cylinder cars in 1924, after which its smallest engine was a straight-six. The Buick Model 24 was sturdy and adequate, although a little underpowered.

◁ Opel 4/14 1924

Origin Germany

Engine 1,018 cc, straight-four

Top speed 50 mph (80 km/h)

The Opel 4PS (4HP) series cars were the first German vehicles to be built on an assembly line: 119,484 of the 4/12, 4/14, 4/16, and 4/18 models were built in seven years.

△ Standard SL04 1922

Origin UK

Engine 1,944 cc, straight-four

Top speed 52 mph (84 km/h)

A series of spacious, four-cylinder cars like the SL04 led to Standard selling 10,000 a year in the 1920s, when "Standard" implied "of a high standard" – not "ordinary", as now.

△ Fiat 509A 1926

Origin Italy

Engine 990 cc, straight-four

Top speed 48 mph (77 km/h)

The 509's lively but economical overhead-cam engine and the option to buy on hire purchase made it a popular car, leading to 90,000 sales from 1925 to 1929.

◁ Austin Twelve 1927

Origin UK

Engine 1,861 cc, straight-four

Top speed 53 mph (85 km/h)

A wide range of competent, dependable cars, such as the Twelve, helped Herbert Austin's company become the UK's most successful car maker of the 1920s.

△ MG 18/80 1928

Origin UK

Engine 2,468 cc, straight-six

Top speed 78 mph (126 km/h)

In 1922, supported by the Morris company, Cecil Kimber began making sporting cars based on Morris components. Later badged as MGs, his cars had attractively styled bodies and gave good performance.

Royce 10 hp car,
1904

Great marques
The Rolls-Royce story

From the earliest days of this famous British marque, the design and manufacture of its cars has focused on quality, refinement, and reliability. As a result, Rolls-Royces have long been known as the best cars in the world, so much so that the Rolls-Royce name has become a term meaning "the best of the best" in any field.

FREDERICK HENRY ROYCE, founder of an electrical engineering business in Manchester, built his first car in 1904. At around the same time, Charles Stewart Rolls was setting up a motor dealership and repair workshop in London with Claude Johnson. Henry Edmunds, a friend of Rolls and a director of Royce's company, persuaded Rolls to meet Royce and drive the new car. Rolls immediately recognized the superior quality and refinement of the vehicle. The pair agreed that Royce would develop a range of cars that Rolls would sell under the Rolls-Royce name.

Rolls-Royce badge
(introduced 1930)

The first models ranged from a two-cylinder, 10 hp chassis at £395, through three-cylinder 15 hp and four-cylinder 20 hp machines to a flagship 30 hp six-cylinder car, which went on sale in 1905 at £890. As with other prestige marques of the time, the body had to be purchased separately from a coachbuilder, at an additional cost of up to £500.

In September 1905 Charles Rolls entered a pair of 20 hp Rolls-Royces into the Isle of Man Tourist Trophy (TT), an event that aimed to find the best touring car rather than the fastest purpose-built racing machine. The regulations stipulated four-seater bodywork, and there was a limit on the amount of fuel the cars could use. The TT Rolls-Royces had lightweight chassis and four-speed gearboxes with overdrive top gear, allowing fast cruising with good fuel economy. Rolls drove one car, which broke its gearbox early on. The other car, in Percy Northey's hands, finished second, gaining valuable publicity for the fledgling marque.

A 40/50 hp model, with a larger, six-cylinder engine and a revised chassis, was launched at the London Motor Show in 1906. The following year, driver Claude Johnson – who has been described as "the hyphen in Rolls-Royce" – completed a 15,000-mile (24,000-km) trial in this car under the supervision of the Royal Automobile Club (RAC). The run took in the Scottish Reliability Trial, in which the car won a gold medal. Johnson's 40/50 was given the name Silver Ghost, after its then unusual colour. This performance, together

Selling the best
"The Best Car in the World" is illustrated in an appropriately aristocratic setting in this Rolls-Royce advertisement from 1917.

Assembling Merlin engines
The Rolls-Royce Merlin was one of the most successful aero engines of World War II. It was used in planes such as the Supermarine Spitfire and Hawker Hurricane.

with the Phantom series of cars introduced in 1925, enhanced the company's growing reputation. In 1930 Rolls-Royce bought Bentley and relocated production to the Rolls-Royce works in Derby. It then developed a new range of "Derby Bentleys", using Rolls-Royce chassis and Bentley engines.

The first Rolls-Royce aero engines were made in World War I, and the company remained an important supplier to Britain's fighting aircraft in

> # "Everyone who buys the **best things** ... buys only **Rolls-Royce** motor cars"
> LORD NORTHCLIFFE, NEWSPAPER PROPRIETOR, IN A LETTER TO CLAUDE JOHNSON, 1912

World War II. A factory was set up at Crewe, 50 miles (80 km) from Derby, to increase aero-engine production, and all car making moved there after the war. Post-war production began in 1946 with the Mark VI Bentley and the Rolls-Royce Silver Wraith. Both had the same new chassis and an "F-head" engine with overhead inlet valves for more efficient breathing. First Bentley, then Rolls-Royce, adopted standardized

bodywork built in-house, although customers could still choose to order a bare chassis to be clothed by a coachbuilder. Bentleys were gradually reduced to little more than Rolls-Royces with Bentley radiator grilles.

In 1959 a V8 engine of 6,230 cc was introduced in the Silver Cloud II and a new full-size saloon, the Phantom V. The key development of the 1960s was the 1965 Silver Shadow saloon (and its Bentley T-series brother). A more modern car with full-width, four-door styling and a monocoque structure, the Shadow sold in greater numbers than any previous Rolls-Royce. Shadow derivatives included the two-door Corniche coupé and convertible, the long-wheelbase Silver Wraith, and the Pininfarina-designed Camargue. Updated with a 6,750 cc engine in 1970

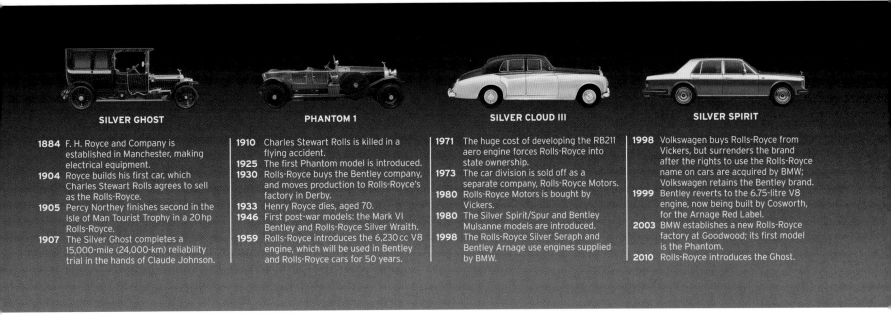

SILVER GHOST

1884 F. H. Royce and Company is established in Manchester, making electrical equipment.
1904 Royce builds his first car, which Charles Stewart Rolls agrees to sell as the Rolls-Royce.
1905 Percy Northey finishes second in the Isle of Man Tourist Trophy in a 20 hp Rolls-Royce.
1907 The Silver Ghost completes a 15,000-mile (24,000-km) reliability trial in the hands of Claude Johnson.

PHANTOM 1

1910 Charles Stewart Rolls is killed in a flying accident.
1925 The first Phantom model is introduced.
1930 Rolls-Royce buys the Bentley company, and moves production to Rolls-Royce's factory in Derby.
1933 Henry Royce dies, aged 70.
1946 First post-war models: the Mark VI Bentley and Rolls-Royce Silver Wraith.
1959 Rolls-Royce introduces the 6,230 cc V8 engine, which will be used in Bentley and Rolls-Royce cars for 50 years.

SILVER CLOUD III

1971 The huge cost of developing the RB211 aero engine forces Rolls-Royce into state ownership.
1973 The car division is sold off as a separate company, Rolls-Royce Motors.
1980 Rolls-Royce Motors is bought by Vickers.
1980 The Silver Spirit/Spur and Bentley Mulsanne models are introduced.
1998 The Rolls-Royce Silver Seraph and Bentley Arnage use engines supplied by BMW.

SILVER SPIRIT

1998 Volkswagen buys Rolls-Royce from Vickers, but surrenders the brand after the rights to use the Rolls-Royce name on cars are acquired by BMW; Volkswagen retains the Bentley brand.
1999 Bentley reverts to the 6.75-litre V8 engine, now being built by Cosworth, for the Arnage Red Label.
2003 BMW establishes a new Rolls-Royce factory at Goodwood; its first model is the Phantom.
2010 Rolls-Royce introduces the Ghost.

and a host of detail improvements in 1977, the Silver Shadow remained in production until 1980, when the Silver Spirit and long-wheelbase Silver Spur (and Bentley Mulsanne) took over.

Crippled by the costs of developing the RB211 aero engine, Rolls-Royce was taken into state ownership in 1971. The car division was sold off as a separate entity, Rolls-Royce Motors, in 1973. The rights to the Rolls-Royce name remained with the aero-engine company, but were licensed to the car maker. In 1980 the British engineering group Vickers bought Rolls-Royce Motors. Bentleys now started to diverge from their Rolls-Royce counterparts, with the launch of the Mulsanne Turbo. In 1998 a new range of cars, the Rolls-Royce Silver Seraph and Bentley Arnage, were for the first time powered by bought-in engines, supplied by BMW.

In 1998 Volkswagen acquired Rolls-Royce and Bentley from Vickers, paying £430m for the car designs, the factory, the brand names, and the two Rolls-Royce trademarks – the Spirit of

Rocking Rolls
Rolls-Royces have long been associated with the glamour of rock and roll. Here, Elvis Presley poses by his Silver Cloud outside the entrance to his Gracelands mansion in Memphis, Tennessee.

Ecstasy mascot and the "Grecian" radiator grille. However, Volkswagen neglected to acquire the rights to use the Rolls-Royce name on cars, which were still owned by the aero-engine company. BMW bought the licence to those rights for just £40m, leaving Volkswagen little option but to surrender the Rolls-Royce brand and concentrate on Bentley – claiming that was all it ever wanted. In 2003 BMW opened a new Rolls-Royce factory at Goodwood, Sussex, where production began of the new Phantom. That was joined in 2010 by a smaller model, the Ghost. The motoring media praised both cars, giving Rolls-Royce a stable start to its latest era of making what some, at least, continue to argue are the best cars in the world.

Small Cars

In the 1920s manufacturers competed to produce practical motor cars at prices the middle classes could afford, finally enabling car ownership to extend beyond the wealthy elite. Some of these vehicles were desperately primitive, others almost too small to be usable. But there were also those that showed the way in which small cars would develop, with four-cylinder engines, four wheels, and brakes on each wheel.

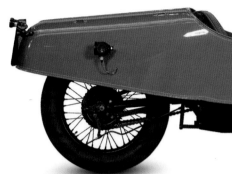

◁ **Tamplin 1919**
Origin UK
Engine 980 cc, V2
Top speed 42 mph (68 km/h)

Edward Tamplin bought the rights to the Carden cyclecar and produced it under his own name. It had a JAP engine on the side, an oiled fibreboard body, and tandem seats.

◁ **Leyat Hélica (replica) 1919**
Origin France
Engine 1,203 cc, fan-three
Top speed 60 mph (97 km/h)

Marcel Leyat's vision for motorized road transport was a propeller-driven "plane without wings". It had a light body, tandem seating, and rear-wheel steering. Only 30 were sold.

▷ **Citroën Type C 5CV 1922**
Origin France
Engine 856 cc, straight-four
Top speed 38 mph (61 km/h)

The two- (later three-) seater Type C was promoted as being ideal for female drivers, since it had an electric starter rather than a hand crank. The marketing ploy worked, and about 81,000 were sold in four years.

△ **SIMA-Violet 1924**
Origin France
Engine 496 cc, flat-two
Top speed 68 mph (109 km/h)

This narrow, two-seat cyclecar had a plywood body on a tubular-steel frame. It performed well, especially with its two-stroke engine upgraded to 750 or even 1,500 cc for competition purposes.

◁ **Trojan 10HP PB 1922**
Origin UK
Engine 1,488 cc, square-four
Top speed 41 mph (66 km/h)

Based on a 1913 prototype, the very cheap Trojan with an ultra-simple underfloor engine, two-speed epicyclic gearbox, and solid tyres, was made until 1930.

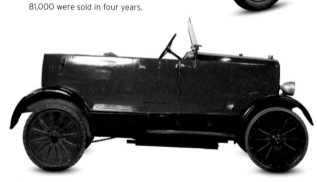

◁ **Hanomag 2/10PS 1925**
Origin Germany
Engine 503 cc, one-cylinder
Top speed 40 mph (64 km/h)

Hanomag started making steam engines in 1835, turning to petrol-engined cars in the 1920s. The bizarre looks of this model won it the nickname *Kommissbrot*, after a loaf of army bread, but also limited sales.

Austin Sevens

Herbert Austin and his 18-year-old draughtsman Stanley Edge drew out Herbert's dream of a car for the people in secret at Austin's home. This was to be a "proper car" in miniature: practical and reliable, with four wheels, a front-mounted, four-cylinder engine driving the rear wheels, and four-wheel brakes. Despite its tiny dimensions, the Austin Seven took the UK market by storm, selling 290,924 between 1922 and 1939.

▷ **Austin Seven 1922**
Origin UK
Engine 696 cc, straight-four
Top speed 52 mph (84 km/h)

Although the Seven would later be a huge success, at first it really was too small. The length, width, and engine size were all increased within a year of the model's launch.

▽ **Morgan-JAP Aero 1929**

Origin UK

Engine 1,096 cc, V2

Top speed 70 mph (113 km/h)

With a front-mounted, V-twin engine and single rear-wheel drive, the sporty Aero was the latest in Morgan's long line of excellent three-wheelers that began in 1910.

◁ **Dixi 3/15PS 1927**

Origin Germany

Engine 747 cc, straight-four

Top speed 48 mph (77 km/h)

Dixi of Eisenach built the Austin Seven under licence as the 3/15PS. When BMW took over Dixi in 1928, the 3/15PS became BMW's first car. It remained in production until 1932.

▷ **Opel 4/12 1924**

Origin Germany

Engine 951 cc, straight-four

Top speed 45 mph (72 km/h)

This little two-seater, named the *Laubfrosch* (tree frog), was built on a production line inspired by the one at Ford. A three-seater followed in 1924, and a four-seater in 1925.

◁ **Triumph Super Seven 1927**

Origin UK

Engine 832 cc, straight-four

Top speed 50 mph (80 km/h)

Triumph's response to the Austin Seven was the slightly larger and more powerful Super Seven. In competition, it took seventh place in the Monte Carlo Rally of 1930.

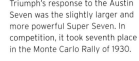

▽ **Morris Minor 1928**

Origin UK

Engine 847 cc, straight-four

Top speed 50 mph (80 km/h)

Larger and more user-friendly than the Austin Seven, and with a modern overhead-camshaft engine, the Minor was the first of Morris's successful economy cars.

△ **Austin Seven 1926**

Origin UK

Engine 747 cc, straight-four

Top speed 50 mph (80 km/h)

In the enlarged Seven, Britain at last had an affordable car for the lower middle classes. Austin kept it popular with improvements to the chassis, body, and brakes.

△ **Austin Seven 1928**

Origin UK

Engine 747 cc, straight-four

Top speed 50 mph (80 km/h)

The improvements continued in 1928, with front-mounted headlights, a nickel-plated radiator, coil ignition, and shock absorbers on all four wheels.

△ **Austin Seven 1930**

Origin UK

Engine 747 cc, straight-four

Top speed 52 mph (84 km/h)

Engine refinements helped to counter the additional weight of a deepened chassis and extra crossmember on this "Chummy" open tourer.

Louis Renault
in his 1899
Type A Voiturette

Great marques
The Renault story

Unmistakably French in style and yet universal in outlook, Renault remains one of the world's most successful car makers. For more than 100 years Renault's reputation for design flair has been matched by its accomplishments in all the major motor-sport arenas, from rallying to Formula 1 and the Le Mans 24-hour race.

THE HISTORY OF FRANCE'S motor industry would be very different had Louis Renault chosen to work in the family button-making business. Born in 1877 and the youngest of five brothers, his ambitions lay elsewhere. In 1898, at the age of 21, Louis built a "quadricycle" in a small workshop at the family home in Billancourt, Paris. Although he intended to build only one car for himself, the demand for replicas was such that he became a full-time car builder a year later, with two of his siblings providing the funding. By the end of 1899 Société Renault Fréres had made 71 cars, and in 1902 Renault began making its own engines. The cars proved successful in city-to-city races, with Marcel Renault winning the 1903 Paris–Vienna event in a 3.8-litre Type K model.

Renault badge
(introduced 1992)

By 1907 Louis Renault had acquired most of the company's shares and set about building cars in greater volume. In 1913 Renault was producing more than 10,000 cars and commercial vehicles per year, making it the largest vehicle manufacturer in France. The bulk of these were small, two-cylinder cars, many of which were sold as taxis – at the time there were over 3,000 Renault cabs on the streets of Paris alone.

Emerging from World War I with greatly increased coffers due, in part, to the manufacture of lorries and tanks for the French army, Renault nonetheless began losing ground to its competitors in the civilian market. By the mid-1920s the firm's models seemed old-fashioned, many having a distinct pre-war look. Citroën, in particular, consistently produced superior cars. Renault responded with a range of handsome six-cylinder cars, and also the striking eight-cylinder Reinastella model of 1929. The Nervastella, the Reinastella's smaller sister, triumphed at the 1930 Moroccan Rally, and the Nervasport, a more agile version of the Nervastella, won the Monte Carlo Rally of 1935.

Production of large Renault models ceased at the outbreak of World War II in September 1939, but the smaller four-cylinder Juvaquattre, Novaquattre, and Primaquattre models continued to be made until France fell to Germany in June 1940.

Believing the war would soon end, Louis Renault kept his factory open, keen to preserve his employees' jobs. It was a disastrous decision, and the German army took control of his factories for its own ends. After Paris was liberated in August 1944, Renault was arrested as a collaborator and imprisoned. Poorly treated and in ill health, he died just three months later.

a wheelbase of just 210 cm (82½ in). The 4CV was an instant success, and over 1 million 4CVs were made until production ended in 1961. Although an unlikely competition car, the 4CV triumphed in Italy's daunting Mille Miglia road race from 1952 to 1957. Renault followed the 4CV with the 845 cc Dauphine in 1956, which was hugely popular despite its reputation

> "My aim is to make the **best car** at the **lowest price** so that one day each **family in France** may have its **own car.**"
>
> LOUIS RENAULT, c.1928

In 1945 the firm was nationalized and refocused on making mainstream cars for the masses. Chief among the new models was the 4CV, which at its launch in September 1946 was one of the smallest four-door saloon cars ever made. Powered by a rear-mounted, 760 cc, four-cylinder engine, it had

for poor handling and a propensity to rust. Some 200,000 Dauphines were sold in the US alone up until 1960, and the Dauphine was also made under licence in Italy and Brazil.

The arrival in 1961 of the R4 marked the wholesale adoption by Renault cars of front-wheel drive. The much-copied

In tune with the modern age
With motorists in a convertible gazing up at a passing aircraft, this Renault poster of 1913 captures the pioneering spirit of engineering in the early 20th century.

Renault 6CV taxi, 1926
Although simple in looks, the 6CV proved very popular, being sturdy and extremely economical.

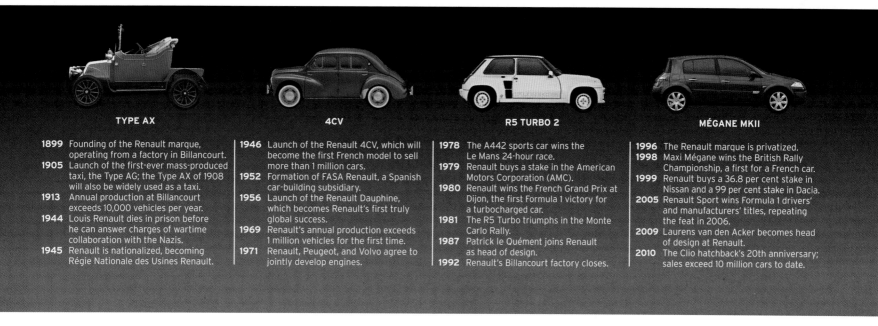

TYPE AX

4CV

R5 TURBO 2

MÉGANE MKII

1899 Founding of the Renault marque, operating from a factory in Billancourt.	**1946** Launch of the Renault 4CV, which will become the first French model to sell more than 1 million cars.	**1978** The A442 sports car wins the Le Mans 24-hour race.	**1996** The Renault marque is privatized.
1905 Launch of the first-ever mass-produced taxi, the Type AG; the Type AX of 1908 will also be widely used as a taxi.	**1952** Formation of FASA Renault, a Spanish car-building subsidiary.	**1979** Renault buys a stake in the American Motors Corporation (AMC).	**1998** Maxi Mégane wins the British Rally Championship, a first for a French car.
1913 Annual production at Billancourt exceeds 10,000 vehicles per year.	**1956** Launch of the Renault Dauphine, which becomes Renault's first truly global success.	**1980** Renault wins the French Grand Prix at Dijon, the first Formula 1 victory for a turbocharged car.	**1999** Renault buys a 36.8 per cent stake in Nissan and a 99 per cent stake in Dacia.
1944 Louis Renault dies in prison before he can answer charges of wartime collaboration with the Nazis.	**1969** Renault's annual production exceeds 1 million vehicles for the first time.	**1981** The R5 Turbo triumphs in the Monte Carlo Rally.	**2005** Renault Sport wins Formula 1 drivers' and manufacturers' titles, repeating the feat in 2006.
1945 Renault is nationalized, becoming Régie Nationale des Usines Renault.	**1971** Renault, Peugeot, and Volvo agree to jointly develop engines.	**1987** Patrick le Quément joins Renault as head of design.	**2009** Laurens van den Acker becomes head of design at Renault.
		1992 Renault's Billancourt factory closes.	**2010** The Clio hatchback's 20th anniversary; sales exceed 10 million cars to date.

R16, introduced in 1964, later set the template for five-door hatchbacks, and the 1972 R5 supermini had a similar influence on the mid-price, small-car market. All these models sold in vast numbers, even if each ultimately failed to keep pace with the rivals that followed in their tracks.

The 1980s was a tumultuous decade for the company. Renault returned to the Grand Prix arena and gained its first Formula 1 triumph at Dijon, France, in 1980, which also marked the maiden victory for a turbocharged car. The following year the R5 Turbo won the Monte Carlo Rally on its debut. However, away from the glamorous world of motor sport there was upheaval. In 1979 Renault had begun a major sales drive in the US as it attempted to penetrate a market it had largely ignored since the 1960s. It subsequently acquired a large stake in the American Motors Corporation marque, the deal briefly proving fruitful before Chrysler bought Renault's AMC shares in 1987. Falling sales compounded by internal disarray after the assassination of Renault's cost-cutting principal, Georges Besse, in 1986, led to the company making vast losses. After fighting its way back to profitability, it was privatized in 1996. Renault formed an alliance with Nissan in 1999 and also acquired the majority stake in Dacia of Romania.

In the early 1980s Renault became a style leader again, spearheaded by its Espace MPV. The renaissance continued into the 1990s under design director Patrick le Quément. The chic Twingo city car (1992) won fans across Europe, and the Mégane Scénic (1996) established a new class of car – the compact MPV. Not every model was a success: the Avantime of 2001 was withdrawn after two years, having failed in its attempt to redefine the luxury car. This enduring marque also returned to prominence in Formula 1, with World Championship victories in both 2005 and 2006.

Renault Dauphine
Elegant, low-priced, and small enough to negotiate congested city streets, the 1956 Dauphine was an everyday car for the masses. It sold more than 2 million worldwide.

Sports Cars

By the end of World War I the sports-car formula for the next half century was clearly established. An in-line engine was mounted in front of the driver, driving the rear wheels. There were many different ways of achieving the ultimate performance: some manufacturers favoured complex and advanced engineering; others concentrated on minimizing weight or reducing wind resistance with low, streamlined bodywork.

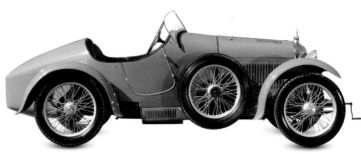

▷ Amilcar CGS 1924
Origin France
Engine 1,047 cc, straight-four
Top speed 75 mph (121 km/h)

The C Grand Sport was a rapid small sports car, with full-pressure engine lubrication, allowing prolonged high engine speeds. It also had four-wheel brakes when most had only two.

◁ Mercedes 28/95 1924
Origin Germany
Engine 7,280 cc, straight-six
Top speed 95 mph (153 km/h)

One of the last Mercedes built before the merger with Benz, this model used an all-aluminium overhead-camshaft engine derived from a World War I aircraft engine.

△ Briggs & Stratton Flyer 1919
Origin USA
Engine 201 cc, one-cylinder
Top speed 25 mph (40 km/h)

Lawnmower engine maker Briggs & Stratton sold the Flyer until 1925. At $125, it was the cheapest new car ever. A motorized fifth wheel lowered to drive the flexible wood chassis.

▷ Vauxhall Velox 30/98 1922
Origin UK
Engine 4,224 cc, straight-four
Top speed 85 mph (137 km/h)

With a powerful overhead-valve engine, the 30/98 was a superb sports car despite its largely pre-World War I design. It is now highly sought after.

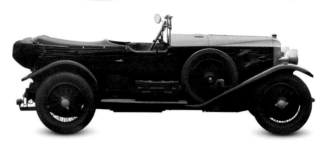

▷ Aston Martin 1½-litre 1921
Origin UK
Engine 1,486 cc, straight-four
Top speed 80 mph (129 km/h)

Lionel Martin built a Special in 1913 using a Coventry-Simplex engine, and began limited production in 1921. Output stepped up when AC Bertelli bought the marque in 1925.

△ Alvis FWD 1928
Origin UK
Engine 1,482 cc, straight-four
Top speed 85 mph (137 km/h)

The first front-wheel-drive, all-independently sprung sports car was too unconventional for its time to sell well. Still, it had great success on the racetrack.

▽ Bugatti Type 43 1927
Origin France
Engine 2,262 cc, straight-eight
Top speed 110 mph (177 km/h)

With its supercharged engine straight from the Grand Prix-winning Type 35 and light, sporting bodywork, the Type 43 Bugatti was a very rapid touring car indeed.

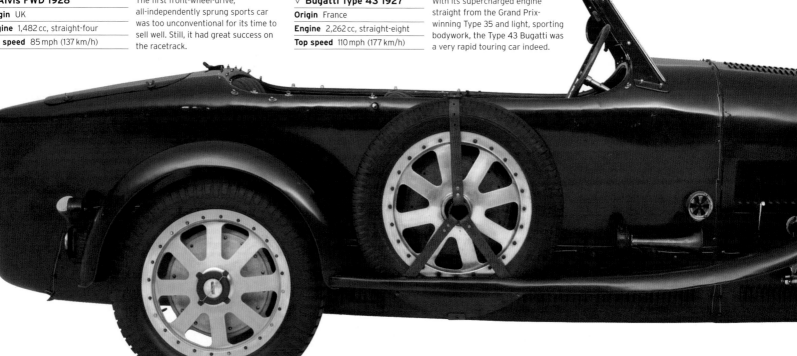

◁ **Sunbeam 16HP 1927**

Origin UK

Engine 2,035 cc, straight-six

Top speed 60 mph (97 km/h)

Sunbeam made high quality cars but this smaller-engined model suffered from an overweight chassis that dulled its performance. It was made until 1933.

▷ **Sunbeam 20/60HP 1924**

Origin UK

Engine 3,181 cc, straight-six

Top speed 80 mph (129 km/h)

This Sunbeam was highly praised for its refinement and advanced features, such as four-wheel brakes. Sunbeam's double-overhead-camshaft 3-litre model was derived from this car.

△ **Bentley 3-litre 1921**

Origin UK

Engine 2996 cc, straight-four

Top speed 85 mph (137 km/h)

With a 16-valve overhead-cam engine, the first Bentley was superbly built and sold with a five-year chassis guarantee. Four-wheel brakes were added in 1924.

▷ **Bentley 4½-litre 1927**

Origin UK

Engine 4398 cc, straight-four

Top speed 95 mph (153 km/h)

WO Bentley's fine engine, with overhead camshaft, twin plugs, and four valves per cylinder, propelled this heavy sports car well. However, Ettore Bugatti called it "a lorry".

▷ **Isotta-Fraschini Tipo 8A 1924**

Origin Italy

Engine 7,372 cc, straight-eight

Top speed 97 mph (156 km/h)

More expensive than a Duesenberg, Italy's first straight-eight was often clad with heavy limousine bodies. This sporting model showed its performance potential.

▽ **Lea-Francis Hyper 1927**

Origin UK

Engine 1,496 cc, straight-four

Top speed 85 mph (137 km/h)

The Hyper was a very successful sports car, winning the Tourist Trophy thanks to its supercharged Meadows engine, light weight, and good roadholding.

▷ **Alfa Romeo 6C 1750 Gran Sport 1929**

Origin Italy

Engine 1,752 cc, straight-six

Top speed 90 mph (145 km/h)

Alfa increased its 1,500 cc sports car to 1,750 in 1929, boosting sales over the next few years by adding a supercharger as well as this stunning Zagato body.

Alfa Romeo 6C 1750

One of the finest models ever produced by Alfa Romeo, the 6C 1750 is often considered to be the first true Grand Tourer. Equally at home on the road and the racetrack, the 6C was supplied as a rolling chassis upon which specialists ranging from British company James Young to the Italian Zagato studio would construct the bodywork. It was a winning combination, with supercharged versions trouncing the opposition from 1929 to 1931 and providing Alfa Romeo with its first major crossover hit.

HIRING DESIGNER Vittorio Jano from Fiat in 1923 paid immediate dividends for Alfa Romeo. It was his genius that resulted in the awesome Alfa P2 winning the first ever Grand Prix World Championship in 1925. In the same year he took elements of the racing model to develop the 6C 1500. Jano united a light frame with a small but high-revving powerplant to create an exceptionally nimble car. Four years later, the six-cylinder engine was enlarged, resulting in the 6C 1750 that was unveiled at the Rome Motor Show. As with the original 6C,

a selection of specialist coachbuilders clothed the chassis, with Zagato creating some of the most popular designs. In addition to standard Turismo and Gran Turismo versions, Super Sport and Gran Sport variants were offered with ultra-reliable, supercharged engines that made them ideal for endurance racing. Victories at the 1929 and 1930 Mille Miglia events in Italy cemented the legacy of the 6C 1750 as a classic Alfa racer. Larger-engined 6Cs took up the mantle and continued the marque's illustrious competition success well into the 1930s.

SPECIFICATIONS	
Model	Alfa Romeo 6C 1750 (1929-33)
Assembly	Milan, Italy
Production	2,579
Construction	Aluminium body on ladder frame
Engine	1,752 cc, straight-six
Power output	46-102 bhp at 4,000-4,600 rpm
Transmission	Four-speed manual
Suspension	Live axle, semi-elliptic leaf springs
Brakes	Drums front and rear
Maximum speed	68-106 mph (110-170 km/h)

Combined effort
First used in 1920, the Alfa Romeo name was a combination of the original ALFA (Anonima Lombarda Fabbrica Automobili) company with the surname of industrialist Nicola Romeo, who was a director of the fledgling marque from 1915 to 1928.

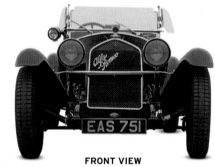

FRONT VIEW

REAR VIEW

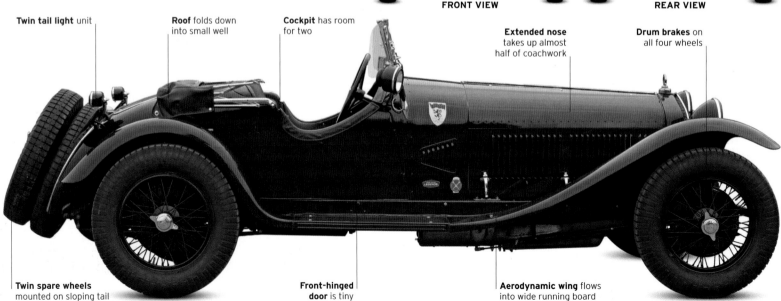

Twin tail light unit

Roof folds down into small well

Cockpit has room for two

Extended nose takes up almost half of coachwork

Drum brakes on all four wheels

Twin spare wheels mounted on sloping tail

Front-hinged door is tiny

Aerodynamic wing flows into wide running board

Statement of intent
With its large grille to allow air in
to help cool the smooth six-pot
engine, huge headlamps mounted
on a chrome brace, and a small
windscreen to reduce aerodynamic
drag, the 6C looked as though it
meant business. The all-new,
low-slung chassis in the preceding
1500 model was so sublime that
it remained virtually unchanged
on this larger 1750 variant.

THE EXTERIOR

Weight-saving and aerodynamics were specialities of Zagato. The Milan-based coachbuilder used aluminium over the rigid ladder chassis – slightly shortened on competition cars – to craft light but strong racing versions of the 6C 1750. Most of the examples were painted racing red or scarlet as pictured here – though some buyers chose a less-flattering white. Black wire-spoked wheels were standard.

1. Hood ornament features green victory laurels to represent Alfa's racing success **2.** Large headlamp essential for night stages of endurance races **3.** Front leaf-spring suspension unit attached directly to chassis **4.** Spoked wheels measured 18 in in diameter **5.** Engine cover lock **6.** Auxiliary light beside windscreen **7.** Badge of this particular model's Italian coachbuilder **8.** Tail light unit **9.** Fuel filler-cap positioned on driver's side adjacent to luggage compartment **10.** Two spare wheels doubled-up at rear

11

THE INTERIOR

The 6C's spartan interior reflected its underlying character as essentially a race model. An array of dials and switches kept the driver up to date on what was happening under the bonnet. Leather and wood were used by some coachbuilders to fit out the small cockpit, but luxuries were kept to the minimum – even the small windscreen and side windows provided negligible protection from the elements.

11. Cramped cockpit dominated by large, four-spoke steering wheel **12.** Two of the control pedals, either side of brake pedal, inscribed with manufacturer's name **13.** Door-mounted leather storage pouch

12

13

UNDER THE BONNET

Base models featured a single-overhead-cam arrangement on the straight-six, while more performance-orientated variants incorporated a double-overhead-cam set-up. A few pure race-bred competition cars were given a fixed-head (*Testa Fissa*) block. When combined with larger valves, a higher compression ratio, and a supercharger working flat out, it enabled a power output of 100 bhp or above.

14. Crankcase, cylinder head, and exhaust manifold featuring outlets for each of the six cylinders **15.** Twin-breathing horizontal carburettor **16.** Ribbed Roots supercharger positioned at front of crankshaft **17.** Iron, aluminium alloy, and bronze used for engine components

14

15

16

17

Chrysler, 1929
The Wall Street Crash of 1929 was a disaster for the car industry, killing off several great marques and expensive models. As a result, second-hand cars, such as this luxury Chrysler, became a new market commodity.

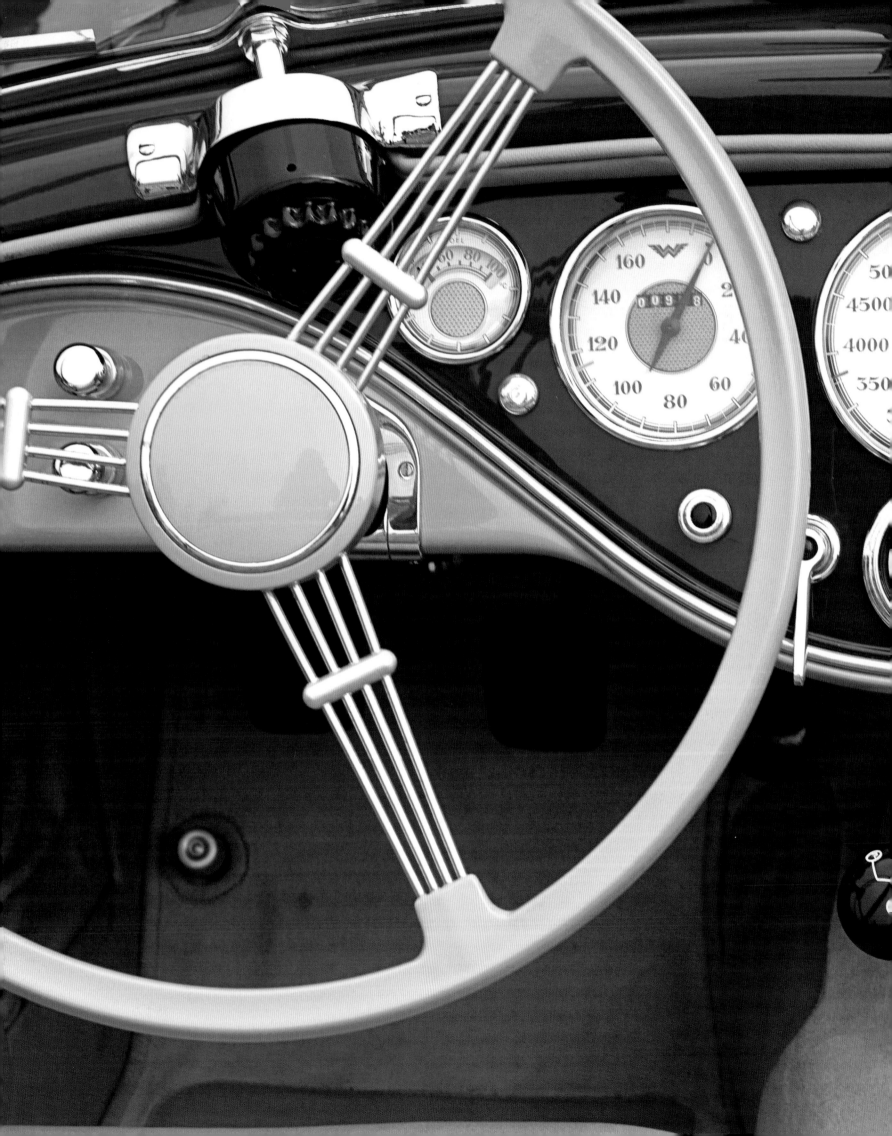

The
1930s

Great Depression & Detroit | Streamliners & superchargers | **Low slung & highly strung**

Economy Models of the Post-Depression Era

The Great Depression that struck the US in 1929 and spread around the world hit car sales hard. Some people still wanted cars, though their aspirations were lower. Upmarket car makers introduced smaller, more affordable versions for the new decade, and manufacturers of small cars made improvements to their models. The new low-price cars were mostly very usable four-seat saloons, much better equipped than earlier economy vehicles.

△ **Singer Junior 8HP 1927**

Origin	UK
Engine	848 cc, straight-four
Top speed	55 mph (89 km/h)

Cars such as this one with its lively but economical overhead-camshaft engine made Singer one of the best-selling UK manufacturers in the 1920s. In the 1930s sales declined due to lack of development.

△ **DKW FA 1931**

Origin	Germany
Engine	490 cc, straight-two
Top speed	47 mph (76 km/h)

DKW turned its little two-stroke engine sideways and mounted it behind a transverse gearbox to drive the front wheels. This achieved a much lighter and more compact powertrain.

▷ **Goliath Pionier 1931**

Origin	Germany
Engine	198 cc, one-cylinder
Top speed	28 mph (45 km/h)

From 1924 Carl Borgward made small commercial vehicles. During the economic crisis he adapted the designs to make this small fabric-bodied car, 4,000 of which were sold.

▷ **Ford Model Y 1932**

Origin	UK
Engine	933 cc, straight-four
Top speed	57 mph (92 km/h)

Built in the UK, France, and Germany, the Model Y was perfect for the European market, and cheap enough to give Ford market leadership, a position it held for decades.

△ **Adler Trumpf Junior 1934**

Origin	Germany
Engine	995 cc, straight-four
Top speed	57 mph (92 km/h)

This front-wheel-drive "people's car" sold over 100,000 before the war. In two-seat sports form it achieved many successes, including second in class at the Le Mans race in 1937.

△ **Austin Seven Ruby 1934**

Origin	UK
Engine	747 cc, straight-four
Top speed	50 mph (80 km/h)

Austin kept the Seven modern with synchromesh on the top three gears, effective four-wheel brakes, shock absorbers, and a sturdy body. However, the extra weight slowed it down.

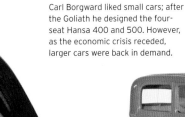

△ Hansa 500 1934

Origin Germany

Engine 465 cc, straight-two

Top speed 40 mph (64 km/h)

Carl Borgward liked small cars; after the Goliath he designed the four-seat Hansa 400 and 500. However, as the economic crisis receded, larger cars were back in demand.

△ Fiat Topolino 500 1936

Origin Italy

Engine 569 cc, straight-four

Top speed 53 mph (85 km/h)

Dante Giacosa designed this "Fiat for the people", with a proper water-cooled engine up front, and two seats – though often more people were crammed in.

△ Hillman Minx Magnificent 1936

Origin UK

Engine 1,185 cc, straight-four

Top speed 62 mph (100 km/h)

Hillman's affordable Minx saloon series began in 1932. In 1936 Hillman offered a better-equipped model with a much improved interior space compared with rival 10 HP saloons.

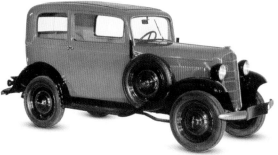

△ Opel P4 1936

Origin Germany

Engine 1,074 cc, straight-four

Top speed 55 mph (89 km/h)

The P4 was developed from Opel's earlier "Laubfrosch". Conventional in both styling and engineering, it was well constructed and reliable, and popular for those reasons.

△ Morris Eight 1936

Origin UK

Engine 918 cc, straight-four

Top speed 58 mph (93 km/h)

The Eight saved Morris when Austin and Ford had knocked it into third place in the UK. In terms of layout, size, and mechanical specification, it copied the Ford Eight, but it sold well.

△ American Bantam 60 1937

Origin USA

Engine 747 cc, straight-four

Top speed 55 mph (89 km/h)

Production of Austin Sevens under licence in the US had a chequered history from 1929. This restyle by Alexis de Sakhnoffsky did look American, but was too tiny to sell well.

△ Škoda Popular 1938

Origin Czechoslovakia

Engine 995 cc, straight-four

Top speed 62 mph (100 km/h)

Škoda produced innovative small cars in the 1930s. This model featured a wet-liner engine, single-tube backbone chassis, and swing-axle, independent rear suspension.

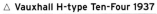

△ Vauxhall H-type Ten-Four 1937

Origin UK

Engine 1,203 cc, straight-four

Top speed 60 mph (97 km/h)

Vauxhall's entry-level car was a little bigger than its rivals' and boasted monocoque construction, independent front suspension, and hydraulic brakes. Sales reached 42,245.

▷ Lancia Aprilia 1937

Origin Italy

Engine 1,352 cc, V4

Top speed 80 mph (129 km/h)

Probably the most advanced pre-war saloon, the monocoque Aprilia had all-independent suspension, a narrow-angle V4 engine with overhead cam, hydraulic brakes, and pillarless doors.

Racing Cars and Single-Seaters

The 1930s saw Italian marques take the lead in European motor racing as French and British opposition waned. However, it wasn't long before German government investment created immensely fast and dominant racing machines. These German cars left other manufacturers looking at lesser formulae where they could compete on an equal footing; only the Italian manufacturers battled on to collect an occasional Grand Prix win.

◁ **Riley Brooklands 1929**

Origin UK

Engine 1,087 cc, straight-four

Top speed 88 mph (142 km/h)

The light, sporting build of Riley cars made them ideal for creating a sports-racing version. The Brooklands raced with great success, winning the 1932 Tourist Trophy.

△ **Bugatti Type 51 1931**

Origin France

Engine 2,262 cc, straight-eight

Top speed 140 mph (225 km/h)

Jean Bugatti developed the Type 51 from the Type 35 and added a new twin-cam engine. The car won the 1931 French GP, but later struggled to match German and Italian racers.

△ **Hudson Eight Indianapolis 1933**

Origin USA

Engine 3,851 cc, straight-eight

Top speed 130 mph (209 km/h)

To combat reduced race entries during the Great Depression, Indianapolis started the "Junk Formula", welcoming Specials built on production chassis, like this Hudson.

▷ **Auto Union Type A 1934**

Origin Germany

Engine 4,360 cc, V16

Top speed 171 mph (275 km/h)

Ferdinand Porsche designed this revolutionary Grand Prix car, more like modern racers than anything in its day, with a hugely sophisticated engine in front of the rear wheels.

△ **Auto Union Type D 1938**

Origin Germany

Engine 2,990 cc, V12

Top speed 205 mph (330 km/h)

Auto Union designer Eberan von Eberhorst produced this complex machine for the new 3-litre Grand Prix category in 1938. Its mid-mounted, three-camshaft V12 produced 420 bhp.

Alfa Romeo

The only racing marque that successfully challenged the all-conquering Germans through the 1930s was Italy's Alfa Romeo, owned and partly financed by the government of dictator Benito Mussolini. With Vittorio Jano as designer, Enzo Ferrari as team manager, and drivers like Tazio Nuvolari, Achille Varzi, and Rudolf Caracciola, Alfa Romeo was able to keep a toehold, but in the end it was an impossible challenge.

▷ **Alfa Romeo 8C 2300 1931**

Origin Italy

Engine 2,336 cc, straight-eight

Top speed 135 mph (217 km/h)

At the start of the decade racing cars still had mechanics on board and, in the case of this Alfa Romeo, even four seats. Built to win Le Mans, this model won it four years in a row.

◁ **Alfa Romeo Tipo B 1932**

Origin Italy

Engine 2,650 cc, straight-eight

Top speed 140 mph (225 km/h)

This was the first successful centre-line single-seater after riding mechanics were dropped. It won the Italian Grand Prix on its debut, challenging German supremacy.

◁ Maserati 8C 3000 1932

Origin Italy

Engine 2,991 cc, straight-eight

Top speed 149 mph (240 km/h)

Maserati's new Grand Prix car for the 1933 season had an ultra-light alloy engine. It beat the Alfa Romeos to win the 1933 French Grand Prix.

▷ Morgan 4/4 Le Mans 1935

Origin UK

Engine 1,098 cc, straight-four

Top speed 80 mph (129 km/h)

Morgan's first four-wheel car was a lively performer with a Coventry Climax engine. Several were raced, and Prudence Fawcett finished 13th in hers at Le Mans (France) in 1938.

△ Maserati 8CTF 1938

Origin Italy

Engine 2,991 cc, straight-eight

Top speed 180 mph (290 km/h)

The double-overhead-camshaft, twin-supercharged 8CTF was built to challenge German domination in European Grands Prix. However, it proved more successful in the US.

◁ Mercedes-Benz W25 1934

Origin Germany

Engine 3,360 cc, straight-eight

Top speed 180 mph (290 km/h)

Encouraged by German government incentives, Mercedes-Benz invested heavily to produce this clean and competitive racer for the new 750 kg (1,654 lb) maximum weight formula.

△ Mercedes-Benz W125 1937

Origin Germany

Engine 5,660 cc, straight-eight

Top speed 205 mph (330 km/h)

The only restriction for the 1937 Grand Prix season was a maximum weight of 750 kg (1,654 lb). Rudolf Uhlenhaut took full advantage to build one of the most powerful GP cars ever.

△ Issigonis Lightweight Special 1938

Origin UK

Engine 750 cc, straight-four

Top speed 90 mph (145 km/h)

Built by Alec Issigonis, who designed the Morris Minor and the Mini, this car has an ultra-light semi-monocoque with all-independent suspension incorporating rubber belts at the rear.

△ Mercedes-Benz W154 1938

Origin Germany

Engine 2,962 cc, V12

Top speed 192 mph (309 km/h)

For 1938 engines were limited to 3.0-litre supercharged or 4.5-litre unsupercharged; Mercedes still managed to achieve 430 bhp with this twin-supercharged, four-cam, V12 racer.

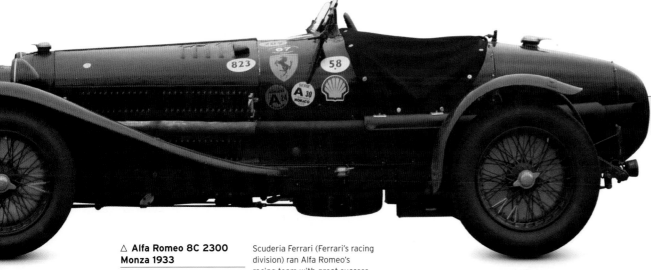

▽ Alfa Romeo 12C-37 1937

Origin Italy

Engine 4,475 cc, V12

Top speed 193 mph (311 km/h)

Alfa Romeo battled bravely to match the dominant German marques in the late 1930s. Vittorio Jano's answer was this 430 bhp V12, but it did not handle well.

△ Alfa Romeo 8C 2300 Monza 1933

Origin Italy

Engine 2,556 cc, straight-eight

Top speed 135 mph (217 km/h)

Scuderia Ferrari (Ferrari's racing division) ran Alfa Romeo's racing team with great success in the 1930s. This may look like a roadgoing sports car, but it won numerous Grands Prix.

Louis Chevrolet (right) at the wheel of a 1915 Cornelian

Great marques
The Chevrolet story

Cars like the Corvette, Camaro, and Blazer carry the name of one of the most charismatic racing drivers pre-World War I. Yet Louis Chevrolet had precious little to do with the products that have sold in their tens of millions – his heart was always at the race track, rather than in the humming industry of Detroit.

LOUIS CHEVROLET, THE SON OF A clockmaker, was born on Christmas Day 1878 in Switzerland. The family later moved to Burgundy, France. The Chevrolets were far from wealthy; while still a boy, Louis was duty-bound to find work in a vineyard, where he immediately showed the mechanical inventiveness he had learned from his father. To speed up the process of decanting wine from one barrel to another, he designed a pump. It worked beautifully. Louis had no idea he was taking the first step in a process that would see the family name adorn automobiles – barely invented then –

Chevrolet badge
(introduced 1913)

car company De Dion-Bouton (at the time, the world's biggest) employed him as a mechanic; a similar spell with Fiat followed. Louis had always loved bicycle racing, and now he made his mark in motor sport too.

He became a familiar figure at race circuits and, after clinching the international speed record for covering 1 mile (1.6 km) in 52.8 seconds, he joined the ranks of the fastest men on earth. Louis' exploits brought him into contact with entrepreneurs in the burgeoning automobile industry centred around Detroit. Soon after being hired as a racing driver by Buick, he met William C. Durant – the founder,

it was capable (roads permitting) of 65 mph (105 km/h). Priced at $2,150, the car had respectable sales figures.

The partnership between the two men, however, soon turned sour. Chevrolet wanted to make high-quality cars with a pedigree enhanced by motor sport, but Durant wanted to churn out low-priced products for the US mass market. In 1913 Durant bought out Louis Chevrolet. The company subsequently grew so

Racing Corvettes
Replacing the Corvette's straight-six engine with a small-block V8 turned it into a superb racer. Here, three Corvettes led by Red Faris (car 11) battle it out on a US track in 1962.

fast that Durant was able to negotiate a takeover of General Motors and assume control once again.

Chevrolet went from strength to strength, selling over 1 million cars for the first time in 1927 and nudging Ford into second place to become the US's best-selling car maker (and the world's largest car manufacturer). From 1936 until 1976 it remained the best-selling marque in the US – an astounding achievement. For Chevrolet to establish and

"I sold you **my car** and I sold you **my name**, but I am not going to sell **myself** to you."
LOUIS CHEVROLET TO WILLIAM DURANT, 1913

of such popularity that, by 2007, one in every 16 cars around the world would carry the Chevrolet brand.

As a teenager, Louis Chevrolet became an apprentice in a bicycle workshop. The work suited him, and he was soon enthusiastically improving cycle gear systems. At 18, he briefly worked for the Mors car company in Paris before departing for Canada to seek his fortune as a chauffeur-mechanic. From there, he went to New York, where the French

in 1908, of General Motors (GM). Durant's over-ambitious plans saw him ousted from GM by its financiers in 1910, but he immediately saw in Louis Chevrolet the kind of buccaneering partner he needed to start all over again. The would-be tycoon did not need to be asked twice. The pair co-founded the Chevrolet Motor Car Company in 1911, and a year later they unveiled a five-seater touring car with a 4.9-litre, six-cylinder engine. Called the Classic Six,

SERIES C CLASSIC SIX

1911 Company set up by Swiss-French racing driver Louis Chevrolet and American founder of GM, William C. Durant.

1912 The Series C Classic Six becomes the first car to be sold by Chevrolet.

1913 First use of Chevrolet logo.

1918 Chevrolet incorporated into GM; the Model D is introduced, available in both four-passenger roadster and five-passenger tourer configurations.

1927 Chevrolet overtakes Ford to become best-selling marque in the US.

CORVETTE

1929 The Stovebolt Six engine introduced; it will be Chevy's principal powerplant for the next three decades.

1941 Chevrolet sells a record 1.6 million cars and trucks in this year.

1950 First fully automatic Powerglide transmission on a Chevy.

1953 Debut of the Corvette, billed as "The first all-American sports car".

1955 Chevrolet introduces its small-block V8 engine – the most successful of its kind – which is still in use today.

BEL AIR

1957 Chevrolet becomes the first US automobile manufacturer to place a fuel-injected engine in some of its models, including the Bel Air.

1967 The Camaro model is introduced.

1969 The Corvair model is discontinued, in part because of bad press it receives in a book by journalist Ralph Nader called *Unsafe At Any Speed*.

1975 The Chevette model is introduced.

1983 GM and Toyota join forces to produce a new small Chevy.

CAMARO

1993 Further venture with Toyota, to build right-hand-drive Cavalier models that Toyota will then sell in Japan.

2001 Chevrolet Cruz, a joint project with Suzuki, becomes first GM model to be built in Japan since the 1930s.

2003 50th anniversary of Corvette model sees 5,000 Corvettes converging on National Corvette Museum in Kentucky.

2008 Chevrolet survives GM's brush with bankruptcy and reorganization.

Appealing to youth
"You're only young twice!" claims this 1954 advert: once when you take your first "old jalopy" to heart, and again when you "put your first brand-new Chevrolet on parade".

maintain this performance, it had to mount an almost constant product offensive. This began in 1918 with the launch of a powerful V8 model, the Model D, but the battle for customers' hearts and minds intensified with the 1925 Superior, featuring gleaming disc wheels and cellulose paint for just $625. The first General Motors vehicle assembled outside the US was a Chevrolet, a truck bolted together in a plant in Copenhagen in January 1924. It was the spearhead for the corporation's global expansion. Throughout the 1930s Chevrolet consolidated its market lead by offering an ever-wider choice of cars, and by 1941 the range included station wagons and power-top convertibles. In 1950 automatic transmission made its debut in Chevrolet cars.

The next big milestone came in 1955, when Chevrolet introduced its small-block V8 engine – the most successful unit of that configuration ever, with many millions being made. The little V8 also rescued the fortunes of the Corvette sports car, transforming it from a feeble performer into a road rocket. This ingenious roadster, introduced in 1953, pioneered glassfibre bodywork on a production car and, with a V8 transplant, became a venerable US institution, which is currently in its sixth generation.

Just when it seemed that Chevrolet could do no wrong in the eyes of US car-buyers, disaster struck in the shape of the 1960 Corvair. The Corvair's rear-mounted engine (in imitation of the VW Beetle) made it tail-heavy, leading to accidents and allegations from consumer groups that Chevrolet had launched the car despite knowing it had shortcomings. As a result of the ensuing furore, US car makers were eventually obliged to adopt safety measures such as seatbelts, crumple zones, and airbags.

Throughout the 1960s and 70s Chevrolets exemplified the American automobile, whether it was the full-size Impala (first seen in 1958), the compact Chevelle, the stylish Monte Carlo coupé, the El Camino pickup, or the brawny, off-road Blazer. Like other US marques, Chevrolet suffered in the economic crises of the late 1970s and early 1980s. To offer more fuel-efficient vehicles in the 1980s, the Chevrolet name fronted several imported and joint-venture small cars from Isuzu, Toyota, and Suzuki. This strategy eventually resulted in GM's purchase in 2001 of a controlling stake in Daewoo of South Korea, and the use of the Chevrolet name on Daewoo's small export models.

The global banking crisis of 2008 almost sounded the death knell for Chevrolet, with GM facing vast debts and bankruptcy. But the US government intervened and took a controlling stake in General Motors. Chevrolet survived.

As for Louis Chevrolet, he fulfilled his dream to create competitive racing cars, but died in poverty on 6 June 1941 and was buried not far from Indianapolis Motor Speedway.

Corvette small-block V8 Engine
Used in Chevrolets and other GM divisions, this powerful, compact V8 became the basis of American "hot-rod" culture for a generation.

Luxury Cars

The 1930s may have been the decade of worldwide depression, but there were still enough wealthy customers to support a fine selection of luxury car manufacturers in the US and Europe. Elegant, comfortable, and often speedy, these cars were usually the first to receive new developments like power brakes, synchromesh gears, and hydraulic brakes.

▷ **Rolls-Royce 20/25 1930**
Origin UK
Engine 3,699 cc, straight-six
Top speed 75 mph (121 km/h)

As the increasing weight of formal luxury coachwork made cars slower, Rolls-Royce upgraded its 20 hp model into the 20/25 with more power.

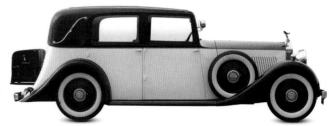

◁ **Rolls-Royce 20/25 1930**
Origin UK
Engine 3,699 cc, straight-six
Top speed 75 mph (121 km/h)

The 20/25 was steadily improved through its seven-year production, with synchromesh gears from 1932, but it struggled to maintain the "Best Car in the World" claim.

△ **Rolls-Royce Phantom II 1930**
Origin UK
Engine 7,668 cc, straight-six
Top speed 90 mph (145 km/h)

Magnificent engineering, effortless power, and the ultimate in elegance defined the Rolls-Royce Phantom, even if it could hardly be called advanced mechanically.

△ **Cadillac 60 Special 1938**
Origin USA
Engine 5,676 cc, V8
Top speed 92 mph (148 km/h)

Cadillac built some of the most prestigious cars of the 1930s, using not just a large V8, but V12 and V16 engines too. The 60 Special heralded post-war styling in 1938.

Packard

At the top of the luxury car tree in the US stood Packard: it launched the world's first production V12 engine in 1915 and maintained its position through the 1920s. The Great Depression meant a shift of emphasis was vital, broadening its range and appeal, but Packard failed to spot the market turning in the late 1930s, allowing Cadillac to steal its crown.

△ **Packard Super 8 1930**
Origin USA
Engine 6,318 cc, V8
Top speed 100 mph (161 km/h)

Opulent, and beautifully built, the Packard Super 8 was one of the top luxury cars at the start of the decade. Buyers were not concerned by its huge fuel consumption.

▽ **Packard Super 8 1932**
Origin USA
Engine 6,318 cc, straight-eight
Top speed 100 mph (161 km/h)

A new chassis design allowed Packard to build lower body styles with a better ride afforded by hydraulic dampers. Power-assisted brakes were fitted from 1933.

◁ **Buick NA 8/90 1934**

Origin USA

Engine 5,644 cc, straight-eight

Top speed 85 mph (137 km/h)

The Buick was spacious and surprisingly good to drive, with a synchromesh gearbox attached to an overhead valve engine – both advanced features at the time.

◁ **Buick Master Series 60 1930**

Origin USA

Engine 5,420 cc, straight-six

Top speed 75 mph (121 km/h)

Buick entered the 1930s with an ancient and thirsty six-cylinder engine, but the cars were still impressive touring machines that found a ready market.

△ **Buick Century Series 60 1936**

Origin USA

Engine 5,247 cc, straight-eight

Top speed 95 mph (153 km/h)

A luxurious family car with a surprising turn of speed, thanks to its 120 bhp engine, the Series 60 Buick proved popular worldwide, offering great value for money.

△ **Talbot 65 1932**

Origin UK

Engine 1,665 cc, straight-six

Top speed 65 mph (105 km/h)

In 1926 chief engineer Georges Roesch gave Talbot one of the smoothest-running six-cylinder engines ever, making this British saloon refined and desirable.

△ **Lincoln K V12 1934**

Origin USA

Engine 6,735 cc, V12

Top speed 100 mph (161 km/h)

Lincoln's luxurious V12 model offered the best of everything, and had pioneering styling updates such as integral, sloping headlights and aerodynamic lines.

◁ **La Salle V8 1931**

Origin USA

Engine 5,840 cc, V8

Top speed 80 mph (129 km/h)

General Motors launched La Salle as a slightly cheaper alternative to its Cadillac brand. Offering similar running gear at a lower price, these elegant and impressive cars sold well.

△ **Packard Super 8 1936**

Origin USA

Engine 5,342 cc, straight-eight

Top speed 90 mph (145 km/h)

Another new chassis design kept Packard at the head of the field, with refinements such as hydraulic brakes. However, competition affected sales.

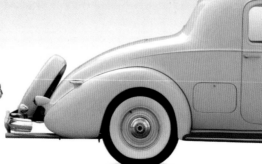

△ **Packard Super 8 1938**

Origin USA

Engine 5,342 cc, straight-eight

Top speed 95 mph (153 km/h)

The last of Packard's top-of-the-range Super 8s to have their own distinctive coachwork were built in 1938, with a V-screen and more curvaceous lines.

Rytecraft Scoota-car, c.1937
Dwarfed by a US sedan on a London street, this two-seater microcar was powered by a 250 cc Villiers engine capable of 40 mph (60 km/h). Only 1,000 Scoota-cars were made, but microcars continued into the 21st century.

CUW 231

Sports Cars

New events such as the Mille Miglia in Italy and the Le Mans 24-hour race in France in the 1920s meant that by the following decade competitive automobile racing was thriving. It led to many manufacturers developing models that could be used on both road and track, with marques such as Alfa Romeo and Aston Martin producing fast cars designed to appeal to customers with a competitive edge.

△ **Salmson S4 1929**
Origin France
Engine 1,296 cc, straight-four
Top speed 56 mph (90 km/h)

French carmaker Salmson offered the S4 in a range of body styles, and fitted it with a modern double-overhead-cam powerplant.

△ **Austin Seven Ulster 1930**
Origin UK
Engine 747 cc, straight-four
Top speed 80 mph (129 km/h)

This aluminium-bodied race version of the Austin Seven, first launched in 1922, added competition success to the model's mainstream popularity.

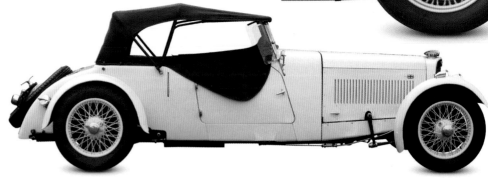

◁ **Aston Martin MkII 1932**
Origin UK
Engine 1,495 cc, four-cylinder
Top speed 80 mph (129 km/h)

The epitome of the small British sports car of the period, the MkII was lower than its predecessor, thanks to a redesigned chassis.

△ **Aston Martin Le Mans 1932**
Origin UK
Engine 1,495 cc, straight-four
Top speed 85 mph (137 km/h)

Aston's two-seater Le Mans sports model was named in recognition of the marque's participation in the celebrated French endurance event since 1928.

▷ **Alfa Romeo 8C 2600 1933**
Origin Italy
Engine 2,556 cc, straight-eight
Top speed 105 mph (169 km/h)

This later version of the famed 8C featured a bigger powerplant and was used with further success by Alfa's official racing team.

△ **Alfa Romeo 8C 1934**
Origin Italy
Engine 2,336 cc, straight-eight
Top speed 105 mph (169 km/h)

Among the many Italian coachbuilders to clothe Vittorio Jano's iconic 8C model was the legendary Pinin Farina with a typically beautiful interpretation.

▽ **Alfa Romeo 8C 2300 1931**
Origin Italy
Engine 2,336 cc, straight-eight
Top speed 105 mph (169 km/h)

Designed by the automotive genius Vittorio Jano in 1931, the celebrated 8C dominated Blue Riband races such as the Mille Miglia in Italy during the early 1930s.

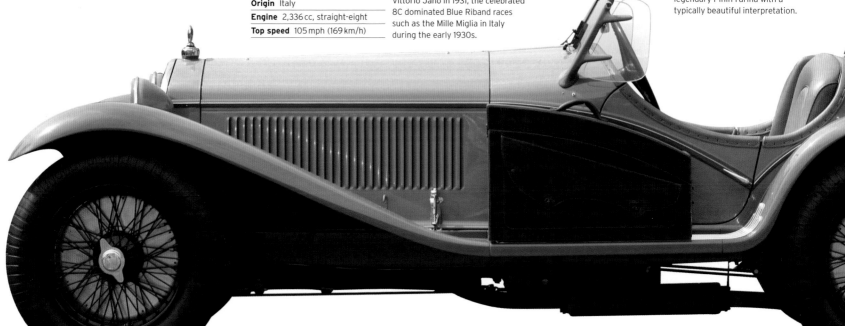

▷ **MG PB 1935**

Origin UK

Engine 939 cc, straight-four

Top speed 76 mph (122 km/h)

Revising the 1934 MG PA led to the larger-engined PB a year later, which was available in coupé and convertible body styles.

◁ **MG TA Midget 1936**

Origin UK

Engine 1,292 cc, straight-four

Top speed 79 mph (127 km/h)

Introduced as a replacement for the PB, the sportier TA Midget featured MG's first hydraulic brakes and, on later models, a synchromesh gearbox.

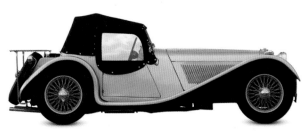

▷ **Fiat Balilla 508S 1933**

Origin Italy

Engine 995 cc, straight-four

Top speed 70 mph (113 km/h)

A year after Fiat's new Balilla was launched in 1932, a Sports (S) version of the family model was made available with extra horsepower.

△ **Jaguar SS100 1936**

Origin UK

Engine 2,663 cc, straight-six

Top speed 95 mph (153 km/h)

Less than 200 examples were made of the SS100 sports model, one of the last before the "SS" was dropped from the company's name.

▷ **Morgan Super Sport 3-wheeler 1936**

Origin UK

Engine 1,096 cc, V-twin

Top speed 70 mph (113 km/h)

In the 1930s Morgan expanded the technology on its three-wheelers so that buyers could now choose models with three speeds rather than just two.

▽ **Morgan 4/4 1936**

Origin UK

Engine 1,122 cc, straight-four

Top speed 80 mph (129 km/h)

After 27 years of building three-wheeled vehicles, in 1936 Morgan launched its first four-wheeler in the form of the evergreen 4/4 model.

△ **AC 16/80 1936**

Origin UK

Engine 1,991 cc, straight-six

Top speed 80 mph (129 km/h)

The six-cylinder engine in the elegant 16/80 was first introduced in 1919, and would go on to power ACs until the early 1960s.

▽ **BSA Scout 1935**

Origin UK

Engine 1,075 cc, straight-four

Top speed 60 mph (97 km/h)

Known as a manufacturer of cars, motorcycles, and three-wheelers, BSA launched its first modern-looking sports tourer, the Scout, in 1935.

△ **BMW 328 1936**

Origin Germany

Engine 1,971 cc, straight-six

Top speed 93 mph (150 km/h)

A Le Mans and Mille Miglia winner, the streamlined 328 was one of the finest sports models of the late 1930s.

▷ **Wanderer W25K 1936**

Origin Germany

Engine 1,963 cc, straight-six

Top speed 90 mph (145 km/h)

The svelte and stylish W25K came from German carmaker Wanderer, which was part of the Auto Union car manufacturing group that included Audi.

Mass-Market Models

In the 1930s motoring became popular for the middle classes of Europe and the US, with discerning buyers choosing cars for reliability and power, spaciousness and price. In the US new marques such as Pontiac were created to cater to the mass market and innovations were comfort related, such as automatic transmission to smooth the ride. In Europe Citroën popularized front-wheel drive and monocoque construction.

△ **Citroën 11 Large 1935**

Origin	France
Engine	1,911 cc, straight-four
Top speed	76 mph (122 km/h)

André Citroën flouted convention with the monocoque construction, front-wheel-drive Traction Avant series. They functioned well, and were produced until 1957.

◁ **Singer Nine Le Mans 1933**

Origin	UK
Engine	972 cc, straight-four
Top speed	70 mph (113 km/h)

Singer's powerful overhead-camshaft engine was its strongest selling point. This was an excellent small sports car to rival MG in the UK.

▷ **Austin 10/4 1935**

Origin	UK
Engine	1,125 cc, straight-four
Top speed	55 mph (89 km/h)

The 10/4 was Austin's best-selling model from 1932 to 1940, as customers traded up from the tiny Austin Seven of the 1920s to get a little more space and speed.

△ **Pontiac Six 1935**

Origin	USA
Engine	3,408 cc, straight-six
Top speed	75 mph (121 km/h)

Pontiac provided six-cylinder power and stylish bodywork featuring a fencer's mask grille and turret-top lines. The Six saw the company fifth in the US sales league by 1939.

◁ **Ford V8-81 1938**

Origin	USA
Engine	3,622 cc, V8
Top speed	85 mph (137 km/h)

Ford's V8 engine gave more performance for the price than any rivals could offer. This helped it to become a worldwide best-seller to follow Models A and T.

△ **Rover 14 1934**

Origin	UK
Engine	1,577 cc, straight-six
Top speed	69 mph (111 km/h)

Stylish and solidly middle class with the additional appeal of a six-cylinder engine, Rover's 14HP sold steadily in the UK throughout the 1930s.

▷ **Renault Juvaquatre 1938**

Origin	France
Engine	1,003 cc, straight-four
Top speed	60 mph (97 km/h)

An estate version of Renault's first unitary construction model was produced until 1960. It had conventional running gear with mechanical brakes and three gears.

△ **Chevrolet EA Master 1935**

Origin	USA
Engine	3,358 cc, straight-six
Top speed	85 mph (137 km/h)

Chevrolet sold over half a million E-series cars in 1935 as car ownership increased massively in the US. Responsive, stylish, and modern, they had a clear appeal.

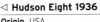

▷ Plymouth P3 1937

Origin USA

Engine 3,300 cc, straight-six

Top speed 75 mph (121 km/h)

Chrysler's bargain basement marque was a sales phenomenon in the US, with its simple, rugged cars at an excellent price. In 1937 566,128 Plymouths were sold.

△ Oldsmobile Six 1935

Origin USA

Engine 3,530 cc, straight-six

Top speed 80 mph (129 km/h)

Oldsmobile was General Motors' mainstream marque, selling on its pioneering features such as hydraulic brakes and synchromesh gears or an optional automatic gearbox.

◁ Hudson Eight 1936

Origin USA

Engine 4,168 cc, straight-eight

Top speed 90 mph (145 km/h)

Hudson moved gradually upmarket in the 1930s, and lost some market share, but this rugged and powerful straight-eight sold well for its size.

▷ Dodge D5 1937

Origin USA

Engine 3,570 cc, straight-six

Top speed 85 mph (137 km/h)

Though its body styling was very similar to other cars in the Chrysler group, this didn't stop Dodge selling 295,000 of the D5 in 1937, thanks to strong US demand for mid-range cars.

◁ Mercedes-Benz 260D 1936

Origin Germany

Engine 2,545 cc, straight-four

Top speed 60 mph (97 km/h)

Claimed to be the first production car with a diesel engine, the 260D was durable but rather slow and noisy. However, the diesel engine was a sign of things to come.

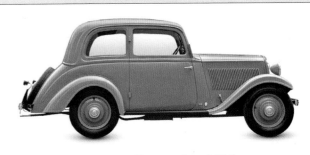

△ Hanomag Garant 1936

Origin Germany

Engine 1,097 cc, straight-four

Top speed 52 mph (84 km/h)

A more conventional car than the 1920s Kommisbrot, the Garant proved very popular. Hanomag built no more cars after World War II, despite creating a promising prototype in 1951.

◁ Dodge D11 1939

Origin USA

Engine 3,570 cc, straight six

Top speed 85 mph (137 km/h)

Absorbed by Chrysler in 1928, Dodge celebrated its 25th anniversary with this modern vee-screen, faired-headlight model that anticipated post-war styling.

▽ Mercedes-Benz 170H 1936

Origin Germany

Engine 1,697 cc, straight-four

Top speed 68 mph (109 km/h)

When Adolf Hitler demanded a "people's car" to mobilize Germany, Mercedes-Benz came up with the unsuccessful, rear-engined 130H and 170H, which offered open-top motoring with side protection.

Volkswagen
flat-four

Commissioned to create a people's car *(Volks Wagen)* by Adolf Hitler, Ferdinand Porsche designed an engine that was cooled by air rather than water, saving the weight and complication of a radiator, water pump, and hoses. When car production resumed after World War II, the simple, rugged engine went on to sell in huge numbers worldwide, until manufacture ceased in 2003.

PACKING A PUNCH

A key feature of the engine's design is properly termed the horizontally opposed layout of its four cylinders, although such a configuration is more often called "flat-four" or "boxer". Much less common today than the in-line four, a flat-four has two main advantages: a lower centre of gravity (which aids roadholding) and reduced vibration (which enhances refinement). In each pair of opposed cylinders, positioned to either side of the central crankshaft, the pistons move in opposition, like boxers trading punches. As a result, secondary vibrations produced by the unbalanced motion of masses within the engine are significantly reduced.

ENGINE SPECIFICATIONS	
Dates produced	1936-2003
Cylinders	Four cylinders, horizontally opposed
Configuration	Rear-mounted, longitudinal
Engine capacities	1,131 cc (increased to 2.0 litre)
Power output	24 bhp @ 3,300 rpm, ultimately 70 bhp
Type	Conventional four-stroke, air-cooled
Head	ohv actuated by pushrod and rocker; two valves per cylinder
Fuel System	Single carburettor
Bore and Stroke	75 mm x 64 mm (2.95 in x 2.52 in)
Power	21.2 bhp/litre
Compression Ratio	5.8:1

▷ See pp.346-347 How an engine works

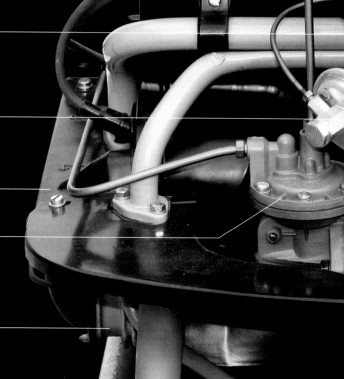

Fuel pipe
This pipe carries petrol from the fuel pump to the carburettor.

Ignition coil
Acting as a transformer, the ignition coil converts battery voltage into high-voltage pulses that are fed to the spark plugs.

Distributor

Vacuum advance
This device adjusts the timing of the ignition according to the engine load.

Engine shape
Because of its opposed-piston layout, the engine is low and wide, giving it a low centre of gravity.

Mechanical fuel pump

Cylinder head
The heads carry one inlet valve and one exhaust valve per cylinder, operated via pushrods and rocker arms from a camshaft in the crankcase.

Silencer
This smoothes out the pulsing of the exhaust gases to reduce engine noise.

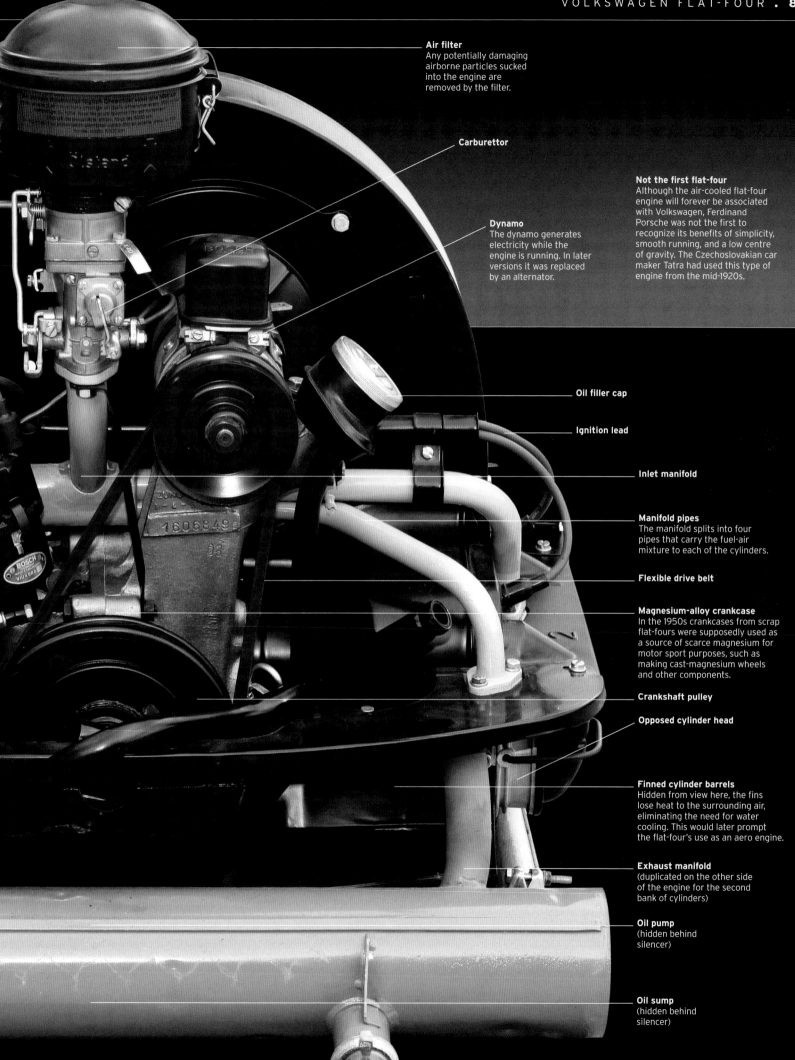

Air filter
Any potentially damaging airborne particles sucked into the engine are removed by the filter.

Carburettor

Dynamo
The dynamo generates electricity while the engine is running. In later versions it was replaced by an alternator.

Not the first flat-four
Although the air-cooled flat-four engine will forever be associated with Volkswagen, Ferdinand Porsche was not the first to recognize its benefits of simplicity, smooth running, and a low centre of gravity. The Czechoslovakian car maker Tatra had used this type of engine from the mid-1920s.

Oil filler cap

Ignition lead

Inlet manifold

Manifold pipes
The manifold splits into four pipes that carry the fuel-air mixture to each of the cylinders.

Flexible drive belt

Magnesium-alloy crankcase
In the 1950s crankcases from scrap flat-fours were supposedly used as a source of scarce magnesium for motor sport purposes, such as making cast-magnesium wheels and other components.

Crankshaft pulley

Opposed cylinder head

Finned cylinder barrels
Hidden from view here, the fins lose heat to the surrounding air, eliminating the need for water cooling. This would later prompt the flat-four's use as an aero engine.

Exhaust manifold
(duplicated on the other side of the engine for the second bank of cylinders)

Oil pump
(hidden behind silencer)

Oil sump
(hidden behind silencer)

Sunbeam Silver Bullet, Daytona Beach, 1930
The Silver Bullet was a British contender for
the world Land Speed Record in 1930. Despite
its 4000 bhp aircraft engine and astonishing
streamlined shape, the Sunbeam failed to achieve
its anticipated 250 mph (402 km/h) top speed.

Streamlined Cars

The vast majority of drivers in the 1930s were perfectly happy with their spacious, easily-accessed, upright, slab-fronted cars. But now that cars were capable of comfortably exceeding 80 mph (129 km/h) a small number of stylists and engineers, in Europe and the US, were turning their attention to aerodynamics and exploring its potential to increase maximum speeds dramatically and boost stability.

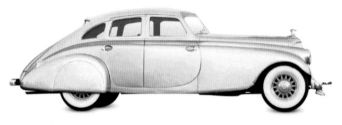

△ Pierce Silver Arrow 1933

Origin USA

Engine 7,566 cc, V12

Top speed 115 mph (185 km/h)

A concept car designed by James R. Hughes, only five Silver Arrows were built in this form. It caused a sensation at the 1933 New York Show, but was too expensive.

▽ Bugatti Type 50 1931

Origin France

Engine 4,972 cc, straight-eight

Top speed 110 mph (177 km/h)

Jean Bugatti styled this Profilée coupé that had the most extreme raked windscreen yet seen on a road car. It combined a luxury road chassis with a double-overhead-camshaft engine.

△ Peugeot 402 1935

Origin France

Engine 1,991 cc, straight-four

Top speed 75 mph (121 km/h)

Far more successful than most streamlined cars of the 1930s, mainly due to its low price, 75,000 of the 402 were sold. Retaining a separate chassis allowed Peugeot to offer 16 body styles.

▷ Cord 810 1936

Origin USA

Engine 4,730 cc, V8

Top speed 93 mph (150 km/h)

The brilliant Cord didn't just boast aerodynamic styling with pop-up headlights: it was front-wheel drive with trailing arm suspension and electric gearchange.

△ Renault Viva Gran Sport 1936

Origin France

Engine 4,085 cc, straight-six

Top speed 89 mph (143 km/h)

With its swept-back, V-shaped grille forming part of the body rather than standing vertically, plus laid-back headlights faired into the front wings, this was an advanced car for its time.

▽ Cord Phantom Corsair 1938

Origin USA

Engine 4,730 cc, V8

Top speed 115 mph (185 km/h)

Designed by millionaire Rust Heinz and built by California coachbuilders Bohmann & Schwartz, based on a Cord 810, this one-off dream car featured in the 1938 film *The Young in Heart*.

▷ Alfa Romeo 6C 2300 Aerodinamica 1935

Origin Italy

Engine 2,309 cc, straight-six

Top speed 120 mph (193 km/h)

Developed secretly on Benito Mussolini's request by Vittorio Jano and Gino and Oscar Jankovits, this car was to have been a V12, but was fitted with a six-cylinder engine.

▷ Alfa Romeo 8C 2900B Le Mans Coupé 1938

Origin Italy

Engine 2,905 cc, straight-eight

Top speed 140 mph (225 km/h)

This sensational aerodynamic coupé, driven by Raymond Sommer and Clemente Biondetti, set the fastest lap at 97 mph (156 km/h), and led for 219 laps at the 1938 Le Mans race – until a tyre blew.

△ **Steyr 50 1936**

Origin Austria

Engine 978 cc, straight-four

Top speed 53 mph (85 km/h)

This teardrop-shaped Austrian people's car was more powerful than some, so it could climb steep Alpine passes. Some 12,000 Steyr 50s were sold up to 1940.

△ **Mercedes-Benz 150H Sport Roadster 1934**

Origin Germany

Engine 1,498 cc, straight-four

Top speed 78 mph (125 km/h)

Designers Hans Nibel and Max Wagner at Mercedes created this mid-engined sports racing prototype, of which just 20 were made. It had great handling, and innovative features such as a coil-sprung, swing-axle rear suspension, and disc wheels.

▷ **Tatra T87 1936**

Origin Czechoslovakia

Engine 2,968 cc, V8

Top speed 99 mph (159 km/h)

With exceptionally aerodynamic bodywork by Paul Jaray and Hans Ledwinka, the rear-engined Tatra was as effective as it was unconventional.

◁ **Chrysler CU Airflow Eight 1934**

Origin USA

Engine 5,301 cc, straight-eight

Top speed 90 mph (145 km/h)

With its wind-tunnel-developed monocoque body, low build, and great handling, the Airflow was way ahead of its time. But the car suffered quality problems, and its sales were poor.

◁ **Lincoln-Zephyr 1936**

Origin USA

Engine 4,378 cc, V12

Top speed 90 mph (145 km/h)

Faired-in headlights and aerodynamic styling made the monocoque-construction Zephyr look very modern, but it still had a side-valve engine and mechanical brakes.

△ **Lagonda V12 Lancefield Le Mans Coupé 1939**

Origin UK

Engine 4,479 cc, V12

Top speed 128 mph (206 km/h)

Lagonda improved its fortunes in the 1930s with a superb V12 engine, which powered two roadsters to 3-4 at Le Mans in 1939. This coupé was finished too late to join them.

▷ **Panhard et Levassor X77 Dynamic 1936**

Origin France

Engine 2,863 cc, straight-six

Top speed 90 mph (145 km/h)

Despite advanced monocoque construction, torsion-bar independent front suspension, and a near-central driving position, the "Art Deco" Dynamic was, however, not popular.

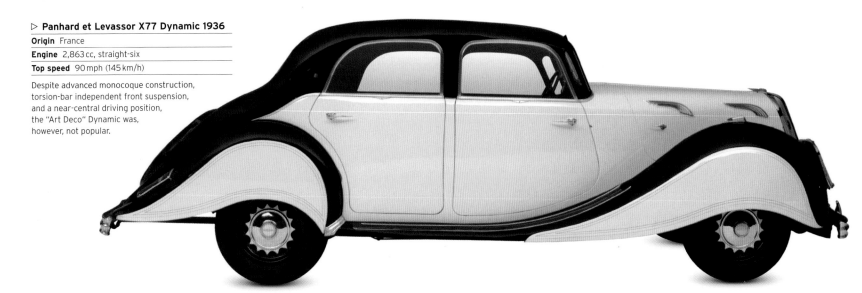

Lincoln-Zephyr

Traditionally associated with high-priced luxury, the Ford-owned Lincoln marque offered buyers its cheapest model to date with the 1936 Zephyr. Featuring Lincoln's first unibody construction – in all-steel – and powered by a new V12 engine, the Zephyr thrilled with its daring, sleek design. Launched at the 1936 New York Auto Show, the Zephyr became one of the marque's best-selling cars of the 1930s and proved that streamlining was the future.

AERODYNAMIC STYLING may not have paid off for Chrysler in 1934 with its radical Airflow range, but that didn't prevent Ford from introducing its own sleek model two years later. Though a risky venture, the Lincoln-Zephyr was underpinned by a smart marketing move – offering cut-price luxury at a time when other top-end manufacturers were going to the wall. Initially available as a two-door fastback sedan or four-door sedan coupé, this three-window coupé and a convertible coupé were added to the range in 1937. World War II put car production on hold until 1942. When the model returned in 1946, the Zephyr name was dropped but the car continued for two more glorious years under the Lincoln banner.

The sweeping, teardrop lines of the Zephyr were in marked contrast to offerings from other contemporary luxury manufacturers such as Cadillac and Packard, and would influence the direction their future ranges would take. Within Lincoln, the model provided the blueprint for one of America's most seminal automobiles, the first-generation Continental from 1939 to 1948.

SPECIFICATIONS	
Model	Lincoln-Zephyr (1936)
Assembly	Detroit, USA
Production	29,997 (1937)
Construction	Steel unibody (monocoque)
Engine	267 cu in (4,378 cc), V12
Power output	110 bhp
Transmission	Three-speed manual
Suspension	Front and rear transverse-leaf springs
Brakes	Drums front and rear
Maximum speed	90 mph (145 km/h)

Rail to road
The Zephyr model name came from a futuristically styled, steel-bodied diesel locomotive called the Pioneer Zephyr. It operated from 1934 and set several speed records during its time spent promoting rail travel in the US.

FRONT VIEW

REAR VIEW

Roof with gentle curve was efficient aerodynamically

Slatted, V-shaped grille was a signature

Bonnet ornament epitomized model's Art Deco styling

Sleek air vent drew hot air away from the V12 engine

Boot was improbably small for such a large car

Bumper with extended over-riders

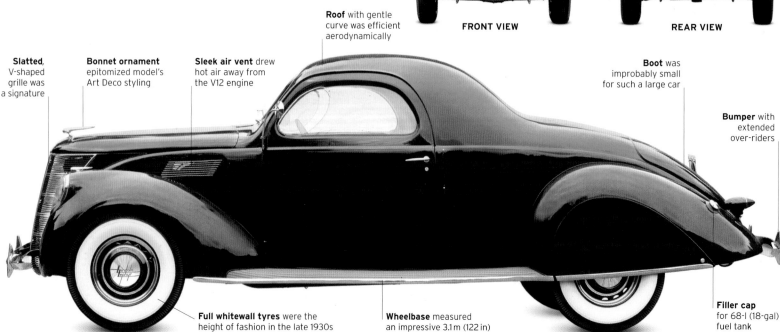

Full whitewall tyres were the height of fashion in the late 1930s

Wheelbase measured an impressive 3.1 m (122 in)

Filler cap for 68-l (18-gal) fuel tank

Road presence
Dominated by its distinctive grille and dramatic, sweeping curves, the front of the Lincoln-Zephyr oozed Art Deco panache. The model was originally conceived by John Tjaarda of the Briggs Manufacturing Company that had supplied Ford and other car makers with bodies for several years. The Zephyr's front end was then reworked by Edsel Ford and in-house designer Eugene "Bob" Gregorie.

THE EXTERIOR

Attention to detail was evident on the Lincoln-Zephyr, but marketing material also stressed the benefits of the combined chassis and body unit – "No other gives the same protection, the same comfort." Although the svelte profiles were gradually given straighter edges from 1942 onwards, by this time the Zephyr had made its mark as America's aerodynamic style leader.

1. Bonnet ornament also serves as bonnet-opening mechanism   2. Grille-mounted badge
3. Teardrop headlights in Art Deco style   4. In 1938 the grille was reduced in size and moved lower down the front end   5. Cooling vent imitates style of grille   6. External hinge on door   7. Elegant door handles   8. Whitewall tyres on 17 in wheels   9. Pop-up indicator   10. "Wing" side window and door mirror   11. Tail light continues the fluid styling theme   12. Boot-release handle

THE INTERIOR

Despite being the cheapest Lincoln to date, there was no corner-cutting inside the Zephyr cockpit. Some models, mainly convertibles, were upholstered in red, brown, or grey leather, and featured wooden dashboards. From 1937 to 1940 the Zephyrs had an unusual instrument layout with the main dials positioned in the centre of the dashboard; from 1940, the speedometer was moved in front of the driver. The dashboard colour was matched to the exterior paint colour.

13. Speedometer dial tops out at 100 mph (161 km/h)   14. Minor control knobs   15. Split-screen fuel and oil-pressure gauges   16. Bench seat accommodates three occupants   17. Window winder handle   18. Parking brake lever

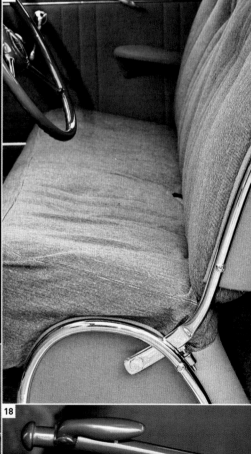

UNDER THE BONNET

Advertised by Lincoln as a "silent, alert powerhouse", the Zephyr's V12 block was based on Ford's flathead V8 engine. It was the only engine of this type available in its sector at the time. Capable of returning a respectable 14–18 miles per gallon (6–8 kilometres per litre), the 110 bhp unit was expanded in 1940 to 292 cu in (4,785 cc), which generated an additional 10 bhp. The final capacity change came in 1942, when a power plant with 302 cu in (4,949 cc) was fitted.

19. Safety horn **20.** Two-barrel Stromberg carburettor **21.** Original aluminium cylinder heads later replaced by cast-iron versions in 1942 **22.** Spare wheel and brace in boot

Magnificent and Exotic Body Styles

The 1930s saw the ultimate flowering of the coachbuilder's art. The most exotic chassis, often adapted from state-of-the-art racing cars into roadgoing performance machines, were dressed in the most stylish, streamlined, luxurious, and even decadent bodywork the world had yet seen. It is no surprise that style-conscious France contributed much to this period; even medium-sized French cars were given stunning bodywork.

△ **Cadillac V16 two-seater roadster 1930**

Origin	USA
Engine	7,413 cc, V16
Top speed	95 mph (153 km/h)

The ultimate US status symbol, the Cadillac V16 was a vast car with effortless performance. This rare two-seater belonged to Otis Chandler, publisher of the *Los Angeles Times*.

▷ **Alfa Romeo 8C 2900B Coupé 1938**

Origin	Italy
Engine	2,905 cc, straight-eight
Top speed	100 mph (161 km/h)

Based on the 8C 35 Grand Prix chassis, the 2900B was the finest roadgoing supercar from Alfa Romeo. A handful were sold with this elegant body by Touring.

◁ **Hispano-Suiza K6 1934**

Origin	France
Engine	5,184 cc, straight-six
Top speed	90 mph (145 km/h)

The final model from this illustrious Paris car maker was given some fine bodies. This close-coupled saloon had distinctive overlapping doors - a style that saw a revival 70 years later.

▷ **Lancia Astura 1931**

Origin	Italy
Engine	2,973 cc, V8
Top speed	79 mph (127 km/h)

With its narrow-angle overhead-cam V8 engine, the Astura was one of Italy's finest pre-war chassis. This 4th Series Cabriolet was bodied by Pinin Farina.

▷ **Auburn Speedster 1935**

Origin	USA
Engine	4,596 cc, straight-eight
Top speed	104 mph (167 km/h)

Just 500 Speedsters were built in 1935-36, making them highly sought after. Each was tested at 100 mph (160 km/h), which was achievable thanks to 148 bhp from the supercharged engine.

◁ **Bugatti Type 57SC Atalante 1935**

Origin	France
Engine	3,257 cc, straight-eight
Top speed	120 mph (193 km/h)

A mere 17 of these supremely elegant vehicles with low suspension were built. Designed by Jean Bugatti, they had twin-cam engines and independent front suspension.

◁ **Mercedes-Benz 500K Special Roadster 1934**

Origin	Germany
Engine	5,018 cc, straight-eight
Top speed	102 mph (164 km/h)

Using the world's first all-independent suspension, with coil springs and shock absorbers, the 500K offered unparalleled comfort and matching performance.

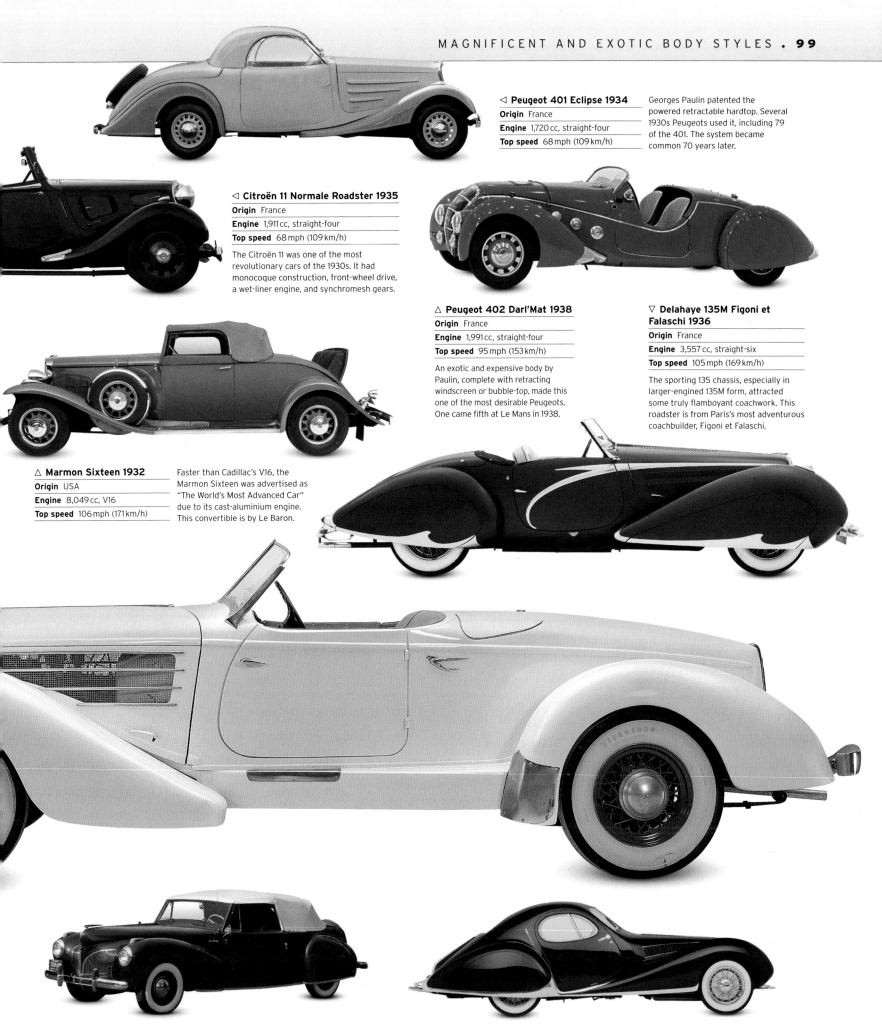

◁ **Peugeot 401 Eclipse 1934**

Origin France

Engine 1,720 cc, straight-four

Top speed 68 mph (109 km/h)

Georges Paulin patented the powered retractable hardtop. Several 1930s Peugeots used it, including 79 of the 401. The system became common 70 years later.

◁ **Citroën 11 Normale Roadster 1935**

Origin France

Engine 1,911 cc, straight-four

Top speed 68 mph (109 km/h)

The Citroën 11 was one of the most revolutionary cars of the 1930s. It had monocoque construction, front-wheel drive, a wet-liner engine, and synchromesh gears.

△ **Peugeot 402 Darl'Mat 1938**

Origin France

Engine 1,991 cc, straight-four

Top speed 95 mph (153 km/h)

An exotic and expensive body by Paulin, complete with retracting windscreen or bubble-top, made this one of the most desirable Peugeots. One came fifth at Le Mans in 1938.

▽ **Delahaye 135M Figoni et Falaschi 1936**

Origin France

Engine 3,557 cc, straight-six

Top speed 105 mph (169 km/h)

The sporting 135 chassis, especially in larger-engined 135M form, attracted some truly flamboyant coachwork. This roadster is from Paris's most adventurous coachbuilder, Figoni et Falaschi.

△ **Marmon Sixteen 1932**

Origin USA

Engine 8,049 cc, V16

Top speed 106 mph (171 km/h)

Faster than Cadillac's V16, the Marmon Sixteen was advertised as "The World's Most Advanced Car" due to its cast-aluminium engine. This convertible is by Le Baron.

△ **Lincoln Continental 1939**

Origin USA

Engine 4,378 cc, V12

Top speed 90 mph (145 km/h)

Originally hand-built, the Continental was Lincoln's finest car. It began as a one-off made for Edsel Ford, but was so admired that Edsel put it into production.

△ **Talbot T150C SS 1937**

Origin France

Engine 3,994 cc, straight-six

Top speed 115 mph (185 km/h)

Anthony Lago revived Talbot with modern engines and suspension. The "Teardrop", designed by Figoni et Falaschi, was equally at home at Le Mans as cruising the Riviera.

BMW 319, 1937

Great marques
The BMW story

BMW began as a maker of aero engines, later diversifying into motorcycles and then cars. From near-certain bankruptcy in the 1950s, BMW bounced back in the 1960s with the landmark Neue Klasse models. It has since grown into one of the most respected European marques and a leading manufacturer of sports saloons.

BMW WAS BORN in the boom years of the aviation industry. Gustav Otto (son of Nikolaus Otto, the petrol-engine pioneer) had founded an aircraft factory near Munich, Germany, in 1911, and in 1913 Karl Rapp started an aero-engine works nearby. After Rapp left, his company was reorganized as the Bayerische Motoren Werke (Bavarian Engine Works), or BMW. In 1917 BMW merged with the aircraft company, from which Otto had retired due to illness the previous year.

BMW entered car manufacturing in 1929 after buying the Dixi company, which built Austin Sevens under licence at a factory in Eisenach. In 1932 BMW began producing its own cars, beginning with the 3/20 AM-1. The 303 of 1934 had a six-cylinder engine and was the first model with the twin kidney-shaped grille, which is still seen on BMWs today. The finest BMW of the inter-war years was the 328 sports car of 1936, which dominated European sports-car racing in the late 1930s. During World War II BMW made cars, motorcycles, and

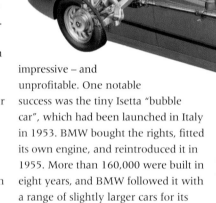

BMW badge
(introduced 1917)

aero engines for the German government, and its factories were severely damaged by Allied bombing. After the post-war division of Germany, the company's Eisenach factory lay in the Soviet-controlled Eastern Zone. Motorcycle and car production resumed, with vehicles being badged as EMW (Eisenacher Motoren Werke). The factory was later home to the long-running Wartburg marque, which endured until 1991. Cars based on BMW's designs were also built in England by Bristol.

The Munich factory, in the Western Zone under Allied control, restarted motorcycle production in 1948. It then

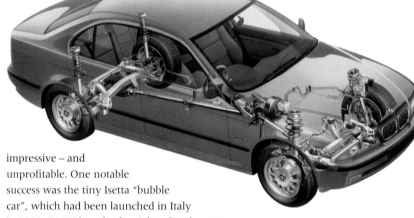

BMW 5 Series suspension
In 1995 the third generation of BMW's 5 Series used aluminium for the suspension and steering to offset the weight of structural improvements and slight increase in size.

impressive – and unprofitable. One notable success was the tiny Isetta "bubble car", which had been launched in Italy in 1953. BMW bought the rights, fitted its own engine, and reintroduced it in 1955. More than 160,000 were built in eight years, and BMW followed it with a range of slightly larger cars for its increasingly prosperous clientele.

> ## "They have this **amazing ability** to produce ... **gutsy** and **reliable engines.**"
> GORDON MURRAY, DESIGNER OF THE BMW-ENGINED MCLAREN F1, 1994

embarked on a range of luxury cars, beginning in 1951 with the 501. However, the 501 cost four times the average German salary, and even those who could afford it were more likely to buy a model from the more established Mercedes-Benz marque. BMW's V8-engined models, including the rapid 507 sports car, were equally

BMW Isetta "bubble car"
This tiny, two-seater car was powered by a one-cylinder, four-stroke motorcycle engine.

The company still struggled financially, and in 1959 it was nearly bankrupt. It was saved by the investment of the Quandt family, who installed a fresh management team.

The first fruit of this successful management change was the Neue Klasse Series – starting with the 1500 of 1961 – which at last put BMW on the road to financial security. Crisp, square-jawed styling and new, overhead-cam engines made these cars extremely desirable. To meet the increased demand for the Neue Klasse

cars, BMW needed more production capacity, so it took over Glas – an ailing car manufacturer at Dingolfing.

The New Six Series of six-cylinder luxury saloons and coupés expanded BMW's range during the late 1960s, while the 5-Series, initiated in 1972, redefined the mid-range executive car by offering efficient engines, clean-cut styling, and class-leading safety. Meanwhile, the 3.0CSL, a lightweight development of BMW's New Six coupé, beat Ford's RS Capri in the European Touring Car Championship. But the oil crisis of 1973 ensured that neither the road-going CSL nor a turbocharged 2002 unveiled that year were great successes. BMW also struggled with a supercar project, the M1, which began limited production in 1979.

Instead, BMW established a well-structured range during the 1970s, introducing the compact

501

507

3.0CSL

M3

1911	Gustav Otto establishes his aircraft company near Munich.
1913	Karl Rapp opens his aero-engine works.
1917	Rapp leaves; his firm is renamed Bayerische Motoren Werke (BMW) and merges with the aircraft company.
1923	BMW produces is first motorcycle, the R32.
1929	BMW buys the Austin-based Dixi brand; the Dixi 3/15 DA-2 is BMW's first car.
1932	The 3/20 AM-1 is the first all-German BMW car.

1936	BMW introduces the 328, which dominates sports-car racing.
1945	BMW's Eisenach factory comes under Soviet control after World War II.
1948	Post-war production of motorcycles resumes at the Munich factory.
1951	The 501 is the first new model to be produced by the Munich factory.
1955	BMW launches its own version of the Isetta "bubble car".
1959	The Quandt family steps in to prevent the sale of BMW to Daimler-Benz.

1961	The 1500 is the first Neue Klasse car.
1967	BMW takes over the Glas marque.
1972	Launch of the E12 5-Series.
1973	The 3.0CSL wins the European Touring Car Championship.
1975	BMW 3-Series is introduced.
1979	Production of the M1 supercar begins.
1983	BMW turbo engine powers Brabham driver Nelson Piquet to the Formula 1 World Championship.
1987	The M3 wins the European Touring Car Championship, and again in 1988.

1990	BMW begins supplying engines for the McLaren F1 road car.
1994	BMW buys Britain's Rover Group.
1998	Rolls-Royce marque is bought by BMW.
2000	BMW sells Rover; it also becomes Formula 1 engine supplier to Williams.
2001	"Flame surfaced" 7-Series and new Mini are unveiled, styled by Chris Bangle.
2003	BMW's new Rolls-Royce factory at Goodwood, southeast England, launches its first model, the Phantom.
2009	Design chief Chris Bangle leaves BMW.

3-Series in 1975, the 6-Series coupé in 1976, and the large 7-Series in 1977. A second-generation 5-Series followed in 1981, the same year that BMW became engine supplier to the Brabham Formula 1 team, providing it with a mighty 1.5-litre turbo. Based on the Neue Klasse engine of 1961, the turbo powered Nelson Piquet to the 1983 World Championship.

In the mid-1980s BMW installed the M1's 24-valve engine into 5- and 6-Series cars to produce the rapid yet refined M-car Series. The engine was also tried in a 3-Series, but its weight ruined the handling. Instead, BMW engine boss Paul Rosche developed a 16-valve, four-cylinder engine for the M3 of 1988, which enabled the car to dominate touring-car racing grids just as the 328 had done half a century earlier. In 1990 BMW provided the engine for the McLaren F1 road car, and in 1999 it won the Le Mans 24-hour race with Williams. The following year BMW developed a V10 Formula 1 engine for Williams, for whom it remained engine supplier until 2005. After breaking with Williams, BMW owned the Sauber Grand Prix team from 2006 to 2009.

BMW augmented its range from 2000 onwards, with new generation 3-, 5-, and 7-Series models, Z-Series sports cars, and the X-Series SUVs. In 2001 design chief Chris Bangle restyled the cars with "flame surfacing" – using a car's curves and angles to capture the essence of a burning flame.

BMW had expanded its operations in the 1990s, buying Britain's Rover Group in 1994 and the Rolls-Royce marque in 1998. It sold Rover in 2000 but kept the Mini brand, reinventing it in 2001 with spectacular success. Two years later BMW set up a new Rolls-Royce factory at Goodwood, southeast England.

Despite poor market conditions in recent years, BMW's sales have held up well, its core models bolstered by new technology such as stop-start and mild-hybrid systems. Introduced in 2007 as "Efficient Dynamics", these systems automatically turn off the engine when it is not needed to save fuel.

BMW 328
Produced from 1936 to 1940, the 328 was one of the finest sports cars of its time. It had a beautifully styled streamlined body, a light tubular frame, and a 1,971 cc, six-cylinder engine with hemispherical combustion chambers.

Powerful Sports Tourers

Despite the 1929 Wall Street Crash that precipitated a worldwide recession, the 1930s saw small manufacturers continue to make large-engined sports tourers, with ever-increasing refinement as the global economy recovered. The widespread building of high-quality surfaced roads allowed wealthy drivers to cruise at hitherto unimagined speeds and travel hundreds of miles in a few hours, making journeys such as Paris to Monte Carlo or London to Edinburgh a comfortable reality.

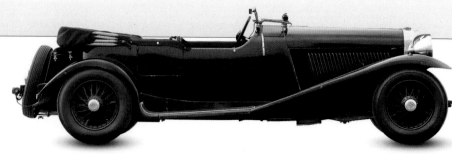

△ Bentley 4-litre 1931

Origin UK

Engine 3,915 cc, straight-six

Top speed 80 mph (129 km/h)

The magnificent 8-litre and less-impressive 4-litre models were the swansongs of the independent Bentley company, which would shortly be taken over by Rolls-Royce.

△ Railton Eight 1933

Origin UK

Engine 4,010 cc, straight-eight

Top speed 90 mph (145 km/h)

Reid Railton had the idea of mounting English sporting coachwork on the powerful US Terraplane chassis. The result was the Eight – a fast sporting car available at a competitive price.

▷ Delahaye T135 1935

Origin France

Engine 3,227 cc, straight-six

Top speed 100 mph (161 km/h)

Named "Coupe des Alpes" after success in the challenging Alpine Rally, the T135 had a truck-derived engine, but it performed well on road and track – and looked fabulous.

△ SS I 1933

Origin UK

Engine 2,552 cc, straight-six

Top speed 75 mph (121 km/h)

William Lyons initially built motorcycle sidecars, and then bodies for Austin Sevens. His first complete car was the SS 1 coupé of 1931. It was also available as a tourer from 1933.

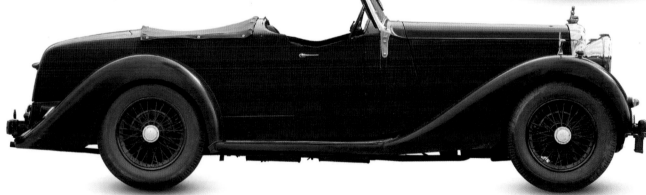

◁ Daimler LQ20 Special 1934

Origin UK

Engine 2,700 cc, straight-six

Top speed 75 mph (121 km/h)

Daimler's owner-driver range had Lanchester-derived engines, fluid flywheel transmission, and servo brakes. Unlike the light Special tourer shown here, the cars were usually heavy-bodied saloons.

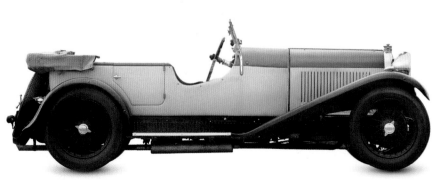

◁ Lagonda 3-litre 1933

Origin UK

Engine 3,181 cc, straight-six

Top speed 82 mph (132 km/h)

Lagonda found its luxury tourers hard to sell in the recession, but its 3-litre model was still a fine sporting car that performed well. It offered pre-selector transmission as an option.

△ Mercedes-Benz 540K 1936

Origin Germany

Engine 5,401 cc, straight-eight

Top speed 106 mph (171 km/h)

Twice the price of a V16 Cadillac, the Mercedes-Benz 540K was a magnificent grand tourer with all-independent suspension, power brakes, and a supercharged engine that gave 180 bhp.

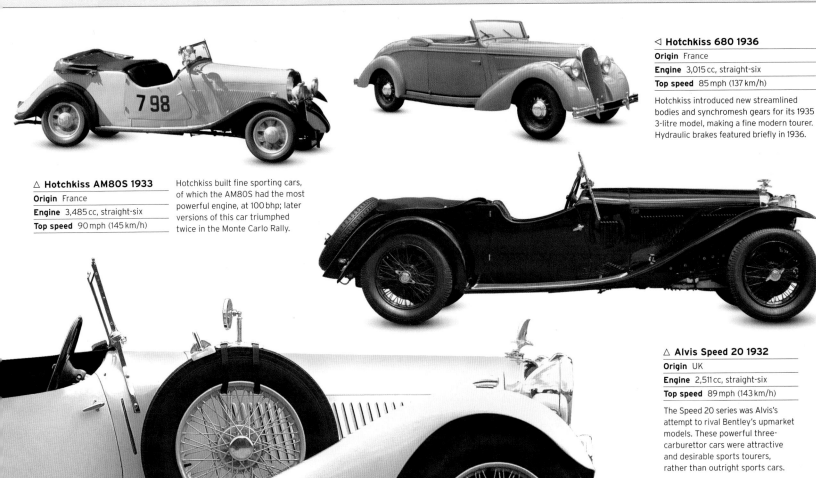

◁ Hotchkiss 680 1936
Origin France
Engine 3,015 cc, straight-six
Top speed 85 mph (137 km/h)

Hotchkiss introduced new streamlined bodies and synchromesh gears for its 1935 3-litre model, making a fine modern tourer. Hydraulic brakes featured briefly in 1936.

△ Hotchkiss AM80S 1933
Origin France
Engine 3,485 cc, straight-six
Top speed 90 mph (145 km/h)

Hotchkiss built fine sporting cars, of which the AM80S had the most powerful engine, at 100 bhp; later versions of this car triumphed twice in the Monte Carlo Rally.

△ Alvis Speed 20 1932
Origin UK
Engine 2,511 cc, straight-six
Top speed 89 mph (143 km/h)

The Speed 20 series was Alvis's attempt to rival Bentley's upmarket models. These powerful three-carburettor cars were attractive and desirable sports tourers, rather than outright sports cars.

◁ Alvis Speed 25 1937
Origin UK
Engine 3,571 cc, straight-six
Top speed 97 mph (156 km/h)

Alvis refined the Speed 20 with independent front suspension and an all-synchromesh gearbox. It then added a larger engine and servo brakes to create this Speed 25.

△ Jensen S-type 1937
Origin UK
Engine 3,622 cc, V8
Top speed 81 mph (130 km/h)

The S-type was the first car made by brothers Alan and Richard Jensen, who began as coachbuilders. They offered it as a drophead coupé, saloon, or tourer, and with a 2.2-litre engine option.

▷ Triumph Dolomite Roadster 1938
Origin UK
Engine 1,991 cc, straight-six
Top speed 80 mph (129 km/h)

With its three-carburettor engine and waterfall grille, the Walter Belgrove-designed Dolomite was a striking car. Accommodation was three seats abreast in the front, and a two-seat dickey behind.

▷ Delage D6-75 1938
Origin France
Engine 2,998 cc, straight-six
Top speed 95 mph (153 km/h)

Despite near bankruptcy and a takeover by Delahaye in 1935, Delage continued making superb sporting cars throughout the 1930s. This replica TT version is more sporty than most D6-75s.

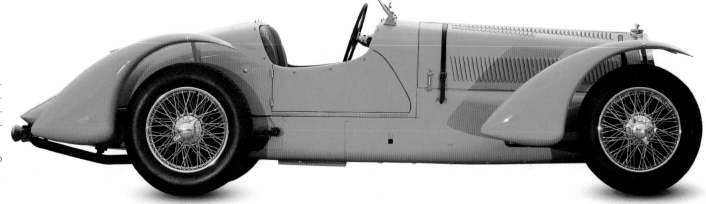

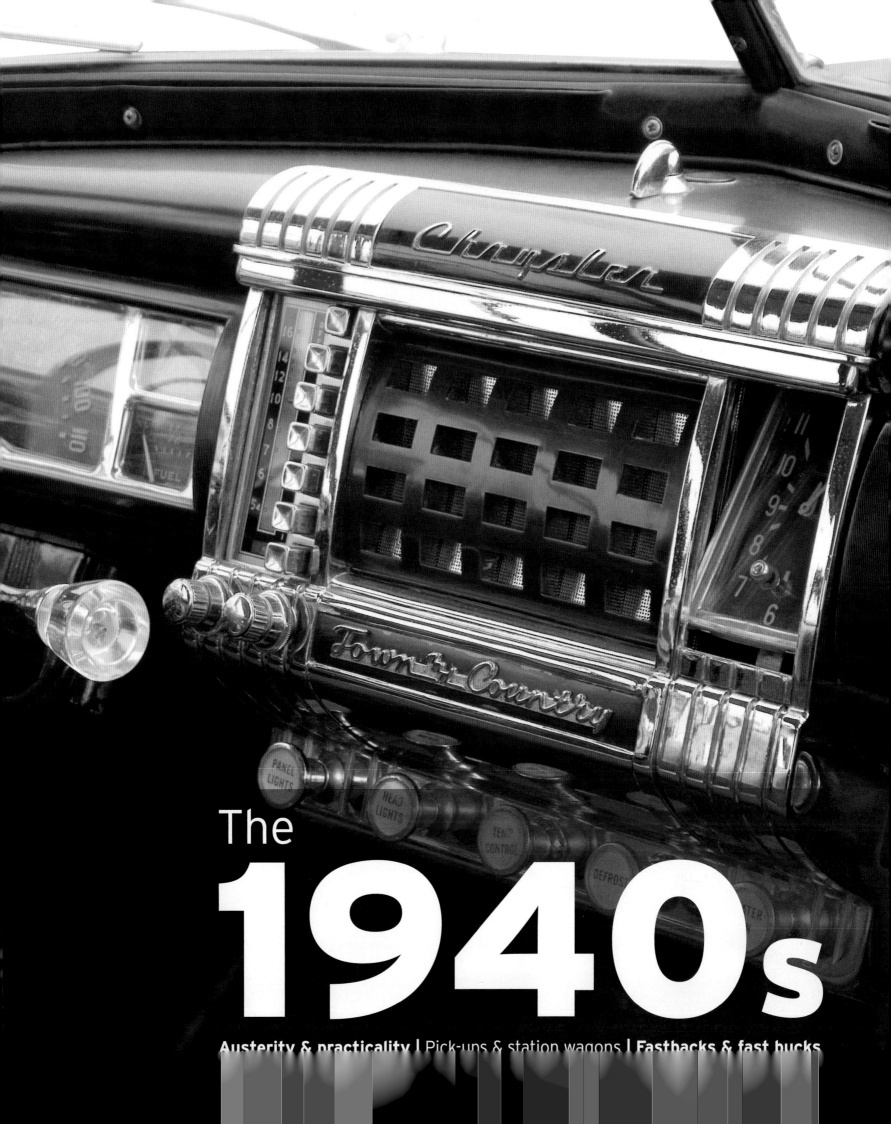

The
1940s

Austerity & practicality | Pick-ups & station wagons | **Fastbacks & fast bucks**

Large Cars

After World War II few people in Europe could afford large, luxurious saloons. Instead, designs were conservative and only figures such as government ministers, ambassadors, or doctors could justify a large, powerful car for their work. Cars were mostly updated pre-war creations with heavy and ponderous engines, many still with side valves and three-speed gearboxes.

▷ **Isotta-Fraschini 8C Monterosa 1947**

Origin Italy

Engine 3,400 cc, V8

Top speed 100 mph (161 km/h)

Inspired by Tatra, engineer Fabio Rapi planned an advanced luxury car, with a rear-mounted V8 engine, rubber springs, and aerodynamic monocoque body. Only five of these were ever built.

▷ **Daimler DE36 1946**

Origin UK

Engine 5,460 cc, straight-eight

Top speed 83 mph (134 km/h)

This huge post-war Daimler was supplied to seven royal families around the world, including the Windsors. It had the UK's last production straight-eight engine.

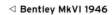

◁ **Bentley MkVI 1946**

Origin UK

Engine 4,257 cc, straight-six

Top speed 100 mph (161 km/h)

Post-war Bentleys were priced just below the equivalent Rolls-Royce; 80% were sold with factory-built "Standard Steel" bodies, which was cheaper than coachbuilding.

▷ **Opel Kapitän 1948**

Origin Germany

Engine 2,473 cc, straight-six

Top speed 78 mph (126 km/h)

Re-introduced in 1948, the monocoque Kapitän helped Opel get back on its feet after the war. It was a practical and popular car: 30,431 were sold up to 1951.

△ **Wolseley 6/80 1948**

Origin UK

Engine 2,215 cc, straight-six

Top speed 79 mph (127 km/h)

This reliable saloon became the standard police car in the UK in the 1940s, used for both patrol and pursuit duties. It had a factory-supplied, heavy-duty specification.

▷ **Humber Pullman II 1948**

Origin UK

Engine 4,086 cc, straight-six

Top speed 78 mph (126 km/h)

This imposing limousine was a favourite of British government officials. The chassis was an extended Super Snipe, requiring a two-part propeller shaft.

◁ **Humber Super Snipe II 1948**

Origin UK

Engine 4,086 cc, straight-six

Top speed 82 mph (132 km/h)

Preferred by bank managers and government officials, the Super Snipe was the epitome of conservative taste. It inherited its engine from the wartime British army staff car.

▽ **Rolls-Royce Silver Wraith 1946**

Origin UK

Engine 4,257 cc, straight-six

Top speed 85 mph (137 km/h)

The top UK post-war luxury car had its body custom-made, generally panelled in aluminium. It gradually grew in length and engine size until 1959.

△ **Ford V8 Pilot 1947**

Origin UK

Engine 3,622 cc, V8

Top speed 79 mph (127 km/h)

An extremely tough car, the Pilot's flathead V8 engine dated back to the 1930s. Its pulling power was legendary, but it was out of step with the UK's post-war austerity.

▷ **Lagonda 2.6-litre 1948**

Origin UK

Engine 2,580 cc, straight-six

Top speed 90 mph (145 km/h)

A luxury convertible and saloon designed by the great WO Bentley, the Lagonda had all-independent suspension and a double-camshaft 2.6-litre engine that subsequently powered Aston Martins.

△ **Delahaye 235 1951**

Origin France

Engine 3,557 cc, straight-six

Top speed 110 mph (177 km/h)

An updated version of the pre-war 135, Delahaye built 85 of the 235 between 1951 and 1954. Coachbuilt bodywork proved too expensive and was replaced by a factory body.

▷ **Austin A135 Princess 1947**

Origin UK

Engine 3,995 cc, straight-six

Top speed 88 mph (142 km/h)

Triple carburettors and more modern-looking, aluminium bodywork from coachbuilder Vanden Plas helped improve performance. This is the later, long-wheelbase limousine.

◁ **Austin A125 Sheerline 1947**

Origin UK

Engine 3,995 cc, straight-six

Top speed 81 mph (130 km/h)

Razor-edged styling and huge headlamps helped this large Austin resemble a contemporary Bentley, but performance from its truck-derived engine was limited.

US Style-Setters

There was a huge appetite for new cars in post-war America, so manufacturers rushed into production, working with essentially pre-war body styles. These styles, however, had seen three seasons' more development than European makes, since the US had joined the war that much later. By 1949 pent-up demand was satisfied, and manufacturers were competing head-on with aerodynamic new styles and with the first signs of fins and chrome.

△ **Lincoln 1946**

Origin USA

Engine 4,998 cc, V12

Top speed 92 mph (148 km/h)

Lincoln, Ford's upmarket brand, was still making pre-war-styled cars in 1946. These were fine cars, but the public was looking for something more modern than this.

△ **Kaiser Frazer F47 1946**

Origin USA

Engine 3,707 cc, straight-six

Top speed 82 mph (132 km/h)

The first US car with true post-war styling – a full-width bodyshell with no front or rear wing mouldings – the Frazer was styled by Howard "Dutch" Darrin.

◁ **Buick Roadmaster Sedanette 1949**

Origin USA

Engine 5,247 cc, straight-eight

Top speed 87 mph (140 km/h)

Buick's 1949 Sedanette was superbly proportioned, its fastback style enhanced by tapering chrome sidebars, spats over the rear wheels, and fighter-aircraft-style "ventiports".

△ **Chrysler Windsor Club Coupé 1946**

Origin USA

Engine 4,107 cc, six-cylinder

Top speed 82 mph (132 km/h)

The Chrysler Windsor was a Chrysler Royal with better trim, including two-tone wool broadcloth seats. This coupé has distinctively post-war rear-end styling, despite still-protruding wings.

▷ **Buick Super 1946**

Origin USA

Engine 4,064 cc, straight-eight

Top speed 82 mph (140 km/h)

Buick's post-war style was a light update of its 1942 models, but it was still more modern than most of its rivals. Elegant and attractive, the convertibles were particularly desirable.

△ **Chevrolet Stylemaster 1946**

Origin USA

Engine 3,548 cc, straight-six

Top speed 80 mph (132 km/h)

The US's best-selling car was a competitively priced, pre-war-styled machine whose Stovebolt Six engine dated back to 1937.

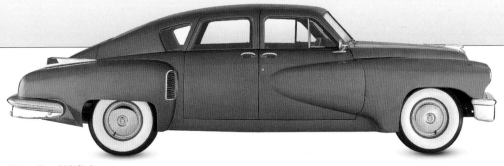

◁ Tucker 48 1948
Origin USA
Engine 5,475 cc, flat-six
Top speed 131 mph (211 km/h)

Even without the personality of its mercurial sponsor, Preston Tucker, this car would have made headlines with its rear-mounted helicopter engine and storming performance.

▽ Pontiac Chieftain Convertible 1949
Origin USA
Engine 4,079 cc, straight-eight
Top speed 85 mph (137 km/h)

Low, sleek, full-width bodies were the hit of 1949 at Pontiac. This was some compensation for the rather unexciting pre-war L-head six- and eight-cylinder engines.

◁ Ford Custom V8 1949
Origin USA
Engine 3,917 cc, V8
Top speed 85 mph (137 km/h)

Ford's new styling came in 1949. It was clean, low, modern, and boxy – all of which was soon to be seen on European Fords too. The public flocked to buy the new models.

▽ Dodge Coronet 1949
Origin USA
Engine 3,769 cc, straight-six
Top speed 80 mph (129 km/h)

Dodge's boxy new look arrived in 1949. Apart from the chrome, US cars were not too different in profile from European cars at this time, but this was soon to change.

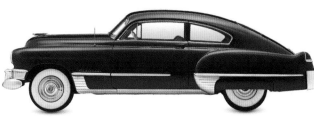

△ Cadillac Fleetwood 60 Special 1947
Origin USA
Engine 5,670 cc, V8
Top speed 90 mph (145 km/h)

In 1947 Cadillac was still building a pre-war-styled car, dressing it up with ever more chrome. Slightly wider doors were fitted to the luxury Fleetwood model.

◁ Hudson Super Six 1948
Origin USA
Engine 4,293 cc, straight-six
Top speed 90 mph (145 km/h)

One of the few small firms in post-war US car production, Hudson excelled with its low-built "step down" 1948 models and new, powerful, Super Six engine.

△ Cadillac Series 62 Club Coupé 1949
Origin USA
Engine 5,424 cc, V8
Top speed 92 mph (148 km/h)

General Motors' 1948 body design featured tailfins inspired by the P38 Lockheed fighter plane. 1949 brought a new OHV engine.

▽ Chevrolet Fleetline Deluxe 1949
Origin USA
Engine 3,548 cc, straight-six
Top speed 80 mph (129 km/h)

Chevrolet adopted fully blended front wings in 1949. The wings were still a conservative style, but the marque remained the market leader.

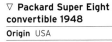

▽ Packard Super Eight convertible 1948
Origin USA
Engine 5,359 cc, straight-eight
Top speed 98 mph (158 km/h)

1948 was Packard's finest post-war year, as its clean, modern, "bathtub" styling was a hit with buyers. However, the small company could not afford annual restyles like its rivals.

△ Oldsmobile 88 Club Sedan 1949
Origin USA
Engine 4,977 cc, V8
Top speed 100 mph (161 km/h)

Futuramic styling, plus the new high-performance Rocket V8 engine and effective Hydramatic automatic transmission, made the 1949 Oldsmobiles hugely desirable.

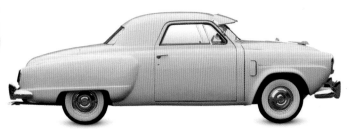

◁ Studebaker Champion 1950
Origin USA
Engine 2,779 cc, straight-six
Top speed 82 mph (132 km/h)

In 1947 Studebaker was the first big name to introduce post-war styling. By 1950 the Champion was onto its first major revision, with longer nose and aerodynamic lines.

Jeep, 1942
The Jeep, built by Ford and Willys, was a battlefield taxi for the US Army. These soldiers, based in Tennessee, had little idea that their "GP" (General Purpose vehicle) would start a sport-utility vehicle phenomenon in peace-time.

Practical Everyday Transport

The demands and shortages of World War II meant that transport in the 1940s had to concentrate on practicality without frills or luxuries – vans and pick-ups were vital to move food and supplies to where they were needed, and off-road vehicles were required to carry troops over rough terrain. After the war simple, sturdy vehicles were in demand as the world's economies began to recover.

△ **Humber Super Snipe staff car 1938**

Origin UK

Engine 4,086 cc, straight-six

Top speed 78 mph (126 km/h)

This Humber was the perfect vehicle for transporting British officers during World War II. Despite being large and lumbering, it was rapid and very strong.

△ **Ford F1 1948**

Origin USA

Engine 3,703 cc, V8

Top speed 70 mph (112 km/h)

Attractive, well proportioned, and adequately powerful in V8 form, the 1948 truck was styled by Bob Gregorie along the lines of the 1939 Ford range and has always been popular.

▽ **International Harvester K-series pick-up 1941**

Origin USA

Engine 3,507 cc, straight-six

Top speed 65 mph (105 km/h)

The pick-up truck became standard transport in rural America by the 1940s. Agricultural machinery maker International Harvester started building light trucks in 1909.

△ **Citroën 11 Large 1935**

Origin France

Engine 1,911 cc, straight-four

Top speed 65 mph (105 km/h)

The longest of the innovative front-wheel-drive Citroëns was over 4.5 m (15 ft) long with a huge turning circle. Ideal for the larger family, or as a taxi, it had three rows of seats.

△ **Volkswagen Kübelwagen 1940**

Origin Germany

Engine 985 cc, flat-four

Top speed 50 mph (80 km/h)

Ferdinand Porsche's Beetle-based military transport served in all fields of war, despite being only two-wheel drive. A remarkable 50,435 of these were built from 1940 to 1945.

△ **Volkswagen Schwimmwagen Type 166 1941**

Origin Germany

Engine 1,131 cc, flat-four

Top speed 47 mph (76 km/h)

A highly effective amphibian of which 15,584 were built, the Schwimmwagen had a propeller for water propulsion. It was four-wheel drive in first gear only, with two limited-slip differentials.

▷ **Chevrolet Stylemaster Van 1946**

Origin USA

Engine 3,548 cc, straight-six

Top speed 87 mph (140 km/h)

This capacious van was ideal for transporting loads in rural areas. Great value, the durable "Stovebolt Six" engine introduced in 1937 made it a best-seller.

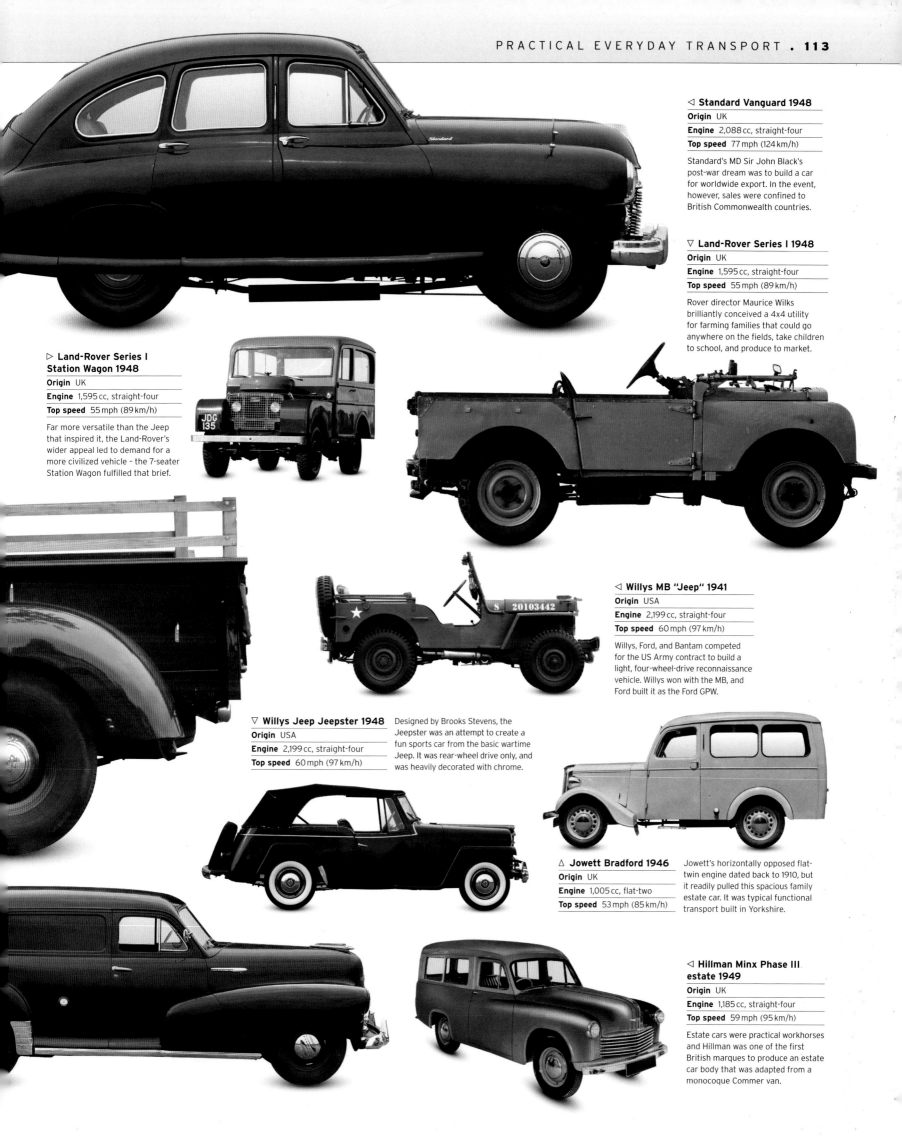

◁ **Standard Vanguard 1948**

Origin UK

Engine 2,088 cc, straight-four

Top speed 77 mph (124 km/h)

Standard's MD Sir John Black's post-war dream was to build a car for worldwide export. In the event, however, sales were confined to British Commonwealth countries.

▽ **Land-Rover Series I 1948**

Origin UK

Engine 1,595 cc, straight-four

Top speed 55 mph (89 km/h)

Rover director Maurice Wilks brilliantly conceived a 4x4 utility for farming families that could go anywhere on the fields, take children to school, and produce to market.

▷ **Land-Rover Series I Station Wagon 1948**

Origin UK

Engine 1,595 cc, straight-four

Top speed 55 mph (89 km/h)

Far more versatile than the Jeep that inspired it, the Land-Rover's wider appeal led to demand for a more civilized vehicle – the 7-seater Station Wagon fulfilled that brief.

◁ **Willys MB "Jeep" 1941**

Origin USA

Engine 2,199 cc, straight-four

Top speed 60 mph (97 km/h)

Willys, Ford, and Bantam competed for the US Army contract to build a light, four-wheel-drive reconnaissance vehicle. Willys won with the MB, and Ford built it as the Ford GPW.

▽ **Willys Jeep Jeepster 1948**

Origin USA

Engine 2,199 cc, straight-four

Top speed 60 mph (97 km/h)

Designed by Brooks Stevens, the Jeepster was an attempt to create a fun sports car from the basic wartime Jeep. It was rear-wheel drive only, and was heavily decorated with chrome.

△ **Jowett Bradford 1946**

Origin UK

Engine 1,005 cc, flat-two

Top speed 53 mph (85 km/h)

Jowett's horizontally opposed flat-twin engine dated back to 1910, but it readily pulled this spacious family estate car. It was typical functional transport built in Yorkshire.

◁ **Hillman Minx Phase III estate 1949**

Origin UK

Engine 1,185 cc, straight-four

Top speed 59 mph (95 km/h)

Estate cars were practical workhorses and Hillman was one of the first British marques to produce an estate car body that was adapted from a monocoque Commer van.

Ford F-Series

Pick-up trucks have been part of the fabric of American society for almost a century, and none more so than Ford's F-Series. The first all-new offering from Ford following the post-war resumption of civilian car manufacture, the F-Series was advertised as "Built Stronger To Last Longer". The models proved so successful that the series went on to become the US's best-selling vehicles for over two decades, and has remained in continuous production ever since its launch in 1948.

FORD'S EXPERIENCE of producing pick-up trucks from the 1920s onwards meant that after World War II the company was well placed to construct a brand new line of utility vehicles. Known as "Bonus Built" trucks due to their extra features, the F-Series from 1948 consisted of ½-ton (F-1), ¾-ton (F-2), and 1-ton (F-3) payload variants, plus larger workhorses, such as the F-5, with massive load capacities. The F-Series looked like no pick-ups before, with individually designed cabs separated from their flat beds instead of adapted automobiles that had passed for pick-ups

prior to the war. Ford trumpeted the originality of its trucks with lines such as "Star-Spangled New! Excitingly Modern! Strikingly Different!". Beneath the shiny exteriors were new engines that promised more power and economy than ever before in a pick-up. It was a winning blend that immediately appealed to US buyers; just under 110,000 F-1s were sold in 1948, making it the most successful year for Ford truck sales for almost two decades. Such was the strength of the original template that the descendents of the F-Series are still going strong more than 60 years later.

SPECIFICATIONS	
Model	Ford F-1 (first generation, 1948-52)
Assembly	USA
Production	628,318
Construction	Ladder-frame chassis
Engine	215/226 cu in straight-six, 239 cu in V8
Power output	95-106 bhp at 3,300-3,800 rpm
Transmission	Three- or four-speed manual
Suspension	Front and rear leaf springs
Brakes	Drums front and rear
Maximum speed	70 mph (113 km/h)

Pick-up heritage
The renowned Ford script was patented in 1909 after being used by the company in various forms during the first few years of the decade. A couple of years later an oval background was added to the design, but on the F-1 just the script was pressed into the steel of the tailgate.

FRONT VIEW

REAR VIEW

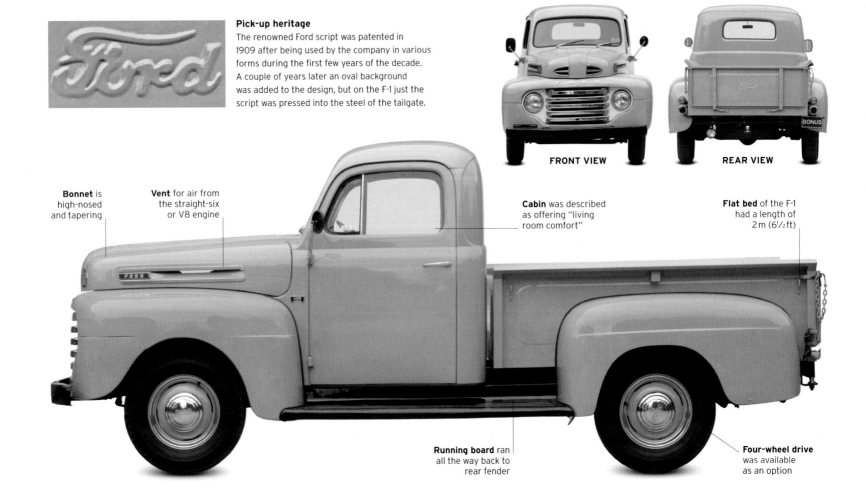

Bonnet is high-nosed and tapering

Vent for air from the straight-six or V8 engine

Cabin was described as offering "living room comfort"

Flat bed of the F-1 had a length of 2 m (6½ ft)

Running board ran all the way back to rear fender

Four-wheel drive was available as an option

Easy rider
The F-Series' much-vaunted "Million-Dollar Truck Cab" was the result of a development programme that sought to provide the driver and up to two passengers with comfort, space, and visibility that had not previously been available in a pick-up. Externally, as seen on this 1948 F-1, the front end was a bold design statement consisting of a high bonnet line with nostril-style air vents, five-bar horizontal chrome grille, and headlights positioned either side of the bars.

THE EXTERIOR

By constructing the cab separately from the working area at the rear, Ford was able to offer over 139 body-chassis combinations. This meant that the F-Series was available in a variety of styles, including panel van, pick-up, and platform trucks, with gross load capacities up to 10,000 kg (22,000 lb), inclusive of vehicle weight. The extensive research and development that Ford put into the series aimed to combine form with function, and its objectives were achieved in a series of forward-thinking utility vehicles.

1. F-1 designation was changed to F-150 in 1953 **2.** Bonnet air vents **3.** Headlight and grille radically redesigned for the 1951 model **4.** Alternative block Ford script **5.** External door handle **6.** Filler cap for cabin-mounted 64-l (17-gal) fuel tank **7.** Ford hubcaps were an optional extra **8.** Chain release for tailgate **9.** Tail light and directional indicator **10.** Fold-down tailgate **11.** Wooden truck bed

THE INTERIOR

Ride quality was given prominence in Ford's new pick-ups, with the inclusion of additional pads and additional rubber bushings (energy-absorbing sleeves) enabling near-automobile levels of handling and roadholding. Previously seen spartan interiors, where the emphasis was solely on functionality, gave way to luxuries that included a "coach-type" bench seat, three-way cabin air control, and a maximum-visibility windscreen. Extras included a passenger-side sun visor and windscreen wiper, plus an additional horn.

12. Bare painted metal of cabin indicates strictly utilitarian character
13. Window winder and internal door handle   **14.** Air ventilation slots
15. Small ashtray on dashboard   **16.** Large storage panel on dashboard
17. Coil-sprung bench seat could accommodate three   **18.** Heater unit
19. Brake and clutch pedals

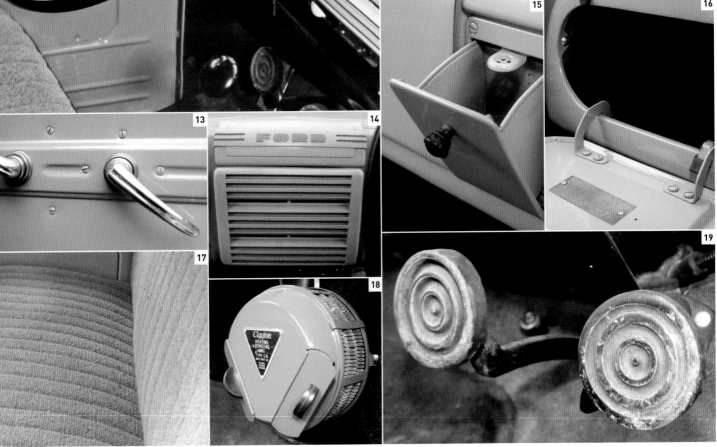

UNDER THE BONNET

The post-war economic landscape demanded appropriately economical vehicles. For the F-1, this meant two new units, a 226 cu in (3,703 cc) straight-six and a 239 cu in (3,916 cc) V8, shown here. The former was replaced in 1952 – the last year of the first-generation models – by a 215 cu in (3,523 cc) overhead-valve six that almost matched the performance output of the V8. Besides being strong and reliable, these engines were also especially frugal, with modest fuel and servicing bills, leading to attractively low running costs.

20. F-Series powerplants marketed as "Most modern engine line in the truck field"

Roadsters and Sports Cars

Instructed to help restore the UK's devastated balance of payments after World War II, British car manufacturers hurried to build sports cars to sell on the lucrative US market, where home-grown products were too bulky to match nimble European cars on twisty roads. Few of these British products would last long into the next decade (the Jaguar XK120 being an exception), and mainland Europe saw only a handful of expensive sports cars produced.

△ Bristol 400 1947
Origin UK
Engine 1,971cc, straight-six
Top speed 94 mph (151 km/h)

Bristol Aeroplanes entered the car market with a repackaged pre-war BMW design, brought back to the UK as "war reparations". It was a good sporting car and sold well.

△ Riley RMC Roadster 1948
Origin UK
Engine 2,443cc, straight-four
Top speed 100 mph (161 km/h)

A somewhat half-hearted attempt to make a sports car out of a four-door sports saloon, the Roadster had a single row of three seats and a very long tail. In all, 507 were made.

▷ Bristol 402 1948
Origin UK
Engine 1,971cc, straight-six
Top speed 98 mph (158 km/h)

Touring of Italy gave Bristol an attractive post-war style for the 401 saloon and this rare, four-seat convertible, which has a concealed hood and wind-up windows.

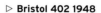

△ Ferrari 166 MM Barchetta 1949
Origin Italy
Engine 1,995cc, V12
Top speed 125 mph (201 km/h)

The first true production Ferrari sports car, usually fitted with this fabulous Touring Barchetta body, won the Mille Miglia, Spa, and Le Mans races in 1949.

◁ Jaguar XK120 1948
Origin UK
Engine 3,442cc, straight six
Top speed 125 mph (201 km/h)

William Lyons designed his 120 as simply a test bed for the new twin-cam XK engine. Huge demand, however, persuaded him to put it into production.

Grand Prix Cars

When Grand Prix racing resumed in 1946, in the wake of World War II, the German "Silver Arrows", almost unbeatable in the late 1930s, were nowhere to be seen. The new rules allowed 1.5-litre supercharged or 4.5-litre unsupercharged engines, and saw the small supercharged Italian racers from Alfa Romeo and Maserati dominate. The only car to beat them in the 1940s was the lumbering French Talbot-Lago.

△ Alfa Romeo 158 Alfetta 1948
Origin Italy
Engine 1,479cc, straight-eight
Top speed 180 mph (290 km/h)

One of the most successful Grand Prix cars ever, the supercharged 158/159 won 47 of the 54 Grands Prix it entered. Colombo's superb engine put out up to 350bhp.

▷ **Talbot-Lago T26 Grand Sport 1947**

Origin	France
Engine	4,482 cc, straight-six
Top speed	120 mph (193 km/h)

The ultimate Grand Tourer of the 1940s enjoyed a wide range of fabulous coachbuilt bodies, with none finer than this model by Saoutchik. A lighter version won Le Mans in 1950.

◁ **MG TC 1945**

Origin	UK
Engine	1,250 cc, straight-four
Top speed	75 mph (121 km/h)

Attractive, light, and fun – if very old-fashioned in its design – the TC sold as fast as MG could build it in the early post-war years.

▽ **MG YT 1948**

Origin	UK
Engine	1,250 cc, straight-four
Top speed	71 mph (114 km/h)

An MG sports car tailored for family use, the versatile YT was built only for export. Just 877 were sold between 1948 and 1950.

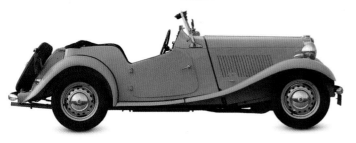

△ **MG TD 1949**

Origin	UK
Engine	1,250 cc, straight-four
Top speed	80 mph (129 km/h)

It still looked like a pre-war car, but the TD was beautifully rounded, readily tunable, and had a left-hand drive version too. Worldwide, 29,664 were sold between 1950 and 1953.

◁ **Austin A90 Atlantic 1949**

Origin	UK
Engine	2,660 cc, straight-four
Top speed	91 mph (146 km/h)

Leonard Lord's attempt at making a car that would appeal to US buyers was too small and costly to catch on, despite great PR generated by the records it set at the Indianapolis Speedway.

△ **Healey Silverstone 1949**

Origin	UK
Engine	2,443 cc, straight-four
Top speed	107 mph (172 km/h)

Donald Healey added the powerful twin-camshaft Riley engine to his own chassis, which had excellent handling qualities. The result was this ideal club-racing road car.

◁ **Allard P1 1949**

Origin	UK
Engine	3,622 cc, V8
Top speed	85 mph (137 km/h)

Sydney Allard put the readily available "flathead" Ford V8 engine in a sporting chassis with light bodywork to produce the P1. In it, he won the Monte Carlo Rally in 1952.

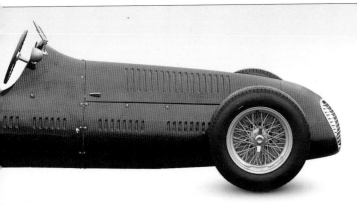

◁ **Maserati 4CLT/48 1948**

Origin	Italy
Engine	1,491 cc, straight-four
Top speed	168 mph (270 km/h)

With a new tubular chassis and twin superchargers for 1948, the 16-valve 4CLT became more competitive, and won numerous Grands Prix in 1948 and 1949.

△ **Talbot-Lago T26C 1948**

Origin	France
Engine	4,482 cc, straight-six
Top speed	168 mph (270 km/h)

Despite being heavy (it was even burdened with a pre-selector gearbox) and lacking a supercharger, the T26C scored two Grand Prix victories in 1949, thanks to its endurance and reliability.

Jaguar XK
straight-six

One of the most iconic powerplants in motoring history, Jaguar's XK straight-six was light, powerful, and reliable, and it remained essentially unchanged for almost 40 years. As well as featuring in the original XK120, the unit was used in XK140, XK150, and E-type sports cars, C- and D-type racers, and several saloon ranges.

AN ICONIC SPORTS-CAR ENGINE

Before World War II, when Jaguar was known as SS Cars, engines had been bought in from rival company Standard. The idea that Jaguar should produce its own engine was born during the war. Led by company founder William Lyons, an engineering team including William Heynes, Walter Hassan, and Claude Baily planned the engine in minute detail while on fire-watch duty on the roof of Jaguar's Coventry factory. Harry Weslake was drafted in to create the crucial aluminium cylinder-head design. The XK engine finally freed the renamed Jaguar Cars from dependence on outside suppliers.

ENGINE SPECIFICATIONS	
Dates produced	1949-1986
Cylinders	Straight-six
Configuration	Front-mounted, longitudinal
Engine capacities	2.4 litre, 2.8 litre, 3.4 litre, 3.8 litre, and 4.2 litre
Power output	133 bhp (2.4) to 265 bhp (3.8 and 4.2)
Type	Conventional four-stroke, water-cooled, petrol engine with reciprocating pistons, distributor ignition, and a wet or dry sump
Head	dohc with bucket tappets; two valves per cylinder
Fuel System	Triple HD.8 SU carburettors
Bore and Stroke	87 mm x 106 mm (3.42 in x 4.17 in)
Power	260 bhp @ 4,000 rpm
Compression Ratio	9.0:1

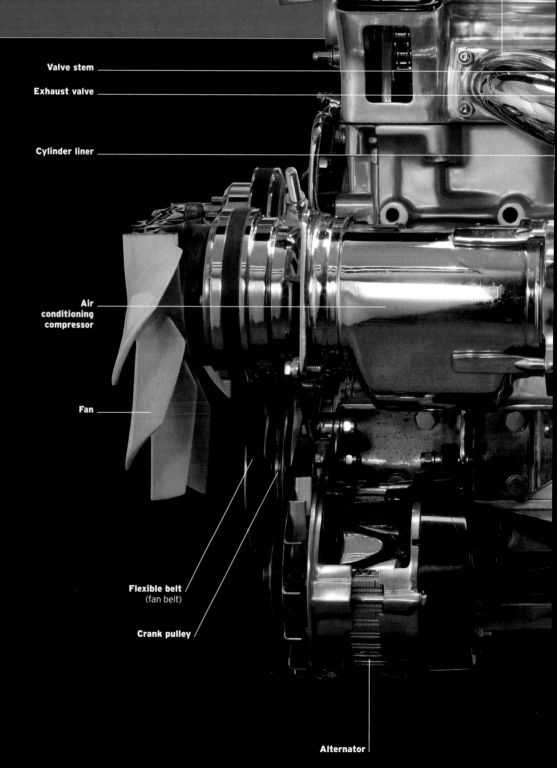

Duplex chains
These carry drive from the crankshaft (mostly hidden in this view of the engine) to the double overhead camshafts

Oil filler cap

Exhaust manifold

Valve stem

Exhaust valve

Cylinder liner

Air conditioning compressor

Fan

Flexible belt (fan belt)

Crank pulley

Alternator

▷ **See pp.346-347** How an engine works

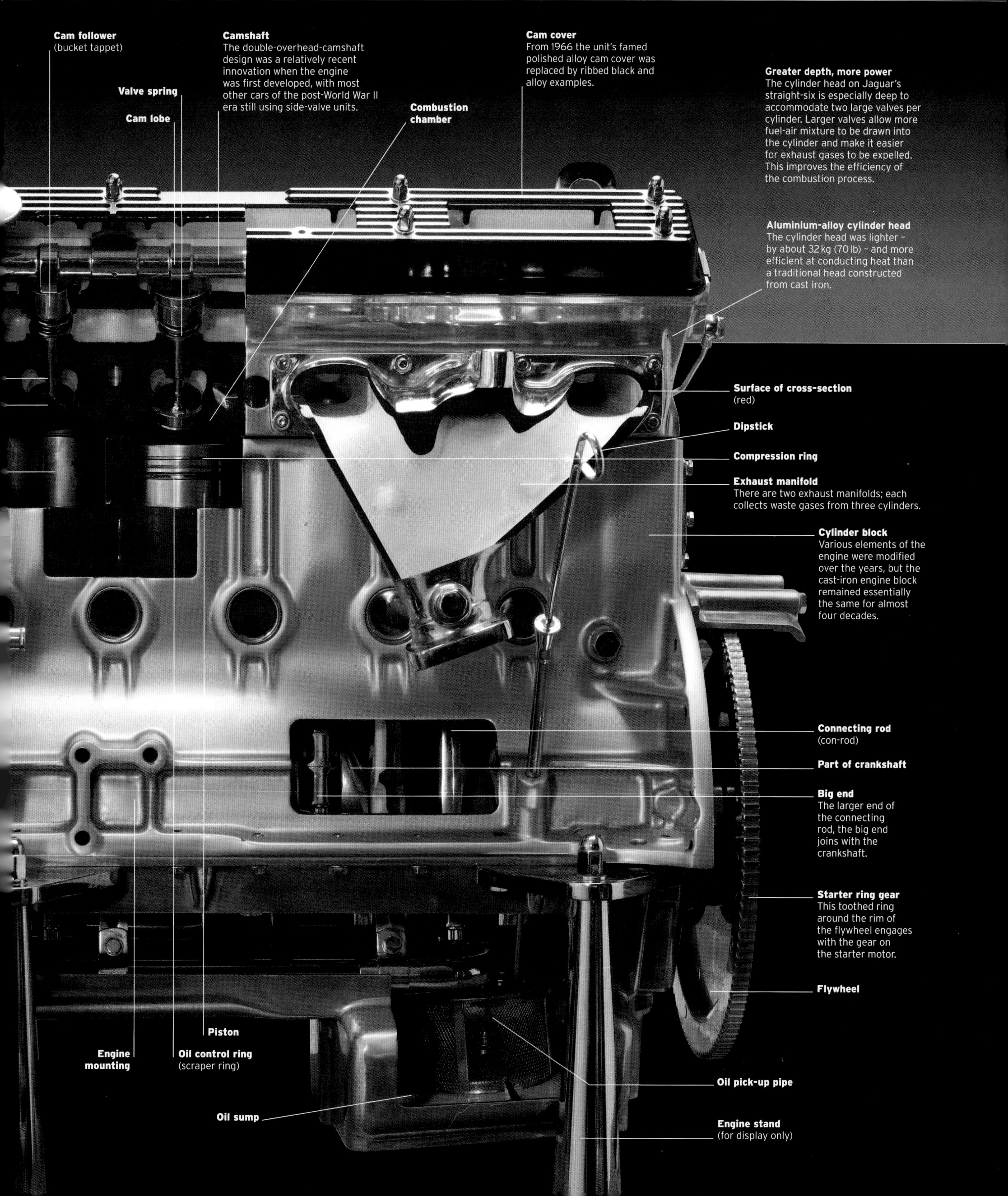

Cam follower
(bucket tappet)

Valve spring

Cam lobe

Camshaft
The double-overhead-camshaft design was a relatively recent innovation when the engine was first developed, with most other cars of the post-World War II era still using side-valve units.

Combustion chamber

Cam cover
From 1966 the unit's famed polished alloy cam cover was replaced by ribbed black and alloy examples.

Greater depth, more power
The cylinder head on Jaguar's straight-six is especially deep to accommodate two large valves per cylinder. Larger valves allow more fuel-air mixture to be drawn into the cylinder and make it easier for exhaust gases to be expelled. This improves the efficiency of the combustion process.

Aluminium-alloy cylinder head
The cylinder head was lighter – by about 32 kg (70 lb) – and more efficient at conducting heat than a traditional head constructed from cast iron.

Surface of cross-section
(red)

Dipstick

Compression ring

Exhaust manifold
There are two exhaust manifolds; each collects waste gases from three cylinders.

Cylinder block
Various elements of the engine were modified over the years, but the cast-iron engine block remained essentially the same for almost four decades.

Connecting rod
(con-rod)

Part of crankshaft

Big end
The larger end of the connecting rod, the big end joins with the crankshaft.

Starter ring gear
This toothed ring around the rim of the flywheel engages with the gear on the starter motor.

Flywheel

Piston

Engine mounting

Oil control ring
(scraper ring)

Oil pick-up pipe

Oil sump

Engine stand
(for display only)

Jaguar D-Type at Le Mans, 1957

Great marques
The Jaguar story

From building motorcycle sidecars in a tiny workshop in a seaside town in northwest England, William Lyons's company evolved into a manufacturer of high-quality sports cars and saloons. Over the decades, the Jaguar marque established a reputation for fast, refined cars, which it continues to live up to today.

MOTORCYCLE ENTHUSIASTS

William Lyons and William Walmsley started the Swallow Sidecar Company in Blackpool, Lancashire, in 1922. Swallow sidecars quickly became known for their high quality and stylish looks. In 1927 Swallow began making coachbuilt bodywork for the Austin Seven. Swallow's bodywork, designed by Lyons, gave the Seven a touch of flair and individuality that appealed to 1920s motorists.

Jaguar badge
(introduced 1935)

The company relocated in 1928 to the Midlands city of Coventry, and Lyons gradually expanded the range of Swallow bodies. In 1931 Swallow launched into car manufacture with its own creations, the SS1 and SS2. Both cars had rakish Lyons bodywork on chassis made by Standard, another Coventry firm. Swallow was renamed SS Cars in 1934, at which time Walmsley left the company. In 1935 Lyons unveiled his first sports car, the SS Jaguar 90. It was followed the next year by the most celebrated of Lyons's early cars, the SS Jaguar 100 – a sports car with a top speed of 100 mph (160 km/h).

After World War II the company dropped the letters SS, because of their Nazi connotations, and adopted the name Jaguar for all its cars. During the war Jaguar engineers had begun working on a new 3.4-litre, twin-cam

Alongside the XK line of sports cars, which progressed through the XK140 and XK150 of the late 1950s, Jaguar offered fast, refined saloons. The MkVII was the definitive Jaguar saloon of this era. Combining sleek good looks with the power of the XK engine and a sophisticated chassis, it handled superbly and gave a cosseting ride. The advertising of the time (and for many years to come) used the slogan "Grace, space, pace", which summed up perfectly the company's product range.

In 1961 Lyons's E-type impressed the motoring world with its performance, stunning looks, and price, just as the XK120 had done back in 1948. Again powered by the XK engine, this time in 3.8-litre form, the E-type was based on the same kind of monocoque

company. The second was that the Pressed Steel Company, which built Jaguar bodies, had been taken over by a rival car maker, BMC. The solution to both problems came in 1966 when BMC and Jaguar merged to form British Motor Holdings, which itself merged with the Leyland group two years later to form British Leyland. Lyons fought hard to retain as much independence for Jaguar as possible.

While the XJ saloon of 1968 and the V12 engine introduced in the E-type in 1971 were great technical achievements, the 1970s also saw the introduction of the controversially styled XJ-S and the unsuccessful XJ coupé racing programme. Within the vast British Leyland conglomerate, now state owned, the quality of

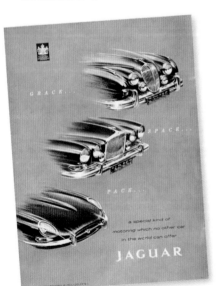

"Grace, space, pace" advert, early 1960s
Letting the cars' front ends do the talking, this advert shows (top to bottom) the MkII, MkX, and E-type offering "a special kind of motoring which no other car in the world can offer".

> "The **outstanding impression** ... is its combination of **extravagant performance** and silent, **effortless functioning**."

WILLIAM BODDY ON THE XK120, *MOTOR SPORT MAGAZINE*, 1951

engine, which would become a Jaguar fixture for the next four decades. It premiered in the new XK120 sports car at the 1948 London Motor Show. The XK120 gave high performance levels at a bargain price of less than £1,000. The famous C- and D-types – racing cars using the XK120 engine and equipped with innovations such as disc brakes and low-drag aerodynamics – won the Le Mans 24-hour race for Jaguar on five occasions during the 1950s.

construction as the Le Mans-winning D-type. The car also used aspects of the D-type's sleek, wind-cheating shape. Available in fixed-roof coupé and open roadster versions, the E-type was a hit on both sides of the Atlantic. It sold well, as did Jaguar's 1960s saloons – the huge MkX and the compact MkII.

Jaguar faced two problems in the mid-1960s. The first was that William Lyons was close to retirement and there was no obvious successor in the

Jaguar V12
First used in the Series 3 E-type of 1971, the V12 engine powered Jaguar cars until 1996, when it was replaced by the AJ-V8. It was based on design intended for a Le Mans prototype car, the XJ13, which never raced.

XK120

D-TYPE

E-TYPE

XJS

1922 William Lyons and William Walmsley form Swallow Sidecars.
1927 Swallow makes Austin Seven bodies.
1931 Swallow's first car, the SS1, is launched.
1933 The company changes its name to SS Cars Limited.
1935 The SS90 and SS100 are launched.
1945 SS Cars becomes Jaguar Cars.
1948 Jaguar launches the XK120 sports car and the XK engine.
1951 Peter Walker and Peter Whitehead win at Le Mans in a Jaguar C-type.

1953 Tony Rolt and Duncan Hamilton win at Le Mans in a Jaguar C-type.
1955 The D-type Jaguar wins at Le Mans, and repeats the feat in 1956 and 1957.
1956 Launch of the 2.4-litre, the first Jaguar with a monocoque construction.
1960 Jaguar buys Daimler from BSA.
1961 Introduction of both the E-type and the MkX saloon; Jaguar buys the truck maker Guy Motors.
1962 Launch of the first Jaguar–Daimler hybrid, the Daimler 2.5-litre.

1963 Jaguar buys Coventry Climax, a manufacturer of engines and forklifts; launch of the S-type.
1964 Jaguar buys Henry Meadows, which produces engines.
1966 Jaguar merges with the British Motor Corporation to form British Motor Holdings (BMH).
1968 BMH and Leyland merge to form the British Leyland Motor Corporation.
1988 Johnny Dumfries, Andy Wallace, and Jan Lammers win Le Mans in the XJR-9.

1988 Martin Brundle wins the World Sports Car Championship driving for Jaguar.
1989 Ford buys Jaguar for £1.6 billion.
1990 John Nielsen, Price Cobb, and Martin Brundle win the Le Mans 24-hour race in the Jaguar XJR-12.
1998 The all-new S-type model is a success.
1999 Jaguar becomes part of Ford's Premier Automotive Group.
2001 The rationale of the new X-type compact executive saloon is criticized.
2008 Ford sells Jaguar to Tata.

Jaguar cars suffered. Privatization came in 1984, not a moment too soon, and under the leadership of Sir John Egan Jaguar thrived once again. The XJ-S had already proved successful in touring-car racing in the hands of the Tom Walkinshaw Racing team, and Jaguar built on this by returning to Le Mans with a works team in 1988. Using V12 engines based on Jaguar's road car units, the XJR-9 and XJR-12 sports car won at Le Mans in 1988 and 1990 respectively.

In 1989 GM, Daimler-Benz, and Ford were all rumoured to be bidding for Jaguar, but it was Ford who won with a £1.6 billion takeover plan. Ford re-equipped Jaguar's factories, which

one Ford executive claimed were so primitive they reminded him of communist-era Russia. The now rejuvenated Jaguar developed new XJ saloons and a V8-engined XK sports coupé, while at the same time cutting costs and improving quality. In 1999 Jaguar became part of Ford's Premier Automotive Group, which included the Aston Martin, Land Rover, Lincoln, and Volvo marques. Ford also bought Jackie Stewart's Formula 1 team and rebranded it as Jaguar, but this racing venture was unsuccessful.

Under pressure to concentrate on its core businesses as its market share shrank in the new millennium, Ford sold Jaguar and Land Rover

to the Indian group Tata in 2008 for £1.15 billion. Tata inherited well-advanced plans for new models, including a mid-sized XF saloon and a new XJ, both of which were launched to wide acclaim. By 2010 Jaguar was back in profit and

had more new models ready for launch, pointing to a secure future for one of Britain's best-loved car brands.

Jaguar XK140, 1954
The follow-up to the highly successful XK120, Jaguar's XK140 had a more powerful engine. Other improvements included uprated brakes and suspension.

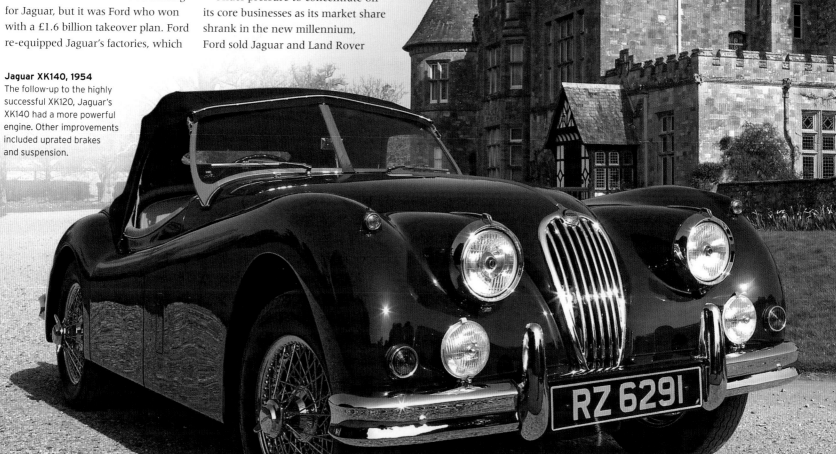

RZ 6291

Small Cars

After World War II there was a new motoring revolution. Most soldiers posted overseas had experienced long-distance travel for the first time. On their return home they wanted to be mobile and take their families much further afield than their fathers had been able to. To meet this demand, manufacturers around the world strove to develop cars for the masses, many of which went on to sell by the million.

◁ Morris Eight Series E 1938
Origin UK

Engine 918 cc, straight-four

Top speed 58 mph (93 km/h)

A pre-war model just modern enough in looks to continue in production post-war, the Series E Morris sold well until the new Morris Minor was ready to take over.

▷ Morris Minor 1948
Origin UK

Engine 918 cc, straight-four

Top speed 62 mph (100 km/h)

Alec Issigonis's brilliant people's car had a monocoque construction, torsion-bar front suspension, four gears, and modern lines – but not the flat-four engine he had wanted.

△ Volkswagen 1945
Origin Germany

Engine 1,131 cc, flat-four

Top speed 63 mph (101 km/h)

Designed by Ferdinand Porsche before the war, the "Beetle" would eventually become the best-selling car of all time thanks to its reliable engine, good space, and low price.

▷ Ford Taunus G93A 1948
Origin Germany

Engine 1,172 cc, straight-four

Top speed 60 mph (97 km/h)

This German version of Britain's E93A Ford Prefect had much more modern styling than its counterpart, but it was exactly the same beneath the bonnet.

△ Toyota Model SA 1947
Origin Japan

Engine 995 cc, straight-four

Top speed 58 mph (93 km/h)

Japan's first new post-war model, the SA mimicked many features of Volkswagen's Beetle, although its Ford-like engine was mounted at the front rather than the rear.

◁ Standard 8HP 1945
Origin UK

Engine 1,009 cc, straight-four

Top speed 60 mph (97 km/h)

Standard rushed its pre-war Eight back into production in 1945, having improved it with a four-speed gearbox. A competent if unexciting car, it sold 53,099 in three years.

◁ **Datsun DB 1948**

Origin Japan

Engine 722 cc, straight-four

Top speed 50 mph (80 km/h)

With styling copied from the US-built Crosley, this was Japan's first modern-looking car. The DB used a pre-war Datsun truck chassis and a side-valve car engine.

▷ **Crosley 1948**

Origin USA

Engine 721 cc, straight-four

Top speed 70 mph (113 km/h)

The slab-sided Crosley showed great promise with its unique sheet-steel, overhead-camshaft engine, but it failed to win over the US car-buying public.

▽ **Fiat 500C 1949**

Origin Italy

Engine 569 cc, straight-four

Top speed 60 mph (97 km/h)

This was the final version of Dante Giacosa's brilliant 1937 "Topolino" (Little Mouse), which mobilized the population of Italy with its well-packaged conventional layout.

△ **Citroën 2CV 1948**

Origin France

Engine 375 cc, flat-two

Top speed 39 mph (63 km/h)

Derived from a 1930s plan to develop a car to replace the horse and cart in rural France, the 2CV became a favourite in both town and country. The 2CV's crude looks belied its high-quality, innovative engineering.

◁ **Renault 4CV 1946**

Origin France

Engine 760 cc, straight-four

Top speed 57 mph (92 km/h)

The 4CV looked similar to its British rival, the Morris Minor, but it had all-independent suspension and a rear-mounted engine; it was also quicker to reach a million sales.

◁ **MG Y-type 1947**

Origin UK

Engine 1,250 cc, straight-four

Top speed 71 mph (114 km/h)

MG lengthened its little TC sports car chassis and added pre-war Morris Eight body panels to create this antiquated but charming saloon, which sold 6,158 from 1947 to 1951.

△ **Austin A40 Devon 1947**

Origin UK

Engine 1,200 cc, straight-four

Top speed 67 mph (108 km/h)

Modelled on a pre-war Chevrolet, Austin's first post-war design was slightly awkward and bulbous-looking, but it sold well thanks to its new overhead-valve engine.

▷ **Panhard Dyna 110 1948**

Origin France

Engine 610 cc, flat-two

Top speed 68 mph (109 km/h)

Designed by Jean Albert Grégoire, the Dyna 110 had an aluminium structure, an air-cooled aluminium engine, front-wheel drive, and independent suspension.

◁ **Bond Minicar 1948**

Origin UK

Engine 122 cc, one-cylinder

Top speed 38 mph (61 km/h)

Petrol rationing and cheap tax for three-wheelers made this two-seater ideal for the austerity of post-war Britain. The two-stroke engine pivoted with the car's front wheel.

▷ **Saab 92 1949**

Origin Sweden

Engine 764 cc, straight-two

Top speed 65 mph (105 km/h)

Aircraft maker Saab gave its 92 the most aerodynamic styling of the time, along with front-wheel drive and a two-stroke engine. The 92 proved a very successful rally car.

Volkswagen Beetle

Surely the most extraordinary success story in the history of the motor car, the Beetle began life as a pet project of Adolf Hitler, who commissioned famed engineer Ferdinand Porsche to design a low-cost vehicle for the German people. Production eventually began post World War II, under the British army then occupying much of Germany. Its manufacture lasted in Germany until 1978 – or 1980 for the cabrio – but continued in Latin America, latterly in Mexico, until 2003. In all, over 21 million Beetles were made, an all-time record for a single model.

THE BEETLE was designed to be cheap to build, and suitable for road conditions in late 1930s Germany, even in the hands of inexperienced motorists. An air-cooled engine was mechanically simple, and meant the car could not boil over; a low power output assured reliability. Positioning the engine at the back saved weight by eliminating the heavy axle and propshaft of a conventional rear-wheel-drive car, while the alloy engine kept weight down. Good aerodynamics meant easy cruising on Hitler's new autobahns, despite the engine's small size. Supple torsion-bar suspension and big wheels helped the Beetle cope with Germany's rough rural roads and cobbled town streets. Costs were kept down by using an unsynchronized gearbox and cable brakes, features that continued on the rarely ordered base model until the early 1960s.

FRONT VIEW

REAR VIEW

The name that survived Hitler
The *Volkswagen*, or "People's Car", was re-baptised the *KdFWagen*, or "Strength-through-Joy Car", in 1938, in reference to the leisure division of the Nazi trade-union movement. When production began, the car went back to its original name.

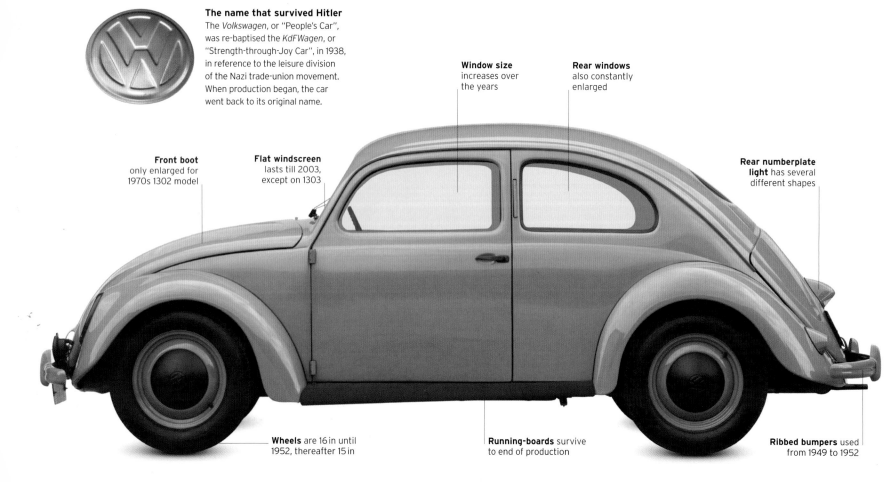

Window size increases over the years

Rear windows also constantly enlarged

Front boot only enlarged for 1970s 1302 model

Flat windscreen lasts till 2003, except on 1303

Rear numberplate light has several different shapes

Wheels are 16in until 1952, thereafter 15in

Running-boards survive to end of production

Ribbed bumpers used from 1949 to 1952

SPECIFICATIONS

Model	Volkswagen Beetle, 1945-2003
Assembly	Mainly Wolfsburg, Germany
Production	21,529,464
Construction	Platform chassis, steel body
Engine	1,131 cc, air-cooled flat-four
Power output	24 bhp at 3,300 rpm
Transmission	Four-speed manual
Suspension	All-independent by torsion bars
Brakes	Drum
Maximum speed	70 mph (113 km/h)

Evolution not revolution
This 1948 Beetle is a stripped-bare standard model
rather than the better-presented and much more
common export model available from 1949. The basic
Beetle style lasted to the end of production, with
the laid-back headlamps only being replaced by
more upright units in the facelift for 1968.

THE EXTERIOR

Ferdinand Porsche drew on 1930s streamlining trends to give the Beetle a smooth shape. This reduced fuel consumption and allowed for relaxed cruising on the new German motorways. Seen as old-fashioned at one stage, the Beetle was eventually regarded as timeless. It had only two significant restyles: in 1968, when the front was squared up, and in 1972, when the 1302 got a curved windscreen to become the 1303.

1. Basic model has no chromework **2.** Bonnet handle lacks exterior lock **3.** Externally mounted horn on early standard models **4.** Pop-up indicators stay until 1960 for European cars **5.** "Pope's Nose" boot light used until 1952 **6.** Round rear lights give way to oval units for 1953 **7.** Split rear window on all cars until March 1953

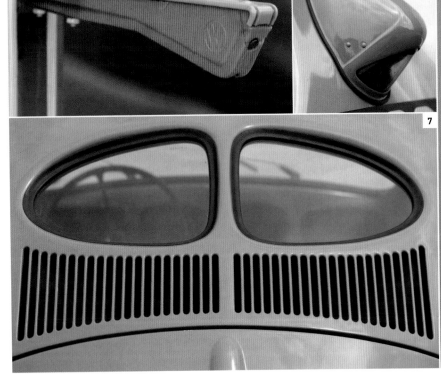

THE INTERIOR

The Beetle's interior was never hugely spacious, and nor was boot space particularly generous – at least until the 1302 came along, with its luggage capacity increased by an impressive 85 per cent. It was therefore useful that there was a deep trough behind the rear seat, whose backrest usefully folded forward. The dashboard was always sparse, with only the 1303 having a modern moulded-plastic dashboard.

8. Original centre-dial dash found on all but very last "split-window" cars **9.** Slim-spoke black steering wheel used on base model **10.** Choke knob on the floor **11.** Indicator switch is integrated into dashboard top **12.** Wicker parcel shelf under dashboard is a period accessory **13.** Cloth seat covers typical of European cars of the 1940s **14.** Pivoting backrest aids access to rear

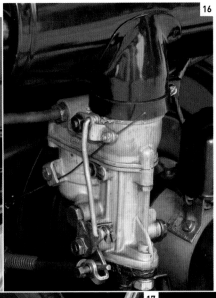

UNDER THE BONNET

Originally a 985 cc unit, the air-cooled flat-four engine entered production after World War II with a capacity of 1,131 cc and a power output of 24 bhp. In 1954 the engine was enlarged to 1,192 cc. A new 1300 model was introduced for 1966, and was joined by a 1500 variant for 1967. In 1970 the 1,584 cc 1302S replaced this. The new engine had an output of 50 bhp – a modest figure true to the Volkswagen philosophy.

15. Simplicity of engine compartment; later cars more cluttered **16.** Downdraught carburettor from supplier Solex **17.** Spare wheel always stowed in prow of car **18.** Fuel filler remains under bonnet until 1968 model

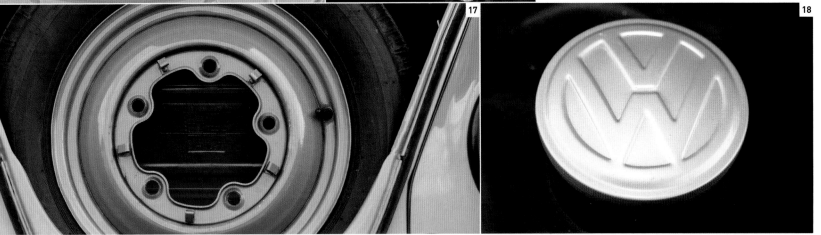

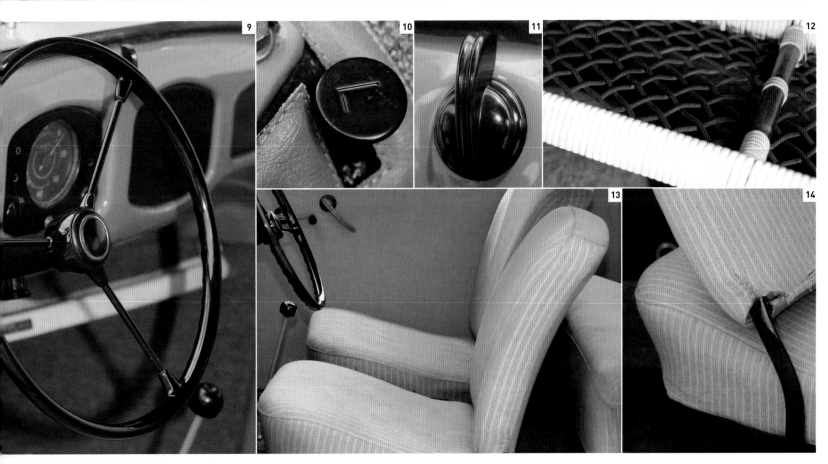

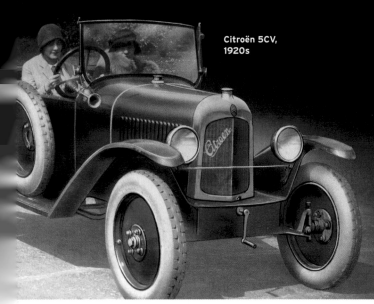

Citroën 5CV, 1920s

Great marques
The Citroën story

André Citroën was one of the automotive industry's earliest visionaries. Despite humble beginnings, his Citroën marque came to embody all that was original and daring about car design. Citroën produced an array of landmark automobiles that were uniquely French, appealing to the heart as well as the intellect.

BORN IN PARIS in 1878, André Citroën's interest in engineering was sparked by a visit in 1901 to an uncle in Poland who had patented a gear mechanism with double-helical teeth – the same shape that would later lend itself to Citroën's famous logo. On his return, Citroën set up a small factory in the French capital from which to manufacture the gears, while also allowing other companies, including Škoda, to produce them under licence.

After the outbreak of World War I in 1914, the astute Citroën managed to raise the finance to become a munitions producer. When the war ended in 1918, his business had supplied over 23 million shells to the French army. By now a wealthy man, Citroën began making cars a year

Citroen badge
(introduced 2009)

later. When his Type A 10CV prototype emerged in May 1919, it caused a furore because it significantly undercut established rivals on price. At the time it was commonplace to order just the chassis from a manufacturer and then have the car's body made by a coachbuilder; yet here was a complete car kitted out with many items found only on more expensive machines. Citroën received 16,000 orders in just two weeks.

Spurred on by this success, André Citroën then set about developing an entire model range. He was quick to recognize the value of marketing, conceiving new and inventive ways of persuading the public to buy his products. Launched in 1922, the tiny 5CV three-seater, with its 856 cc engine, was clearly an entry-level car. Citroën's masterstroke was to target the car at women. It came with an electric starter motor, and the advertising claimed that it was an ideal car for female drivers because there was no need to crank a handle to get it going. Women flocked to buy this accomplished little car.

André Citroën could never rein in his spending as he searched for the next "big thing" in motoring. By early 1934 his range consisted of 76 models, with endless permutations of chassis and bodies. Furthermore, few parts were interchangeable between the different models, and the expense of re-tooling the factory to manufacture each new model ate away at the company finances. Nevertheless,

Towering advertisement
André Citroën's most famous publicity stunt was to have his name emblazoned in lights on the Eiffel Tower between 1925 and 1934.

André Citroën continued to push the boundaries. The innovative 7CV, which made its debut in April 1934, had front-wheel drive and an integrated chassis and body. Even Citroën's choice of stylist for the 7CV was inspired: he

> "The **first words** that a **baby should learn** to pronounce are mummy, daddy, and **Citroën.**"
> ANDRE CITROËN, 1927

could have had his pick of the best contemporary coachbuilders, but instead he chose the Italian sculptor Flaminio Bertoni, despite Bertoni's lack of prior automobile experience.

The 7CV was the first of a new family of front-wheel-drive cars that would be united under the "Traction Avant" banner. While these models would be rightly acknowledged as automotive classics in generations to come, customers were initially poorly served, with gearboxes often breaking and cracks appearing in bodyshells. Most of these issues were quickly rectified, but the firm's reputation was tarnished. André Citroën's obsession with spending whatever it took to outshine the rival Renault marque – allied to the dizzying rate at which he launched new models – reached a head in December 1934, when creditors forced the company into bankruptcy. The tyre maker Michelin, the largest creditor, assumed control.

André Citroën died just six months later, but the firm continued to evoke his pioneering spirit, in particular

with the 2CV. Introduced in 1948, this twin-cylinder, four-door car was initially met with derision, but it was cheap and rugged, and remained in production for a staggering 42 years. By contrast, the DS19 was as daring as the 2CV was simplistic. Launched in 1955, it featured self-levelling suspension and a streamlined body that was styled, once more, by Bertoni.

In 1963 Citroën acquired the ailing Panhard marque while also working closely with Fiat on joint projects. However, in 1968 Citroën had to be bailed out by the French government after buying the Italian sports-car maker Maserati. The purchase was a costly error and in terms of new models it produced little more than the much-admired but unprofitable Maserati-powered SM supercar.

Citroën continued to lose money. New models such as the small GS saloon – voted European Car of the Year in 1971– temporarily helped to boost Citroën's finances, but this idiosyncratic

Universal appeal
Simple and almost rustic in looks, the 2CV was designed to handle uneven rural roads with little maintenance. Yet its small size and economic running made it equally well suited to urban driving, as seen here in Paris.

TYPE A 10CV

2CV

DS DÉCAPOTABLE

CX

1919 André Citroën launches his first car, the Type A 10CV.
1922 Introduction of the tiny, 856 cc 5CV.
1922 A Citroën-Kegresse crosses the Sahara Desert.
1924 Citroën introduces the B10, the first car in Europe with an all-steel body.
1925 Citroën begins a nine-year sponsorship of the Eiffel Tower.
1933 The Rosalie model is the first standard production car in the world to be fitted with a diesel engine.

1934 The front-wheel-drive Traction Avant series is launched, beginning with the 7CV model.
1934 Citroën declared bankrupt; the tyre manufacturer Michelin takes control.
1935 André Citroën dies.
1948 The low-cost 2CV is launched at the Paris Motor Show.
1955 The streamlined DS19 saloon is introduced at the Paris Motor Show.
1963 Citroën takes over former rival Panhard; it ceases making Panhard cars in 1967.

1967 Citroën begins joint-venture with NSU to develop rotary engines.
1968 Citroën acquires Maserati.
1971 GS is voted European Car of the Year.
1974 Peugeot takes a 38.2 per cent stake in Citroën.
1975 CX saloon is European Car of the Year.
1976 Peugeot increases its shareholding in Citroën to 90 per cent.
1986 Citroën Sport makes an aborted attempt at winning the World Rally Championship with the BX 4TC.

1993 Production of the 2CV ends.
1993 Citroën factory team wins its first Rally Raid Manufacturers' title.
2004 Sébastien Loeb wins the first of his six consecutive World Rally Championships with Citroën.
2009 Citroën launches the "anti-retro" DS3 hatchback.
2009 New brand identity to celebrate Citroën's 90th birthday, with the launch of new logo and the "Créative Technologie" slogan.

marque finally lost its independence in 1974, when arch-rival Peugeot bought a 38.2 per cent stake. Two years later Peugot completed its takeover, raising its stake to 90 per cent. Some consider the CX, which emulated the GS by being voted European Car of the Year in 1975, to be the last "true" Citroën, since there was a gradual change of ethos under Peugeot. In an attempt to appeal to a wider market, 1980s Citroën products, such as the 1986 AX supermini hatchback,

became more conventional. This trend continued in the 1990s, with Citroën models – including the strong-selling Saxo of 1995 and Xsara of 1997 – increasingly resembling their Peugeot counterparts. The Citroën marque suffered an image problem as a result, yet it still managed sales of nearly 1.4 million cars in 2003.

In recent years Citroën has gained a formidable reputation in rallying, founded on its commitment to

showcasing new technology in its competition cars. In 2004 the French star Sébastien Loeb won the first of six consecutive World Rally Championships with Citroën. As well as being technologically innovative, Citroën has also undergone a design renaissance. The attractively styled DS3, launched in 2009, was the first in a new range of premium cars under the DS banner.

Xsara Picasso
In 1998 Citroën introduced the Xsara Picasso to compete with Renault's Megane Scenic compact MPV. This ghosted image shows how the components of the regular Xsara were incorporated into a compact MPV package.

Mid-Range Family Saloons

Once hostilities were over, factory owners flush with money from war contracts hurried to fill their factories' capacities with car manufacture again. However, shortages of raw materials – especially steel – meant that many stayed initially with old-fashioned construction techniques like wood body frames, aluminium body panels, and fabric-covered roofs. Some rushed pre-war models back into production, while others took the time to develop all-new models.

△ **Rover 10 1945**

Origin UK

Engine 1,389 cc, straight-four

Top speed 65 mph (105 km/h)

The 10HP was a luxuriously trimmed but underpowered 1930s saloon. It stayed in production post-war and looked identical to the more powerful 1948–49 P3 model that followed.

▷ **Riley RMB 1946**

Origin UK

Engine 2,443 cc, straight-four

Top speed 95 mph (153 km/h)

Pre-war in appearance only, the RM was among Britain's first new post-war models and, in 2.5-litre form, was a dynamic sports saloon, built to high standards.

▷ **Daimler DB18 1945**

Origin UK

Engine 2,522 cc, straight-six

Top speed 72 mph (116 km/h)

Daimler's smallest car from directly before the war was the obvious choice to re-introduce post-war. Well engineered and sensible, it exuded quality, but not opulence.

▷ **Alvis TA14 1946**

Origin UK

Engine 1,892 cc, straight-four

Top speed 74 mph (119 km/h)

Alvis re-entered the market post-war with a quality coachbuilt saloon. Its styling and chassis were firmly rooted in the 1930s, with beam axles and mechanical brakes.

◁ **Mercedes-Benz 170V 1946**

Origin Germany

Engine 1,697 cc, straight-four

Top speed 67 mph (108 km/h)

Launched in 1936 and very successful due to its quality construction, smooth running, and all-independent suspension, the 170V was re-introduced post-war.

▽ **Peugeot 203 1948**

Origin France

Engine 1,290 cc, straight-four

Top speed 71 mph (114 km/h)

Post-war Peugeots were built to be resilient. The 203, in particular, had a spacious modern body, a powerful engine for its size, and hard-wearing running gear. It was made until 1960.

△ **AC 2-litre 1947**

Origin UK

Engine 1,991 cc, straight-six

Top speed 80 mph (129 km/h)

AC quickly launched a quality car with attractive, post-war styling, although it had a pre-war chassis with beam axles. Its powerful engine was designed in 1919.

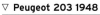

◁ **Triumph 1800 1946**

Origin UK

Engine 1,776 cc, straight-four

Top speed 75 mph (121 km/h)

Standard bought Triumph in 1945, and relaunched it as an upmarket marque with razor-edge styling. The 1800's engine was enlarged in 1949, and it lasted until 1954.

△ Jowett Javelin 1947
Origin UK
Engine 1,486 cc, flat-four
Top speed 78 mph (126 km/h)

The Javelin was the result of a brave attempt by a small Yorkshire company to build an all-new post-war car. It had a modern engine and was aerodynamic, with good handling.

△ Volvo PV444 1947
Origin Sweden
Engine 1,414 cc, straight-four
Top speed 76 mph (122 km/h)

With monocoque construction and a new overhead-valve engine – later tuned to give double the power and a top speed of 95 mph (153 km/h) – the new Volvo was ahead of its time.

▽ Sunbeam-Talbot 90 1948
Origin UK
Engine 1,944 cc, straight-four
Top speed 77 mph (124 km/h)

Produced as a quality four-door saloon or two-door drophead, the 90 had an attractive post-war look but still had a beam front axle.

△ Vauxhall Velox 1948
Origin UK
Engine 2,275 cc, straight-six
Top speed 74 mph (119 km/h)

A pre-war design with minimal enhancements, the Velox had a strong six-cylinder engine and sold on value for money and reliability. Full post-war styling came in 1951.

△ Tatra T600 Tatraplan 1948
Origin Czechoslovakia
Engine 1,952 cc, flat-four
Top speed 80 mph (129 km/h)

With a drag coefficient of just 0.32, the brilliant T600 was extremely aerodynamic. The air-cooled engine was mounted at the rear, giving a spacious interior for six people.

△ Humber Hawk III 1948
Origin UK
Engine 1,944 cc, straight-four
Top speed 71 mph (114 km/h)

One of the first British cars to have curved windscreen in a modern body, the Mk III had a pre-war side-valve engine and chassis, but now with independent front suspension.

△ Morris Oxford MO 1948
Origin UK
Engine 1,476 cc, straight-four
Top speed 71 mph (114 km/h)

The Oxford MO was a large Morris Minor, with the same torsion-bar front suspension, rack-and-pinion steering, and hydraulic brakes. It sold 159,960 in six years despite its slow performance.

△ Holden 48-215 "FX" 1948
Origin Australia
Engine 2,171 cc, straight-six
Top speed 80 mph (129 km/h)

General Motors acquired Australia's Holden in 1931, but Holden forged its own identity post-war with this monocoque car – intended first as a Chevrolet but too small for the US.

△ Fiat 1500 1949
Origin Italy
Engine 1,493 cc, straight-six
Top speed 75 mph (121 km/h)

This was the final version of a car introduced in 1935. Very advanced with aerodynamic styling, it had a backbone chassis, independent front suspension, and overhead valves.

△ Hansa 1500 1949
Origin Germany
Engine 1,498 cc, straight-four
Top speed 75 mph (121 km/h)

Strikingly modern for its time, the Hansa had a backbone chassis and all-independent suspension, and even pioneered flashing indicators. It could seat six people.

The 1950s

Curves & tailfins | Convertibles & chrome | **Pinks & pastels** | Bubble cars & spiders

Economical Cars

Europe specialized in the small, economical family car in the 1950s, producing a wide range of practical and often surprisingly civilized vehicles with much more space, pace, and comfort than their pre-war equivalents. However, some marques, such as Ford, bucked the modernizing trend by continuing throughout the decade to sell pre-war cars at rock bottom prices, undercutting the more advanced models.

◁ **Wolseley 1500 1957**

Origin UK

Engine 1,489 cc, straight-four

Top speed 78 mph (126 km/h)

Morris recycled the Minor's floorpan and fitted it with a bigger engine to make this upmarket Wolseley (also available under the Riley name); a popular car, it sold over 140,000.

△ **Ford Prefect E493A 1949**

Origin UK

Engine 1,172 cc, straight-four

Top speed 60 mph (97 km/h)

Ford added faired-in headlamps and quality fittings inside to distract buyers from the car's pre-war origins. The Prefect sold well in the car-starved UK of the post-war era.

△ **Ford Popular 103E 1953**

Origin UK

Engine 1,172 cc, straight-four

Top speed 60 mph (97 km/h)

A hangover from the 1930s, the 103E had rod brakes, a side-valve engine, three gears, and pre-war styling. It was basic and very cheap, and remained in production until 1959.

▷ **Ford Anglia 100E 1953**

Origin UK

Engine 1,172 cc, straight-four

Top speed 70 mph (113 km/h)

Ford built pre-war cars through the 1950s, but this modern-looking saloon brought their small cars up to date. It sold well, despite having a side-valve engine and three gears.

△ **Ford Anglia 105E 1959**

Origin UK

Engine 997 cc, straight-four

Top speed 76 mph (122 km/h)

The 105E, the final model in the Anglia series, was right up to date with its ultra-modern, US-influenced styling, oversquare, free-revving new engine, and slick, four-speed gearbox; the 1,197 cc Super is shown.

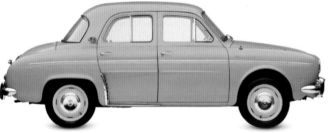

◁ **Renault Dauphine 1956**

Origin France

Engine 845 cc, straight-four

Top speed 66 mph (106 km/h)

The Dauphine was an update of the rear-engined, post-war 4CV. With a slightly larger engine, more space inside, and an appealing new body, it sold over 2 million in 12 years.

△ **DKW Sonderklasse 1953**

Origin Germany

Engine 896 cc, straight-three

Top speed 75 mph (121 km/h)

With its light, air-cooled, two-stroke engine and aerodynamic styling, the DKW Sonderklasse was faster than its small engine size suggested; later models could reach 88 mph (142 km/h).

▷ **Morris Minor Traveller 1953**

Origin UK

Engine 1,098 cc, straight-four

Top speed 62 mph (100 km/h)

The attractive, practical, timber-clad Traveller was a popular addition to the hugely successful Morris Minor range. It had side-hinged rear doors and a rear seat that folded away to increase space.

◁ **Simca Aronde Plein Ciel 1957**

Origin France

Engine 1,290 cc, straight-four

Top speed 82 mph (132 km/h)

Simca started by making Fiats under licence, and the Aronde was its first new design. The body of this good-looking but expensive Plein Ciel coupé was built by Facel.

◁ **Nash Metropolitan 1954**

Origin UK/USA

Engine 1,489 cc, straight-four

Top speed 75 mph (121 km/h)

Built in Britain primarily for the North American market, this little coupé was marketed at female drivers, as an about-town car for wealthy housewives.

△ **Fiat 600 1955**

Origin Italy

Engine 633 cc, straight-four

Top speed 62 mph (100 km/h)

The first rear-engined Fiat, with all-independent suspension and monocoque construction, the 600 was a brilliant small car with adequate space for four people.

△ **Fiat 600 Multipla 1956**

Origin Italy

Engine 633 cc, straight-four

Top speed 55 mph (89 km/h)

The well-packaged Multipla could seat six adults yet was only about 3.5 m (11 ft 6 in) long. It pioneered the "MPV" (Multi-Purpose Vehicle) concept, which became especially popular in the 1990s.

△ **Austin A40 1958**

Origin UK

Engine 948 cc, straight-four

Top speed 72 mph (116 km/h)

After Prince Philip remarked on the dumpy look of Austin cars, the company called in Pinin Farina, who turned the staid A40 into this stylish saloon.

△ **Škoda Octavia 1959**

Origin Czechoslovakia

Engine 1,089 cc, straight-four

Top speed 75 mph (121 km/h)

Launched in 1954 as the 440, this Czech people's car was good value for money, but the swing-axle rear suspension could cause problems when cornering for unwary drivers.

De Soto, mid-1950s
The post-war economic boom in the US saw a steep rise in the number of car owners, and the proliferation of new highways and service stations. Here, a De Soto driver stops to refuel at a Phillips 66 gasoline and service station.

Detroit Fins and Chrome

Post-war prosperity in the US brought the most indulgent and flamboyant period ever in car design, as carmakers at all levels of the market dressed up their cars with ever increasing amounts of chrome plating and wild styling excesses: fins, bullets, and aircraft-inspired detail. Cars and engines grew to enormous proportions, peaking in 1959 before blander styling arrived in 1960.

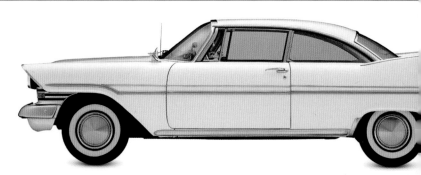

▷ Chevrolet Bel Air 1953

Origin USA

Engine 3,859 cc, straight-six

Top speed 87 mph (140 km/h)

A quarter of a million Bel Air sedans, Chevrolet's luxury model, were made in 1953, helped by competitive pricing and attractive styling with increasing amounts of chrome.

◁ Chevrolet Bel Air 1957

Origin USA

Engine 4,343 cc, V8

Top speed 106 mph (171 km/h)

Seen as a "baby Cadillac" with its iconic finned styling and hot V8 options, the 1957 Chevrolets are among the marque's most popular classics today.

▷ Lincoln Continental Mark II 1956

Origin USA

Engine 6,030 cc, V8

Top speed 108 mph (174 km/h)

Lincoln reintroduced its top-of-the-line Continental in 1956 with an exceptionally well-proportioned, if large, two-door coupé body style. The price tag was almost $10,000.

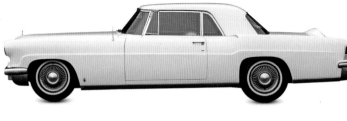

◁ Lincoln Capri 1958

Origin USA

Engine 7,046 cc, V8

Top speed 110 mph (177 km/h)

Believing biggest had to be best, Ford's top brand built the largest car of the post-war era. The Capri was over 5.8 m (20 ft) long, with a 375 bhp V8 to lug it along.

▷ Pontiac Bonneville Custom 1959

Origin USA

Engine 6,375 cc, V8

Top speed 114 mph (183 km/h)

The late 1950s saw Pontiac reinvent itself as a sporty marque with low-slung styling and hot V8 engine options, resulting in many stock-car race wins in 1959.

△ Plymouth Fury 1959

Origin USA

Engine 5,205 cc, V8

Top speed 105 mph (167 km/h)

Plymouth was on the way up from 1955, with dramatic new Virgil Exner styling and a lively V8 engine. The Fury two-door coupé was one of its most stylish models.

△ Chrysler New Yorker 1957

Origin USA

Engine 6,424 cc, V8

Top speed 116 mph (187 km/h)

Designer Virgil Exner's new "forward look", plus new torsion-bar front suspension, helped Chrysler win *Motor Trend*'s Car of the Year in 1957 and turn its falling fortunes around.

▽ Edsel Corsair 1959

Origin USA

Engine 5,440 cc, V8

Top speed 119 mph (192 km/h)

Ford introduced the Edsel in 1957 to target the mid-range market in the US, but it did not succeed and closed in 1959. Only 1,343 of this attractive and powerful Corsair were built.

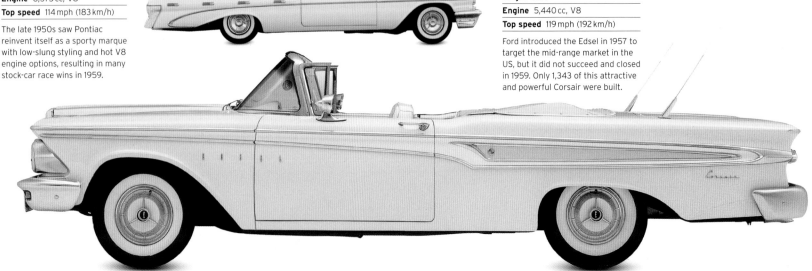

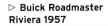

▷ **Ford Fairlane 500 Club Victoria 1959**

Origin USA

Engine 4,785 cc, V8

Top speed 98 mph (158 km/h)

The 1959 Fords won the Gold Medal for Exceptional Styling at the Brussels World Fair, and sold well. This two-door Club Victoria was a relative rarity; with just 23,892 sold.

△ **Studebaker Silver Hawk 1957**

Origin USA

Engine 4,736 cc, V8

Top speed 115 mph (185 km/h)

One of the world's oldest road vehicle producers, Studebaker introduced distinctive styling after the war; this two-door body style began in 1953, with fins growing steadily to this 1957 peak.

▷ **Buick Roadmaster Riviera 1957**

Origin USA

Engine 5,965 cc, V8

Top speed 117 mph (188 km/h)

Buick's hardtop Riviera appeared in 1954. By 1957 it had ladles of chrome and big fins, but Buick's popularity was in decline despite 250/300 bhp engines.

▽ **Buick Limited Riviera 1958**

Origin USA

Engine 5,965 cc, V8

Top speed 115 mph (185 km/h)

For 1958 Buick went for heavy emphasis on its already massive fins. The 300 bhp Limited models were the most luxurious and longer than ever, but sales flagged.

▽ **Cadillac Series 62 Club Coupe 1952**

Origin USA

Engine 5,424 cc, V8

Top speed 98 mph (158 km/h)

Cadillac was the style innovator at the top end of the US market and was a pioneer of big fins, as seen on the back of this luxurious 190 bhp coupé.

▷ **Cadillac Series 62 Convertible Coupe 1958**

Origin USA

Engine 5,981 cc, V8

Top speed 116 mph (187 km/h)

All-new styling brought Cadillac up to the minute in 1957 and the fins grew even bigger in 1958; the engine had grown too, now boasting 310 bhp in standard form.

▷ **Cadillac Series 62 Sedan 1959**

Origin USA

Engine 6,391 cc, V8

Top speed 114 mph (183 km/h)

The massive fins of the 1959 Cadillac were divided by twin-bullet tail lamps and the engine now had 325 bhp. It was surely the most flamboyant of 1950s American car designs.

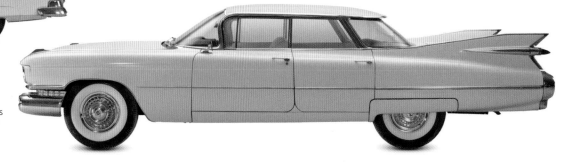

Opulence and High Performance

The 1950s saw prosperity slowly return after World War II, and with it increasing demand for cars of the highest luxury. But now, as roads improved and people's horizons broadened, ultimate performance was a goal too. The best post-war cars were expected to cruise all day at 100 mph (161 km/h) – more if they claimed to be serious sports cars – and before long, that's what they did.

△ Rolls-Royce Silver Dawn 1949

Origin	UK
Engine	4,566 cc, straight-six
Top speed	87 mph (140 km/h)

Rolls-Royce claimed to make the best cars in the world and on engineering integrity, it did. This was its "smallest" car: still the ultimate opulence for four.

◁ Rolls-Royce Silver Cloud I 1955

Origin	UK
Engine	4,887 cc, straight-six
Top speed	106 mph (171 km/h)

Still being built on a separate chassis meant that Rolls-Royces could easily be fitted with coachbuilt luxury bodies: this one by Hooper & Co. exudes grace.

▽ Bristol 403 1953

Origin	UK
Engine	1,971 cc, straight-six
Top speed	104 mph (167 km/h)

Still clearly derived from the outstanding pre-war BMWs, the Bristol 403 had 100 bhp, which was put to great effect in this aerodynamic, high-quality four-seater.

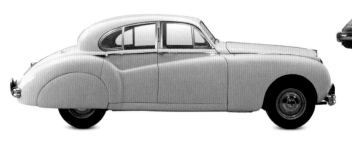

▷ Jaguar MkVII 1951

Origin	UK
Engine	3,442 cc, straight-six
Top speed	102 mph (164 km/h)

The Mark VII was the car William Lyons was preparing for when he produced the stunning XK120. Fast, stylish, and luxurious, the MkVII was a great saloon.

◁ Jaguar XK140 FHC 1955

Origin	UK
Engine	3,442 cc, straight-six
Top speed	124 mph (200 km/h)

Seeing the insatiable demand for its XK sports cars, Jaguar produced variants including this fixed-head coupé with a wood and leather interior.

△ Jaguar XK150 FHC 1957

Origin	UK
Engine	3,781 cc, straight-six
Top speed	132 mph (212 km/h)

Sold first in slightly less potent 3.4-litre form, the XK150 FHC was a very civilized sports 2+2, capable of cruising happily all day at 100 mph (161 km/h) in relative silence.

▽ Jaguar MkIX 1959

Origin	UK
Engine	3,781 cc, straight-six
Top speed	114 mph (183 km/h)

Jaguar's last separate-chassis saloon boasted 220 bhp, power steering, and all-disc brakes, making it a highly civilized, if heavyweight, gentleman's express.

△ Facel Vega FVS 1954

Origin France

Engine 5,801cc, V8

Top speed 134mph (216km/h)

One of the first European marques to use US V8 power (in this case, from Chrysler), Facel Vega offered an outstanding "Grand Routier" in the extremely stylish FVS.

△ Mercedes-Benz 300 1951

Origin Germany

Engine 2,996cc, straight-six

Top speed 103mph (166km/h)

Germany's first prestige car after World War II was built with quality and durability as priorities: around 1,000 a year were built over 10 years.

◁ Lancia Aurelia B20 GT 1953

Origin Italy

Engine 2,451cc, V6

Top speed 115mph (185km/h)

Brilliantly engineered with the world's first production V6 engine and semi-trailing arm rear suspension, the Aurelia was built to perfection, regardless of cost.

△ Mercedes-Benz 300SL 1954

Origin Germany

Engine 2,996cc, straight-six

Top speed 129mph (208km/h)

One of the most iconic cars of the 1950s, the 300SL with its gullwing doors and 250bhp fuel-injected, dry-sump engine was an outstanding sports coupé.

▷ Tatra 603 1956

Origin Czechoslovakia

Engine 2,474–2,545cc, V8

Top speed 100mph (161km/h)

This top-quality, streamlined saloon was built mainly for Czech diplomats. The 603 has a compact, air-cooled V8 engine, which is mounted at its back.

△ Ferrari 250GT 1956

Origin Italy

Engine 2,953cc, V12

Top speed 145mph (233km/h)

Ferrari's first volume production GT, the 250 boasted tremendous performance from the triple-Weber carburettor V12, within a luxurious 2+2 coupé styled by Pinin Farina.

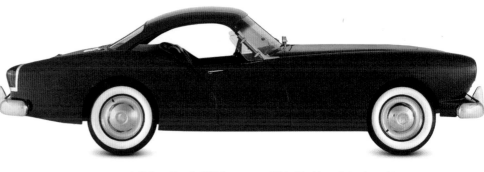

△ Kaiser Darrin 1954

Origin USA

Engine 2,641cc, straight-six

Top speed 96mph (154km/h)

Shipbuilder Henry Kaiser turned to cars after World War II. The glassfibre-bodied Darrin with doors that slid into the front wings was the brainchild of designer Howard "Dutch" Darrin.

△ Bentley R-type Continental 1952

Origin UK

Engine 4,566cc, straight-six

Top speed 120mph (193km/h)

Rolls-Royce finally cashed in on subsidiary Bentley's sporting heritage with this magnificent coachbuilt Grand Touring saloon, the epitome of luxury and speed.

◁ Bentley S2 1959

Origin UK

Engine 6,230cc, V8

Top speed 113mph (182km/h)

Rolls-Royce and Bentley were at a disadvantage in the US, as their six-cylinder engines were considered downmarket. But this changed when this silken V8 was launched.

△ Aston Martin DB2/4 1953

Origin UK

Engine 2,580cc, straight-six

Top speed 116mph (187km/h)

Expensive and exclusive, with W.O. Bentley's twin-overhead-camshaft engine in a tubular chassis, the Aston Martin epitomized racing pedigree and class.

△ Aston Martin DB4 1958

Origin UK

Engine 3,670cc, straight-six

Top speed 141mph (227km/h)

By the end of the decade the Aston Martin had grown into a true luxury supercar, with exotic Italian styling by Touring and 240bhp from its new twin-cam engine.

Henry Ford pictured in 1946, sitting in the "horseless carriage" he built in 1896

Great marques
The Ford story

Henry Ford was the first automobile manufacturer to make the most of mass production techniques, and his Model T sold by the million. Since then, the Ford Motor Company has grown into a global giant, the only big US car maker to survive the recession of the first decade of the new millennium without government aid.

HENRY FORD was born on a farm in Dearborn, Michigan, in 1863. Aged 16, he moved to nearby Detroit to train as a mechanic. In 1891 Ford went to work for the Detroit Edison company, and he began experimenting with engines in his spare time. He built his first "horseless carriage" in 1896. Ford's second car, completed in 1898, impressed entrepreneur William H. Murphy so much that Murphy was

Ford badge
(introduced 1927)

willing to finance a car-making venture with Ford in charge of the technical side of the business. Ford struggled to turn his prototype into a production vehicle and the Detroit Automobile Company, as this firm was known, made big losses. A restructuring of the company gave Ford more chance to test out new ideas. The result was a racer that beat the renowned Winton

car in a 10-mile (16-km) race in October 1901. But the company still had no profitable products, and it was wound up at the end of the year. A new company, the Henry Ford Motor Company, concentrated on road cars, but it still failed to get a complete car into production. When the directors hired Henry M. Leland as a consultant, Ford decided to move on, and the company later became Cadillac.

Ford eventually founded his own successful venture, the Ford Motor Company, in June 1903. The first

Ford production car was the two-cylinder Model A. In 1904 Ford used another of his early racing cars, the "999", to set a new land speed record of 91 mph (147 km/h). Ford's business partner, Alexander Malcomson, was keen to take the company upmarket, and the result was the four-cylinder Model B and six-cylinder Model K. Ford, on the other hand, wanted to focus on low-priced cars. In 1906 he bought Malcomson's share of the business and re-focused the company on smaller, cheaper models. The most

Ford Mustang Cobra Jet 428
The Mustang of 1964 inspired the term "pony car", used to describe a new class of compact, affordable, large-engined car with a sporty image. The 1968 Cobra Jet 428 was one of the fastest production cars of its day.

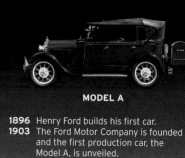

MODEL A

THUNDERBIRD LANDAU

CAPRI

SIERRA COSWORTH RS500

1896	Henry Ford builds his first car.
1903	The Ford Motor Company is founded and the first production car, the Model A, is unveiled.
1908	The Model T is introduced.
1922	Ford buys Lincoln.
1927	Production of the Model T finally ends after more than 15 million have been made; a new Model A is introduced to replace the Model T.
1932	The Ford Model 18 is the first affordable V8-powered car.

1943	Edsel Ford dies of cancer aged 49.
1945	Henry Ford II takes over as president of the Ford Motor Company.
1947	Henry Ford dies at the age of 83.
1954	Mid-way between a sports car and a grand tourer, the Thunderbird creates a new class of car – the "personal car".
1963	Ford of Britain unveils the Cortina family saloon, beginning a line of vehicles that will become best-sellers across Europe until the 1980s.

1964	Launch of the Mustang "pony car", a new type of car featuring a high-performance engine in a compact body.
1967	Ford finances the Cosworth DFV V8 engine; it will be the most successful engine family in Formula 1 history.
1969	In Europe Ford launches the Capri coupé, which will sell into the 1980s.
1978	In the US Ford recalls the Pinto for safety modifications.
1982	Aerodynamically styled Sierra debuts.
1987	Ford buys Aston Martin.

1989	Ford buys Jaguar.
1990	Launch of the Explorer; it becomes the most popular SUV in the US.
1998	The Ford Focus wins praise for its comfort, suspension, and performance.
1999	Ford buys the Stewart Formula 1 team.
2000	Faulty tyres apparently cause Explorers to roll over, leading to a recall.
2008	Ford, General Motors, and Chrysler present plans for the future of the US car industry, but Ford later decides not to accept government aid.

Ford Consul Cortina toy
Launched by Ford in the UK in 1962, initially as the Consul Cortina, the Cortina was a popular mid-size family car. The spacious estate version was a class leader.

man who had caused Ford's departure from the company bearing his own name in 1902. For the next five years there were no new Ford models, only revised versions of the Model T. In 1927 Ford was finally forced to admit that the Model T was outdated – and that there was nothing to replace it. Production halted for six months while an all-new Model A was created. Other models followed through the 1930s, including 1932's Model Y – the first Ford specifically designed for the European market.

planning, resulting in such successes as the sporty but luxurious Thunderbird of 1954, and the stylish, compact Mustang of 1964. In Europe Ford led sales charts with its Anglia, Taunus, Cortina, and Escort. Ford's "Total Performance" campaign of the 1960s saw it focus on taking the lead in motor sport. It won the classic 24-hour race at Le Mans, France, with the GT40 and began to dominate Formula 1 with a Cosworth-designed V8 engine. By the 1970s Ford's RS Escorts had propelled it to the forefront of European rallying.

The company's reputation suffered a severe blow in the 1970s when it was forced to recall the US Ford Pinto, amid

Aerodynamic body shapes, derided by some as resembling jelly moulds, became a Ford trademark on both sides of the Atlantic in the 1980s with the introduction of the Taurus and Sierra. From the late 1990s striking design became a Ford strength under the design leadership of J. Mays, and class-leading handling became standard in Ford products thanks to the efforts of technical chief Richard Parry-Jones.

Ford suffered significant losses from 2006 onwards, in common with other US car makers, but avoided relying on government help to survive the global economic slump. It sold acquisitions such as Hertz, Aston Martin, Jaguar, Land Rover, and Volvo, and mortgaged factories, intellectual property, and other assets to release working capital. The move appeared to work, and by 2010 Ford looked to be in the best shape of the three major US car makers as it headed into a new era of electric cars, hybrids, and alternative fuels.

successful of these was the Model T, introduced in 1908. With a new four-cylinder engine, easy-to-use epicyclic transmission, and modern styling, the Model T was far more advanced than anything else available for $850. As word spread and sales increased, the price actually fell, driven by improvements in the manufacturing process. In 1913 Ford became the first marque to produce cars on a moving assembly line, reducing the time taken to build a Model T from 14 hours to a mere 93 minutes. The Model T provided the basis for numerous Allied military vehicles during World War I, including field ambulances.

Henry Ford appointed his son, Edsel, as president of the company in 1919. In 1922 Ford bought the troubled Lincoln company, which, ironically, had been set up by Henry Leland – the

"I reduce the charge for our car by one dollar, I get a thousand new customers."

HENRY FORD ON THE MODEL T, 1913

During World War II Ford's finely honed mass-production techniques were applied to making Jeeps, tank engines, aircraft, and other hardware for the Allied forces. In 1943 Henry Ford had to take charge of the company again when his son Edsel died of cancer. Edsel's own son, Henry Ford II, became president in 1945 and assumed sole control after his grandfather, Henry Ford, died in 1947.

After the war Ford concentrated on good-value cars for the mass market, both in the US and in its satellite operations in Europe. The marque's great strength was clever product

allegations that this sub-compact car had safety failings. Ford in the US struggled to cope in the energy crisis of the early 1980s, when oil supplies were interrupted after 1979's Iranian Revolution. Ford's gas-guzzlers lost out to more economical models imported from Japan, and the company had to rely on the profits from its better-performing European offshoots.

2010 Ford Ecoboost 1.6L engine
Ford's Ecoboost engine uses twin turbos and direct injection to generate power consistent with a larger engine size, but with greater efficiency and reduced emissions.

Racing Cars

The 1950s was the decade of successful front-engined racing cars, especially in sports-car racing. European marques derived from roadgoing sports cars dominated, gradually becoming more and more different from their street origins. Disc brakes proved a huge advantage and would be rapidly adopted, along with other improvements such as fuel injection that would filter through to improve road cars in time.

▷ **Talbot-Lago T26 Grand Sport 1951**

Origin France

Engine 4,483 cc, straight-six

Top speed 125 mph (201 km/h)

Based on the chassis and engine from a successful Grand Prix racer, the Grand Sport was an early post-war sports racing car that won at Le Mans in 1950.

△ **Ferrari 375 MM 1953**

Origin Italy

Engine 4,522 cc, V12

Top speed 150 mph (241 km/h)

Built primarily as a competition car, the 375 Mille Miglia won the Spa 24-hour race, Pescara 12-hour race, and Buenos Aires 1,000 km at the start of its glittering racing career.

△ **Kurtis-Chrysler 500S 1953**

Origin USA

Engine 6,424 cc, V8

Top speed 145 mph (233 km/h)

Typical of the effective US-built racers that contested the Carrera Panamericana and US endurance races, this car has the Chrysler Hemi V8 in a light, aluminium body.

◁ **Ferrari 250GT SWB 1959**

Origin Italy

Engine 2,953 cc, V12

Top speed 160 mph (257 km/h)

The gorgeous Pinin Farina-designed SWB dominated the Group III (2-3 litre) racing class, winning many races outright. It was equally at home on the road.

△ **Abarth 205 1950**

Origin Italy

Engine 1,089 cc, straight-four

Top speed 108 mph (174 km/h)

The first complete car from legendary engine tuner Carlo Abarth, the 205 used a tuned Fiat engine in a body styled by Giovanni Michelotti. It was a successful endurance racer.

▽ **Lotus Eleven 1956**

Origin UK

Engine 1,098 cc, straight-four

Top speed 112 mph (180 km/h)

The elegant Lotus Eleven marked a step forward in professionalism from Lotus and proved hugely successful. It came 7th overall at Le Mans in 1956, racing against many larger-engined cars.

△ **Pupulidy-Porsche Special 1954**

Origin USA

Engine 1,582 cc, flat-four

Top speed 130 mph (209 km/h)

American racer Emil Pupulidy built a body inspired by Mercedes' Silver Arrows, fitted it to a VW floorpan, and went racing. He won the car's first race at the Nassau Speed Week in the Bahamas.

▷ **Porsche 550/1500RS 1953**

Origin Germany

Engine 1,498 cc, flat-four

Top speed 136 mph (219 km/h)

When Porsche designed a new engine with double overhead camshafts on each side for its mid-engined 550 racer, it became a race winner. The actor James Dean had a fatal crash in his.

◁ **Porsche 550 Coupé 1953**

Origin Germany

Engine 1,488 cc, flat-four

Top speed 124 mph (200 km/h)

This was Porsche's first purpose-built works racing car. Mid-engined 550s won their class in 1953 events from Le Mans to the Carrera Panamericana.

△ Aston Martin DBR1 1956
Origin UK
Engine 2,922 cc, straight-six
Top speed 155 mph (249 km/h)

The most successful Aston Martin racing car until 2010, the DBR1 had six major international race wins, including Le Mans, Nürburgring, Goodwood, and Spa.

△ OSCA MT4 1953
Origin Italy
Engine 1,490 cc, straight-four
Top speed 120 mph (193 km/h)

Superb design by the Maserati brothers and a twin-camshaft, twin-spark engine made the MT4 more competitive than it looked. In 1954 it won the Sebring 12-hour race in the US.

△ Aston Martin DBR2 1957
Origin UK
Engine 3,670 cc, straight-six
Top speed 160 mph (257 km/h)

Aston built two cars to race its new 3.7-litre engine, with semi-backbone chassis and styling like the DBR1; they later raced with 4.2-litre engines in the US.

△ Maserati 250F 1954
Origin Italy
Engine 2,494 cc, straight-six
Top speed 180 mph (290 km/h)

The elegant 250F raced throughout the seven years of the 2.5-litre limit in Formula 1, winning eight Grand Prix and giving Juan Manuel Fangio the 1957 World Championship.

◁ Panhard 750 Spider 1954
Origin France/Italy
Engine 745 cc, flat-two
Top speed 90 mph (145 km/h)

Built by Tino Bianchi on a 1950 Panhard Dyna rolling chassis, with frame by GILCO and body by Colli, this one-off Special competed in the 1955 Mille Miglia in Italy.

▷ Mercedes-Benz W196 1954
Origin Germany
Engine 2,496 cc, straight-six
Top speed 186 mph (299 km/h)

Mercedes-Benz returned to Formula 1 with a complex spaceframe chassis, desmodromic valves, and fuel injection. The W196 gave race driver Juan Manuel Fangio two world titles.

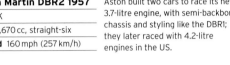

△ Alfa Romeo 1900SSZ 1954
Origin Italy
Engine 1,975 cc, straight-four
Top speed 117 mph (188 km/h)

The Alfa Romeo 1900, marketed as "the family car that wins races", spawned this lightweight special-bodied car by Zagato that was successful in long-distance races.

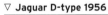

◁ Jaguar C-type 1951
Origin UK
Engine 3,442 cc, straight-six
Top speed 144 mph (232 km/h)

This roadgoing race car was built to win Le Mans, which it did in 1951 and 1953 (pioneering disc brakes in 1953). It was derived from the XK120, with a lightweight tubular chassis.

▽ Jaguar D-type 1956
Origin UK
Engine 3,781 cc, straight-six
Top speed 167 mph (269 km/h)

After the XK-derived C-type, Jaguar developed this lightweight racer with monocoque centre section to win Le Mans in France. It won in 1955, 1956, and 1957.

Sports Cars

Massive demand for sports cars in prosperous post-war America prompted rapid progress in design there and in Europe. This was a golden era for sports cars, as profiles became lower and stylists emphasized this with gorgeous, flowing lines, in the process coming up with some of the most attractive cars ever built.

△ **Chevrolet Corvette 1953**

Origin USA

Engine 3,859 cc, straight-six

Top speed 107 mph (172 km/h)

A Motorama dream car that made it to production, this was the first plastic-bodied car and represented a well-judged leap of faith by Chevrolet.

△ **Sunbeam Alpine 1953**

Origin UK

Engine 2,267 cc, straight-four

Top speed 95 mph (153 km/h)

Based on the four-seat Sunbeam-Talbot 90 chassis, the Alpine was overweight. Good PR from Alpine Rally wins in Europe and a 120 mph (193 km/h) record run were not enough to win sales.

△ **Alfa Romeo Giulietta Spider 1955**

Origin Italy

Engine 1,290 cc, straight-four

Top speed 112 mph (180 km/h)

This beautiful little sports car was built to a very high specification with performance far higher than its 1.3 litres would suggest, thanks to its brilliant twin-cam engine.

▷ **Alfa Romeo 2000 Spider 1958**

Origin Italy

Engine 1,975 cc, straight-four

Top speed 111 mph (179 km/h)

Ahead of contemporary British and US standards, except for its drum brakes, this handsome 2+2 Alfa boasted unitary construction, a five-speed gearbox, and a double-overhead-camshaft engine.

△ **Jowett Jupiter 1950**

Origin UK

Engine 1,486 cc, flat-four

Top speed 84 mph (135 km/h)

Innovative but heavy, Jupiters enjoyed good handling thanks to a low, horizontally opposed engine. Jowett was too small to make it in quantity: 899 of these were sold.

◁ **Triumph TR2 1953**

Origin UK

Engine 1,991 cc, straight-four

Top speed 107 mph (172 km/h)

This fast and entertaining sports car was developed on a shoe-string budget. It was an immediate success in the market, and probably won more rallies than any other car.

△ **Arnolt Bristol 1953**

Origin USA/Italy/UK

Engine 1,971 cc, straight-six

Top speed 109 mph (175 km/h)

S.H. "Wacky" Arnolt of Indiana, USA, commissioned Bristol to build a rolling chassis in England, to be clothed by coachbuilders Bertone of Italy. Just 142 were built.

▷ **Jaguar XK 140 1955**

Origin UK

Engine 3,442 cc, straight-six

Top speed 124 mph (200 km/h)

The XK 120 grew up into the XK 140, with rack-and-pinion steering, more power, and more space inside. Customers could have a roadster, drophead, or fixed-head coupé.

▽ **BMW 507 1956**

Origin Germany

Engine 3,168 cc, V8

Top speed 135 mph (217 km/h)

Just 250 of these gorgeous super sports cars from BMW were built. It was so good, motorcycle World Champion John Surtees has owned one from new.

△ **MGA 1955**

Origin	UK
Engine	1,489 cc, straight-four
Top speed	100 mph (161 km/h)

Beautiful lines, a top speed of 100 mph (just), and a fixed-head coupé option made up for the separate chassis in the MGA. It sold well, especially in the US.

◁ **Mercedes-Benz 190SL 1955**

Origin	Germany
Engine	1,897 cc, straight-four
Top speed	107 mph (172 km/h)

Launched just after the similarly shaped but much faster 300SL Gullwing, the 190 was a luxurious touring car for two, built to traditional Mercedes-Benz quality standards.

△ **Daimler SP250 1959**

Origin	UK
Engine	2,548 cc, V8
Top speed	120 mph (193 km/h)

The maker of staid luxury saloons had a new aluminium V8, and it was used in a glassfibre-bodied sports car with a chassis copied from Triumph.

△ **Austin-Healey 100/4 1952**

Origin	UK
Engine	2,660 cc, straight-four
Top speed	103 mph (166 km/h)

Donald Healey conceived an inexpensive sports car using Austin Atlantic parts, Gerry Coker styled a stunning body, and Austin bought the rights to produce it.

△ **Austin-Healey Sprite 1958**

Origin	UK
Engine	948 cc, straight-four
Top speed	86 mph (138 km/h)

Targeting the bottom-of-the-market preserve of kit cars, the "Frogeye" ("Bugeye" in the US) Sprite showed that sports cars didn't have to be fast to be fun.

◁ **AC Ace 1956**

Origin	UK
Engine	1,971 cc, straight-six
Top speed	117 mph (188 km/h)

Launched in 1954 with AC's own engine, the Ferrari-inspired Ace with all-independently sprung chassis came alive with a 120 bhp Bristol engine, and later spawned the Cobra.

△ **Porsche 356A 1955**

Origin	Germany
Engine	1,582 cc, flat-four
Top speed	100 mph (161 km/h)

The lively 356, launched in 1950, grew from its VW roots until, by the end of the decade, it was a 110 mph (177 km/h) flyer, hitting 125 mph (201 km/h) in its twin-cam Carrera form.

△ **Lotus Elite 1957**

Origin	UK
Engine	1,216 cc, straight-four
Top speed	118 mph (190 km/h)

This was the world's first glassfibre monocoque: complex with excellent aerodynamics, a powerful Coventry Climax engine, and supple suspension. It was highly sophisticated.

△ **Lotus 7 1957**

Origin	UK
Engine	1,172 cc, straight-four
Top speed	85 mph (137 km/h)

Brilliantly simple, Sevens were sold mostly as kits with a choice of engines. Low weight and well-designed suspension made them quick and effective in club racing.

Chevrolet Corvette

Launched in 1953 as a glassfibre two-seater convertible in the style of contemporary European models, the Corvette was America's first production sports car. Initially fitted with a six-cylinder engine, the Corvette began to fulfil its potential only when it was given a V8 powerplant. A series of redesigns – including the 1963 split-screen Sting Ray Coupe and "Mako Shark" 1968 Stingray – kept the model fresh. With around 1.5 million made to date, the Corvette has earned the title of the oldest US sports car still in production.

THE BRAINCHILD of Harley Earl, design chief at General Motors, the Corvette appeared to great acclaim at GM's 1953 Motorama sales show. But the model had a slow start, with just 300 sold in its first year. Despite its racy styling, the Corvette's six-cylinder engine was seen as insufficient for power-hungry US buyers. With the model in real danger of disappearing, Corvette's fortunes were turned around in 1955 by the 265 cu in (4,342 cc) V8 with manual transmission. Coupled with a body redesign in 1956 and engine upgrades over the next few years, the first-generation Corvette became one of America's hottest automobiles. The ornate second generation and muscular third series took the model into the 1980s. Now in its sixth generation, the Corvette's styling sees a return to its European-influenced roots.

FRONT VIEW **REAR VIEW**

Flagged Up
Originally designed in 1953 by Chevrolet's Robert Bartholomew, the Corvette logo consists of two flags, one chequered to reflect its racing character, and the other featuring a fleur-de-lys – a nod to company founder Louis Chevrolet's French roots.

SIDE VIEW WITH CLOSED TOP

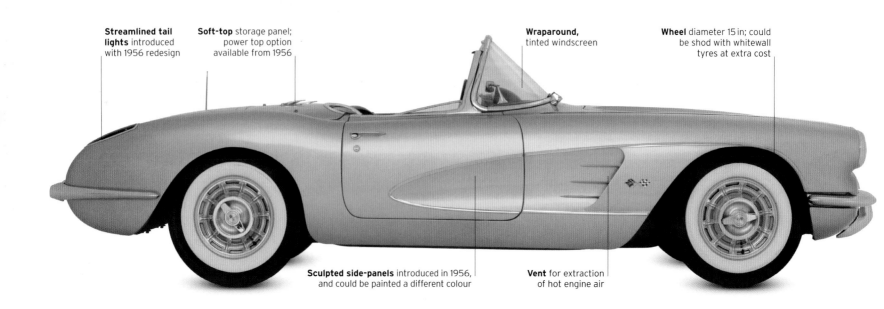

Streamlined tail lights introduced with 1956 redesign

Soft-top storage panel; power top option available from 1956

Wraparound, tinted windscreen

Wheel diameter 15 in; could be shod with whitewall tyres at extra cost

Sculpted side-panels introduced in 1956, and could be painted a different colour

Vent for extraction of hot engine air

SPECIFICATIONS	
Model	Chevrolet Corvette MkI (1953-62)
Assembly	Michigan and Missouri, USA
Production	68,915
Construction	Welded box section
Engine	265 cu in (4,291 cc), V8
Power output	150-360 bhp at 4,200-6,200 rpm
Transmission	Two-speed Powerglide automatic
Suspension	Front independent, rear rigid axle
Brakes	Drums front and rear
Maximum speed	142 mph (229 km/h)

Determined styling

Harley Earl conceded that the open-tooth style of the grill was copied from Ferrari models of the time. When combined with the ridged bonnet and four headlights – introduced in 1958 to replace the two headlights of the early models – it gave this 1959 Corvette an aggressive frontal appearance, one that would become even meaner with later generations of the model.

THE EXTERIOR

The Corvette's unique glassfibre body set it apart from its rivals – a 1959 advertisement led with the line "From a Different Mold". On a practical level, it gave the model significant weight-saving advantages over the competition. A redesign in 1956 included the addition of coved, or sculpted, body panels and revised tail lights. This Inca Silver was one of seven colour options available in 1959.

1. Flags alongside cooling vent 2. Knock-off hubs were elaborate wheel covers 3. Two headlights on either side from 1958 4. Grill "teeth" would disappear in 1961 restyle 5. Tail lights would be restyled into classic, enduring, "duck-tail" variety in 1961 6. Twin exhausts incorporated into rear bumpers

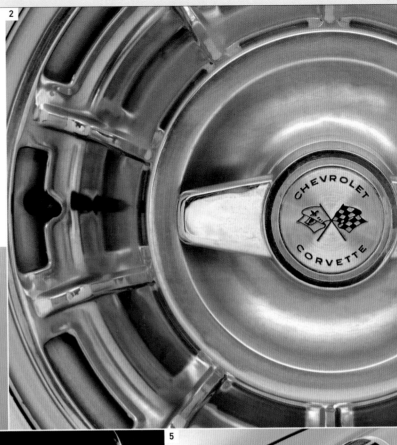

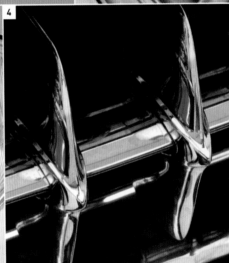

THE INTERIOR

The original 1953 Corvettes inconveniently had their instruments to the right of the steering wheel, but in 1958 they were moved in front of the driver. Interior colours included red, black, and turquoise; options ranged from power windows to courtesy lights. But it was all about the car's performance, and in 1959 Chevy touted the Corvette as "a polished instrument strictly designed for driving pleasure".

7. Cockpit with competition-type steering wheel, vinyl-padded dashboard, and passenger grab bar
8. Speedometer ran to 160 mph (257 km/h); below it was a rev counter; other instruments were a battery charge gauge 9. Radio, heater controls, and electric clock
10. T-shift manual gear stick new for 1959 11. Corvette name taken from type of warship 12. Release for soft-top cover 13. Door release and manual window winder handle 14. Chrome armrest fixing new for 1959

UNDER THE BONNET

The straight-six was dropped in 1956, and from 1957 a larger 283 cu in (4,637 cc) V8 was fitted. When paired with the new fuel-injection option, Chevrolet was able to declare the Corvette as the first to feature "One hp per cubic inch". At a time when speed and horsepower counted most, these output figures catapulted the Corvette into the big league in terms of sales and popularity.

15. Bonnet latch under front of bonnet **16.** Bonnet hinge part of cable-operated release system **17.** Engine choices in 1959 were twin-carburettor (shown here) or fuel-injected versions of the 283 cu in (4,637 cc) V8

Chevrolet
small-block V8

Produced in many variants over a 55-year lifespan, the Chevy small-block epitomizes the tried and trusted American engine recipe of a 90-degree V8 built of cast iron with pushrod valve actuation. It quickly became popular as a drag-racing engine and powered iconic sports and pony cars such as the Chevrolet Camaro and Corvette, and the Pontiac Firebird.

SMALL BLOCK, SHORT STROKE

Dubbed the "Mighty Mouse" after a popular cartoon character, the small-block Chevy lent itself to high performance roles, in part due to its oversquare cylinder dimensions (the bore being greater than the piston stroke). A short piston stroke reduces the peak acceleration, lessening the inertial forces acting on the pistons and allowing the use of higher engine rpm to increase the power output. Lower-powered versions of the small-block saw service in family cars, and the engine was also put to marine use. Over 90 million small-blocks have been made since the engine's introduction.

Chevrolet's second V8
Remarkably, given its subsequent success, this was only the second V8 engine Chevrolet had designed, the first appearing decades earlier in 1917. Despite this lack of V8 experience, Chevy hit on just the right design philosophy of keeping the engine as simple, compact, and light as possible, while engineering in the potential for higher power outputs.

ENGINE SPECIFICATIONS

Dates produced	1955 to present
Cylinders	Eight cylinders in two banks, 90-degree "V"
Configuration	Front-mounted, longitudinal
Engine capacity	265 cu in (4,291 cc), ultimately 400 cu in (6,570 cc)
Power output	162 bhp @ 4,400 rpm, ultimately 375 bhp
Type	Conventional four-stroke, water-cooled petrol engine with reciprocating pistons, distributor ignition, and a wet sump
Head	ohv actuated by pushrod and rocker arms; two valves per cylinder
Fuel System	Carburettor, later fuel injection
Bore and Stroke	3.75 in x 3.00 in (95.3 mm x 76.2 mm)
Specific power	37.8 bhp/litre
Compression Ratio	8.0:1

▷ **See pp.346-347** How an engine works

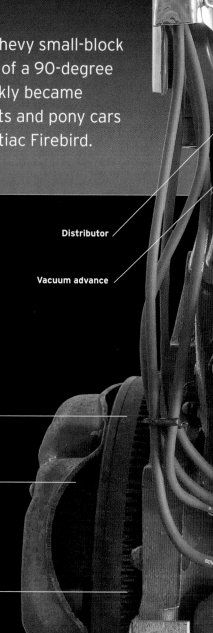

Distributor

Vacuum advance

Flywheel
The flywheel smoothes out variations in the engine's rotation.

Clutch housing

Starter ring gear
Engaging with the starter motor pinion gear when the engine starts up, the ring gear transfers torque to the flywheel to get the engine turning.

Starter motor solenoid
The solenoid connects the starter motor to the battery via high-current cables.

Starter motor

Engine stand

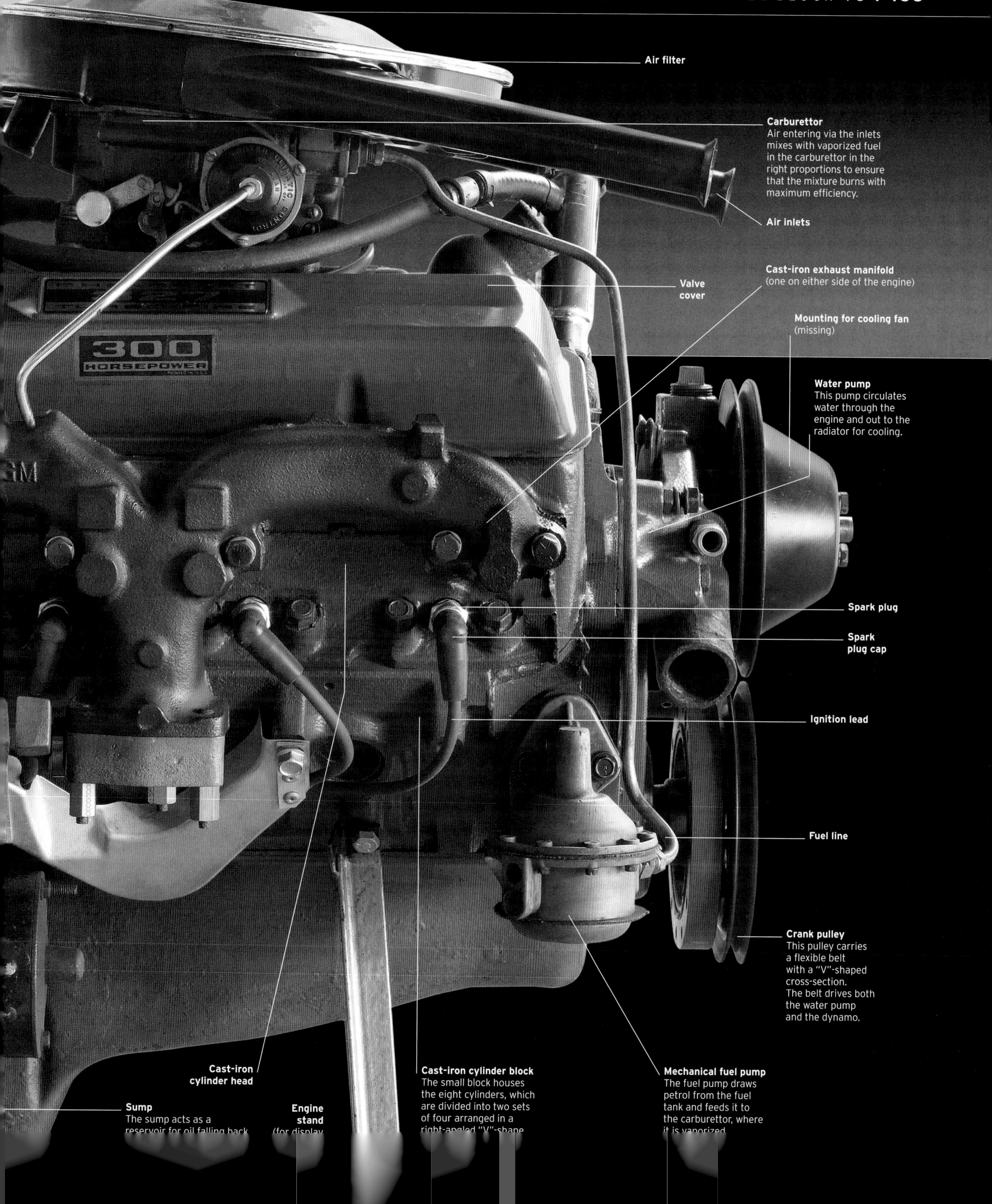

Air filter

Carburettor
Air entering via the inlets
mixes with vaporized fuel
in the carburettor in the
right proportions to ensure
that the mixture burns with
maximum efficiency.

Air inlets

Cast-iron exhaust manifold
(one on either side of the engine)

Valve cover

Mounting for cooling fan
(missing)

Water pump
This pump circulates
water through the
engine and out to the
radiator for cooling.

Spark plug

Spark plug cap

Ignition lead

Fuel line

Crank pulley
This pulley carries
a flexible belt
with a "V"-shaped
cross-section.
The belt drives both
the water pump
and the dynamo.

Cast-iron cylinder head

Sump
The sump acts as a
reservoir for oil falling back

Engine stand
(for display

Cast-iron cylinder block
The small block houses
the eight cylinders, which
are divided into two sets
of four arranged in a
right-angled "V"-shape

Mechanical fuel pump
The fuel pump draws
petrol from the fuel
tank and feeds it to
the carburettor, where
it is vaporized

300
HORSEPOWER

GM

Bubble Cars and Microcars

Inventors had always made tiny, economical motor cars, but consumers rarely bought them. The Suez crisis of 1956 and the subsequent petrol rationing changed that – suddenly fuel economy became a priority. Existing microcars were thrust into the limelight and new models joined the market in droves. But soon these were superseded by small conventional cars like the Fiat 500 and the Mini.

△ Inter 175 Berline 1953

Origin France

Engine 175 cc, one-cylinder

Top speed 50 mph (80 km/h)

Built by a French aircraft company, the tandem-seat Inter's front wheels could be folded in to allow it to pass through a doorway or narrow passage for storage.

△ Heinkel Cabin Cruiser 1957

Origin Germany

Engine 204 cc, one-cylinder

Top speed 50 mph (80 km/h)

Lightweight construction, typical of an aircraft company, plus brilliant packaging enabled the Heinkel to seat two adults and two children and go as fast as a BMW Isetta.

△ Vespa 400 1957

Origin Italy/France

Engine 393 cc, straight-two

Top speed 52 mph (84 km/h)

Designed by Piaggio but built in France, this two-seater was sophisticated for its time, with a fan-cooled engine in the rear, and all-independent suspension.

△ Austin Mini Seven 1959

Origin UK

Engine 848 cc, straight-four

Top speed 72 mph (116 km/h)

The Mini had Issigonis's brilliant packaging, its transverse engine and gearbox-in-sump allowing four seats. Priced competitively, it wiped out the bubble cars.

△ Frisky Family Three 1958

Origin UK

Engine 197 cc, one-cylinder

Top speed 44 mph (71 km/h)

Engine maker Henry Meadows Ltd began building 4-wheel Frisky cars in 1957, based on prototype styling by Michelotti. A 3-wheel model was cheaper to tax in Britain.

△ Fiat Nuova 500 1957

Origin Italy

Engine 479 cc, straight-two

Top speed 51 mph (82 km/h)

Dante Giacosa's brilliant new 500 was only a slow two-seater at first, but repackaged interior space and more power transformed it into a 3.4-million seller.

▷ Berkeley SE492 1958

Origin UK

Engine 492 cc, straight-three

Top speed 80 mph (129 km/h)

This brilliant glassfibre and aluminium monocoque sports car had a transverse engine, front-wheel drive, and all-independent suspension, but was let down by unreliable motorcycle engines.

▷ Goggomobil Dart 1959

Origin Germany/Australia

Engine 392 cc, straight-two

Top speed 65 mph (105 km/h)

Australian Bill Buckle designed this stylish sports body to fit the chassis and running gear of the German Goggomobil. This model sold 700 with 300 cc or 400 cc engines.

◁ **Subaru 360 1958**

Origin Japan

Engine 356 cc, straight-two

Top speed 60 mph (97 km/h)

Though little-known outside Japan, this clever monocoque four-seater with air-cooled rear engine sold 392,000. It was the people's car of Japan in the 1960s.

△ **BMW Isetta 300 1955**

Origin Germany

Engine 298 cc, one-cylinder

Top speed 50 mph (80 km/h)

Built by BMW under licence from Iso, the 300 was the archetypal bubble car. It developed into a dependable car with two seats and single or close-double rear wheels.

△ **Zündapp Janus 1957**

Origin Germany

Engine 250 cc, one-cylinder

Top speed 50 mph (80 km/h)

A mid-mounted engine, back-to-back seating for four adults, and great build quality made this microcar one of the cleverest. However, it was too unconventional to sell well.

▷ **BMW 600 1957**

Origin Germany

Engine 582 cc, flat-two

Top speed 62 mph (100 km/h)

Isetta customers wanted a four-seater, so BMW obliged with the 600 – one side door served the rear seats. Michelotti transformed the 600 into the larger 700 for 1959.

△ **Messerschmitt KR200 1956**

Origin Germany

Engine 191 cc, one-cylinder

Top speed 60 mph (97 km/h)

Fritz Fend's concept for disabled ex-servicemen was transformed into a practical tandem-seat bubble car with aircraft-like canopy and handlebar steering.

△ **Messerschmitt TG500 1958**

Origin Germany

Engine 490 cc, straight-two

Top speed 80 mph (129 km/h)

With over double the power of a KR200, the four-wheel "Tiger" excelled in small-capacity racing and autotests due to its low centre of gravity and tiny dimensions.

△ **Scootacar 1958**

Origin UK

Engine 197 cc, one-cylinder

Top speed 45 mph (72 km/h)

Although it arrived late on the market, around 1,500 of three different models were built in total of this British tandem-seat microcar. Driver and passenger sat scooter-style astride the engine.

△ **Bambino 200 1955**

Origin Netherlands

Engine 191 cc, one-cylinder

Top speed 53 mph (85 km/h)

This rear-engined German Fuldamobil was built under licence in the Netherlands. Versions were also built in South America, Britain, Sweden, Greece, India, and South Africa.

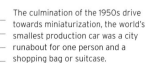

▷ **Peel P50 1963**

Origin UK

Engine 49 cc, one-cylinder

Top speed 38 mph (61 km/h)

The culmination of the 1950s drive towards miniaturization, the world's smallest production car was a city runabout for one person and a shopping bag or suitcase.

Austin Mini Seven

Conceived as an alternative to the "bubble cars" popular at the time of the 1956 Suez Crisis, the Mini revolutionized small-car design. Its front-wheel drive and transverse engine established the pattern for the modern motor car, putting manufacturer BMC (British Motor Corporation) in the technological forefront. It also became an emblem of the freewheeling 1960s, its cheeky charm boosted by the rally successes of the Cooper version. The Mini was assembled in several countries, and over five million had been made when production ended in 2000.

THE MINI'S appeal did not rest just on its small size and trim, functional lines. Above all it had astonishing packaging; its body was 3 metres (10 feet) long and accommodated four people and their luggage as well as an orthodox four-cylinder engine. It also had excellent roadholding and handling, and soon became the darling of keen drivers. Variations included the sportier Cooper, the more luxurious Wolseley Hornet and

Riley Elf, the Jeep-like Moke, a van, and a pick-up. In 1969 the up-market Clubman was introduced, with an extended nose. Mechanically, the car was gradually refined, but the only significant change was a softer rubber-and-fluid independent suspension, introduced in 1964 and removed in 1971. Latterly the car failed to compete with the new generation of bigger and more comfortable "superminis" and sales fell away.

FRONT VIEW

REAR VIEW

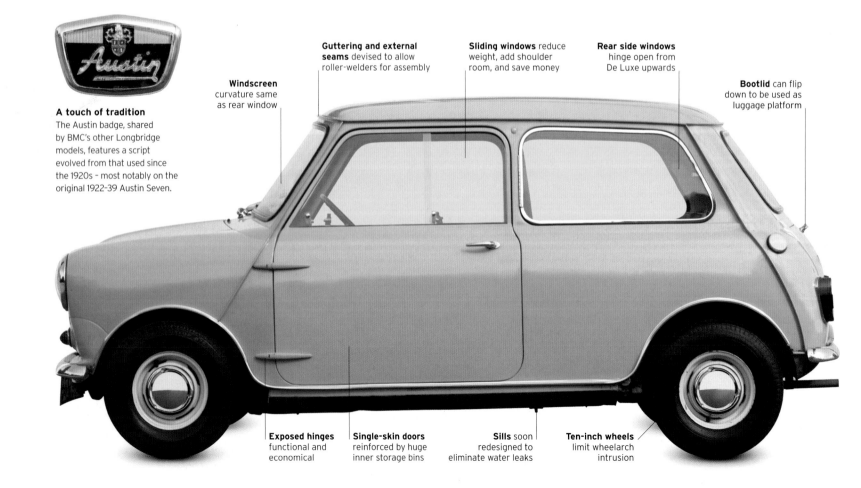

A touch of tradition
The Austin badge, shared by BMC's other Longbridge models, features a script evolved from that used since the 1920s – most notably on the original 1922-39 Austin Seven.

Windscreen curvature same as rear window

Guttering and external seams devised to allow roller-welders for assembly

Sliding windows reduce weight, add shoulder room, and save money

Rear side windows hinge open from De Luxe upwards

Bootlid can flip down to be used as luggage platform

Exposed hinges functional and economical

Single-skin doors reinforced by huge inner storage bins

Sills soon redesigned to eliminate water leaks

Ten-inch wheels limit wheelarch intrusion

Form follows function

The Mini's austere appearance was marked by a distinct lack of embellishment. Its creator, Sir Alec Issigonis, affected a disdain for styling, but he had a fine eye for line. The Mini in its original form was largely his work, refined by his body draughtsman, with limited involvement from BMC's styling chief. Ironically, its simple functionality was what would ultimately establish the Mini as a fashion icon.

SPECIFICATIONS			
Model	Austin Mini MkI, 1959–67	Power output	34 bhp at 5,500 rpm
Assembly	Mainly Longbridge, UK	Transmission	Four-speed manual
Production	435,000	Suspension	Rubber cone or hydrolastic
Construction	Steel monocoque (separate subframes)	Brakes	Drums front and rear
Engine	848 cc, ohv straight-four	Maximum speed	72.4 mph (117 km/h)

THE EXTERIOR

"If it weren't so damn ugly I'd shoot myself," said an admiring Italian automobile engineer after sampling a prototype Mini. Yet top stylist Battista "Pinin" Farina thought it hard to improve on the shape. There were always two schools of thought about the Mini: those who wished it had a bit more panache, and those who appreciated its functionalism and cheeky character.

1. "Seven" name abandoned in 1962 **2.** External access for bonnet catch **3.** Simple frontal treatment **4.** Torpedo-like hinges **5.** Handles were later depressed in "bosses" for pedestrian safety **6.** Full-width hubcaps on De Luxe **7.** Sliding windows used until 1969 **8.** Over-centre catch to open rear side window **9.** Tail lights restyled for MkII **10.** Curved boot handle used in MkI, MkII

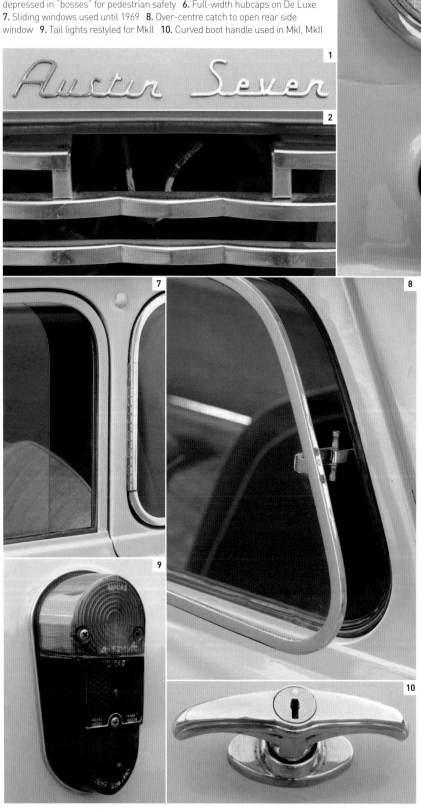

THE INTERIOR

On an early Mini every trick is used to gain room. Besides the famous door bins (discarded in 1969), there are similar bins either side of the rear seat – under which there is further storage space. The bare dashboard, initially with just a single dial, allows a generous parcel shelf and adds to the sense of spaciousness. Thin, upright seats have the same effect, but are notably uncomfortable.

11. Austin crest repeated on horn push **12.** Basic panel for switches **13.** Central speedometer suits LHD and RHD cars **14.** "Magic wand" gear lever was not very precise **15.** Windscreen washer not standard **16.** Upright seats help accommodate four people in car only 3 m (10 ft) long **17.** Thin cushioning gains space in interior **18.** Metal window catches, replaced by plastic versions in 1963 **19.** Non-standard door lever: "bootlace" cable normally used

UNDER THE BONNET

The secret of the Mini's space efficiency is the transversely placed engine, and putting the transmission in the sump rather than having a gearbox on the end of the engine. The four-speed gearbox is operated by a long, willowy lever emerging from the toeboard; Coopers have an easier-to-use remote-control lever.

20. Bonnet release catch   **21.** Transverse A-series engine   **22.** Clutch has hydraulic actuation   **23.** Battery and spare tyre in boot

Fiat Nuova 500, 1957
With the Nuova 500 (or *cinquecento*), Fiat created a cheap and practical city car that scooter owners could aspire to. It was fun, fuel-efficient, and an instant icon for Italy's post-war economic miracle.

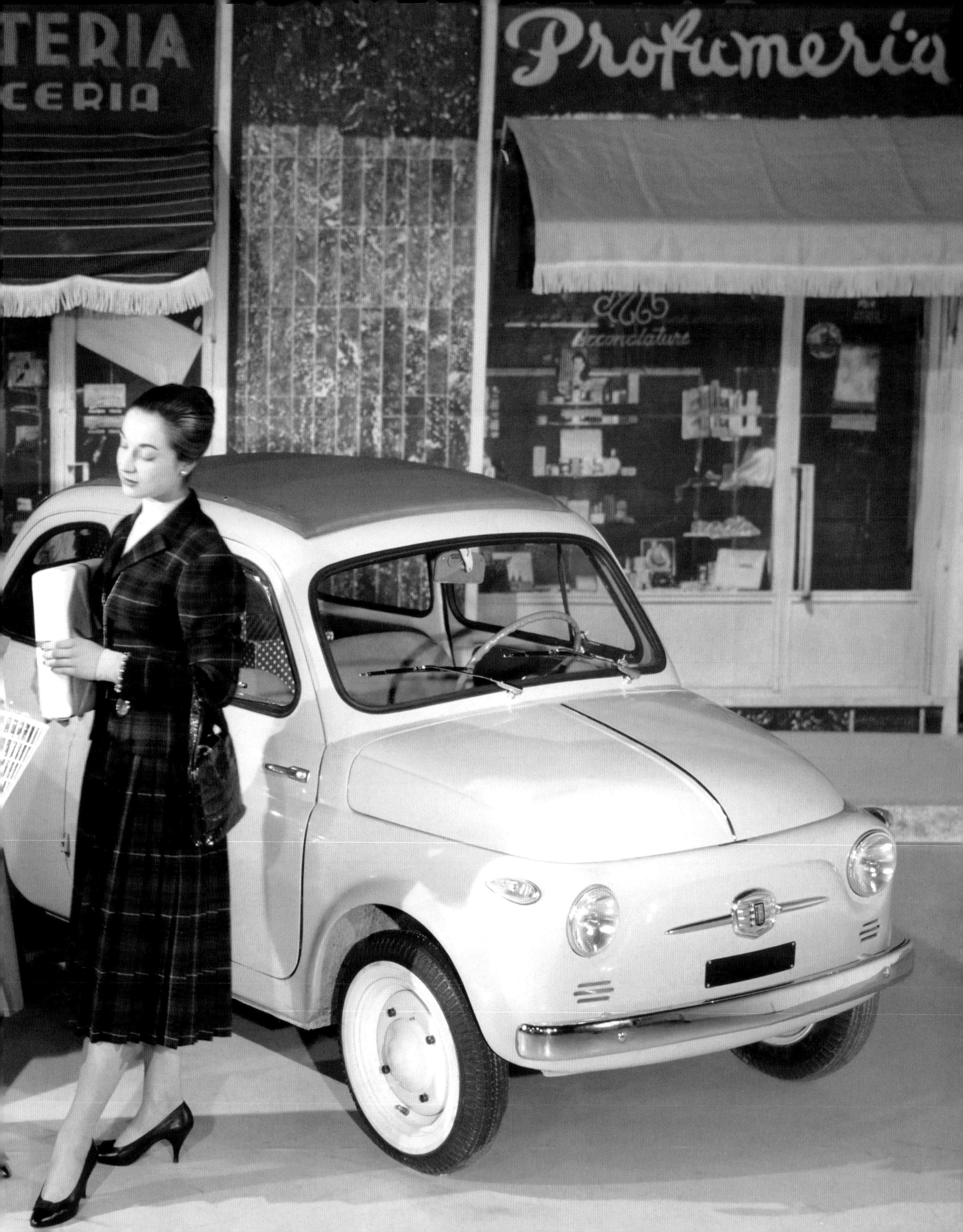
TERIA
CERIA
Profumería

Large Saloons

In 1950s America all saloons were large and sales figures were huge, justifying annual improvements and restyling. In Europe the economic climate was less favourable, with limited demand in the austerity years after World War II. As a result, updated pre-war cars were produced well into the decade in Europe, especially by smaller manufacturers that could not afford the cost of monocoque construction technology or major engineering changes.

▷ **Daimler Conquest Century 1954**

Origin UK

Engine 2,433 cc, straight-six

Top speed 90 mph (145 km/h)

Daimler made good cars, but struggled to update in the 1950s. However, performance modifications on the Century made it much livelier than the basic Conquest.

▽ **Mercury Monterey 1954**

Origin USA

Engine 4,195 cc, V8

Top speed 100 mph (161 km/h)

Mercury's first all-new engine since 1939 powered a clean, modern-styled car that was even available with a green-tinted, plexiglass roof panel, 50 years ahead of its time.

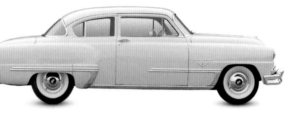

△ **Oldsmobile Super 88 1955**

Origin USA

Engine 5,309 cc, V8

Top speed 101 mph (163 km/h)

With its Futuramic styling and Rocket V8 engine, Oldsmobile was king of NASCAR (the National Association for Stock Car Auto Racing) in the early 1950s.

△ **Hudson Hornet 1954**

Origin USA

Engine 5,047 cc, straight-six

Top speed 106 mph (171 km/h)

This was the last year for Hudson's low-floored "step-down" series, introduced in 1948 with the Super Six engine. It was developed into the NASCAR-winning Hornet in 1951.

△ **De Soto Firedome 1953**

Origin USA

Engine 4,524 cc, V8

Top speed 92 mph (148 km/h)

De Soto introduced the Firedome as its top model in 1952. Its name alludes to the efficient hemispherical combustion chambers in its new V8 engine, which gave 160 bhp.

△ **Alvis TC21/100 Grey Lady 1954**

Origin UK

Engine 2,993 cc, straight-six

Top speed 100 mph (161 km/h)

Alvis kept its post-war big saloon saleable by boosting the engine to 100 bhp, and adding wire wheels and bonnet scoops. Graber saved it with modern styling in 1956.

◁ **Austin A99 Westminster 1959**

Origin UK

Engine 2,912 cc, straight-six

Top speed 98 mph (158 km/h)

Austin's Westminster grew into a distinguished large saloon with Pininfarina styling for the 1960s. It was competitively priced with servo brakes and either overdrive or automatic gearbox.

◁ **Renault Frégate 1951**

Origin France

Engine 1,997 cc, straight-four

Top speed 78 mph (126 km/h)

Nationalized after the war, Renault needed an upmarket saloon. But the Frégate was slow to enter production and was soon outclassed by the Citroën DS.

▷ **Vauxhall Cresta 1955**

Origin UK

Engine 2,262 cc, straight-six

Top speed 80 mph (129 km/h)

Vauxhall's General Motors parentage was conspicuous in the chrome-laden Cresta; the styling was pure 1949 Chevrolet. Despite that, it sold quite well in Britain.

▷ **Rambler Ambassador 1958**

Origin USA

Engine 5,359 cc, V8

Top speed 95 mph (153 km/h)

AMC was formed by the 1954 merger of Nash and Hudson. It was the only major US car maker to increase sales in the recession of 1958, thanks to new Rambler models.

◁ **Chevrolet Bel Air Nomad 1956**

Origin USA

Engine 4,343 cc, V8

Top speed 108 mph (174 km/h)

Mid-1950s Chevrolets had low, sporty styling and a potent V8 engine that made even this estate car model hugely exciting. Of 1.6 million 1956 Chevrolets, a mere 7,886 were Nomads.

△ **Lancia Flaminia 1957**

Origin Italy

Engine 2,458 cc, V6

Top speed 102 mph (164 km/h)

Styling by Pinin Farina gave the Lancia Flaminia a resemblance to the Austin Westminster, but under the skin this was a much more sophisticated car with De Dion transaxle and great handling.

▽ **Armstrong Siddeley Sapphire 1953**

Origin UK

Engine 3,435 cc, straight-six

Top speed 100 mph (161 km/h)

A luxurious car that continued to sell to traditional customers for whom Jaguar appeared too modern, the Sapphire came with pre-selector or Hydramatic gearboxes.

◁ **Rover 90 1957**

Origin UK

Engine 2,639 cc, straight-six

Top speed 91 mph (146 km/h)

Rover's P4 range had radical styling when it was launched in 1950, and stayed fresh into the 1960s. Separate chassis construction and high quality fittings made it a solid car.

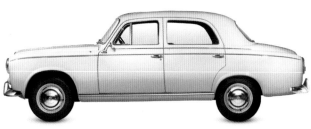

▷ **BMW 502 1955**

Origin Germany

Engine 3,168 cc, V8

Top speed 105 mph (169 km/h)

BMW's aluminium V8 engine appeared in 1954 at 2580cc, but grew the following year to give this big saloon the performance to match its imposing looks and quality fittings.

◁ **Humber Hawk VI 1954**

Origin UK

Engine 2,267 cc, straight-four

Top speed 83 mph (134 km/h)

The last of the separate-chassis Hawks was a solid, well-built, and comfortable saloon. It had good cruising ability thanks to overdrive transmission, but sluggish acceleration.

△ **Peugeot 403 1955**

Origin France

Engine 1,468 cc, straight-four

Top speed 76 mph (122 km/h)

The 403 is a rugged and well-engineered car whose later 404 version can still be seen in Africa and South America. Over a million were sold. Fictional US detective Columbo drove a convertible 403.

△ **Humber Super Snipe 1959**

Origin UK

Engine 2,651 cc, straight-six

Top speed 92 mph (148 km/h)

Humber finally adopted monocoque construction but went for slightly too small a six-cylinder engine in this Super Snipe. Later models had 3-litre engines and better performance.

Family Cars

For space, comfort, and fuel economy, family cars of the 1950s were similar to those of today; the big differences were in style, safety, performance, and noise at higher speeds. Any of these family cars would comfortably take you from London to Edinburgh, or from Calais to Nice, in a day – a big improvement on the much slower family cars of the 1930s.

△ Alfa Romeo 1900 1950
Origin Italy
Engine 1,884 cc, straight-four
Top speed 103 mph (166 km/h)

Dr Orazio Satta set Alfa Romeo on the road to post-war success with this strikingly modern saloon – a monocoque with a twin-cam engine and aerodynamic full-width styling.

△ Volvo Amazon 1956
Origin Sweden
Engine 1,583 cc, straight-four
Top speed 90 mph (145 km/h)

Starting as the 121 in 1956 with four doors and 60 bhp, the strong but light Amazon was steadily improved. In its two-door form it sold until 1970.

◁ Volvo PV444 1957
Origin Sweden
Engine 1,583 cc, straight-four
Top speed 95 mph (153 km/h)

Volvo's PV444 was rugged, lively, and popular in the 1950s – a four-speed, all synchromesh gearbox was a boon. The similar PV544 replaced it from 1958.

△ Riley RME 1952
Origin UK
Engine 1,496 cc, straight-four
Top speed 78 mph (126 km/h)

Also made in a more responsive 2.5-litre form, the Riley was outdated in its construction but remained a quality, sporting saloon car for a select clientèle.

△ Borgward Isabella TS 1954
Origin Germany
Engine 1,493 cc, straight-four
Top speed 93 mph (150 km/h)

A sporty and well-built two-door saloon, the Isabella sold over 200,000 in seven years, but could not save this family company from collapse in 1961.

△ Ford Consul MkII 1956
Origin UK
Engine 1,703 cc, straight-four
Top speed 81 mph (130 km/h)

In Britain Ford's small cars retained pre-war characteristics, but its mid-range family cars had modern US styling. The Consul shared a basic bodyshell with the Zephyr.

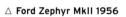

△ Ford Zephyr MkII 1956
Origin UK
Engine 2,553 cc, straight-six
Top speed 90 mph (145 km/h)

A six-cylinder engine plus a light weight gave the Zephyr effortless performance. Overdrive models had six gears to choose from.

▷ Fiat 1200 Granluce 1957
Origin Italy
Engine 1,221 cc, straight-four
Top speed 85 mph (137 km/h)

A small but lively saloon with good road-handling, this car sold over 400,000 in three years. There was also an attractive two-seater convertible version.

◁ MG Magnette ZA 1954
Origin UK
Engine 1,489 cc, straight-four
Top speed 80 mph (129 km/h)

With an engine from Austin and a body from Wolseley, the MG saloon also boasted twin carburettors, rack-and-pinion steering, and leather and wood trim.

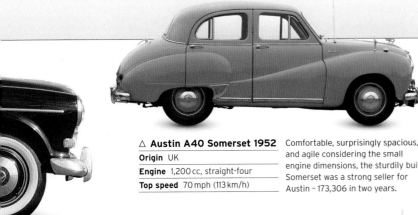

△ **Austin A40 Somerset 1952**

Origin	UK
Engine	1,200 cc, straight-four
Top speed	70 mph (113 km/h)

Comfortable, surprisingly spacious, and agile considering the small engine dimensions, the sturdily built Somerset was a strong seller for Austin – 173,306 in two years.

▷ **Henry J 1951**

Origin	USA
Engine	2,641 cc, straight-six
Top speed	82 mph (132 km/h)

Kaiser-Frazer tried to boost its flagging sales with this cut-price economy saloon with a Willys four- or six-cylinder engine. Production lasted until 1954.

△ **Austin A50/A55 Cambridge 1955**

Origin	UK
Engine	1,489 cc, straight-four
Top speed	75 mph (121 km/h)

Monocoque construction for the Somerset's successor provided lower lines and a lighter weight. The addition of a bigger engine created a serviceable family car for the 1950s.

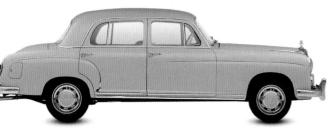

△ **Mercedes-Benz 220 1954**

Origin	Germany
Engine	2,195 cc, straight-six
Top speed	101 mph (163 km/h)

Mercedes' first monocoque construction saloon arrived in four-cylinder form in 1953; the more powerful six-cylinder version joined it in 1954. Sturdy and well built, they sold well.

▷ **Hindustan Ambassador 1958**

Origin	India
Engine	1,489 cc, straight-four
Top speed	73 mph (117 km/h)

India's best-known car, still in production today, is a locally built Morris Oxford Series II. Slowly updated over the years, since 1992 it has used an Isuzu engine.

△ **Vauxhall PA Velox 1957**

Origin	UK
Engine	2,262 cc, straight-six
Top speed	87 mph (140 km/h)

Vauxhall's US-ownership was apparent in the styling of this Velox with its wraparound windscreen. The look put off the more conservative British buyer.

◁ **Volkswagen Kombi 1950**

Origin	Germany
Engine	1,131 cc, flat-four
Top speed	58 mph (93 km/h)

Volkswagen made the most of the Beetle's platform construction and low-mounted, flat engine to produce the Kombi van, pick-up, camper, and minibus range.

△ **Simca Aronde 1958**

Origin	France
Engine	1,290 cc, straight-four
Top speed	82 mph (132 km/h)

The steadily updated Aronde saloon, estate, convertible, and coupé sold over a million in the 1950s. This was a reliable, spacious saloon with modest performance.

△ **Wolseley 15/60 1959**

Origin	UK
Engine	1,489 cc, straight-four
Top speed	77 mph (124 km/h)

Pinin Farina gave the big Wolseley – and soon Austin, Morris, MG, and Riley too – a new look with a strong hint of US design. The Wolseley was a comfortable, durable car.

Walter P. Chrysler in 1924 with the Chrysler Six

Great marques
The Chrysler story

When Walter P. Chrysler decided to compete with the giants of Ford and General Motors (GM), he set a course that would see his firm become one of the world's largest motor manufacturers. Embracing such marques as Dodge, Plymouth, and DeSoto, the Chrysler brand has made some of the US's most innovative, iconic cars.

KANSAS-BORN Walter P. Chrysler had worked his way up through the railroad business before his talents were taken up by the motor industry. Hired as a production manager at the General Motors' marque Buick in 1911, he became president from 1916 until 1919. By then Chrysler had turned Buick into GM's most profitable division.

After leaving Buick, Chrysler was recruited to transform the fortunes of first Willys-Overland and then the Maxwell Motor Corporation. Keen to develop his own model, Chrysler constructed his first car (the Chrysler Six) and

Chrysler badge
(introduced 1962)

unveiled it at the 1924 New York Auto Show. Encouraged by the positive public reaction, he formed the Chrysler Motor Corporation in 1925. The company acquired the car and truck maker Dodge Brothers in 1928; it was a deal that changed the landscape of the American motor industry, putting Chrysler alongside Ford and GM as one of the "Big Three" US automobile manufacturers. In the same year two new subsidiary marques were set up under the Chrysler umbrella: Plymouth, to cater for the low-priced end of the market, and DeSoto, to serve the mid-priced sector.

Chrysler's deft management ensured that the marque was well placed to ride through the global economic depression of the early 1930s. The company even developed a range of avant-garde models; the Airflow styling first seen on 1934 Chryslers introduced the public to a new, streamlined look. However, these sleek, wind tunnel-developed cars had several quality issues, so most US car-buyers opted for the more traditional Plymouths and DeSotos.

By the outbreak of World War II Plymouth had recorded over 3 million sales, but the death of Walter P. Chrysler in 1940 cast a shadow over the company. Even before the US entered the war in December 1941, Chrysler had redirected some of its capacity towards building tanks for the Allies. Car production ceased early in 1942, but resumed after the war with a largely conservative model range.

In 1951 Chrysler introduced the world's first power-steering system, and a new engine, the 330-cu-in (5.4-litre) FirePower V8. Called the "Hemi" because of its hemispherical combustion chamber, the V8 replaced the straight-eight configuration used since the 1930s. Initially fitted into top-of-the-range Chryslers such as the Saratoga, the Hemi would, in smaller capacities, later be fitted to some DeSotos and Dodges.

Virgil Exner, the former GM and Studebaker designer who joined Chrysler in 1949, was responsible for the "Forward Look" styling that transformed the company's dowdy post-war image. The finest examples of Exner's ultra-sleek creations came

Exner's "Forward Look"
This 1957 magazine advert for Chrysler brands shows the flamboyant, fins-and-chrome style of Virgil Exner's "Forward Look" programme.

in 1957, with a stunning new model range that incorporated gorgeous lines, sweeping fins, and chrome detailing. The award-winning 1957 New Yorker was the epitome of this futuristic new direction, while the 1959 Plymouth Fury's bold proportions established it as another Exner classic.

Exner left the corporation in 1961, the same year that Chrysler dropped its DeSoto division. But even without Exner, Chrysler continued to innovate. It began the 1960s as the only one of the Big Three to use monocoque construction, and in 1964 the Plymouth Barracuda became the world's first "pony car" – a new type of car featuring a high-performance engine inside a compact body. However, another "pony", Ford's Mustang – from which the name of this type of car was derived – garnered all the critical plaudits and

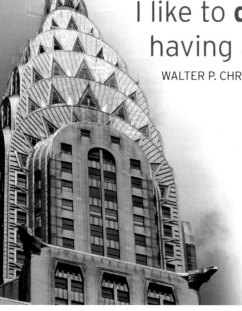

"I like to build things, I like to do things. I am having a lot of fun."

WALTER P. CHRYSLER, 1928

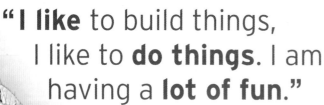

The 1930s saw several innovative Plymouth models, including the 1931 PA. With a steel body, modern styling, and a relatively low price, the PA achieved more than 100,000 sales. In 1931 work finished on the company's new, high-profile office in New York – the iconic Chrysler Building.

Chrysler Building, New York
At 319 m (1,047 ft), this was briefly the world's tallest building. Clad in silvery stone, it is decorated with stylized Chrysler hub and radiator caps and bonnet ornaments.

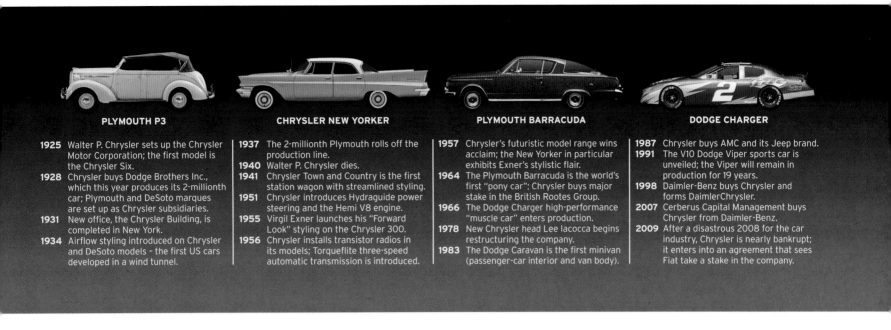

PLYMOUTH P3

CHRYSLER NEW YORKER

PLYMOUTH BARRACUDA

DODGE CHARGER

1925 Walter P. Chrysler sets up the Chrysler Motor Corporation; the first model is the Chrysler Six.
1928 Chrysler buys Dodge Brothers Inc., which this year produces its 2-millionth car; Plymouth and DeSoto marques are set up as Chrysler subsidiaries.
1931 New office, the Chrysler Building, is completed in New York.
1934 Airflow styling introduced on Chrysler and DeSoto models – the first US cars developed in a wind tunnel.

1937 The 2-millionth Plymouth rolls off the production line.
1940 Walter P. Chrysler dies.
1941 Chrysler Town and Country is the first station wagon with streamlined styling.
1951 Chrysler introduces Hydraguide power steering and the Hemi V8 engine.
1955 Virgil Exner launches his "Forward Look" styling on the Chrysler 300.
1956 Chrysler installs transistor radios in its models; Torqueflite three-speed automatic transmission is introduced.

1957 Chrysler's futuristic model range wins acclaim; the New Yorker in particular exhibits Exner's stylistic flair.
1964 The Plymouth Barracuda is the world's first "pony car"; Chrysler buys major stake in the British Rootes Group.
1966 The Dodge Charger high-performance "muscle car" enters production.
1978 New Chrysler head Lee Iacocca begins restructuring the company.
1983 The Dodge Caravan is the first minivan (passenger-car interior and van body).

1987 Chrysler buys AMC and its Jeep brand.
1991 The V10 Dodge Viper sports car is unveiled; the Viper will remain in production for 19 years.
1998 Daimler-Benz buys Chrysler and forms DaimlerChrysler.
2007 Cerberus Capital Management buys Chrysler from Daimler-Benz.
2009 After a disastrous 2008 for the car industry, Chrysler is nearly bankrupt; it enters into an agreement that sees Fiat take a stake in the company.

commercial success. Undeterred, Chrysler developed further high-performance models but with larger bodies; one notable example of these "muscle cars" was the Dodge Charger of 1966. Chrysler also expanded overseas, buying stakes in the British Rootes Group and the French Simca and Spanish Barreiros companies.

By the mid-1970s the global energy crisis rendered Chrysler's range of large-engined cars unpopular. Facing a financial crisis in 1978, Chrysler recruited Lee Iacocca, the former Ford president. He immediately asked the US government for a bail-out, laid off thousands of staff, and sold Chrysler's foreign assets. He also developed some successful models, including a range of compact cars and, in 1983, the world's first minivan – the Dodge Caravan.

Iacocca's measures paid dividends, and with Chrysler back on track, the company bought the American Motors Corporation (AMC) in 1987. This gave Chrysler the iconic Jeep brand, which it would extensively develop. The early 1990s recession hit the company hard, but Chrysler managed to pull through. By the middle of the decade models such as the two-seater Dodge Viper sports car had helped turn it into one of the most profitable US car makers.

In 1998 Daimler-Benz acquired Chrysler, forming the DaimlerChrysler Corporation. Into the new millennium, models such as the executive 300 and compact Neon were global successes. However, after a 2007 takeover by a venture-capital company, Chrysler was brought to its knees by the economic slump that hit the car industry hard in 2008. Despite almost going out of business once more, a deal was made in 2009 that saw the Italian motoring giant Fiat take a stake in Chrysler, providing European support to this most American of companies.

Plymouth Road King
The low-cost Plymouths gave many families their first start in motoring. They were also long-lasting cars: this Road King sedan from around 1940 is pictured here in 1953.

Convertible Style

Before World War II open cars were usually the cheap option. In the 1950s, however, they moved upmarket and became more desirable. As manufacturers turned to monocoque construction, convertibles became more costly to build than they had been on separate chassis. With higher prices, open cars had to become more luxurious and sophisticated, and their role turned to leisure transport.

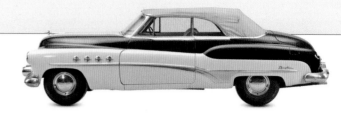

△ Buick Roadmaster 1951

Origin	USA
Engine	5,247 cc, straight-eight
Top speed	85 mph (137 km/h)

Having a Roadmaster parked on your driveway was a status symbol in post-war America. This was Buick's top model, and had automatic transmission; a year later the finned era began.

◁ Healey G-type 1951

Origin	UK
Engine	2,993 cc, straight-six
Top speed	100 mph (161 km/h)

Derived from the far more plentiful Nash-Healey that was built for the US market, just 25 of the Alvis-engined G-type were made by Healey for sale mainly in the UK.

△ Austin-Healey 3000 MkI 1959

Origin	UK
Engine	2,912 cc, straight-six
Top speed	114 mph (183 km/h)

Smooth, stylish, and powerful, the 3000 with its Austin Westminster-derived engine was available either as a two-seater or 2+2 convertible, and sold especially well in the US.

△ Ford Thunderbird 1954

Origin	USA
Engine	4,785 cc, V8
Top speed	115 mph (185 km/h)

Ford's answer to the Chevrolet Corvette and European sports cars, the "T-bird" boasted a 198 bhp V8 engine and a glassfibre hardtop: a soft-top was optional.

◁ Ford Fairlane 500 Skyliner 1958

Origin	USA
Engine	5,440 cc, V8
Top speed	120 mph (193 km/h)

The 1959-model Fords are considered their most elegant ever. This was the last year for the remarkable folding-hardtop Skyliner, a feature that was 50 years ahead of its time.

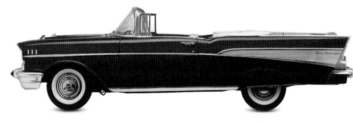

△ Chevrolet Bel Air 1955

Origin	USA
Engine	4,343 cc, V8
Top speed	100 mph (161 km/h)

1955 was Chevrolet's renaissance year, helped by a smart new body style but especially by the hot new V8 engine, it launched in the Bel Air with 162/180 bhp on tap.

▷ Morris Minor 1000 Tourer 1956

Origin	UK
Engine	948 cc, straight-four
Top speed	73 mph (117 km/h)

The brilliant Morris Minor, originally launched in 1948, offered practical, spacious, economical, everyday transport to millions; the 4-5 seat Tourer is still very popular today.

▷ Chevrolet Bel Air Convertible 1957

Origin	USA
Engine	4,638 cc, V8
Top speed	120 mph (193 km/h)

With 283 bhp (one bhp per cubic inch), the Ramjet fuel-injected top-performance option Bel Air is one of the most sought-after Chevrolets, with styling to match.

◁ Nash Metropolitan 1500 1954

Origin	UK
Engine	1,489 cc, straight-four
Top speed	75 mph (121 km/h)

Austin of England built a remarkable 95,000 of these fun little cars for the North American market, badged as Nash or Hudson, plus nearly 10,000 for other markets.

◁ **Mercedes-Benz 300SL Roadster 1957**

Origin Germany

Engine 2,996 cc, straight-six

Top speed 129 mph (208 km/h)

Fast, exotic, and derived from the legendary Gullwing, the 300SL boasted fuel injection, luxury, and impeccable build quality. Expensive, just 1,858 were built.

△ **Morgan Plus Four TR 1954**

Origin UK

Engine 1,991 cc, straight-four

Top speed 96 mph (154 km/h)

One of the most long-lived car shapes ever had its genesis in the roadster version. This model is the drophead coupé, a lusty, fun, and pure sports car.

 ▷ **Volkswagen Karmann Ghia 1957**

Origin Germany

Engine 1,192 cc, flat-four

Top speed 77 mph (124 km/h)

Karmann found a market niche by fitting pretty, Ghia-designed coupé and cabriolet bodies on the VW Beetle floorpan. These were steadily improved as 1,300 and 1,500 cc engines were used.

△ **Renault Floride/Caravelle 1958**

Origin France

Engine 845 cc, straight-four

Top speed 76 mph (122 km/h)

Rather underpowered initially with the Renault 4CV engine, the Floride grew into the Caravelle with 956/1108 cc engines and livelier performance – up to 89 mph (143 km/h).

 △ **Lancia Aurelia B24 Spider 1955**

Origin Italy

Engine 2,451 cc, V6

Top speed 115 mph (185 km/h)

Lancia's Aurelia saloon of 1950 had the world's first production V6 and semi-trailing arm, independent rear suspension: the B24 Spider put these into a gorgeous but expensive open two-seater.

◁ **Škoda Felicia Super 1959**

Origin Czechoslovakia

Engine 1,221 cc, straight-four

Top speed 87 mph (140 km/h)

Ruggedly built on a tubular backbone chassis, the Škoda was an interesting vehicle to drive, with somewhat unpredictable swing-axle rear suspension.

△ **Citroën DS 1961**

Origin France

Engine 1,911 cc, straight-four

Top speed 86 mph (138 km/h)

The DS was introduced in 1955, wowing the public with its high-pressure hydraulic brakes, steering, and suspension. This version, a luxurious cabriolet, followed five years later.

▽ **Cadillac Eldorado 1959**

Origin USA

Engine 6,390 cc, V8

Top speed 120 mph (193 km/h)

The biggest fins came in 1959 and none more dramatic than those on the 345 bhp Eldorado, which also boasted air suspension and powered everything.

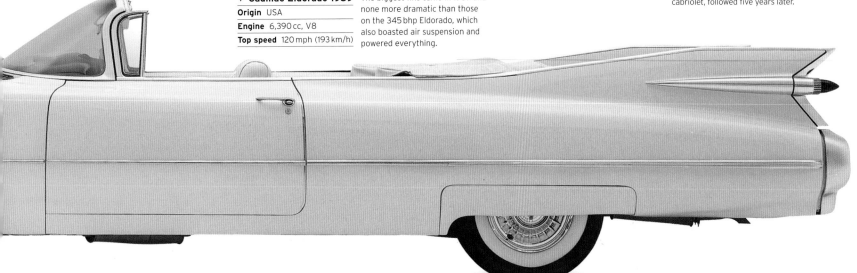

Citroën DS

When introduced in 1955 Citroën's DS was the most advanced car of its time. Under its sleek body was a complex hydropneumatic system, driven off the engine. This powered the self-levelling suspension, the brakes, and the steering, and provided automatic clutch operation and assistance to the gearchange. Nearly 1.5 million of the DS family were made, the last in 1975. Relaxingly seductive to drive, this car became a high-tech emblem of a newly resurgent France.

THE DS was innovative in every aspect of its design, from its aerodynamic body to its unusual construction, with outer panels bolted to an inner "skeleton" base unit. The hydropneumatics were the key technical feature, but other novelties included inboard disc brakes at the front, a special front suspension designed to enhance stability, and the extensive use of many different types of plastic. As with all Citroëns after the Traction Avant of 1934, the DS had front-wheel drive, the engine being mounted in-line, with the gearbox in front of the engine. The unusual front suspension used twin leading arms, while at the rear there were trailing arms. The less well-equipped ID model was launched in 1956, with simplified hydropneumatics, an orthodox clutch, and manual transmission; but over the years its specifications were progressively brought closer to that of the DS.

FRONT VIEW

REAR VIEW

Citroën's chevrons
The Citroën emblem, used from the first car of 1919, has two chevrons. These represent the chevron-pattern helical gears with which marque founder André Citroën made his name and fortune, after he had devised a means of mass-producing this form of gear-wheel.

SIDE VIEW WITH CLOSED TOP

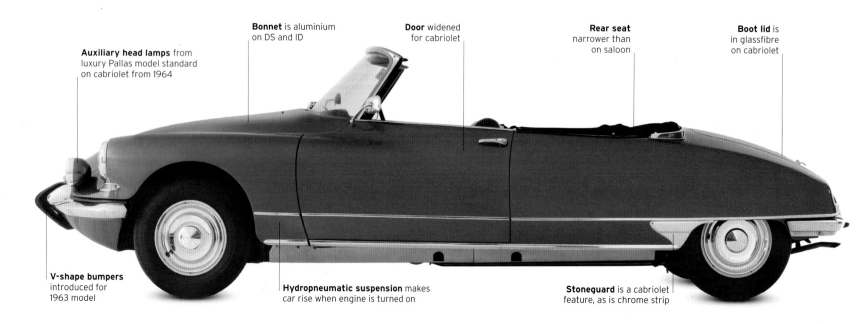

Auxiliary head lamps from luxury Pallas model standard on cabriolet from 1964

Bonnet is aluminium on DS and ID

Door widened for cabriolet

Rear seat narrower than on saloon

Boot lid is in glassfibre on cabriolet

V-shape bumpers introduced for 1963 model

Hydropneumatic suspension makes car rise when engine is turned on

Stoneguard is a cabriolet feature, as is chrome strip

SPECIFICATIONS

Model	Citroën DS/ID, 1955–75
Assembly	Mainly Paris, France
Production	1,455,746
Construction	Steel body-chassis skeleton
Engine	2,175 cc, ohv in-line four (DS21)
Power output	109 bhp at 5,500 rpm (DS21)
Transmission	Four-speed, hydraulic operation
Suspension	All-independent, hydropneumatic
Brakes	Inboard front discs; rear drums
Maximum speed	106 mph (171 km/h)

From "basking shark" to "cat's eye"
The DS21 features low-set air intakes rather than a conventional grille. For 1963 the prow was remodelled, with v-shaped bumpers and three intakes in the below-bumper apron, as seen here. This "basking shark" front was redesigned for 1968. It received twin "cat's eye" lamps behind a plastic cowl; depending on the model, the inner lamps swivelled and the outer were made self-levelling.

THE EXTERIOR

This 1963 DS21 cabriolet was one of 1,365 produced for Citroën by coachbuilder Chapron between 1960 and 1971. The rear wings were formed from two panels, and the doors lengthened using elements from two standard doors. Until 1965 a manual-transmission ID was also available. Thereafter, the DS21 engine was standardized along with certain items previously exclusive to the Pallas.

1. Gold chevrons indicate DS, silver the ID **2.** DS21 tops range from 1965 to 1972 **3.** Auxiliary lamps from luxury Pallas model fitted from '64 and special Pallas chromed indicator **4.** Original door handles replaced by recessed ones in 1971 **5.** Full-diameter hubcaps **6.** Cabriolets always have round tail lights **7.** "Boomerang" rear indicators

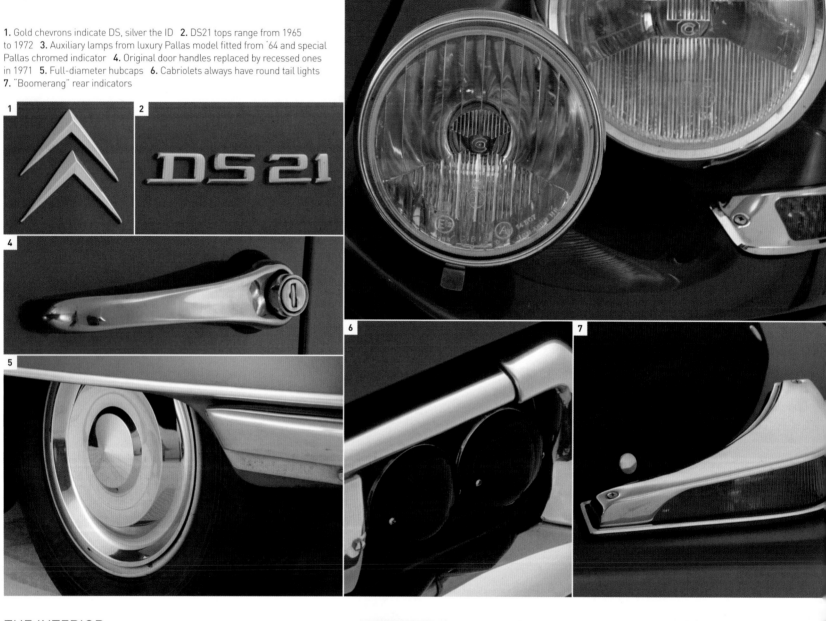

THE INTERIOR

As an expensive top-of-the-range model, the cabriolet always had a high level of trim. Whether ID or DS, the seats were in leather – at first plain at the front, and from 1965 to the Pallas-type, pleated specification. Until 1968 the lower dashboard was painted in the same colour as the exterior. The interior could comfortably seat four, and the well-constructed soft-top folded into a well, so that it lay nicely flat when stowed.

8. Second DS dashboard variant, less flamboyant than plastic original **9.** Single-spoke steering wheel **10.** Low-set interior light substitutes for light on cant rail of Pallas saloon **11.** Lift-out centre armrest found on Pallas models from 1972 **12.** DS always has chrome door furniture; most of ID series use plastic **13.** "Radioën" is Citroën's own brand of car radio **14.** Pallas-type seats introduced for 1966 model

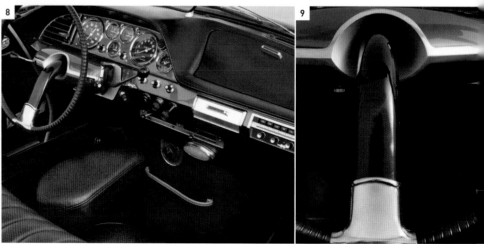

UNDER THE BONNET

The alloy-head crossflow engine with its hemispherical
combustion chambers was originally derived from
Citroën's Traction Avant unit, first seen in 1934.
For 1966 it was comprehensively revised, and
given a bigger bore and a shorter stroke; in ultimate
fuel-injected DS23 format it developed 130 bhp.
From 1963 the DS was also available with a manual
transmission, and from 1970 this was a five-speeder;
a conventional automatic was optional from 1971.

15. DS21 engine develops 109 bhp, with improved torque
16. One of four hydropneumatic spheres for suspension
17. Under-bonnet spare wheel liberates boot space

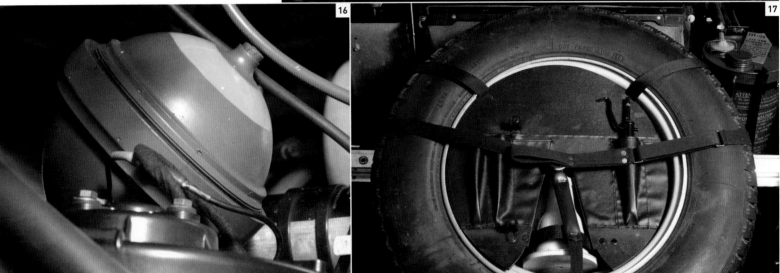

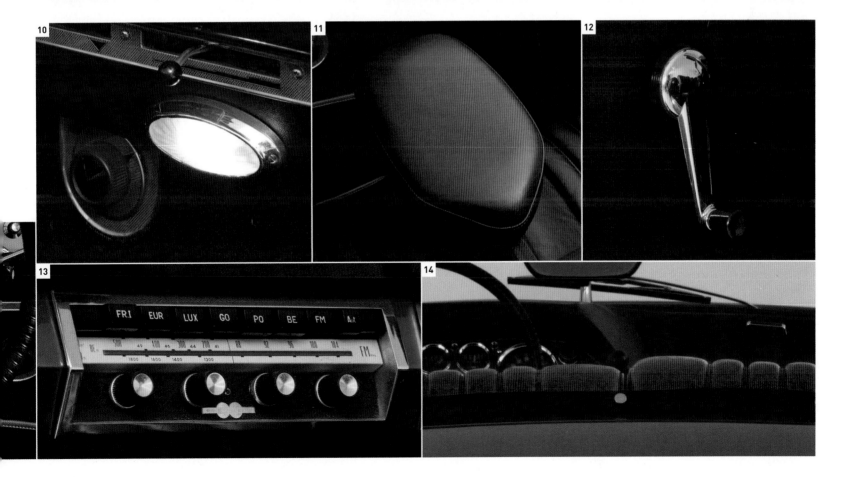

The

1960s

Mustangs & pony cars | Big-blocks & baby-boomers | Minis & muscle cars

Family Cars

In the 1960s engineers in Europe and Japan had considerable freedom with their designs for compact family transport. Manufacturers chose either a front engine with front-wheel drive, a front engine with rear drive, or a rear engine with rear drive. Styling was also flexible, leading to the production of a variety of cars, each with a clear identity.

△ Peugeot 404 1960

Origin	France
Engine	1,618 cc, straight-four
Top speed	84 mph (135 km/h)

Nearly three million of these outstanding family cars were built. Well engineered and durable, they were driven around the world and in some places are still in use.

◁ Wolseley Hornet 1961

Origin	UK
Engine	848 cc, straight-four
Top speed	71 mph (114 km/h)

BMC expanded the Mini's market by giving it a Wolseley grille, larger boot, and better quality trim. From 1963 it had 998cc and from 1964 Hydrolastic suspension.

△ Mini Moke 1964

Origin	UK
Engine	848 cc, straight-four
Top speed	84 mph (135 km/h)

A fun derivative of the Mini, the Moke was originally designed as an off-road, light reconnaissance vehicle for the British Army, but it was more successful as a beach car.

△ Triumph Herald 1200 1961

Origin	UK
Engine	1,147 cc, straight-four
Top speed	77 mph (124 km/h)

Triumph made the most of limited financial resources manufacturing this separate-chassis small car with all-independent suspension, a great turning circle, and luxury trim.

△ Lancia Flavia 1961

Origin	Italy
Engine	1,488 cc, flat-four
Top speed	93 mph (150 km/h)

The Flavia had an aluminium boxer engine and dual-circuit servo disc brakes. In 1963 the engine became 1.8 litres, and fuel injection was added in 1965.

△ Ford Cortina Mk I GT 1963

Origin	UK
Engine	1,498 cc, straight-four
Top speed	94 mph (151 km/h)

Hardly innovative – except for the fresh-air ventilation from 1965 – this car was popular for its low-friction oversquare engine, synchromesh gearbox, and spacious body.

△ MG 1100 1962

Origin	UK
Engine	1,098 cc, straight-four
Top speed	85 mph (137 km/h)

The BMC 1100/1300 range sold well. The increased interior space was the result of a transverse engine and front-wheel drive, while the Hydrolastic suspension gave a comfortable ride.

◁ Hillman Minx/Hunter 1966
Origin UK
Engine 1,725 cc, straight-four
Top speed 92 mph (148 km/h)

Chrysler's Rootes Group produced this no-nonsense family saloon that performed well. It was built for ten years in the UK, then for several decades more in Iran.

△ Sunbeam Rapier IV 1963
Origin UK
Engine 1,592 cc, straight-four
Top speed 92 mph (148 km/h)

Launched in 1955 with 1,390 cc, this two-door saloon based on the Hillman Minx kept Sunbeam's sporting name alive with some rally successes.

▷ Hillman Imp 1963
Origin UK
Engine 875 cc, straight-four
Top speed 78 mph (126 km/h)

The Rootes Group's small car had a superb aluminium engine in the back. The Imp sold around half a million units over 13 years, but it was hugely outsold by the Mini.

△ Renault 8 Gordini 1964
Origin France
Engine 1,108 cc, straight-four
Top speed 106 mph (171 km/h)

All-disc brakes (standard even on basic model R8s) and a five-speed gearbox helped make the rear-engined 8 Gordini remarkably rapid for its small engine size.

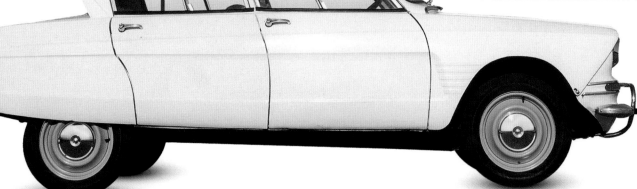

◁ Citroën Ami 6 1961
Origin France
Engine 602 cc, flat-two
Top speed 68 mph (109 km/h)

Giving the 2CV this unusual body helped Citroën sell another 1.8 million small cars between 1961 and 1978. It lost the notchback rear window in 1969.

◁ Amphicar 1961
Origin Germany
Engine 1,147 cc, straight-four
Top speed 70 mph (113 km/h)

Hans Trippel designed this amphibious car after huge investment in research. It used a Triumph Herald engine in the back and steered with the front wheels.

◁ Fiat 124 1966
Origin Italy
Engine 1,197 cc, straight-four
Top speed 85 mph (137 km/h)

Key to Fiat's 1960s success were cars like the 124, which offered excellent carrying capacity and performance with good handling; it lived on for decades more as the Russian Lada.

◁ Volkswagen 1600 Fastback 1966
Origin Germany
Engine 1,584 cc, flat-four
Top speed 83 mph (134 km/h)

Faster than a Beetle and with front disc brakes, the 1600 was improved in 1968 with 12-volt electrics, fuel injection, and MacPherson strut front suspension.

▷ Honda N360 1967
Origin Japan
Engine 354 cc, straight-two
Top speed 72 mph (116 km/h)

Honda extracted 27 bhp from the overhead-cam 360 engine, improving the performance enough for this Japanese-market *kei* car to sell in other markets.

◁ Toyota Corolla 1966
Origin Japan
Engine 1,077 cc, straight-four
Top speed 85 mph (137 km/h)

The first of an incredibly successful line, the Corolla was not exceptional in any way but was well put together and dependable, making it an ideal family car.

Rear/Mid-Engined Racers

In the 1960s many racing-car constructors realized the benefits of moving the engine from its traditional position at the front of the car to the middle or rear. Improved weight distribution was just one of the advantages of this configuration. Marques that adopted the new set-up for their racing models soon reaped the rewards in the form of superior handling and performance on the racetrack.

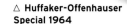

△ Huffaker-Offenhauser Special 1964

Origin USA

Engine 4,179 cc, straight-four

Top speed 180 mph (290 km/h)

Just three Huffaker-Offenhauser Specials were built for Indy Car racing, with the model featuring a liquid suspension system and rear-engine set-up.

△ Simca Abarth GT 1962

Origin France/Italy

Engine 1,288 cc, straight-four

Top speed 143 mph (230 km/h)

Italian tuning company Abarth fitted a new 1,300 cc engine into the French Simca 1000 and transformed it into a winning racer in 1962 and 1963.

△ Maserati Tipo 61 "Birdcage" 1959

Origin Italy

Engine 2,890 cc, straight-four

Top speed 177 mph (285 km/h)

Known as the "Birdcage" because of its intricate tubular chassis, the 61 competed at Le Mans and other endurance events from 1959 to 1961.

▷ Lola T70 1965

Origin UK

Engine 4,736–5,735 cc, V8

Top speed 200 mph (322 km/h)

Raced successfully on home soil in Britain as well as across the Atlantic, the T70 was powered by either a Ford or a Chevrolet V8 engine.

◁ Ford GT40 MkII 1966

Origin USA

Engine 6,997 cc, V8

Top speed 200 mph (322 km/h)

Two years after its 1964 launch, the legendary GT40 was upgraded and the MKII secured a clean sweep at the 1966 Le Mans 24-hour race in France.

▷ Jaguar XJ13 1966

Origin UK

Engine 4,994 cc, V12

Top speed 175 mph (282 km/h)

Jaguar built just one stunning XJ13 model, which despite its new 502 bhp V12 engine was deemed not competitive enough to race at Le Mans.

▷ Eisert Indy racer 1964

Origin USA

Engine 4,949 cc, V8

Top speed 180 mph (290 km/h)

Influenced by Lotus Formula 1 racers of the period, the Eisert was specially built to compete in Indy Car racing in the mid-1960s.

△ Alfa Romeo Tipo 33.2 1967

Origin Italy

Engine 1,995 cc, V8

Top speed 162 mph (261 km/h)

Alfa's decision to develop a new sports prototype model in the 1960s bore fruit with the Tipo 33.2, which won its debut race in 1967.

△ Howmet TX 1968

Origin USA

Engine 2,958 cc, gas turbine

Top speed 180 mph (290 km/h)

Competing in high-profile endurance events during the 1968 season, the Howmet featured a novel gas-turbine powerplant.

△ Lotus 49 1967
Origin UK
Engine 2,993 cc, V8
Top speed 180 mph (290 km/h)

The fruits of a collaboration between Lotus, Ford, and Cosworth, the legendary 49 was piloted by the finest Grand Prix drivers of the late 1960s.

△ Matra Cosworth MS10 1968
Origin France
Engine 2,993 cc, V8
Top speed 180 mph (290 km/h)

Matra started out in Formula 1 in 1967 with the MS10, which shared the same impressive Cosworth engine as the Lotus 49.

△ Ferrari 312/68 1968
Origin Italy
Engine 2,989 cc, V12
Top speed 193 mph (310 km/h)

The 1968 version of Ferrari's 312 F1 racer first unveiled two years previously was the best yet, with Jacques "Jacky" Ickx winning that year's French Grand Prix.

▽ Ferrari 312P 1969
Origin Italy
Engine 2,990 cc, V12
Top speed 199 mph (320 km/h)

First raced in 1969, Ferrari's 312P prototype competed in high-profile endurance events such as the Spa 1,000 km and the Le Mans 24-hour race.

△ March 707 1970
Origin UK
Engine 8,226 cc, V8
Top speed 200 mph (322 km/h)

Designed in the late 1960s, March competed in the North American CanAm racing series with the 707 model, which was powered by a mighty Chevrolet V8 engine.

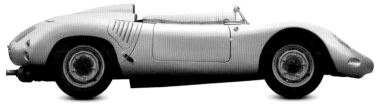

△ Porsche 718 RS 1957
Origin Germany
Engine 1,587 cc, flat-four
Top speed 140 mph (225 km/h)

Porsche's 718 open-topped endurance racer recorded a number of podium finishes, including third place at the 1958 Le Mans 24-hour race. It continued winning races into the early 1960s.

△ Porsche 906 1966
Origin Germany
Engine 1,991 cc, flat-six
Top speed 174 mph (280 km/h)

The first Porsche to incorporate gullwing doors, the 906 from 1966 hit the ground running with class and overall victories in its debut year.

◁ Porsche 917K 1970
Origin Germany
Engine 4,494 cc, flat-twelve
Top speed 199 mph (320 km/h)

Conceived in the 1960s with the aim of winning the 1970 Le Mans 24-hour race, the fabled 917 did just that and also won in 1971.

Sports and Executive Saloons

A new breed of saloon, these cars were aimed at hard-driving businessmen. The cars were well able to sustain foot-to-the-floor overtaking and relaxed high-speed cruising, in contrast to earlier counterparts that would shake themselves to pieces, or overheat their engines. Much of the know-how behind these cars was directly derived from the racing track, where saloon cars had fired the minds of engineers.

△ **Vauxhall Cresta PB 1962**
Origin UK
Engine 3,294 cc, six-cylinder
Top speed 93 mph (150 km/h)

The Cresta was a large, comfortable car from the British branch of General Motors. From 1965 automatic transmission was introduced.

▷ **Austin/Morris Mini Cooper 1961**
Origin UK
Engine 1275 cc, four-cylinder
Top speed 100 mph (161 km/h)

The Mini was never meant to be a performance saloon, but Formula 1 boss John Cooper spotted its potential. Tuned engines and disc brakes exploited its fantastic roadholding.

△ **Ford Zephyr MkIII 1962**
Origin UK
Engine 2,553 cc, six-cylinder
Top speed 95 mph (153 km/h)

Ford offered four- or six-cylinder engines in its biggest British saloon. This car came with front disc brakes, an all-synchromesh gearbox, and an optional automatic transmission.

△ **Volvo 122S 1961**
Origin Sweden
Engine 1,778 cc, four-cylinder
Top speed 100 mph (161 km/h)

The ultimate engine in this rugged yet capable sports saloon car was a 100 bhp unit. It was a spirited performer, especially with optional overdrive, and was called the Amazon in Sweden.

△ **Ford Falcon 1964**
Origin Australia
Engine 3,277 cc, six-cylinder
Top speed 105 mph (169 km/h)

This Falcon was the first car designed in – and for – Australia, and its toughened-up specification laid the foundations for sporty Falcons to come.

▷ **Wolseley 6/110 1961**
Origin UK
Engine 2,912 cc, six-cylinder
Top speed 101 mph (163 km/h)

The 6/110 was a heavy car, so it had no real spark despite a 120 bhp engine. An already luxurious specification could be enhanced with optional air conditioning and power steering.

▽ **Rover P6 2000 TC 1963**
Origin UK
Engine 1,978 cc, four-cylinder
Top speed 108 mph (174 km/h)

In 1963 the P6 broke new ground for safety and sportiness in saloon cars. The TC (twin carburettor) added extra zest. A later version, the P6 3500, had a V8 engine.

∇ **Jaguar XJ6 1968**

Origin	UK
Engine	4,235 cc, six-cylinder
Top speed	124 mph (200 km/h)

Widely hailed as the finest saloon car in the world, the beautiful XJ6 offered a superb compromise between high performance, ride comfort, and roadholding.

◁ **Daimler 2.5-litre V8-250 1962**

Origin	UK
Engine	2,548 cc, V8
Top speed	112 mph (180 km/h)

After Jaguar had taken over Daimler in 1960, it created this compact luxury model by uniting the SP250's refined V8 engine with the Jaguar MkII body. Almost all were automatic.

△ **Jaguar Mk2 1959**

Origin	UK
Engine	3,781 cc, six-cylinder
Top speed	125 mph (201 km/h)

For many, this lithe Jaguar is the epitome of the 1960s sports saloon. The 3.8-litre version was a great saloon racer, although the 3.4 litre was more popular on the road.

▷ **Triumph 2000 1963**

Origin	UK
Engine	1,998 cc, six-cylinder
Top speed	93 mph (150 km/h)

A stylish and well-liked car among business executives of the 1960s, the 2000 featured all-round independent suspension, front disc brakes, and Italian styling by Giovanni Michelotti.

▷ **Humber Hawk MkIV 1964**

Origin	UK
Engine	2,267 cc, four-cylinder
Top speed	83 mph (134 km/h)

Humber's largest executive cars received a styling revision around the rear window for their final three years, like this MkIV. They still featured a column gearchange.

◁ **Isuzu Bellett 1963**

Origin	Japan
Engine	1,991 cc, four-cylinder
Top speed	118 mph (190 km/h)

Little known in the West, the neat Bellett was one of Japan's first sports saloons and, in GT-R form, a star of Japanese production car racing. Over 170,000 were built.

▷ **Holden Monaro 1968**

Origin	Australia
Engine	5,736 cc, V8
Top speed	115 mph (185 km/h)

The Monaro was a sporty, four-seater coupé derived directly from the HK series Kingswood/Brougham saloon. The ultimate edition of the Monaro was the 5.7-litre GTS 327 Bathurst.

△ **Nissan Skyline GT-R 1969**

Origin	Japan
Engine	1,998 cc, six-cylinder
Top speed	124 mph (200 km/h)

The twin-camshaft engine in the GT-R turned the humdrum Skyline saloon into a serious race winner that notched up 50 race wins in its first three years.

Aston Martin
1.5-litre, 1922

Great marques
The Aston Martin story

World-renowned for prestige and driving excitement – and as the maker of James Bond's favourite cars – Aston Martin is a prime example of a small British marque: building sports cars against the commercial odds, yet surviving decade after decade thanks to the support of devoted owners and dogged backers.

ASTON MARTIN BEGAN in 1913 in a London garage founded by Robert Bamford and Lionel Martin. Keen drivers, the pair soon built their own sports car using an old Isotta Fraschini chassis and a Coventry-Simplex 1.4-litre engine, and entered it in time-trial events. It performed so strongly in a 1914 hill-climb at Aston Clinton, Buckinghamshire, that the machine was christened the Aston Martin, and registered for the road in 1915. World War I prevented the car from going into production, with Martin and Bamford being called up for military service and the machinery sold to Sopwith, the aircraft manufacturers. The partnership resumed after the war, but it was beset by financial problems. Bamford eventually left in 1920.

Aston Martin badge
(introduced 1932)

DBS advertisment, 1968
Produced from 1967 to 1972, the DBS was the last model of the David Brown era. It came with four full-size seats and a 4.0-litre engine.

Martin, with the help of his wife, Kate, then became a fully fledged car maker. He relaunched the Aston Martin as a simple sports car in 1921, featuring a bespoke and lightweight 1.5-litre four-cylinder engine. While the car forged a formidable reputation on the race track, its manufacture was slow and chaotic. After several changes of ownership, the company moved to Feltham, Middlesex, in 1926. A year later a new 1.5-litre car was designed by the Italian Bertelli brothers, with Augusto overseeing the engineering and Enrico the low-slung bodywork.

Despite the near-constant internal upheaval, in the eyes of the public, Aston Martin produced fast, robust, exclusive sports cars that inspired enormous loyalty from their owners. The cars proved well able to cope with the Le Mans 24-hour race in France, making their debut in 1928.

During World War II Aston Martin made aircraft components. After the war Aston Martin, almost bankrupt as ever, was bought by David Brown, a Yorkshire industrialist. He had seen it for sale in the classified advertisements of *The Times* newspaper. Brown also acquired the Lagonda marque and combined the best of both traditions in the DB2 sports car, which married Aston's capable chassis with Lagonda's superb 2.6-litre, six-cylinder engine. The DB2 completed Le Mans in 1949, while still in protoype form.

Aston Martin's future as a great marque was sealed at Le Mans in 1950, when Abecassis/Macklin

brought a DB2 home fifth overall and won the 3-litre class; Parnell/Brackenbury finished an overall sixth and came second in the 3-litre class. For the 1951 race, the factory team excelled itself, with DB2s finishing third, fifth, and seventh, while two privately entered DB2s came 10th and 11th. Five finishes from five starters in this 24-hour killer was an astounding achievement for a near-standard, two-seater street machine like the DB2. Another highlight saw Aston Martin clinch the World Sports Car Championship constructors' title in 1959 with the DBR1 racing car.

Brown realized that, to be profitable, Aston Martin's expensive, hand-built road cars had to be sumptuous as well as brawny. After Brown took over the Tickford coachbuilding company in 1955, Aston Martin interiors became increasingly luxurious and the cars' paintwork more lustrous. Modern technology such as disc brakes and overdrive were added, but automatic transmission arrived only in 1959.

For the DB4 of 1958, Aston Martin turned to Italian bodywork specialists Carrozzeria Touring, who provided the sleek styling and the method of lightweight construction. But the DB4 retained a steely edge: DB4 GTs and GT Zagatos were fearsome track cars.

Launched in 1964, the DB5 might have seemed just a more powerful and aerodynamic evolution of the DB4, were it not for a starring role as James Bond's car in the 1964 film *Goldfinger*. This big-screen fame made the Aston Martin marque synonymous with the suave, ruthless secret agent. And the movie mystique endures: an original DB5 film car sold at auction for £2.6 million in 2010.

"It must be placed **high on the list** of the **world's most desirable** grand touring cars."

AUTOSPORT MAGAZINE ON THE DB4GT, 1962

The DB6 of 1965 and DBS of 1967 preceded a brand new V8 engine in 1969, but the golden era ended three years later when David Brown sold the company. Aston Martin muddled its way through the 1970s and 80s, kept afloat by the wedge-shaped Lagonda limousine, which found favour with Middle Eastern buyers. A firm financial footing came only after Ford's purchase of Aston Martin in 1987.

The new management decided to retain the entirely hand-built Aston Martin, now in its Virage incarnation, alongside a new production-line model, called the DB7, which would be smaller and cheaper. The DB7, which used some Jaguar components, was launched in 1993. It proved highly popular, as has its DB9 successor (there was no DB8), which was introduced in 2003. Aston

1.5-LITRE MKII

DB4

V8

V12 VANTAGE

1913	Bamford & Martin Limited is founded in London.
1915	The first Aston Martin car is registered.
1921	The first 1.5-litre production cars arrive, and the first competition car makes its appearance.
1927	The 1.5-litre is launched in "T" touring and "S" sports forms.
1928	Aston Martin International uses dry-sump lubrication.
1936	The 2.0-litre 15/98 replaces the 1.5-litre car; it has a simplified specification.

1949	Prototype DB2s compete at Le Mans.
1955	Aston Martin buys the Tickford coachbuilding company.
1958	The DB4 is unveiled with an all-new, 3.7-litre, 240 bhp engine.
1959	Aston Martin wins the World Sports Car Championship constructors' title with the DBR1.
1964	Aston Martin introduces the DB5.
1965	The DB6 replaces the DB5.
1967	The DBS offers modernized styling and later, from 1969, a new V8 engine.

1976	The four-door Aston Martin Lagonda unveiled, reaching customers four years later.
1978	The Volante, a convertible, joins the V8 range.
1984	The 10,000th Aston Martin is built.
1990	Sales of the Aston Martin Virage start.
1987	Ford buys Aston Martin, bringing financial stability to the company.
1993	The DB7 – a smaller, cheaper Aston Martin – is launched; 5,000 DB7s will be built by 2001.

2001	Aston Martin introduces the V12 Vanquish.
2003	The DB9 replaces the DB7, with a V12 engine as standard; a purpose-built factory opens at Gaydon.
2005	The V8 Vantage, a Porsche 911 rival, goes on sale.
2006	The 30,000th Aston Martin is built.
2009	The V12 Vantage and One-77 supercar are launched, along with the Cygnet city car – a joint venture with Toyota.
2010	The Rapide is a new four-door model.

decided next to confront the Porsche 911 with its own compact sports car. It built an all-new assembly plant in Gaydon, Warwickshire – the firm's first purpose-built home – to make the highly acclaimed V8 Vantage, which reached eager fans in 2005.

In 2007 Ford sold Aston Martin to a Kuwaiti-funded consortium led by David Richards, founder of rally team Prodrive. Even before this change, Aston Martin had returned to the world of motor sport. Consecutive wins at Le Mans in the GT1 class in 2007 and 2008 were followed by a fourth place overall at the 2009 event with a new LMP1-class car – the fastest petrol car in the field. In 2009 the V12 Vantage GT claimed victory in its class at the Nürburgring 24-hour race on its competitive debut.

In 2009, showing pragmatism rarely seen under previous owners, Aston Martin unveiled the Cygnet city car, a joint venture with Toyota. This new addition to the Aston Martin range gives the owners of today's Vantage, DB9, DBS, Rapide, or One-77 models a matching urban runabout. It also helps the company meet legal obligations for car manufacturers to reduce average fuel consumption and missions ss their ranges.

Aston Martin DB7
Introduced in 1993, when Aston Martin and Jaguar were both owned by Ford, the DB7 used the running gear of the Jaguar XJS, although the DB7's styling was very different.

Licence to thrill
Since 1964 Aston Martins have featured alongside 007 in many James Bond films. Most recently this DB5 featured in *Casino Royale* (2006), while a DBS V12 appeared in *Quantum of Solace* (2008).

NASSAU
56526
BAHAMAS

Sedans and Sporty Coupés

Clean, smooth lines and hot-rod performance
options were the big trends in 1960s America, as
car stylists reacted against the excessive fins and
chrome of the previous decade. American carmakers
finally found their sports-car niche with the
Ford-inspired, compact, and affordable "pony cars".
"Coke bottle" styling was to be seen right across
the marketplace and, before long, around the world.

△ Buick Skylark 1961

Origin	USA
Engine	3,528 cc, V8
Top speed	105 mph (169 km/h)

Buick introduced the Skylark sport coupé
to wide acclaim. With its clean, low
lines Buick finally abandoned the fins
of the 1950s for a popular new look.

△ Studebaker Gran Turismo Hawk 1962

Origin	USA
Engine	4,736 cc, V8
Top speed	110 mph (177 km/h)

Packard's takeover in 1954
did not help Studebaker for long;
it struggled, closing in 1966. The
Hawk boosted sales briefly in 1962.

△ Buick Riviera 1963

Origin	USA
Engine	6,571 cc, V8
Top speed	120 mph (193 km/h)

One of the cleanest examples of the
"Coke bottle" styling that swept across
the industry in the 1960s was on the
long, low, lithe, luxury 1963 Buick Riviera.

△ Chrysler 300F 1960

Origin	USA
Engine	6,768 cc, V8
Top speed	120 mph (193 km/h)

The 300 Series "Letter cars" were Chrysler's
most powerful machines: the 1960's F went
to monocoque construction and ram-tuned
induction, but forgot to chop the fins.

△ Plymouth Barracuda 1964

Origin	USA
Engine	4,473 cc, V8
Top speed	106 mph (171 km/h)

Plymouth struggled in the 1960s
until the Barracuda heralded a
remarkable recovery - yet it
never came close to the sales
success of Ford's Mustang rival.

◁ Ford Thunderbird Landau 1964

Origin	USA
Engine	6,392 cc, V8
Top speed	118 mph (190 km/h)

The year Ford launched the
Mustang, the Thunderbird also
received a total new look, with
a longer bonnet, shorter roof,
and power bulge. Sales went
up by 50 per cent.

Ford Mustang

After the record-breaking
success of the compact Falcon
saloon, Ford saw a niche for
a mini-Thunderbird based on
the Falcon platform – and
created a whole new market
with the hugely popular
Mustang. It set a new world
record, selling 418,000 in
its first year: it would have
sold more if Ford could
have built them faster.

▷ Ford Mustang hardtop coupe 1964

Origin	USA
Engine	4,727 cc, V8
Top speed	116 mph (187 km/h)

The Mustang sold in coupé,
convertible, and, later, fastback
coupé forms, with engines
ranging from 3.3-litre straight-six
to 4.7-litre V8. This V8 hardtop
coupé was by far the most popular.

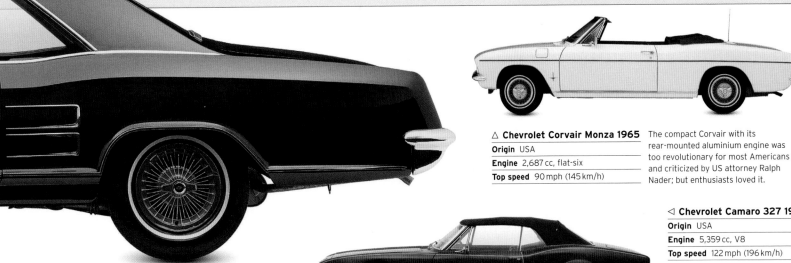

△ **Chevrolet Corvair Monza 1965**

Origin	USA
Engine	2,687 cc, flat-six
Top speed	90 mph (145 km/h)

The compact Corvair with its rear-mounted aluminium engine was too revolutionary for most Americans and criticized by US attorney Ralph Nader; but enthusiasts loved it.

◁ **Chevrolet Camaro 327 1967**

Origin	USA
Engine	5,359 cc, V8
Top speed	122 mph (196 km/h)

It took Chevrolet three years to respond to Ford's Mustang, but when it came, the Camaro offered a great range of performance packages in a smooth, attractive body.

△ **Pontiac Tempest GTO 1966**

Origin	USA
Engine	6,375 cc, V8
Top speed	122 mph (196 km/h)

The Tempest compact helped make Pontiac the third best-selling US marque of the 1960s and the GTO confirmed its performance credentials: it was a real hot rod.

◁ **Oldsmobile Starfire 1964**

Origin	USA
Engine	6,456 cc, V8
Top speed	108 mph (174 km/h)

Oldsmobile moved into the personal luxury market with the Starfire, using its most powerful engine option in an imposing, squared-off, two-door bodyshell.

△ **Mercury Cougar 1967**

Origin	USA
Engine	4,727 cc, V8
Top speed	112 mph (180 km/h)

Mercury entered the "pony car" market in 1967, pitting parent Ford against the Chevrolet Camaro. Handsome styling ensured it caught on, selling 150,000 in its first year.

◁ **Dodge Charger R/T 1968**

Origin	USA
Engine	5,211 cc, V8
Top speed	113 mph (182 km/h)

"Dodge Fever" arrived with the restyle for 1968 as the marque saw record sales, helped by the new, super-smooth "Coke bottle" styled Charger V8.

△ **Mercury Cyclone 1968**

Origin	USA
Engine	4949 cc, V8
Top speed	115 mph (185 km/h)

The Cyclone was Mercury's macho Grand Tourer model from 1964, given "Coke bottle" styling from 1966 that looked best on the most popular Fastback Coupe body.

△ **Ford Mustang 1965**

Origin	USA
Engine	4,727 cc, V8
Top speed	116 mph (187 km/h)

More than a million Mustangs were sold in the first two years of production. The styling was so universally loved that it won the Tiffany Award for Excellence in American Design.

△ **Ford Mustang Fastback 1965**

Origin	USA
Engine	4,727 cc, V8
Top speed	116 mph (187 km/h)

The stylish Fastback bodystyle, sold as the 2+2, joined the range in 1965 and immediately outsold the convertible; in 1966 Mustang took 7.1 per cent of all US car sales.

◁ **Ford Mustang Boss 302 1969**

Origin	USA
Engine	4,942 cc, V8
Top speed	121 mph (195 km/h)

Faced with competition from the Camaro, Mustang grew for 1969, both in size and performance, up to the ultimate Boss 302 and Boss 429 monsters.

Lotus/Ford Cosworth
DFV V8

When Lotus founder Colin Chapman - dissatisfied with the engines available to him - asked Ford to commission a new powerplant for Formula 1, Ford turned to Cosworth's Keith Duckworth. The engine he designed became legendary, winning 12 driver's titles between 1968 and 1982.

FORMULA 1 SUPERSTAR

Cosworth called this engine the DFV (Double Four Valve) because it had two banks of four cylinders arranged in a 90-degree "V", with each cylinder having twin inlet and exhaust valves. The former were on top of the engine to give an unobstructed path to air drawn in through the inlet trumpets. A flat crankshaft operated each bank of cylinders as an in-line four to exploit wave effects in the exhaust pipes, which helped extract spent cylinder gases. Powerful, reliable, compact, and sturdy, the DFV was also popular for its precise construction.

ENGINE SPECIFICATIONS	
Dates produced	1967-1986
Cylinders	Eight cylinders in two banks, 90-degree "V"
Configuration	Mid-mounted, longitudinal
Engine capacity	2,993 cc
Power output	408 bhp @ 9,000 rpm, ultimately 510 bhp @ 11,200 rpm
Type	Conventional four-stroke, water-cooled petrol engine with reciprocating pistons, designed to form part of the car's structure
Head	dohc per bank with bucket tappets; four valves per cylinder
Fuel System	Lucas port fuel injection
Bore and Stroke	85.7 mm x 64.8 mm (3.37 in x 2.55 in)
Specific power	136 bhp/litre, 2.52 bhp/kg
Compression Ratio	11.0:1

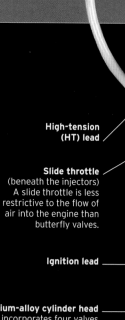

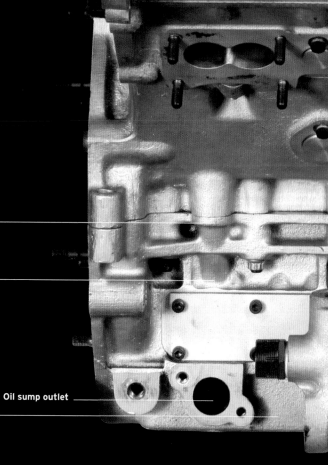

Ignition coil

High-tension (HT) lead

Slide throttle
(beneath the injectors)
A slide throttle is less restrictive to the flow of air into the engine than butterfly valves.

Ignition lead

Aluminium-alloy cylinder head
The head incorporates four valves per cylinder (hidden under the casing) to maximize the flow of gas through the engine. Although this configuration already had a long history by 1967, most racing engines of the time used only two valves per cylinder. Cosworth's spectacular success with the DFV changed that, making four-valve racing engines increasingly popular, and eventually led to four-valve heads being used in high-performance road-car engines too.

Aluminium-alloy cylinder block

Aluminium-alloy lower crankcase

Dry sump
Oil falling through the engine into the sump is removed immediately and stored in a separate oil tank, so the sump is "dry". This allows the sump to be shallower, enabling the engine to be mounted lower in the car.

Oil sump outlet

▷ See pp.346-347 How an engine works

Coarse gauze air filter
The large holes in the gauze ensure that air entering via the inlet trumpets encounters minimum resistance.

Inlet trumpets
These create a "wave ram" effect, in which pressure waves reflected from the trumpets' open ends force more air-fuel mixture into the cylinders at critical engine speeds.

Port fuel injector
Fuel is fed to the injectors by a Lucas shuttle-type injector pump.

Inlet camshaft
(beneath cover)

Engine mounting bracket
Secured to the car by brackets, the engine forms an integral part of the chassis structure.

Cam cover

Exhaust camshaft
(beneath cover)
Like the inlet cam, the exhaust camshaft is driven by a high-precision geartrain rather than a belt or chain.

A hidden issue
When the DFV won its first Formula 1 race in the Lotus 49 in 1967, few onlookers could have suspected that it had a serious design problem. Brief episodes of excessive torque (twisting force) in the gear drive to the camshafts risked damage to the engine. The problem was solved by Duckworth adding a springy "quill shaft" that reduced the severity of these spikes in torque.

Exhaust manifold mounting stud

Exhaust port

Drive belt
Beneath this cover a toothed belt drives engine ancillaries such as the oil and water pumps.

Water pump

Ancillary drive linkage

Scavenge oil pump
This transfers oil from the sump to the oil tank. It incorporates a rotary oil/air separator, which removes air and combustion gases that have become mixed with the oil.

Ultimate Luxury Limousines

The 1960s saw the final flowering of the separate chassis luxury car. These huge, heavy, traditional, and opulent cars were gradually replaced by lighter, more efficient, modern, monocoque luxury models, with significantly higher performance and sleeker, lower lines. The decade also saw the appearance of much smaller luxury cars based on mainstream models, ideal for city-centre driving.

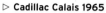

◁ **GAZ Chaika 1959**

Origin USSR

Engine 5522 cc, V8

Top speed 99 mph (159 km/h)

A close copy of a 1955 Packard, the Chaika was built until 1981. It was strictly for party officials, academics, scientists, and other VIPs who were approved by the Soviet government.

▷ **Cadillac Calais 1965**

Origin USA

Engine 7030 cc, V8

Top speed 120 mph (193 km/h)

Every Cadillac was a luxury car; this model featured curved side windows, remote-controlled exterior mirrors, variable ratio steering, and heated seats.

△ **Nissan Cedric 1962**

Origin Japan

Engine 1,883 cc, straight-four

Top speed 90 mph (145 km/h)

Rarely seen outside Japan at the time, Nissan's large saloon was inspired by US styling but fitted with a 1.5–2.8-litre engine. It was Nissan's first monocoque design.

△ **Nissan President 1965**

Origin Japan

Engine 3,988 cc, V8

Top speed 115 mph (185 km/h)

Nissan's ultimate car for 1965 was a better model than the Cedric, with a 3.0-litre V6 or 4.0-litre V8 and, from 1971, ABS. One was used by Japan's prime minister.

▷ **Mercedes-Benz 300SEC 1962**

Origin Germany

Engine 2996 cc, straight-six

Top speed 124 mph (200 km/h)

One of Germany's finest cars of the early 1960s, the 300SEC had a race-proven, fuel-injected six-cylinder engine in a sophisticated coupé or convertible shell.

△ **Mitsubishi Debonair 1964**

Origin Japan

Engine 1991 cc, straight-six

Top speed 96 mph (154 km/h)

This luxury car for the Japanese market was styled like an early 1960s US car, and stayed almost unchanged until 1986. A bigger engine was added in the 1970s.

△ **Mercedes-Benz 600 1963**

Origin Germany

Engine 6332 cc, V8

Top speed 130 mph (209 km/h)

From 1963 until as recently as 1981, Mercedes offered this large saloon for VIPs to travel in an insulated cabin at speeds of up to 120 mph (193 km/h). Only 2,677 of them were built.

▷ **Rolls-Royce Silver Cloud III 1962**

Origin UK

Engine 6230 cc, V8

Top speed 110 mph (177 km/h)

The last of the separate-chassis mainstream Rolls-Royces was traditional and indulgent, but with a wonderful wood and leather interior; it also had V8 power and modern twin headlamps.

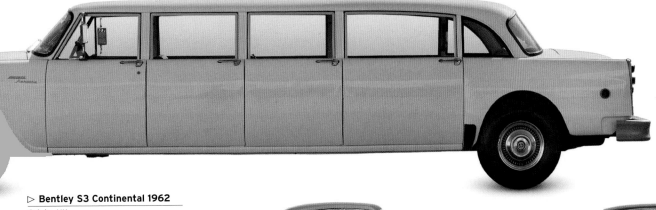

◁ **Checker Marathon Limousine 1963**

Origin USA

Engine 4637 cc, V8

Top speed 90 mph (145 km/h)

Checker built taxis from 1923 to 1959, and then produced a few taxi-derived cars, estates, and limos. This eight-door limo offered a roomy interior.

▷ **Bentley S3 Continental 1962**

Origin UK

Engine 6,230 cc, V8

Top speed 113 mph (185 km/h)

The stately Bentley S3 also came in a coachbuilt "Continental" version. This was a faster and lighter model with an aluminium body and sportier lines.

◁ **Lincoln Continental Convertible 1961**

Origin USA

Engine 7,043 cc, V8

Top speed 115 mph (185 km/h)

The 1961 Continental was one of the most influential auto designs of the decade. It had power-assisted seats, windows, brakes, steering, and gearbox.

▽ **Chrysler New Yorker 1960**

Origin USA

Engine 6,767 cc, V8

Top speed 122 mph (196 km/h)

In 1960 Chrysler began producing its first monocoque construction bodyshells. The New Yorker was the longest and most luxurious, with 350 bhp to speed it along the freeways.

△ **Humber Imperial 1964**

Origin UK

Engine 2,965 cc, straight-six

Top speed 100 mph (161 km/h)

The ultimate Imperial model was discontinued for 10 years by Chrysler's Rootes Group, but they brought it back in 1964–67 as this comfortably equipped, big saloon.

△ **Rolls-Royce Phantom VI 1968**

Origin UK

Engine 6230 cc, V8

Top speed 101 mph (163 km/h)

Huge, heavy, and entirely custom-made, this was the ultimate status symbol for rock stars or royalty. Based on a 1950s design with twin headlamps added, 409 were built up to 1992.

◁ **Radford Mini De Ville 1963**

Origin UK

Engine 1,275 cc, straight-four

Top speed 95 mph (153 km/h)

Harold Radford coachbuilders offered Minis completely reworked with luxury interiors, tuned engines, and special exterior finishes. Customers included British actor Peter Sellers.

△ **Jaguar MkX 1962**

Origin UK

Engine 3,781 cc, straight-six

Top speed 120 mph (193 km/h)

A wide 1960s luxury model with monocoque construction, independent rear suspension, and wood and leather interior, this car was ideal for the US market.

△ **Daimler DS420 1968**

Origin UK

Engine 4,235 cc, straight-six

Top speed 110 mph (177 km/h)

Jaguar based this classy limousine on its MkX/420G platform but extended it at the back. This model was built by Vanden Plas, then by Jaguar from 1979 to 1992.

BMC Mini, 1968
One of the great enablers of the "classless society", the Mini was practical and enjoyable to drive. It appealed to aristocrats and personalities such as fashion model Twiggy, here driving the Mini in which she passed her driving test in 1968.

Austin Seven, 1920s

Great marques
The Austin story

A mainstay of the British motor industry until its demise in 1988, Austin introduced millions of ordinary people to the joys of motoring with models such as the Seven, A30, Mini, and Metro. Other highlights of the marque's history included Austin-Healey sports cars and the Maxi – Britain's first hatchback.

HERBERT AUSTIN, the son of a Buckinghamshire farmer, was born in 1866. When he was 17 a visiting Australian uncle persuaded him to return with him to Melbourne. There, Austin learned mechanical skills at an engineering firm by day, and studied art and design at night. In 1887 Austin became manager of a small Melbourne engineering company, through which he met Irish immigrant Frederick Wolseley, a manufacturer of sheep-shearing machines. Austin's firm made components for Wolseley, and together the two men refined the design of Wolseley's machines. When Wolseley decided to move to Britain, he took the 27-year-old Austin with him to set up a factory in Birmingham.

Under Austin's stewardship, the Wolseley Sheep Shearing Machine Company expanded profitably into machine tools and cycle parts. Austin's thoughts then turned to cars. He saw his first automobile in Paris in 1894, and the following year built a two-horsepower, three-wheeled

Austin badge
(introduced 1931)

prototype. The Wolseley board agreed to invest in Austin's venture, and the first Wolseley car was unveiled at the National Cycle Exhibition held at Crystal Palace, London, in 1896. Named the Wolseley Autocar Number 1, it completed a 250-mile (400-km) road test from Birmingham to Rhyl and back in 1898. The Wolseley Voiturette, a four-wheeled development of the Autocar, followed in 1899 and the next year won first prize in an Auto Club of Great Britain 1,000-mile (1,600-km) rally.

Herbert Austin yearned for his own car company, and in September 1905 he chose a disused printing works at Longbridge, near Birmingham, as the site for his factory. After assembling the necessary finance from banks and business contacts, he established the Austin Motor Company there in December 1905. Following a frenzied four months of activity, the first 20hp model left the works in April 1906. By the end of the year Austin's 50 workers had produced 26 cars. To market his cars, Herbert Austin opened showrooms in Norwich,

"The Austin"
Workers put finishing touches to Austin 12 saloons and vans at the Longbridge factory in 1947. The plant was affectionately referred to as "The Austin" by its workforce.

Manchester, and then London. He promised to "motorize the masses" and create "one huge machine in which cars are produced from start to finish". At one point the firm made everything on site apart from wheels and glass.

The company's meteoric growth in World War I was driven by orders for tanks, aircraft, and ammunition. The payroll had reached 20,000 by 1918, but in post-war Britain the dwindling demand for Austin's large, stately cars brought the firm to near-bankruptcy. As a last resort, Herbert Austin asked his staff to forgo their pay for a month; they did, and the company survived.

(although it would soon be overtaken by Volkswagen). Licensed manufacture of Austin cars had helped found BMW as a car maker in 1930s Germany, and it would also trigger massive growth at Nissan in Japan.

Austin and its close British rival, the Nuffield Organization, makers of Morris cars, merged in 1952 to form the British Motor Corporation (BMC). In the same year a joint venture with the automotive engineer and designer Donald Healey led to the Austin-Healey range of sports cars, beginning with the 100/4. The Austin-Healey association was to last for 20 years.

> "If a motor car is **British, best, and cheapest,** what more can anyone ask?"
>
> HERBERT AUSTIN, 1924

The marque found success in 1922 with the Austin Seven. It was ideally suited to the times, being a cheap and thrifty "real car in miniature". However, the Seven's low price also meant that the profit margin was slim. During World War II Austin continued building cars but also made trucks and aircraft, including Lancaster bombers. By the time of his death in 1941, Herbert Austin had manufactured more than 865,000 cars.

In 1947 the 1-millionth Austin was made, signed by the entire production force, and the firm's 2-millionth car rolled off the production line in 1952. By this stage, Austin was the world's largest exporter of cars to the US

In response to fuel shortages in the UK resulting from the 1956 Suez Crisis, BMC launched the compact and cheap-to-run Mini in 1959. Designed by Sir Alec Issigonis and produced under both the Austin and Morris marques, the Mini revolutionized small-car design with its front-wheel drive and transverse gearbox. The public fell in love with this quirky little car, and it remained in production until 2000.

Austin's Longbridge factory made 377,000 cars in 1965 – its highest annual output ever – with the main vehicles being the Mini and 1100/1300 ranges. BMC and Austin went through several further

AUSTIN SEVEN ULSTER

AUSTIN 12

AUSTIN-HEALEY 100/4

AUSTIN/MORRIS MINI

1905 Austin Motor Company established in Birmingham, UK.
1906 The first Austin, the 20hp, is launched featuring a vertical engine and a rear-mounted fuel tank.
1922 The Austin Seven is the smallest four-cylinder car on sale in Britain.
1930 An American-built version of the Austin Seven goes on sale.
1932 The Austin 12 is introduced, quickly becoming one of the best-selling familycars on the British market.

1936 Austin builds its own single-seater racing car with a double-overhead-camshaft, 750cc engine.
1945 The 16 saloon is Austin's first production model to have an overhead-valve engine.
1948 The A90 Atlantic tries unsuccessfully to win US customers.
1951 The 803cc A30 economy car is a big hit; it is also Austin's first model with a monocoque construction (integrated chassis and body).

1952 Launch of the Austin-Healey sports-car range with the 100/4; Austin and Nuffield Organization merge to form the British Motor Corporation (BMC).
1954 Austin begins building the Metropolitan for Nash Motors.
1958 The A40 is notable for its styling by the Italian company Pinin Farina.
1959 The Austin/Morris Mini is a landmark design for a small car.
1962 The Austin/Morris 1100 family car features novel Hydrolastic suspension.

1968 Austin is now part of British Leyland.
1969 Britain's first hatchback, the Austin Maxi, goes on sale.
1973 The Austin Allegro family car debuts.
1980 The Metro is introduced.
1982 British Leyland becomes Austin Rover.
1983 The Maestro offers a "talking dashboard" with a voice synthesizer that alerts drivers to problems.
1984 The Montego is the last new model produced under the Austin marque.
1988 The last Austin car is made.

Cheap and cheerful
Launched in 1951, the curvy little A30 was designed to replace the Austin Seven and compete with the Morris Minor. It sold well, its low cost making it a first car for many families.

amalgamations in the mid-1960s, leading to the creation in 1968 of the British Leyland conglomerate. Although cars with the Austin name continued to be produced by British Leyland, the 1970s proved to be a chequered time for the marque, with the Austin Allegro of 1973 suffering from poor design and quality. Facing insolvency, British Leyland was nationalized in 1975.

Amid the gloom there were notable successes. The Metro supermini of 1980 – the first Austin model to be built with the aid of computers and welding robots – proved a credible rival to the Ford Fiesta and Renault 5.

Still struggling, British Leyland was rebranded as Austin Rover in 1982. Austin remained the mainstream brand, with sporty editions being given the MG badge; the Rover marque concentrated on more luxurious models. Launched in 1983, the Maestro – the five-door hatchback that replaced the Allegro and Maxi

models – captured a sizable slice of the family-car market in the UK. The Montego of 1984 was the last model to be launched under the Austin banner. The marque name was axed in 1988, two years after Austin Rover was privatized and sold to British Aerospace, becoming the Rover Group. All cars made thereafter were badged either as Rovers or MGs.

Austin Maxi, 1969
The five-door, five-speed Maxi was the last car designed by Sir Alec Issigonis. This publicity photo emphasises the leisure opportunities opened up by Britain's first hatchback.

Compact Coupés

Small, specialist manufacturers created many GT cars in Europe in the 1960s, which, owing to their ingenuity and inventiveness, rivalled those of the big car makers. Hardtop coupés became increasingly popular, and trends towards front-wheel drive or even mid-engine layouts were appearing. Aerodynamic testing produced some very efficient shapes.

◁ **TVR Grantura 1958**

Origin UK

Engine 1,798 cc, straight-four

Top speed 108 mph (174 km/h)

The TVR wasn't styled, it grew. Its cheeky, chunky looks and lively performance due to its light weight brought small yet steady volume sales and competition success into the 1960s.

△ **Porsche 356B 1959**

Origin Germany

Engine 1,582 cc, flat-four

Top speed 111 mph (179 km/h)

By 1960 Porsche's brilliant VW-based sports car of 1950 had moved a long way from its roots. This sophisticated 2+2 coupé was well built and reassuringly expensive.

△ **Gilbern GT 1959**

Origin UK

Engine 1,622 cc, straight-four

Top speed 100 mph (161 km/h)

Wales' only successful carmaker used a spaceframe chassis, attractive glassfibre body, and high quality interiors to sell this handsome MGA/B/Midget-powered coupé.

△ **Volvo P1800 1961**

Origin Sweden

Engine 1,778 cc, straight-four

Top speed 106 mph (171 km/h)

Initially assembled in Britain by Jensen, but soon transferred to Sweden to improve quality, the P1800 was a stylish and incredibly durable two-seat Grand Tourer.

△ **NSU Sport Prinz 1959**

Origin Germany

Engine 598 cc, straight-two

Top speed 76 mph (122 km/h)

Italian styling house Bertone worked wonders to create this winsome little coupé for the bravely independent NSU. Over 20,000 were sold in the 1960s.

△ **Ogle SX1000 1962**

Origin UK

Engine 1,275 cc, straight-four

Top speed 110 mph (177 km/h)

Industrial designer David Ogle designed this bubble-like coupé, which successfully hid the Mini-Cooper running gear below. Sadly, few were made.

△ **Matra Djet 1962**

Origin France

Engine 1,108 cc, straight-four

Top speed 118 mph (190 km/h)

Designed by René Bonnet and built by Matra, the aerodynamic Djet pioneered the mid-engine layout for roadgoing sports cars, and was fast with Renault Gordini power.

◁ **Marcos 1800 1964**

Origin UK

Engine 1,778 cc, straight-four

Top speed 115 mph (185 km/h)

Dennis Adams styled this ultra-low two-seater, with fixed lay-back seats and adjustable pedals. A wide range of engines found their way under the long, low bonnet.

△ **Broadspeed GT 1965**

Origin UK

Engine 1,275 cc, straight-four

Top speed 113 mph (182 km/h)

Broadspeed founder Ralph Broad took the Mini Cooper 1275S and added a glassfibre fastback rear body that, with some engine tuning, made it a real flyer.

◁ **Ford Consul Capri 1961**

Origin UK

Engine 1,498 cc, straight-four

Top speed 83 mph (134 km/h)

Ford's first attempt to make a sporty coupé for Europe just didn't catch on – it was far too American in its styling. Only 18,000 were sold in three years.

◁ **Lancia Fulvia Coupé 1965**

Origin Italy

Engine 1,216 cc, V4

Top speed 100 mph (161 km/h)

Lancia flouted convention with beautifully built, compact, twin-cam V4 engines and front-wheel drive in designer Pietro Castagnero's 2+2 coupé – the last true Lancia.

△ **Ford Capri 1969**

Origin UK

Engine 1,599 cc, straight-four

Top speed 100 mph (161 km/h)

Five years after the Mustang took the US market by storm, Ford managed the same in Europe with the brilliant Capri, helped by engine options from 1,300 cc to 3,000 cc.

◁ **Lotus Elan +2 1967**

Origin UK

Engine 1,558 cc, straight-four

Top speed 123 mph (198 km/h)

Not wanting to lose its keen two-seater buyers when they started families, Lotus developed this upmarket 2+2 Elan, still on the superb-handling, backbone chassis.

△ **Saab Sonett 1966**

Origin Sweden

Engine 1,498 cc, V4

Top speed 100 mph (161 km/h)

Front-wheel drive, a freewheel, and a column gearchange were unusual features derived from the Sonett's saloon parent, but the neat glassfibre body looked good.

△ **Triumph GT6 1966**

Origin UK

Engine 1,998 cc, straight-six

Top speed 112 mph (180 km/h)

Triumph neatly combined the Spitfire chassis and 2000 engine in a pretty, Michelotti-styled body to make the GT6, soon dubbed a "mini E-type". This is the 1970 restyle.

△ **Unipower GT 1966**

Origin UK

Engine 1,275 cc, straight-four

Top speed 119 mph (192 km/h)

The best-looking Mini-based sports car of all, the Unipower had its Mini engine over the rear wheels in a lightweight spaceframe chassis bonded to its glassfibre body.

◁ **Alfa Romeo 1750 GTV 1967**

Origin Italy

Engine 1,779 cc, straight-four

Top speed 116 mph (187 km/h)

Alfa Romeo's Giulia series, launched in 1962–63, was hugely successful. This car was the perfect compact four-seater sporting coupé, with twin-cam power and great handling.

△ **Sunbeam Rapier H120 1969**

Origin UK

Engine 1,725 cc, straight-four

Top speed 106 mph (171 km/h)

Sunbeam's US ownership was clear in the Plymouth Barracuda-derived styling, but the Rapier became an effective sports coupé with Holbay tuning.

Powerful GT Cars

In terms of performance, the most powerful GT cars of the 1960s were on a par with their equivalents today, so efficient were their aerodynamics and engineering. Modern supercar drivers might notice differences in electronic gadgetry, soundproofing, and driver aids – but not in performance. The 1960s also produced some of the finest styling ever seen in this genre.

△ Bristol 407 1962
Origin UK
Engine 5,130 cc, V8
Top speed 122 mph (196 km/h)

The British Bristol marque used a Chrysler V8 engine in the 407, giving this upmarket four-seater the power it needed to merit its pretensions as a status symbol.

△ Aston Martin DB5 1964
Origin UK
Engine 3,995 cc, straight-six
Top speed 148 mph (238 km/h)

Adding the cowled headlamps from the DB4 GT created a much sportier look for the DB5, which was justified by an upgrade to a 314 bhp Vantage engine and a five-speed ZF gearbox.

◁ Aston Martin DB6 1965
Origin UK
Engine 3,995 cc, straight-six
Top speed 140 mph (225 km/h)

The body of this luxurious, heavy model was slightly more spacious than that of the DB5. The flick-up tail balanced the cowled-light front and improved aerodynamic stability.

△ Ferrari 400 GT Superamerica 1961
Origin Italy
Engine 3,967 cc, V12
Top speed 160 mph (257 km/h)

Each 400 Superamerica was built to order and customized for individual owners. With an aerodynamic body styled by Pininfarina, the GT gave shattering levels of performance.

△ Ferrari 275GTB 1965
Origin Italy
Engine 3,286 cc, V12
Top speed 153 mph (246 km/h)

Perfectly proportioned styling by Pininfarina, a five-speed gearbox, and all-independent suspension showed that Ferrari was moving with the times; six-carburettor versions did 165mph (265 km/h).

△ Chevrolet Corvette Sting Ray 1963
Origin USA
Engine 5,360 cc, V8
Top speed 147 mph (237 km/h)

A dramatic 1963 restyling gave the Corvette a new, aerodynamic profile, with the headlamps hidden behind electrically operated panels. For the first time it was offered as a hardtop coupé as well as a convertible.

△ Dino 246GT 1969
Origin Italy
Engine 2,418 cc, V6
Top speed 148 mph (238 km/h)

Enzo Ferrari named this mid-engined two-seater after his son Dino, who died in 1956; later versions went out under simply the Ferrari name. The stunning styling is by Pininfarina.

▷ Jaguar E-type 1961
Origin UK
Engine 3,781cc, straight-six
Top speed 140 mph (225 km/h)

With the E-type, Jaguar's Malcolm Sayer and William Lyons created one of the most beautiful and effective sports cars of all time. The E-type was just as at home on the road as it was on the racetrack.

△ Facel Vega Facel II 1962
Origin France
Engine 6,286 cc, V8
Top speed 133 mph (214 km/h)

Big, bold, unquestionably French, and powered by a Chrysler V8, the Facel II was firmly in the Grand Routier tradition. Only 180 of this expensive, exclusive car were made.

△ **Ford Mustang GT500 1967**

Origin USA

Engine 7,010 cc, V8

Top speed 134 mph (216 km/h)

Carroll Shelby shoe-horned the big-block Ford V8 engine into the Mustang to create the 355 bhp GT500, which offered serious hot-rod performance in a luxury package.

△ **Gordon-Keeble 1964**

Origin UK

Engine 5,395 cc, V8

Top speed 136 mph (219 km/h)

British engineering, a powerful American V8 engine, and delicately beautiful Italian styling by Bertone created this excellent GT, which some see as offering the perfect combination of speed and style.

△ **Iso Grifo A3C 1965**

Origin Italy

Engine 5359 cc, V8

Top speed 170 mph (274 km/h)

Giotto Bizzarrini designed the Grifo A3C for racing, and it triumphed in its category at Le Mans in 1965. It was based on Bizzarrini's stunning V8-powered Grifo two-seat coupé.

△ **Lamborghini 400GT Monza 1966**

Origin Italy

Engine 3,929 cc, V12

Top speed 156 mph (251 km/h)

Lamborghini and Ferrari fought a constant battle to be the top Italian supercar brand. The 400GT's four-cam V12 engine was far more advanced than anything Ferari could offer. The Monza was a one-off edition of the car.

△ **Lamborghini Miura 1966**

Origin Italy

Engine 3,929 cc, V12

Top speed 177 mph (285 km/h)

Lamborghini eclipsed Ferrari when it introduced the outstanding Miura, the first practical, mid-engined supercar. The breathtaking styling was by Marcello Gandini for Bertone.

◁ **Lamborghini Islero 1968**

Origin Italy

Engine 3,929 cc, V12

Top speed 160 mph (257 km/h)

This simple and elegant restyling of the 2+2 Lamborghini 400GT was by Carrozzeria Marazzi. Unfortunately, it lacked the commercial appeal that the top stylists could create.

△ **Jensen Interceptor 1967**

Origin UK

Engine 6,276 cc, V8

Top speed 133 mph (214 km/h)

Jensen commissioned the Italian styling company Vignale to design a new body for this Chrysler V8-engined coupé. The result was a truly elegant, practical 2+2.

▷ **Studebaker Avanti 1962**

Origin USA

Engine 4,736 cc, V8

Top speed 120 mph (193 km/h)

The fibreglass-bodied Avanti was a bold move for a small manufacturer such as Studebaker, but it failed to save the company. Small numbers were made privately until 1991.

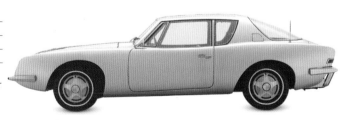

◁ **Maserati Ghibli 1967**

Origin Italy

Engine 4,719 cc, V8

Top speed 154 mph (248 km/h)

Maserati's magnificent four-cam V8 engine enabled this luxurious coupé to perform like a supercar. The car's perfectly proportioned fastback body was styled by Ghia of Italy.

Volkswagen crash test dummies, *c.*1968
With the emergence of strict safety regulations in the 1960s, the responsibility for car safety shifted from the consumer to the manufacturer. Safety features, such as seat belts, became widely tested using life-size plastic dummies.

Sports Cars

Despite a wide choice of attractive, often extremely potent models, the open sports car was in decline in the 1960s as the popularity of civilized, closed-top Grand Touring cars grew: the vast majority of these sports cars were launched in the first half of the decade and many were conceived in the 1950s. Japan now joined the US and Europe on the world market.

△ **MG Midget 1961**

Origin UK

Engine 948 cc, straight-four

Top speed 86 mph (138 km/h)

Tiny, cute, and enormous fun to drive at speeds much lower than it feels, the Midget was a true fun car and was built – with engines up to 1,500 cc – into the 1980s.

△ **Ferrari 250 California Spider 1959**

Origin Italy

Engine 2,953 cc, V12

Top speed 145 mph (233 km/h)

One of the most beautiful and desirable Ferraris ever made, now worth millions, the California Spider was a car of film stars, and became something of a film star itself.

△ **Jaguar E-type 1961**

Origin UK

Engine 3,781 cc, straight-six

Top speed 149 mph (240 km/h)

With double-overhead-camshaft engine, all-disc brakes, and all-independent suspension, the E-type was a bargain compared with other 1960s supercars.

△ **Maserati Mistral Spider 1963**

Origin Italy

Engine 3,692 cc, straight-six

Top speed 145 mph (233 km/h)

Maserati fuel-injected its twin-cam six to get Jaguar-level performance and commissioned Frua to design this understated and sophisticated two-seat body.

△ **Lotus Super Seven 1961**

Origin UK

Engine 1,498 cc, straight-four

Top speed 103 mph (166 km/h)

The Seven was a 1950s design that refused to die, thanks to uncompromising, timeless styling and fabulous, seat-of-the-pants handling. Versions are still made today.

▷ **Lotus Elan 1962**

Origin UK

Engine 1,558 cc, straight-four

Top speed 122 mph (196 km/h)

Lotus cars were engineered for lightness, giving terrific performance. The glassfibre Elan sat on a steel backbone chassis and it went – and handled – superbly.

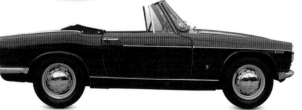

◁ **Austin-Healey 3000 MkIII 1963**

Origin UK

Engine 2,912 cc, straight-six

Top speed 121 mph (195 km/h)

Introduced in 1953 with a four-cylinder engine, the "Big Healey" grew up into a comfortable 2+2 touring sports car. Its low build and swooping curves had huge appeal.

◁ **Innocenti Spider 1961**

Origin Italy

Engine 948 cc, straight-four

Top speed 86 mph (138 km/h)

Innocenti of Milan commissioned Ghia to style a more upmarket body for British Austin-Healey Sprite running gear, with a bootlid, wind-up windows, and a heater.

▷ **Mercedes-Benz 230SL 1963**

Origin Germany

Engine 2,306 cc, straight-six

Top speed 120 mph (193 km/h)

The 230SL may look a sophisticated touring car with its pagoda roof and automatic option, but it won the gruelling Liège-Sofia-Liège rally in 1963: they don't come tougher.

△ **MGB 1962**

Origin UK

Engine 1,798 cc, straight-four

Top speed 103 mph (166 km/h)

Britain's best-selling sports car sold over half a million in 1962–80. Rugged, reliable, and long-legged, it was a perfectly proportioned, truly practical enthusiast's car.

△ **Triumph TR4A 1964**

Origin UK

Engine 2,138 cc, straight-four

Top speed 109 mph (175 km/h)

Designer Giovanni Michelotti restyled the separate-chassis TR sports car for 1961 and Triumph added independent rear suspension in 1964.

△ **Sunbeam Tiger 1964**

Origin UK

Engine 4,261 cc, V8

Top speed 117 mph (188 km/h)

Carroll Shelby helped Rootes develop the Tiger from the excellent Sunbeam Alpine. The new engine gave it all the power it needed to fly, winning races and rallies.

△ **Chevrolet Corvette Sting Ray 1965**

Origin USA

Engine 5,360 cc, V8

Top speed 147 mph (237 km/h)

A stunning restyle in 1963 turned Corvette into Sting Ray, with ultra-modern lines oozing macho potential, fulfilled in the ultimate 375 bhp fuel-injected "L84" model.

△ **AC Cobra 427 1965**

Origin USA/UK

Engine 6,997 cc, V8

Top speed 164 mph (264 km/h)

Designer Carroll Shelby had the idea to put the Ford V8 in the pretty British AC Ace – and topped it with this big block version, a road-legal race car with monstrous acceleration.

▽ **Datsun Fairlady 1965**

Origin Japan

Engine 1,595 cc, straight-four

Top speed 100 mph (161 km/h)

Derived from the 1,500 cc predecessor of 1961, this MGB-beater from Japan was superbly built and tempted US drivers to consider buying Japanese cars.

◁ **Alfa Romeo Duetto Spider 1966**

Origin Italy

Engine 1,570 cc, straight-four

Top speed 111 mph (179 km/h)

Battista Pininfarina styled this exceptionally lovely roadster, which is also a joy to drive with a lively double overhead camshaft engine and all-disc brakes. It continued into the 1990s.

▽ **Fiat Dino Spider 1967**

Origin Italy

Engine 1,987 cc, V6

Top speed 127 mph (204 km/h)

Pininfarina styled this gorgeous Spider, which boasted a Ferrari V6 engine and five-speed gearbox; had it been badged Ferrari, not Fiat, sales would have doubled.

△ **Vignale Gamine 1967**

Origin Italy

Engine 499 cc, straight-two

Top speed 60 mph (97 km/h)

Recognizable to millions of children as Noddy's car, Vignale's Gamine fun car was based on Fiat 500 running gear. But it was too expensive to sell well.

Mercedes-Benz 280SL

The Mercedes-Benz SL class of sports roadsters from the 1960s were known for their supremely elegant styling. Also referred to as W113 within the company, they were manufactured from 1963 to 1971. The "pagoda roof" 230SL of 1963 offered good performance and exceptional handling, together with comfort and sophistication. It was followed by the larger-engined 250SL in 1967, and the 280SL in 1968. Both offered more power but retained the SL's signature styling.

THE MERCEDES-BENZ SL was defined by the graceful styling of its optional hardtop. The 230SL, 250SL, and 280SL models had roofs with raised outer edges. Some commentators likened this shape to the roofs of Chinese buildings, and the "pagoda roof" nickname was born. Styled by Mercedes' master designer Paul Bracq, the car's compactness and elegance was emphasized by its low build and wide track. The SL carried over its basic structural layout from the 1959 Heckflosse or Fintail saloon. It had a steel body welded to a strong load-bearing floorpan, and a protective cage around the cabin with "crumple zones" at the front and rear that absorbed impact. The first sports car in the world with this new safety technology, the SL was the safest roadster of its era.

The original 2,306 cc, 150 bhp, six-cylinder engine of the SL underwent two revisions. In 1967 it was replaced by a longer-stroke, 2,496 cc engine offering more torque. The fuel tank was enlarged and disc rear brakes were added. The 1968 version, shown here, was fitted with a bigger-bore, 2,778 cc M130 engine, which powered the SL until 1971.

SPECIFICATIONS	
Model	Mercedes-Benz 280SL W113 (1968–71)
Assembly	Stuttgart, Germany
Production	23,885
Construction	Unitary steel chassis
Engine	2,778 cc, sohc straight-six
Power output	170 bhp at 5,750 rpm
Transmission	Four-speed automatic
Suspension	Coil spring
Brakes	Discs front and rear
Maximum speed	124 mph (200 km/h)

A German alliance
Daimler and Benz were motor car pioneers of the 19th century. The merger of Daimler (the manufacturer of Mercedes cars) and Benz came in 1926. The Mercedes-Benz badge combines the three-pointed star of Daimler with the Benz laurel wreath.

FRONT VIEW

REAR VIEW

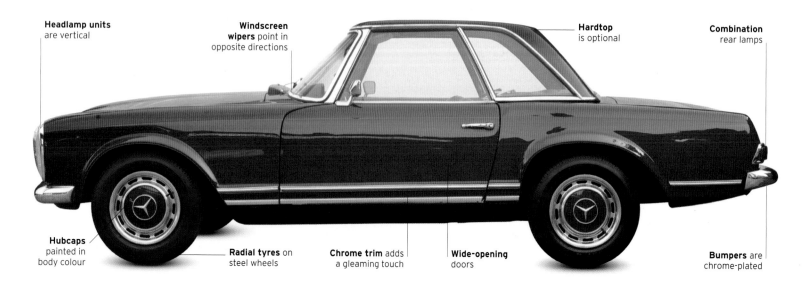

Headlamp units are vertical

Windscreen wipers point in opposite directions

Hardtop is optional

Combination rear lamps

Hubcaps painted in body colour

Radial tyres on steel wheels

Chrome trim adds a gleaming touch

Wide-opening doors

Bumpers are chrome-plated

Sports car sophistication
With its low, wide stance, Lichtenheit, bold vertical lights, and an over-sized three-pointed star, the 280SL shown here, set out its stall as a sophisticated, luxurious, highly personal car that was all about quality and taste. With smooth six-cylinder power and excellent road manners, it had the performance to match its looks.

THE EXTERIOR

The 280SL's styling was a combination of elegance, fine proportion, and just enough ostentation to show what the owner's money had purchased. It was very different from the cars it replaced, the fast but expensive 300SL roadster, and the affordable but slower 190SL with a removable hardtop.

1. Mercedes-Benz three-pointed star logos are prominent
2. 280SL was the last variant of the W113 3. Vertical lights similar to those on Mercedes saloons 4. Safety door handle
5. Filler cap on the tail 6. Opposed windscreen wipers 7. Chrome plating on doors 8. Chrome-rimmed tail light 9. Twin exhaust on all models 10. Steel wheels with body colour hubcaps

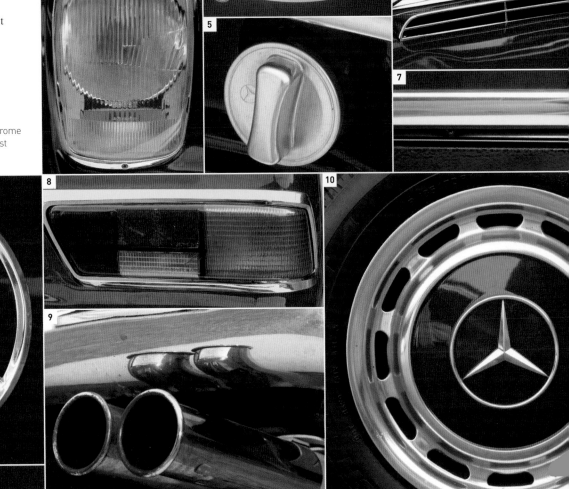

THE INTERIOR

Diehard sports-car enthusiasts were not impressed by the 280SL – it seemed too civilized. The doors opened wide on to a well-trimmed interior, with full carpeting and a choice of vinyl or leather seats. An oddments tray between the seats with an ashtray at the front was a novelty. Chrome trim appeared everywhere, from the steering wheel to the dashboard and even to the seat adjustment controls. The dashboard painted to match the exterior was yet more evidence of Mercedes-Benz's meticulous design approach.

11. Interiors trimmed in leather or vinyl 12. Inner metal ring on the steering wheel acts as horn push
13. Wooden windscreen air vent 14. Spacious glovebox 15. Dashboard air vent 16. Seat controls
17. Automatic transmission selector 18. Sideways facing "jump seat" was optional

UNDER THE BONNET

The engine of the original 230SL was derived from the 230 saloon. It was a 2.3-litre overhead-camshaft, in-line six-cylinder with an alloy block and alloy cylinder head, and four-bearing crankshaft. In 1967 this was replaced by a 2.5-litre, which was more than just a long-stroke version of the same engine. It had seven main bearings for greater smoothness and reliability, though this also made it less eager to rev. For the 280SL, Mercedes moved the cylinders further apart to accommodate larger 8.65 cm (3.3 in) bores, giving 2,778 cc and 170 bhp.

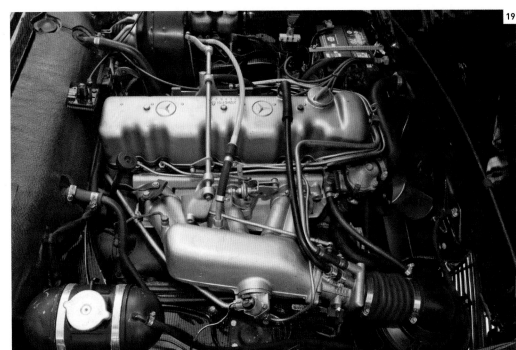

19. The 280SL had the largest engine in the W113 series, a 2.8-litre in-line six; like its predecessors – the 230SL and 250SL – it was fuel-injected

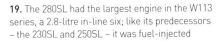

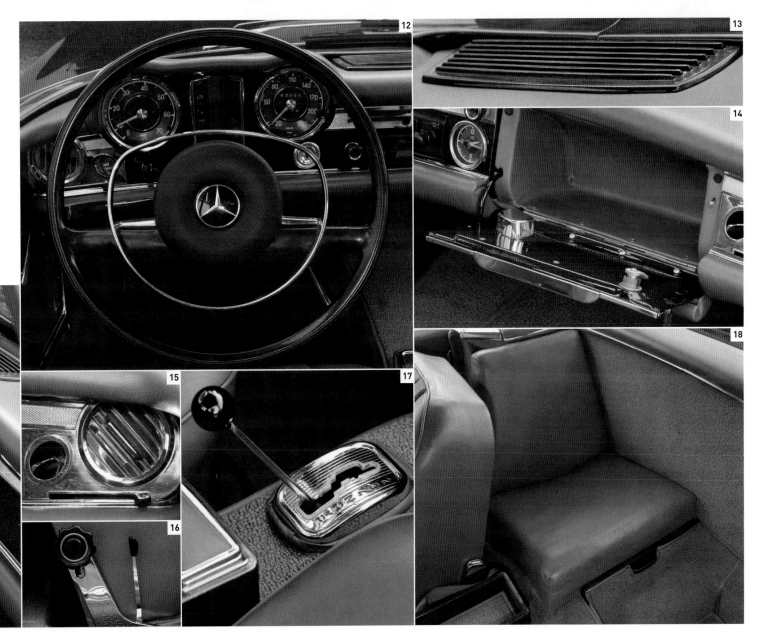

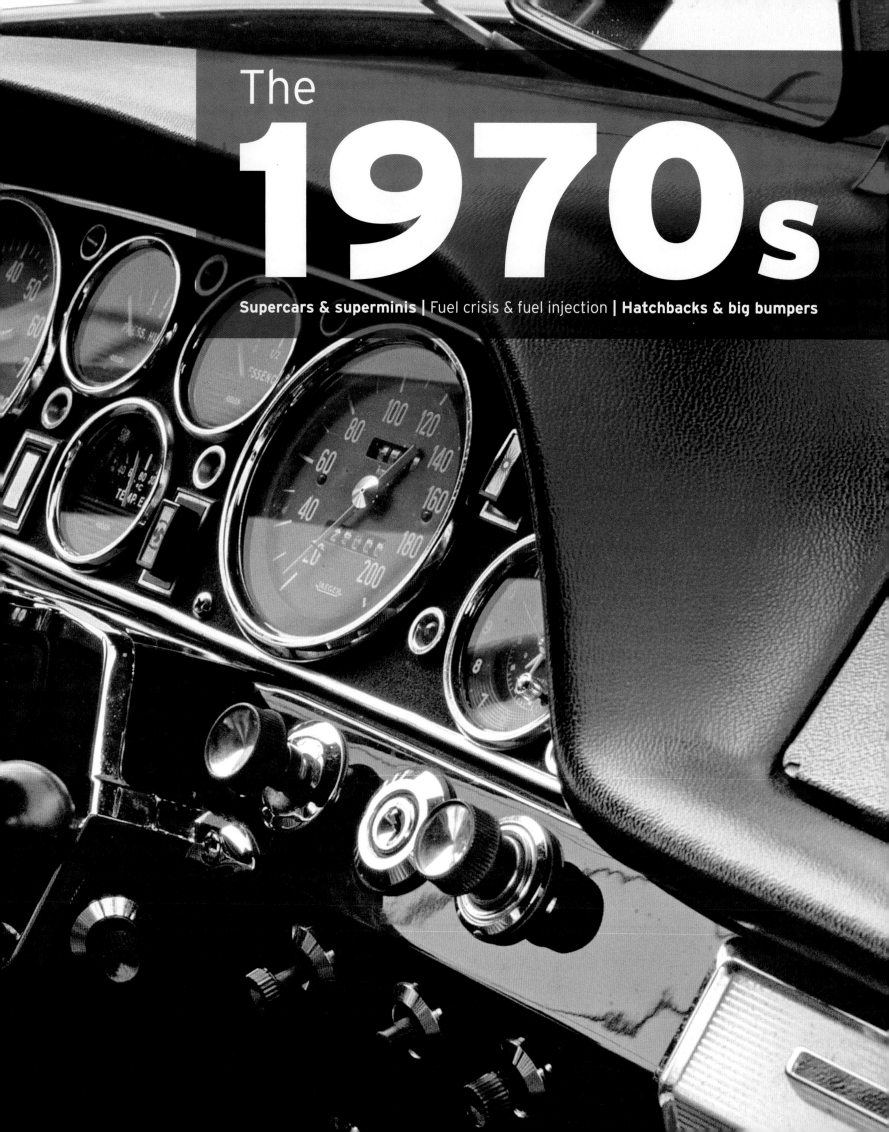

The
1970s

Supercars & superminis | Fuel crisis & fuel injection | **Hatchbacks & big bumpers**

Supercars

The 1970s saw a dramatic shift in car styling away from the flowing curves of the 1960s. Now stark, sharp-edged lines were epitomized by the dramatic wedge profiles that swept the motor show circuit. As television boosted the influence of motor racing, supercars were created by manufacturers who had never made them before, to homologate cars that would grab race-winning headlines.

△ Monteverdi 375C 1967

Origin Switzerland/Italy

Engine 7,206 cc, V8

Top speed 155 mph (249 km/h)

Switzerland's only carmaker commissioned Fissore to style his cars and Frua to build them, with Chrysler "hemi" engines. Only a handful were custom-built annually until 1973.

▷ De Tomaso Pantera 1969

Origin Italy

Engine 5,763 cc, V8

Top speed 160 mph (257 km/h)

A big block Ford V8 in an Italian suit, was styled by Ghia and built by De Tomaso in Italy, initially in partnership with Ford USA. It was so stunning, it was built into the 1990s.

◁ Ferrari 365GTB/4 Daytona 1968

Origin Italy

Engine 4,390 cc, V12

Top speed 174 mph (280 km/h)

The last and fastest of Ferrari's front-engine, rear-drive two-seaters had its heyday in the early 1970s: the 365GTB/4 is simple, brutal, and stunningly effective.

▽ Citroën SM 1970

Origin France

Engine 2,670 cc, V6

Top speed 142 mph (229 km/h)

When Citroën bought Maserati, this was the result: an aerodynamic and hydropneumatic French supercar with a powerful Italian V6 engine.

▷ Ferrari 400GT 1976

Origin Italy

Engine 4,823 cc, V12

Top speed 156 mph (251 km/h)

This executive four-seater is a civilized car with an automatic gearbox, and capable of exceeding 150 mph (241 km/h). A fine Ferrari, even if not as exotic as most.

◁ Ferrari 308 GTS 1978

Origin Italy

Engine 2,926 cc, V8

Top speed 155 mph (249 km/h)

Ferrari dropped the Dino name for its 1970s small sports car and gave it a new four-cam V8, mid-mounted as in the 246GT, with a Pininfarina-styled hardtop or targa body.

▷ Lancia Stratos 1973

Origin Italy

Engine 2,418 cc, V6

Top speed 143 mph (230 km/h)

Lancia's first pure sports car, built to homologate the model for rallying, this Bertone-styled supercar with Dino Ferrari power unit was a winner from the start.

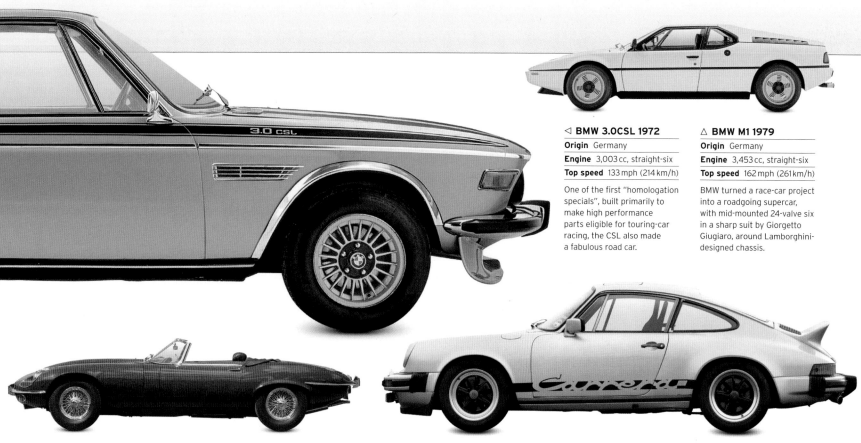

◁ BMW 3.0CSL 1972
Origin Germany

Engine 3,003 cc, straight-six

Top speed 133 mph (214 km/h)

One of the first "homologation specials", built primarily to make high performance parts eligible for touring-car racing, the CSL also made a fabulous road car.

△ BMW M1 1979
Origin Germany

Engine 3,453 cc, straight-six

Top speed 162 mph (261 km/h)

BMW turned a race-car project into a roadgoing supercar, with mid-mounted 24-valve six in a sharp suit by Giorgetto Giugiaro, around Lamborghini-designed chassis.

△ Jaguar E-type Series III 1971
Origin UK

Engine 5,343 cc, V12

Top speed 150 mph (241 km/h)

To replace the XK engine, Jaguar needed something special, with more than six cylinders: what better than this aluminium V12 in an enlarged E-type shell?

△ Porsche 911 1973
Origin Germany

Engine 2,994 cc, flat-six

Top speed 141 mph (227 km/h)

For 1975, Porsche's 911 gained impact-absorbing bumpers to keep it legal in the US; this example has been customized to resemble the earlier 2.7 Carrera RS, which is now a highly-coveted model.

▷ Porsche 934-5 1976
Origin Germany

Engine 2,994 cc, flat-six

Top speed 190 mph (306 km/h)

Derived from the 911 Turbo road car, the 934 was a highly successful sports racer, winning championships in Europe, the US, and Australia into the early 1980s.

△ Mercedes-Benz C111-II 1970
Origin Germany

Engine 4,800 cc (four-rotor Wankel)

Top speed 186 mph (300 km/h)

Mercedes' C111s were experimental cars, starting with a three-rotor Wankel-engined car in 1969. This Phase II version had 350 bhp, but fuel consumption was huge.

◁ Lamborghini Countach LP400 1974
Origin Italy

Engine 3,929 cc, V12

Top speed 170 mph (274 km/h)

When Bertone styled this ultimate wedge-shaped supercar, it could hardly have expected it to enter production and continue being made well into the 1990s.

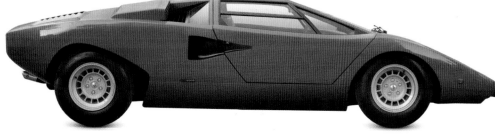

▽ Alfa Romeo Navajo 1976
Origin Italy

Engine 1,995 cc, V8

Top speed 155 mph (249 km/h)

Bertone used the Alfa Romeo Tipo 33 racing car chassis for this dramatic wedge concept car. Its front and rear spoilers change angle as speed rises.

▷ Vauxhall SRV concept 1970
Origin UK

Engine 2,279 cc, straight-four

Top speed 140 mph (225 km/h)

General Motors sent Wayne Cherry to the UK to shake up Vauxhall's styling department. This concept heralded a "droop-snoot" look across the production range.

▷ Aston Martin V8 1972
Origin UK

Engine 5,340 cc, V8

Top speed 162 mph (261 km/h)

The big, macho Aston Martin V8 with 282–438 bhp was sharply styled by William Towns and proved a huge success, continuing in production for two decades.

◁ Lotus Esprit Turbo 1980
Origin UK

Engine 2,174 cc, straight-four

Top speed 148 mph (238 km/h)

Lotus road cars reached supercar status when the exotic Giugiaro-styled Esprit, introduced in 1976, gained a turbocharger, making this light car fly.

Jaguar E-type

Lusted after by generations of motor enthusiasts, the E-type caused a sensation on its 1961 introduction. Sexily styled and technically advanced, the Jaguar promised 150 mph (241 km/h) performance for a fraction of the cost of exotic Italian rivals, and made cars such as the Aston Martin DB4 seem overpriced and under-endowed. As a symbol of the Swinging Sixties, nothing – not even the Mini – comes close. Latterly, the E-type put on middle-aged spread, and the final runs of V12s proved difficult to shift in the key US market.

WITH ITS racing-inspired looks, the E-type could be excused anything. But no excuses were necessary: under the skin it was more sophisticated than any rival. The monocoque body tub, joined to a bolt-on, square-tube front structure, evoked that of the D-type racer. The suspension used torsion bars at the front, but at the rear there was a new, all-independent set-up using coil springs and four dampers. The result was excellent roadholding allied to a genuinely subtle ride, at a time when most sports cars had board-firm suspension. The E-type's engine,

inherited from the preceeding XK150 model, was a 3,781 cc version of Jaguar's famed XK twin-cam straight-six. In 1964 this gave way to a 4,235 cc unit, and the slow-changing gearbox – made by a long-time Jaguar supplier – was replaced by a unit of Jaguar's own design. Two years later a longer-wheelbase 2+2 – with a higher roofline and a taller, more upright windscreen – joined the roadster and two-seater coupé. This longer chassis formed the basis of the V12-powered Series III that was introduced in 1971 to replace the 1968-on Series II.

SPECIFICATIONS	
Model	Jaguar E-type, Series III, 1971-74
Assembly	Coventry, England
Production	72,507
Construction	Steel monocoque
Engine	5,343 cc, ohc V12 (Series III)
Power output	272 bhp at 5,850 rpm (Series III)
Transmission	Four-speed manual; optional auto
Suspension	Independent; torsion-bar front
Brakes	Four-wheel discs
Maximum speed	150 mph (241 km/h)

From Swallow to Jaguar
Jaguar began life as a maker of motorcycle side-cars under the Swallow name. Cars under its own banner arrived in 1931 with the SS1, and in 1935 the SS Jaguar was launched. After World War II the "SS" prefix was dropped for its negative connotations.

FRONT VIEW

REAR VIEW

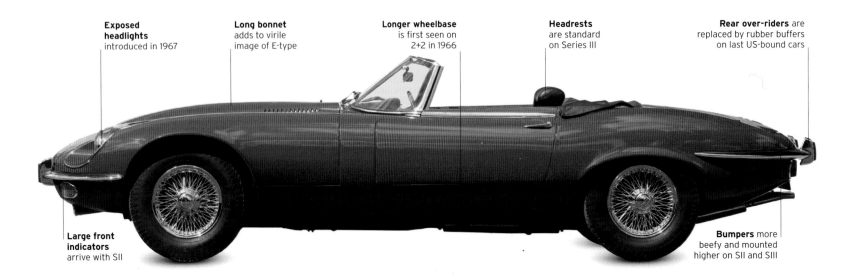

Exposed headlights introduced in 1967

Long bonnet adds to virile image of E-type

Longer wheelbase is first seen on 2+2 in 1966

Headrests are standard on Series III

Rear over-riders are replaced by rubber buffers on last US-bound cars

Large front indicators arrive with SII

Bumpers more beefy and mounted higher on SII and SIII

Compromising on form
The Series III iteration of the E-type was a softer, less overtly aggressive makeover of the 10-year-old original. New features included subtly flared-out wheelarches and a "bird cage" radiator grille. The huge hump in the bonnet top accommodated the V12 engine. As before, there was no place for a number plate – it was usually sported in the form of a large sticker. There was still no other car like it on the road, including in the US where this example featured in a scene from the British-financed 1978 movie *Convoy!*.

THE EXTERIOR

Even in lengthened and over-embellished Series III form, the E-type remains voluptuously impressive. Created by Jaguar stylist and aerodynamicist Malcolm Sayer, the basic long-nosed lines are a development of the shape of the D-type racers that were so successful at the Le Mans 24-hour race in France. At this time all Jaguar styling was evolved with the active participation of marque founder Sir William Lyons, who had a keen eye for design.

1. Jaguar emblem is only found on grille badge **2.** All SIIIs are V12 – although a straight-six was envisaged **3.** Exposed headlights more efficient, but less attractive **4.** "Bird's cage" grille **5.** Typically sparing, yet stylish door handle **6.** Knock-on hubs on optional wire wheels no longer have ears **7.** Bonnet louvres help evacuate engine heat **8.** Fuel filler always under flap on E-type **9.** Bigger tail lights – shared with some Lotuses – come in with 1968 SII **10.** V12's flamboyant four-exit exhaust gives way to twin-pipe design in 1973

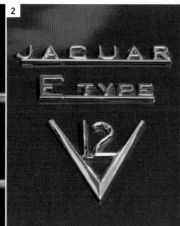

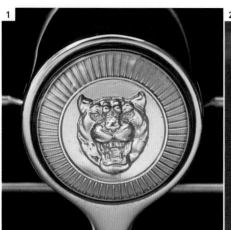

THE INTERIOR

The E-type was never spartan, but from the introduction of the 4.2-litre model in 1964, the interior became a little more plush. Most notably it gained more comfortable seats, square-backed in place of the previous buckets, with headrests as standard on the Series III. It is only 3.8-litre cars that have a patterned-alloy dashboard centre section, accompanied by an alloy-topped centre console on early versions.

11. Interior of SIII largely as SII, but leather-rimmed steering wheel is new **12.** Classic white-on-black instruments are typical Jaguar **13.** E-type always has dials with non-reflecting black rims **14.** Sturdy release for bonnet **15.** Rocker switches replace toggles from "Series 1½" onwards **16.** Four-speed manual is standard; automatic optional on 2+2 and all V12s **17.** Armrests come in with late 3.8s **18.** Broad-pleat leather seats arrive with the 4.2 in 1964

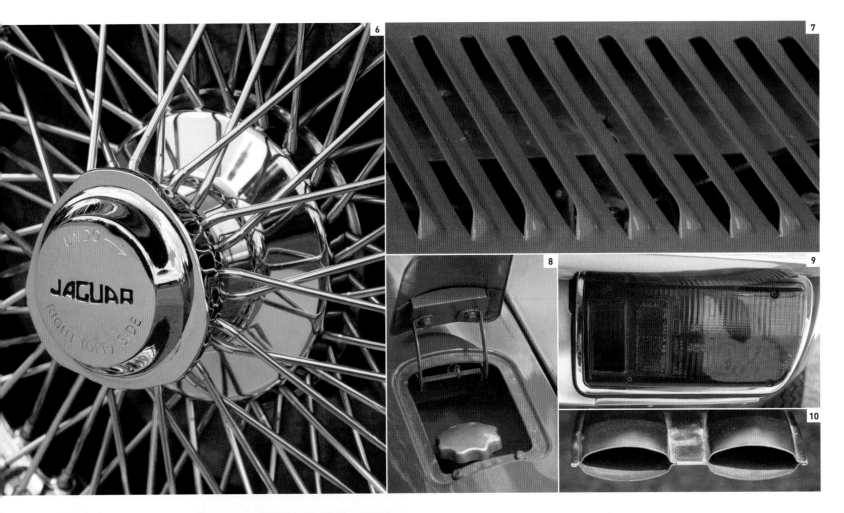

UNDER THE BONNET

The Series III derives its character from the effortless performance of its V12 engine. This gives a maximum speed closer to 150 mph (241 km/h) than was ever possible with a standard six-cylinder car. The 272 bhp quoted is a more realistic DIN figure than the 265 bhp that Jaguar had proclaimed for the 3.8 and 4.2 straight-sixes. It is achieved while using just a single camshaft for each bank of cylinders.

19. The all-alloy V12 is of 5,343 cc and delivers 272 bhp (DIN) at 5,850 rpm, with maximum torque of 304 lb-ft at 3,600 rpm; it breathes through four Stromberg carburettors

Small Cars

The Mini revolutionized small cars in the 1960s, so in the 1970s manufacturers battled for a slice of its market with their own interpretations of what a small car should include. Almost all kept the Mini's front-engine layout and added a hatchback, but not all were transverse and some still had rear-wheel drive. Some offered more space than the Mini, but none matched its brilliant packaging.

△ **Datsun Cherry 100A 1970**

Origin Japan

Engine 988 cc, straight-four

Top speed 86 mph (138 km/h)

The first front-wheel-drive Datsun was inspired by the Mini and sold 390,000 in five years, a period that saw Nissan's worldwide market share grow enormously.

△ **Fiat 127 1971**

Origin Italy

Engine 903 cc, straight-four

Top speed 83 mph (134 km/h)

Fiat had always been brilliant at well-packaged, quick, small cars; the 127 was another success, with sales of 3.7 million. The 1300 Sport option had a 1,300 cc engine and could reach 95 mph (153 km/h).

△ **Mini Clubman 1969**

Origin UK

Engine 998 cc, straight-four

Top speed 75 mph (121 km/h)

By adding a longer, modern-looking front to the Mini, improved trim, and 1- or 1.1-litre engines, British Leyland maintained a presence in the market until the Metro was ready in 1981.

△ **Renault 5 1972**

Origin France

Engine 956 cc, straight-four

Top speed 86 mph (138 km/h)

The class-defining and perhaps most popular supermini, the 5 sold 5.5 million in 12 years. It was reasonably priced, with six engine choices from 782 to 1,397 cc and all-independent suspension.

◁ **Volkswagen Polo 1975**

Origin Germany

Engine 895 cc, straight-four

Top speed 80 mph (129 km/h)

VW completed its modern revolution with the Polo. It had a new overhead-cam front engine, all-independent suspension, and front-wheel drive, with engines from 0.9 to 1.3 litres.

◁ **Mazda Familia/323 1977**

Origin Japan

Engine 985 cc, straight-four

Top speed 80 mph (129 km/h)

First of a long and successful line of small Mazdas, the Familia was old-fashioned, with a front engine and rear-wheel drive, but reliable. Mazda introduced front-wheel drive in 1980.

△ **Mitsubishi/Colt Mirage 1978**

Origin Japan

Engine 1,244 cc, straight-four

Top speed 90 mph (145 km/h)

Sold in some markets as Colt, Mitsubishi's first front-drive car had a two-speed final drive, giving eight forward gears in total, for economy or performance.

△ **Opel Kadett 1973**

Origin Germany

Engine 993 cc, straight-four

Top speed 74 mph (119 km/h)

The German version of the General Motors T-car was sold with engines from 1.0 to 2.0 litres. The car was rear-wheel drive, betraying its US design ethos.

◁ **Citroën 2CV6 1970**

Origin France

Engine 602 cc, flat-two

Top speed 68 mph (109 km/h)

Due to its combination of spacious interior, large sunroof, stylish appearance, and economy, the 2CV stayed in production until 1990, selling almost 3.9 million.

△ **Toyota Starlet 1978**

Origin Japan

Engine 993 cc, straight-four

Top speed 84 mph (135 km/h)

Restricted by its outdated live rear axle, most Starlets were loaded with equipment such as five gears to win sales over the front-wheel-drive, all-independent opposition.

△ **Citroën Visa 1978**

Origin France

Engine 1,124 cc, straight-four

Top speed 89 mph (143 km/h)

Conceived as an economy saloon to replace the Ami, the lightweight Visa became Citroën's choice for rallying in the early 1980s. It was fitted with engines from 653 cc upwards.

◁ **Peugeot 104 1973**

Origin France

Engine 954 cc, straight-four

Top speed 84 mph (135 km/h)

Unusually, Peugeot's first supermini was launched as a 5-door model only; a shorter 3-door followed later. The all-new engine and independent suspension added to its appeal.

△ **Ford Fiesta 1976**

Origin Spain

Engine 957 cc, straight-four

Top speed 79 mph (127 km/h)

Ford's first supermini for Europe was basic, with only four gears, but it had engines up to 1,600 cc and was competitively priced. Sales were 1.75 million by 1983.

△ **Vauxhall Chevette HS 1978**

Origin UK

Engine 2,279 cc, straight-four

Top speed 115 mph (185 km/h)

Vauxhall made a virtue of a live rear axle by adding a big, tuned dual-cam engine. The Chevette went on to win rallies. Most were 1.3-litre hatchbacks.

◁ **Talbot Sunbeam Lotus 1979**

Origin UK

Engine 2,174 cc, straight-four

Top speed 121 mph (195 km/h)

The Talbot Sunbeam had a shortened rear-wheel-drive Avenger platform, so was quite outdated. But adding a big, powerful Lotus engine made it ideal for rallying.

4x4 and Off-Roaders

In the 1970s Jeep and Land Rover finally saw serious opposition in the off-road market. As a trend towards leisure off-roading and even beach cars developed, thousands of home-build dune buggies were sold in the US, UK, and elsewhere. Alongside capable four-wheel-drive off-roaders, there were early examples of the less serious two-wheel-drive soft-roaders that would become popular 30 years later.

▷ **Toyota Land Cruiser FJ40 1960**

Origin Japan

Engine 3,878 cc, straight-six

Top speed 84 mph (135 km/h)

Japan's answer to the Land Rover was this robust off-roader that saw few changes from 1960 to 1984. Front disc brakes and 3.0- and 4.2-litre engines were added between 1974 and 1976.

◁ **Chevrolet Blazer K5 1969**

Origin USA

Engine 5,735 cc, V8

Top speed 98 mph (158 km/h)

Chevrolet shortened its pick-up truck and added a full cab with two- or four-wheel drive and 6-cylinder or 8-cylinder engines to compete against the Jeep, Ford Bronco, and Scout – it sold well.

△ **Ford Bronco 1966**

Origin USA

Engine 2,781 cc, straight-six

Top speed 76 mph (122 km/h)

Conceived by the same team who gave Ford the Mustang, the Bronco was a brave early take on the SUV concept but was too small to capture the US market; models from 1978 onwards were larger.

△ **Subaru Leone Estate 1972**

Origin Japan

Engine 1,595 cc, flat-four

Top speed 87 mph (140 km/h)

The first of the four-wheel-drive, everyday road cars, the Leone (1600 in the UK and US) Estate was a pioneer, and Subarus were still modelled on it 40 years later.

▷ **Suzuki Jimny LJ10 1970**

Origin Japan

Engine 359 cc, straight-two

Top speed 47 mph (76 km/h)

In 1967 Japan's Hope Motor Co. developed a design for a 4x4 with a Mitsubishi engine; Suzuki bought it and fitted its own engine, creating a successful line of tiny 4x4s.

Fun Cars

As the roads became increasingly clogged with traffic and restricted by legislation, adventurous drivers sought excitement off the tarmac. In the US they ripped bodies off old VW Beetles, bolted on light, open shells, and roared off over the sand in their dune buggies. Meanwhile, in France Matra tried to emulate the Range Rover with a two-wheel-drive leisure vehicle, and in the UK even three-wheelers briefly became trendy and fun.

▷ **Meyers Manx 1964**

Origin USA

Engine 1,493 cc, flat-four

Top speed 90 mph (145 km/h)

Californian Bruce Meyers began the dune buggy craze with his Manx, which won the Baja 1000 race. With a glassfibre roadster body and a VW Beetle floorpan, it sold about 6,000 to 1971.

◁ **International Harvester Scout II 1971**

Origin USA

Engine 4,981 cc, V8

Top speed 90 mph (145 km/h)

The Scout was launched in 1960 as the world's first SUV. The Scout II, which had a wheelbase of up to 254 cm (100 in) and a choice of 4-, 6-, or V8-cylinder engines, was in production until 1980.

▷ **Land Rover Series III 1971**

Origin UK

Engine 2,286 cc, straight-four

Top speed 68 mph (109 km/h)

Evolved from the original 1948 Land Rover, the Series III was still the benchmark capable off-roader. With an all-synchromesh gearbox and updated dashboard, it enjoyed a 14-year life.

△ **Jeep Commando 1972**

Origin USA

Engine 4,980 cc, V8

Top speed 90 mph (145 km/h)

The Commando was the ultimate evolution of the 1940s Jeepster, with short or full cab and a range of AMC 6-cylinder or 8-cylinder engines; 20,223 were sold in two years.

▽ **Range Rover 1970**

Origin UK

Engine 3,528 cc, V8

Top speed 99 mph (159 km/h)

This step up from the Land Rover offered superb off-road ability and comfort. With vinyl seats and a plastic dashboard, its interior could be hosed clean. Luxury came later, in the 1980s.

△ **Jeep Wagoneer 1972**

Origin USA

Engine 5,896 cc, V8

Top speed 95 mph (153 km/h)

AMC took over Jeep in 1970 and improved its cars with new engines. The Wagoneer was the original luxury 4x4, with refined Quadra-Trak four-wheel drive added in 1973.

△ **Mercedes-Benz G-Wagen 1979**

Origin Austria

Engine 2,299 cc, straight-four

Top speed 89 mph (143 km/h)

Expensive but tough, this reliable off-roader came with either two- or four-wheel drive. The G-Wagen had low-ratio gears like the Land Rover, but with the benefit of coil springs for its live axles.

△ **Matra-Simca Rancho 1977**

Origin France

Engine 1,442 cc, straight-four

Top speed 89 mph (143 km/h)

While not as rugged as a full-blown 4x4, this front-wheel-drive soft-roader was ideal for rural tracks too challenging for normal road cars. It was rebranded as a Talbot in 1979.

△ **Leyland Mini Moke 1968**

Origin Australia

Engine 998 cc, straight-four

Top speed 75 mph (120 km/h)

Impractical in rainy Britain, Mokes made much more sense in warm, dry climates. Production was in Australia from 1968 to 1981, later transferring to Portugal.

△ **Bond Bug 1970**

Origin UK

Engine 700 cc, straight-four

Top speed 76 mph (121 km/h)

The three-wheeled Bug embodied the spirit of youth, freedom, humour, and optimism with which Britain entered the 1970s. But fewer than 3,000 people were inspired to buy one.

Guy Moll driving an Alfa Romeo P-3 in Berlin, 1934

Great marques
The Alfa Romeo story

Originating in the Italian city of Milan a century ago, the Alfa Romeo marque conjures up images of sophisticated road cars and legendary competition success. In the 1930s Alfa Romeo's racers were the finest in the world and provided the foundation for a wealth of superbly engineered, stylish road-going models.

DESPITE BEING REGARDED as a quintessentially Italian car maker, Alfa Romeo's roots go back to the early 20th century and the French auto manufacturer Alexandre Darracq. Looking to expand his operations into Italy, Darracq set up a factory on the outskirts of Milan in 1906. The venture failed, and four years later a consortium of Italian investors took over to create a company called Alfa – an acronym

Alfa Romeo badge
(introduced 1971)

for Anonima Lombarda Fabbrica Automobili. The first Alfa-badged model was the 24HP, which was designed by the company's chief engineer, Giuseppe Merosi, in 1910 and featured a 4,082 cc, straight-four engine. The model's entry in the 1911 Targa Florio race in Sicily was an early indication of Alfa's sporting intentions. Merosi went on to develop a range of successful models over the next 12 years, with engine capacities

ranging from 2,413 cc to 6,082 cc and featuring innovations that included a double overhead camshaft.

As with many other car makers, World War I initiated a switch at Alfa from automobile manufacture to the production of military components such as aircraft engines. In 1915 businessman Nicola Romeo took a controlling stake in Alfa and, after post-war car manufacture had resumed, the company was renamed Alfa Romeo in 1920. The 6.3-litre, straight-six G1 was the first new offering, and in this model drivers such

as Giuseppe Campari, Enzo Ferrari, and Uvo Sivocci secured competition successes for the marque.

A significant development occurred in 1923, with Vittorio Jano replacing Giuseppe Merosi as Alfa Romeo's chief engineer. The ex-Fiat employee would prove fundamental to Alfa Romeo's future success, developing a number of models that cemented the marque's reputation for producing superb racing cars. His initial creation was Alfa Romeo's first eight-cylinder model, the P2. It won the inaugural Grand Prix World Championship in

Alfasuds in competition
With great styling and superb handling, the Alfasud was one of the marque's best-selling models. A one-model race series called Trofeo Alfasud was staged between 1975 and 1981.

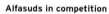

8C 2300

1910	The Alfa company is formed in Milan.
1911	The marque's first model, the 24HP, competes in the Targa Florio race.
1920	Under Nicola Romeo, the company is rebranded Alfa Romeo.
1921	The G1 becomes the first Alfa Romeo model.
1925	An Alfa Romeo P2 wins the first ever Grand Prix World Championship.
1933	The Italian government saves Alfa Romeo from bankruptcy; holding company IRI takes over the firm.

1900SSZ

1938	Alfa Romeo wins the Mille Miglia for the 10th time since 1928.
1946	Car manufacture resumes after the end of World War II.
1950	Nino Farina wins the inaugural Formula 1 World Championship in the Alfa 158.
1959	After more than 20,000 sales since being introduced in 1950, the Alfa 1900 is replaced by the 2000 model.
1966	The Spider roadster is introduced; it will be produced until 1993.

1300 DUETTO SPIDER

1967	The Alfa Romeo Montreal is unveiled as a concept car at Montreal's Expo 67; the Montreal enters production three years later.
1971	The Alfasud is lauded by critics; along with the Sprint variant, more than 1 million will be sold by 1989.
1975	Alfa Romeo wins the World Sports Car Championship; it repeats the feat two years later.
1986	Alfa Romeo is taken over by the Italian Fiat Group.

156

1995	The GTV sports car is introduced; several setbacks cause Alfa Romeo to withdraw from the US market.
1998	The 156 is named European Car of the Year.
2001	The 147 is named European Car of the Year.
2004	Launch of the Bertone-designed GT, followed by the Brera in 2005.
2010	In celebration of Alfa Romeo's centenary, the new Giulietta hatchback is launched, winning critical acclaim.

1925 and continued to take Grand Prix titles to the end of the decade. In the 1930s Jano-designed cars – including the P3, 6C 1750, and 8C 2300 – enabled Alfa Romeo to dominate Grands Prix and races such as Le Mans, France, and Italy's Mille Miglia.

The recession following 1929's Wall Street Crash plunged Alfa Romeo into serious financial difficulty. In 1933 the Italian government stepped in to save the marque. Operating under the state-owned holding company IRI (Instituto per la Ricostruzione Industriale), Alfa Romeo's operations were streamlined so that the company concentrated on producing aircraft engines and cars for wealthy buyers. Coachbuilders, including Pinin Farina (later called Pininfarina) and Touring,

the 1900 was the first Alfa Romeo with an integrated chassis and body. That same year Nino Farina won the first Formula 1 World Championship in the Alfa 158, which had dominated racing since its introduction in 1938. Further success came in 1951, when Juan Manuel Fangio drove the 159 to Alfa Romeo's second Formula 1 World Championship title.

At the 1954 Turin Motor Show, Alfa Romeo revealed the landmark 1,300 cc Giulietta Sprint. This car featured the

20/30 HP ES Sport
This 4,250 cc model was the last in a series of cars derived from the Merosi-designed 24HP of 1910.

"ALFA-ROMEO" TIPO SPORT
E. S. 4 CILINDRI
1921

iconic Spider roadster, unveiled in 1966, which had a starring role in the 1967 film *The Graduate*. The Spider continued in production until 1993.

Back on the track, Alfa Romeo had retired from Formula 1 after 1951, but from the 1960s it competed in the World Sports Car Championship, triumphing in 1975 and 1977. Tuned versions of Alfa Romeo's road cars began to feature in rallying, touring-car, and GT series, amassing a host of titles from the 1960s through to the new millennium.

Alfa Romeo struggled in the global economic slump of the 1970s, but still managed to produce a number of successful new cars. Stylistically daring models like the 1970 Montreal won critical acclaim, and cars such as the million-selling Alfasud of 1971 and the 1972 Alfetta gave the marque a solid backbone, remaining in production for 18 and 15 years respectively. The Alfasud was made in a new factory in Naples, which was funded by the Italian government in an effort to reduce unemployment in the south of the country – hence the car's name (*sud* meaning "south").

The company's continuing financial problems eventually led to Alfa Romeo being taken over by Fiat in 1986. For a

number of years the brand struggled to find a place within the giant Fiat corporation. It was during this period that poor returns on exports to the US, combined with the difficulties of meeting US regulations on safety and emissions, prompted Alfa Romeo to withdraw from the American market.

With the arrival of the sporty GTV, launched to a critical fanfare in 1995, Alfa Romeo seemed to have found its feet once again. Three years later the universally lauded 156 garnered the European Car of the Year award, a feat repeated in 2001 by the compact 147. Since then Alfa Romeo has gone from strength to strength, releasing models such as the GT, Brera, and all-new Giulietta. These new Alfa Romeos hark back to the engineering excellence and cutting-edge styling that captivated car-buyers in the company's formative years.

> "I still have, for Alfa, the **tenderness** of a **first love**. The **pure affection** of a **child** for his **mother**."

ENZO FERRARI, 1952

crafted beautiful bodies on Alfa Romeo chassis, with models such as the 8C 2900B of 1938 exemplifying the company's desire to blend road and race attributes.

World War II saw car production halted once more, and heavy Allied bombing of the company's factories meant that it did not resume until 1946, when the decision was made to produce smaller vehicles for the family market. Launched in 1950,

world's first mass-produced aluminium, double-overhead-cam, four-cylinder engine, which would be used in Alfa Romeo's models for 40 years. Building on the success of the Giulietta, in 1962 Alfa Romeo unveiled the Giulia. The winning formula of a powerful engine in a relatively light body won the Giulia many export orders, and it remained in production through to the late 1970s. Even more enduring was the

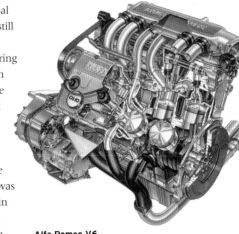

Alfa Romeo V6
Designed by Giuseppe Busso, the V6 powered Alfa Romeo models for more than 25 years. Displacements ranged from 2.0 litres to 3.2 litres. Shown above is the 3.0-litre (2,959 cc) engine from the 164, launched in 1988.

Saloons

The 1970s saw the production of numerous innovative cars, such as the fuel-injected BMWs, the turbocharged Saabs, and the 16-valve Triumphs, but for mainstream saloon cars it was a decade in which time stood still. An extraordinary number of saloons that were already in production in 1970 were still in production in almost unchanged form in 1980.

◁ **Morris Marina 1971**

Origin UK

Engine 1,798 cc, straight-four

Top speed 86 mph (138 km/h)

Mechanically little different from the 1948 Morris Minor, the Marina sold surprisingly well for Britain's struggling car maker. It lasted, as the Ital, until 1984.

▷ **Wartburg Knight 1966**

Origin East Germany

Engine 991 cc, straight-three

Top speed 74 mph (119 km/h)

An East German car with a two-stroke engine, the Knight sold well in Eastern Europe throughout the 1970s. It fared less well in Western Europe, despite incredibly low prices.

△ **Triumph Dolomite Sprint 1973**

Origin UK

Engine 1,998 cc, straight-four

Top speed 115 mph (185 km/h)

Triumph built innovative cars with attractive styling on a tight budget. The Sprint, which challenged the BMW 2002 series, was one of the first 16-valve family saloons.

△ **Citroën CX2400 1974**

Origin France

Engine 2,347 cc, straight-four

Top speed 113 mph (182 km/h)

The Citroën DS's successor combined all its predecessor's innovation with a transverse engine for increased space. It had 2.0-2.5-litre engines, and was made until 1989.

▽ **Saab 99 Turbo 1977**

Origin Sweden

Engine 1,985 cc, straight-four

Top speed 122 mph (196 km/h)

Saab showed the world that turbocharging could be used in a mainstream saloon, not just for racing homologation. It sold well and lifted the company's whole image.

△ **De Tomaso Deauville 1970**

Origin Italy

Engine 5,763 cc, V8

Top speed 143 mph (230 km/h)

Though styled by Ghia, the Deauville suffered from looking like the Jaguar XJ12 – which offered similar performance – while trying to sell for double its price.

△ **Škoda 120S 1970**

Origin Czechoslovakia

Engine 1,174 cc, straight-four

Top speed 86 mph (138 km/h)

The "people's car" for communist Czechoslovakia sold on price alone in Europe, being noisy and difficult to drive. This one did remarkably well in its class in rallying.

◁ **Hillman Avenger 1970**

Origin UK

Engine 1,498 cc, straight-four

Top speed 91 mph (146 km/h)

An all-new design for the 1970s from Chrysler's Rootes Group, the Avenger was thoroughly conventional and lasted until 1981 in various guises.

▷ BMW 2002Tii Alpina A4S 1972

Origin Germany

Engine 1,990 cc, straight-four

Top speed 130 mph (209 km/h)

The 02 series from 1966 established BMW as a serious car maker, selling 750,000 in 10 years. Its finest model (apart from the Turbo) was Alpina's tuned, fuel-injected A4S.

◁ BMW 520 1972

Origin Germany

Engine 1,990 cc, straight-four

Top speed 106 mph (171 km/h)

Key to BMW's success in the 1970s, the 5-Series combined handsome looks with modern running gear. It offered four- and six-cylinder engines from 1.8 to 3.0 litres.

▷ Rover 3500 SD1 1976

Origin UK

Engine 3,528 cc, V8

Top speed 125 mph (201 km/h)

Despite its advanced looks, high specification, and excellent dynamics, the SD1 rapidly gained a reputation for poor quality in the 1970s. Later models fared little better with buyers.

△ Ford Escort Mk2 RS1800 1973

Origin UK

Engine 1,835 cc, straight-four

Top speed 112 mph (180 km/h)

Ford boosted sales through motor sport success, and the RS1800, with its BDA engine, was a formidable rally car. It won the 1979 World Rally Championship.

△ Ford Cortina MkV 1979

Origin UK

Engine 1,993 cc, straight-four

Top speed 103 mph (166 km/h)

The best-selling Cortina changed little from 1970's MkIII to the last MkV in 1982, and sold over two million, mostly in the UK. It was spacious, efficient, and cheap.

△ Cadillac Seville 1975

Origin USA

Engine 5,737 cc, V8

Top speed 115 mph (185 km/h)

General Motors added a more mainstream line to its upper-crust Cadillac marque in 1975. Stylist Bill Mitchell targeted the Mercedes/Rolls-Royce market; it sold well.

△ Maserati Quattroporte II 1975

Origin Italy

Engine 2,965 cc, V6

Top speed 125 mph (201 km/h)

Conceived when Maserati was owned by Citroën, the Quattroporte II had a Merak/SM engine and plenty of SM hydraulic equipment. Just five of these four-door models were built.

turbo

Sports Cars

North American safety laws impacted heavily on sports-car design in this decade, often spoiling pretty shapes with big bumpers, and peppy performance with detuned but low-emission engines. The sports car was declining, as "hot hatchbacks" typified by the Volkswagen Golf GTI grabbed the attention of thrill-seeking drivers.

△ **Morgan 4/4 four-seater 1969**

Origin UK

Engine 1,798 cc, straight-four

Top speed 105 mph (169 km/h)

After almost two decades, Morgan suddenly realized some of its devotees also had families, leading to the reintroduction of a four-seater model for the 1970s.

△ **Peugeot 504 Cabriolet 1969**

Origin France/Italy

Engine 2,664cc, V6

Top speed 110 mph (177 km/h)

This handsome four-seater was designed and built for Peugeot by Pininfarina. There was a coupé version too; both used mechanical parts from the 504 and 604 saloons.

◁ **MG Midget MkIII 1969**

Origin UK

Engine 1,275 cc, straight-four

Top speed 95 mph (153 km/h)

The beloved Sprite/Midget was updated for the 1970s. New features included round rear wheelarches, a Mini Cooper S-type engine, trendy matt-black trim, and a better hood.

◁ **Triumph TR6 1969**

Origin UK

Engine 2,498 cc, straight-six

Top speed 120 mph (193 km/h)

The zenith of the British sports car boasted 150 bhp from the fuel-injected straight-six, rear-wheel drive, fresh air, a loud exhaust, and crisply cool styling.

△ **Triumph Stag 1970**

Origin UK

Engine 2,997 cc, V8

Top speed 118 mph (190 km/h)

Britain's rival to the Mercedes-Benz SL had a distinctive T-shaped rollover bar. The unique V8 engine suffered teething problems, but the Italian styling was a hit.

△ **Triumph TR7 1975**

Origin UK

Engine 1,998 cc, straight-four

Top speed 110 mph (177 km/h)

The TR7 was built to meet anticipated safety laws, which meant a hardtop only; a convertible followed five years later. It was a civilized cruiser and a big seller.

△ **Triumph TR8 1980**

Origin UK

Engine 3,528 cc, V8

Top speed 135 mph (217 km/h)

Fitting Rover's V8 engine gave the TR8 punchy performance as a roadster or coupé. The TR line was axed in 1981, after just 2,500 TR8s had been sold, mostly in the US.

△ **Lotus Elan Sprint 1971**

Origin UK

Engine 1,558 cc, straight-four

Top speed 120 mph (193 km/h)

The fifth, final, and finest incarnation of Colin Chapman's benchmark sports car, this car had superb road manners matched by 126 bhp of power, a five-speed gearbox, and natty livery.

△ **Mercedes-Benz 350SL 1971**

Origin Germany

Engine 3,499 cc, straight-six

Top speed 126 mph (203 km/h)

An all-new SL for the 1970s, this car shared suspension hardware with the S-Class limousine. Powerful, fast, and stylish, it had a standard hardtop for winter.

◁ **Jensen-Healey 1972**

Origin UK

Engine 1,973 cc, straight-four

Top speed 120 mph (193 km/h)

Created by legendary sports-car designer Donald Healey and built by Jensen, this roadster used a Lotus twin-cam engine. It was great to drive and light on fuel, but could be temperamental.

▽ Matra-Simca Bagheera 1973

Origin France

Engine 1,442 cc, straight-four

Top speed 110 mph (177 km/h)

This mid-engined coupé was built by an aerospace company, using engines and transmissions from Simca family cars. Three-abreast seating and a plastic body were among its interesting facets.

△ MGB 1974

Origin UK

Engine 1,798 cc, straight-four

Top speed 90 mph (145 km/h)

The "rubber bumper" MGB era began in 1974. Together with a raised suspension height and a cleaned-up engine, this made the car legal for US sale, but blunted its feisty character.

△ MGB GT 1974

Origin UK

Engine 1,798 cc, straight-four

Top speed 105 mph (169 km/h)

Being more aerodynamic than MG's B Roadster, the GT had a much higher top speed. It was also far more practical, with its rear tailgate and extra luggage space.

△ Lancia Beta Montecarlo/Scorpion 1975

Origin Italy

Engine 1,756 cc, straight-four

Top speed 120 mph (193 km/h)

This exhilarating mid-engined two-seater came with a steel or canvas roof. It suffered from poor brakes and was withdrawn from 1978-80 to fix them, returning in 2-litre form.

△ Fiat X1/9 1972

Origin Italy

Engine 1,290-1,498 cc, straight-four

Top speed 110 mph (177 km/h)

The X1/9 brought mid-engined sports cars to the masses, and remained popular in Europe and the US until 1989. It was designed and built by Bertone.

▽ TVR 3000S 1978

Origin UK

Engine 2,994 cc, V6

Top speed 125 mph (201 km/h)

TVR produced this convertible after three decades of being in business. An open version of the Ford-powered 3000M, abundant power and low weight made it very fast.

△ Panther Lima 1976

Origin UK

Engine 2,279 cc, straight-four

Top speed 115 mph (185 km/h)

A Morgan alternative, this car had a 1930s roadster look but offered a modern driving experience owing to the powerful Vauxhall engine underneath its glassfibre body.

NSU Wankel
rotary

Felix Wankel, a German designer of torpedo motors, came closer than any other engineer to creating a successor to the reciprocating piston engine. His rotary design was small, light, and almost vibration-free. NSU, Curtiss-Wright, Mercedes-Benz, Rolls-Royce, and Citroën all experimented with it, but Mazda developed the rotary engine the furthest.

WHIRLING DERVISH

Wankel disliked the piston engine because of its complexity and its need to turn reciprocating (up-and-down) motion into circular motion at the crankshaft. Wankel's rotary design generated circular motion directly and, like classic two-stroke piston engines, did away with valves and camshafts to control intake and exhaust, replacing them with simple ports. The Wankel engine has an almost triangular ("trochoidal") rotor that turns within a housing shaped like two partly merged circles. Early rotor-tip sealing problems were solved, but lasting concerns about emissions and fuel economy proved fatal, and the design fell out of use.

ENGINE SPECIFICATIONS

Dates produced	1967–1977
Cylinders	Replaced by twin rotors and housing
Configuration	Front-mounted, longitudinal
Engine capacities	1,990 cc
Power output	113 bhp @ 5,500 rpm
Type	Rotary engine with twin rotors, distributor ignition, and a wet sump
Head	Not applicable – valves are replaced by inlet and exhaust ports in the rotor housing, eliminating camshafts, tappets, and valves
Fuel System	Twin Solex carburettors
Bore and Stroke	Not applicable (cylinder-free engine)
Power	56.8b hp/litre
Compression Ratio	9.0:1

▷ See pp.346–347 How an engine works

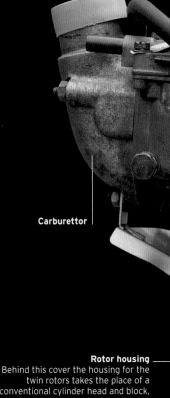

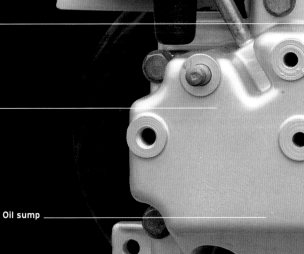

Low-tension (LT) lead
This lead carries low voltage.

High-tension (HT) lead
This lead carries high voltage.

Vacuum advance

Dipstick

Carburettor

Rotor housing
Behind this cover the housing for the twin rotors takes the place of a conventional cylinder head and block, using valveless inlet and exhaust ports.

Housing material
The rotor housing is made of aluminium alloy with a nickel-silicon carbide coating that is electrically deposited on the wearing surface.

Compact powerplant
The engine is so compact that it was mounted longitudinally in the nose of the NSU Ro80. It drove the front wheels via a transmission located behind it.

Oil sump

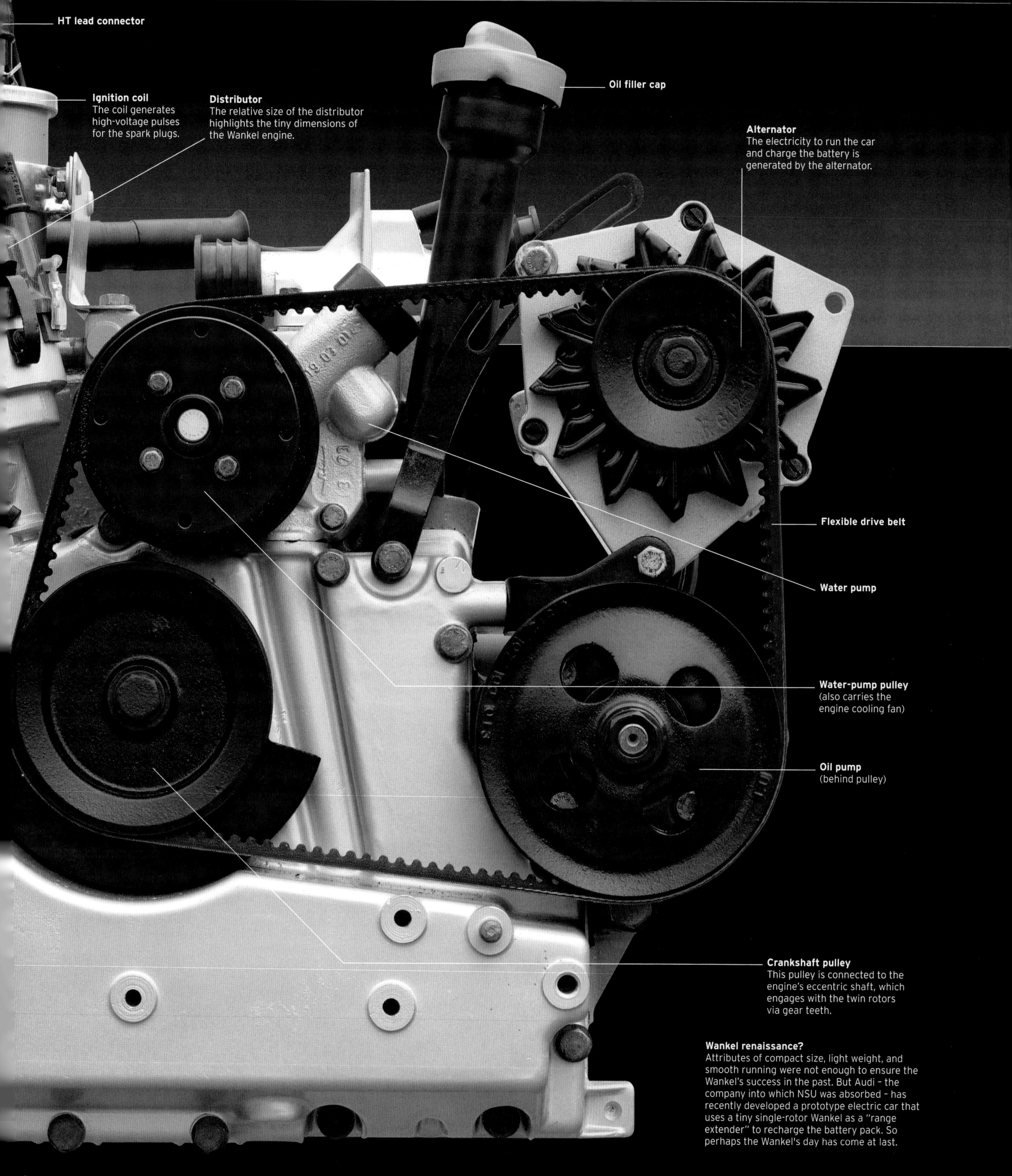

HT lead connector

Ignition coil
The coil generates
high-voltage pulses
for the spark plugs.

Distributor
The relative size of the distributor
highlights the tiny dimensions of
the Wankel engine.

Oil filler cap

Alternator
The electricity to run the car
and charge the battery is
generated by the alternator.

Flexible drive belt

Water pump

Water-pump pulley
(also carries the
engine cooling fan)

Oil pump
(behind pulley)

Crankshaft pulley
This pulley is connected to the
engine's eccentric shaft, which
engages with the twin rotors
via gear teeth.

Wankel renaissance?
Attributes of compact size, light weight, and
smooth running were not enough to ensure the
Wankel's success in the past. But Audi – the
company into which NSU was absorbed – has
recently developed a prototype electric car that
uses a tiny single-rotor Wankel as a "range
extender" to recharge the battery pack. So
perhaps the Wankel's day has come at last.

Stylish Coupés

The flamboyance of the 1950s and curvaceousness of the 1960s had gone: with the 1970s came wedge profiles, straight lines, and angular shapes. Some cars looked better than others; as so often, it was the Italian stylists who seemed to have the best eye for producing a stunning car – though for the first time, Japanese stylists showed they could do it just as well.

△ **Ford Capri RS 3100 1973**

Origin UK

Engine 3,093 cc, V6

Top speed 123 mph (198 km/h)

With its image kept exciting by wild racing cars like this one, the roadgoing Ford Capris continued to notch up healthy sales – around 750,000 in the 1970s.

△ **Opel Manta GT/E 1970**

Origin Germany

Engine 1,897 cc, straight-four

Top speed 116 mph (187 km/h)

Despite attractive styling and almost half-a-million made, most Mantas have rusted away: a shame, as it was a civilized touring car with engines from 1.2 to 1.9 litres.

▷ **Ford Mustang III 1978**

Origin USA

Engine 4,942 cc, V8

Top speed 140 mph (225 km/h)

The third-generation Mustang was a full four-seater for the first time, as it was a larger car based on Ford's "Fox" platform; it continued, with revisions, until 1994.

△ **Jaguar XJ12C 1975**

Origin UK

Engine 5,343 cc, V12

Top speed 148 mph (238 km/h)

To draw sporting kudos for its XJ6/12-derived coupé, British Leyland campaigned this car – the first factory-backed racing activity since 1956. Prepared by Broadspeed, it took pole at Silverstone in 1975.

▽ **Chevrolet Monte Carlo 1970**

Origin USA

Engine 5,735 cc, V8

Top speed 115 mph (185 km/h)

Chevrolet launched a new coupé for the 1970s, bigger than a Chevelle and more luxurious, but still with a useful turn of speed for stock-car racing.

△ **Rolls-Royce Corniche 1971**

Origin UK

Engine 6,750 cc, V8

Top speed 120 mph (193 km/h)

The Silver Shadow was a monocoque but this did not stop Rolls-Royce from adapting the structure into this two-door coupé. The Corniche looked very elegant too.

▷ **Datsun 260Z 1973**

Origin Japan

Engine 2,565 cc, straight-six

Top speed 125 mph (201 km/h)

The 240–280Z series was the world's best-selling sports car in the 1970s, from what, at the time, seemed a most unlikely source. Japanese cars were about to conquer the globe.

◁ **Volkswagen Scirocco GTI 1974**

Origin Germany

Engine 1,588 cc, straight-four

Top speed 115 mph (185 km/h)

This car was styled by Giorgetto Giugiaro and built by Karmann on the VW Golf floorpan. The Scirocco was a hit, selling 504,200 in seven years, with three engine specs: from 1.4- to 1.6-litre GTI.

◁ **Buick Riviera 1971**

Origin USA

Engine 7,458 cc, V8

Top speed 125 mph (201 km/h)

Buick's status symbol coupé had a stunning new look for the 1970s, with a centrally divided wraparound rear window and accentuated rear "hips".

△ Alfa Romeo Junior Zagato 1970

Origin Italy

Engine 1,290 cc, straight-four

Top speed 105 mph (169 km/h)

Ercole Spada at Zagato achieved the impossible: he took an Alfa Romeo GT Junior and turned it into something even more arresting to look at. Only the cost held back sales.

△ Maserati Kyalami 4.9 1976

Origin Italy

Engine 4,930 cc, V8

Top speed 160 mph (257 km/h)

When Alejandro De Tomaso took over Maserati, he developed his 1972 Ghia-designed Longchamp model into the Kyalami, with a choice of potent Maserati V8 engines.

△ Porsche 911S 2.2 1970

Origin Germany

Engine 2,195 cc, flat-six

Top speed 144 mph (232 km/h)

The 911 gained improved handling for the 1970s by moving the rear wheels back by 5.5 cm (2.2 in) and the fuel-injected S took full advantage, becoming a junior supercar.

△ Porsche 911T 2.4 Targa 1972

Origin Germany

Engine 2,341 cc, flat-six

Top speed 128 mph (206 km/h)

Porsche introduced the Targa to offer fresh-air motoring with rollover protection; it was heavier and less sporting than the 911 Coupé, but found a ready market.

◁ Lancia Gamma Coupé 1976

Origin Italy

Engine 2,484 cc, flat-four

Top speed 125 mph (201 km/h)

A striking two-door body by Pininfarina transformed Lancia's big Gamma saloon. Mechanically sophisticated too, it soon became a desirable machine.

▷ Mazda RX-7 1978

Origin Japan

Engine 2,292 cc, two-rotor Wankel

Top speed 117 mph (188 km/h)

Mazda succeeded, where German manufacturer NSU had failed, in persuading the world to accept the rotary engine as a serious option: 570,500 were sold in seven years.

◁ Porsche 924 1976

Origin Germany

Engine 1,984 cc, straight-four

Top speed 125 mph (201 km/h)

Purists disapprove of the VW van engine, but the front-engined 924 was a best-seller for Porsche and expanded its market beyond the dedicated sporting driver.

△ Suzuki SC100 Coupé 1978

Origin Japan

Engine 970 cc, straight-four

Top speed 76 mph (122 km/h)

Suzuki sold 894,000 rear-engined "Whizzkids", mainly on cute looks as they were cramped for four and had poor performance. The Mini was roomier and more nimble.

Ferdinand Porsche with a Volkswagen prototype

Versuchswagen
IIIA - 43011

Great marques
The Volkswagen story

Volkswagen began in 1937 with the humble Beetle, which went on to become the best-selling car of all time. Since then, Volkswagen has grown into Europe's largest automotive group, with a diverse range of products and brands – from the mass-market Škoda and SEAT to luxury brands such as Bugatti, Bentley, and Lamborghini.

VOLKSWAGEN IS GERMAN for "people's car", and it was Adolf Hitler's vision of a car for the German masses that led directly to the establishment of the company. Hitler sketched out his ideas in 1932, and in 1934 the renowned automotive engineer Ferdinand Porsche was engaged to design the real thing, known as the Kdf-Wagen. Prototypes designed by Porsche and Erwin Komenda, which were running by 1938, had many similarities to the products of Tatra, the Czech car manufacturer. In response, Tatra sued Volkswagen; the Czech company was awarded damages many years later.

Only a few production Volkswagens were built before World War II. During the war the design was adapted to produce military vehicles, including the amphibious Schwimmwagen. In 1945 the Volkswagen factory came under the control of the Americans, then the British, but no existing car manufacturer could see a future for the curious German vehicle with its simple

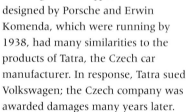

Volkswagen badge
(introduced 1938)

platform chassis, rear-mounted, air-cooled engine, and torsion-bar suspension. It fell to a British army officer, Major Ivan Hirst, to reorganize the war-ravaged factory and finally get the Volkswagen into production. The British forces in Germany ordered 20,000 cars, and soon production was running at 1,000 per month. Output rose as labour and materials became more readily available, and exports began in 1947. A second model line – the Type 2 van – was added in 1950. By 1955 more than 1 million Volkswagen cars and vans had been built.

Simplicity, reliability, and low cost were the major attractions of the Volkswagen. As Europe struggled to repair itself in the aftermath of the war, the Volkswagen proved

Cool camper
Beloved of hippies, surfers, and families, the Type 2 Camper Van combined the freedom of the road with essential home comforts.

to be the right car at the right time. It was even successful in the US, where it grew into a cult car that sold on its anti-establishment, anti-fashion image. The Doyle Dane Bernbach agency produced a classic series of advertisements that turned what many Americans might have seen as the Volkswagen's weaknesses – such as its small size, four-cylinder engine, and lack of annual styling changes – into positive selling points.

The success of the Beetle, as the car was nicknamed, nearly became the company's downfall. Throughout the 1960s Volkswagen relied on the Beetle and its derivatives, ignoring advances in technology and the improvements in living standards that its customers were enjoying in Germany's post-war economic boom. Production of the Beetle hatchback in Germany ended in 1978, and the cabriolet remained on sale until 1980. Manufacture of the

"**Nobody** gave me a **real brief**. I was just told to **go there** and **do something**."

MAJOR IVAN HIRST, THE BRITISH OFFICER WHO
REORGANIZED VOLKSWAGEN AFTER WORLD WAR II

BEETLE (TYPE 1)

KOMBI (TYPE 2 VAN)

SCIROCCO

GOLF RALLYE

1932 Adolf Hitler sketches out his first ideas for a people's car.
1934 Ferdinand Porsche is engaged to design the Kdf-Wagen.
1938 Final Volkswagen prototypes are put on show, but few cars are built before World War II.
1945 Volkswagen factory resumes production under the leadership of British army major Ivan Hirst.
1950 The Type 2 Volkswagen, a van based on the Beetle (Type 1), is launched.

1955 The 1-millionth Volkswagen is built at the Wolfsburg factory.
1965 Volkswagen buys Auto Union, including the brands Audi, DKW, Horch, and Wanderer, from Daimler-Benz.
1969 Volkswagen takes over NSU and adopts an unlaunched NSU saloon as the Volkswagen K70.
1974 Volkswagen launches the Scirocco and Golf, followed by the Polo in 1975, at last replacing the Beetle with modern, water-cooled, front-wheel-drive cars.

1975 The Golf GTI proves an unexpected success, becoming a mainstream part of the Golf range.
1978 Beetle production in Germany ends, but the car is still produced in Brazil and Mexico.
1990 Volkswagen buys the Spanish manufacturer SEAT, whose previous technology partner was Fiat.
1998 Volkswagen buys Lamborghini and Bentley, as well as the rights to the Bugatti name.

1999 Volkswagen buys the Czech car marque Škoda.
2000 Volkswagen founds Bugatti Automobiles SAS at Château Saint Jean in Dorlisheim, France.
2003 Production of the original Beetle finally ends in Mexico, with more than 21 million having been made worldwide.
2009 Volkswagen rescues Germany's Karmann from bankruptcy.
2010 After a battle for control, Volkswagen and Porsche plan a merger.

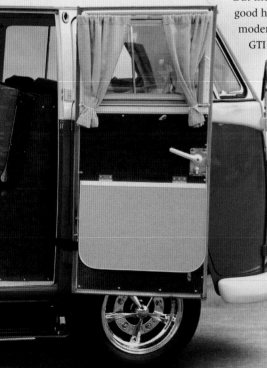

Beetle then moved to Brazil and Mexico, where the car continued to sell strongly.

The Beetle's eventual replacements were the Golf and Polo – modern, front-wheel-drive hatchbacks that first appeared in the mid-1970s. Although they were not the only front-wheel-drive Volkswagens – there had been the K70 and Passat hatchbacks – the Golf and Polo were the first direct alternatives to the Beetle.

New car, retro appeal
The New Beetle evoked its namesake's styling; unlike the original, it had a front-mounted engine and front-wheel drive.

The Golf's arrival was timely, since European and US buyers were switching to small cars in the wake of the early 1970s oil crisis. The Golf took over as the marque's core model, its image being bolstered by the surprising success of the Golf GTI. The fuel-injected GTI of 1975, developed as an after-work project by some Volkswagen engineers, was only expected to sell a few thousand.

But the GTI's combination of pace, good handling, practicality, and modern styling proved irresistible. GTI models became a key part of the Golf range for decades to come.

Volkswagen extended its horizons in the 1980s and 90s, becoming one of the first European car makers to set up a joint venture in

The New Beetle Cabriolet.

China and establish low-cost manufacturing plants in Eastern Europe after the fall of the Berlin Wall in 1989. Volkswagen's Polo, Golf, and Passat ranges gained technical sophistication through successive generations. The marque's reputation for reliable, well-designed products was enhanced by innovations such as narrow-angle, five- and six- cylinder engines in the 1990s and the DSG twin-clutch transmission in 2003.

Meanwhile, the Volkswagen product range was expanding into new market sectors. A small car, the Lupo, was launched in 1998. There was also a special-edition of the Lupo, the 3L, with a 1.2-litre turbodiesel engine that gave a fuel consumption of more than 90 mpg (3 litres per 100 km). At the other end of the range, the Phaeton limousine of 2002 offered both a powerful 6.0-litre W12 engine (effectively two VR6 units merged together) and an extraordinary 5.0-litre V10 diesel – the latter also being used in the Touareg SUV of 2002. More controversial was the New Beetle

of 1998. Critics argued that, apart from styling, it had nothing in common with the original car, but it still became a successful niche model.

Under the leadership of Ferdinand Piëch, grandson of Ferdinand Porsche, Volkswagen acquired Lamborghini and Bugatti in 1998. The same year it also bought Rolls-Royce and Bentley Motor Cars, but failed to secure the rights to the Rolls-Royce name, which went to BMW. Volkswagen claimed it had only ever wanted Bentley; most observers saw it as a missed opportunity.

In 2009 Porsche launched a daring takeover bid for Volkswagen, but it failed to raise enough money to buy the stake it needed and ran up large debts in the process. Volkswagen injected cash into Porsche to help it avoid bankruptcy and the two then planned a friendly merger for 2011.

Meanwhile, Volkswagen's relentless new product offensive continued with excellent cars such as the new Scirocco, Passat CC, and the fifth-generation Polo, capable of superb fuel economy.

High-speed hot hatch
The Golf GTI, one of the first "hot hatches", was a regular on the rally circuit. Here, Franz Wittmann and Matthias Feltz put their GTI through its paces in the 1986 Monte Carlo Rally.

Muscle Cars

In the late 1960s US manufacturers were bitten by the high-performance bug. Sacrificing efficiency for brute force, they installed powerful V8 engines in otherwise humdrum coupés, hardtops, and convertibles. Fearsome competition cars, they were also thrilling to drive on the road. The "muscle cars" reached their pinnacle in 1970, after which power outputs were drastically reduced in the face of the unfolding oil crisis.

△ **Plymouth Road-Runner Superbird 1970**

Origin	USA
Engine	7,213 cc, V8
Top speed	130 mph (209 km/h)

The Superbird, endorsed by the TV cartoon character Road-Runner, was a NASCAR racer made legal for the road. Just 1,900 of these winged wonders were built.

△ **Oldsmobile 442 1970**

Origin	USA
Engine	7,456 cc, V8
Top speed	120 mph (193 km/h)

The 442 was launched in 1964; the figures signified a four-barrel carburettor, four-speed gearbox, and dual exhausts. It was a standalone model from 1968 to 1972.

▷ **Plymouth Hemi 'Cuda 1970**

Origin	USA
Engine	7,210 cc, V8
Top speed	130 mph (209 km/h)

The 'Cuda crowned the large Plymouth Barracuda series, and with its hemispherical-head Chrysler V8 pumping out up to 425 bhp, it was the series powerhouse.

▽ **Pontiac Firebird Trans Am 1973**

Origin	USA
Engine	7,459 cc, V8
Top speed	132 mph (212 km/h)

Often distinguished by a huge bonnet decal sticker depicting a phoenix, the Trans Am was named after the race series in which Firebirds excelled in the late 1960s.

△ **Pontiac Trans Am 1975**

Origin	USA
Engine	6,556 cc, V8
Top speed	118 mph (190 km/h)

The Firebird was restyled with a longer nose and a bigger rear window to become the Pontiac Trans Am. It was still a race contender, despite a cut in power to 185 bhp forced by tighter emissions rules.

◁ **Dodge Challenger R/T 440 1970**

Origin	USA
Engine	6,276 cc, V8
Top speed	114 mph (183 km/h)

This practical hardtop coupé was enlivened by electric acceleration to rival the hottest Mustangs. A 7.2-litre engine option boosted its bhp from 300 to 385.

▷ **Mercury Cougar 1973**

Origin	USA
Engine	7,030 cc, V8
Top speed	125 mph (201 km/h)

For a time in the 1970s, the Mercury Cougar – especially in 390 bhp XR-7 guise – headed Ford's high-power offerings; it was based closely on the Mustang.

▷ **Ford Mustang Mach 1 1972**

Origin USA

Engine 5,753 cc, V8

Top speed 130 mph (209 km/h)

The ultimate performance Mustang of the 1970s was also the largest, and starred in a famous two-wheeled stunt in the James Bond film *Diamonds Are Forever*.

◁ **Ford Falcon XA hardtop 1972**

Origin Australia

Engine 5,673 cc, V8

Top speed 160 mph (257 km/h)

This GT-HO version tore up Australia's race tracks, leading to a public outcry – known as the "Supercar Superscare" – at the prospect of 160 mph (257 km/h) cars speeding on the country's roads.

△ **Chevrolet Camaro 1966**

Origin USA

Engine 6,489 cc, V8

Top speed 136 mph (219 km/h)

The Camaro was Chevrolet's answer to Ford's Mustang, and joined the expanding "pony car" club with its reliable drive train and electric acceleration available for the biggest V8 engine.

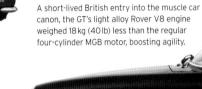

▽ **MGB GT V8 1973**

Origin UK

Engine 3,528 cc, V8

Top speed 125 mph (201 km/h)

A short-lived British entry into the muscle car canon, the GT's light alloy Rover V8 engine weighed 18 kg (40 lb) less than the regular four-cylinder MGB motor, boosting agility.

△ **Chevrolet Nova SS 1971**

Origin USA

Engine 5,736 cc, V8

Top speed 107 mph (172 km/h)

The fastest of the compact Nova SSs could reach 60 mph (97 km/h) from standstill in under 6 seconds. Abundant wheelspin and heavy steering only boosted the car's macho appeal.

▷ **Chevrolet Camaro SS 396 1972**

Origin USA

Engine 6,588 cc, V8

Top speed 120 mph (193 km/h)

A 240 bhp V8 engine was a hot option on the SS. This Camaro, visually updated like the entire range in 1970, was too polluting to be sold in California.

▽ **Chevrolet Corvette 1980**

Origin USA

Engine 5,733 cc, V8

Top speed 125 mph (201 km/h)

Corvettes of the 1970s, like other sporty US cars, gradually surrendered outright performance to tighter emissions laws. This 1980 model offered a relatively tame 190 bhp.

Racing Cars

In the 1970s it became clear that every category of motor racing needed restrictions to power outputs, to prevent cars from taking off at the speeds of over 200 mph (322 km/h) which many were now capable of. Advances in turbocharging then kept legislators on their toes, as speeds continued to rise.

▽ **Tyrrell-Cosworth 001 1970**

Origin	UK
Engine	2,993 cc, V8
Top speed	190 mph (306 km/h)

When Ken Tyrrell was stood up by Matra, he had Derek Gardner design an all-new car to bear the Tyrrell name. This car showed great potential in late 1970.

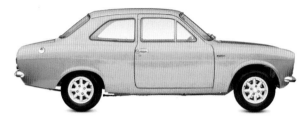

△ **Ford Escort RS1600 1970**

Origin	UK
Engine	1,599 cc, straight-four
Top speed	113 mph (182 km/h)

Fitted with a Cosworth BDA 16-valve double overhead camshaft, which was a development of the basic Ford engine, the RS1600 was a successful rally/race car; around 1,000 were built.

△ **Tyrrell-Cosworth 002 1971**

Origin	UK
Engine	2,993 cc, V8
Top speed	195 mph (314 km/h)

In its first full year as a Formula 1 constructor, Ken Tyrrell's team achieved a fabulous double, World Champion team and driver, the latter for Jackie Stewart.

▷ **Mirage-Cosworth GR7 1972**

Origin	UK
Engine	2,993 cc, V8
Top speed	200 mph (322 km/h)

The 1972 Mirage M6 was the first Cosworth DFV-powered car to win a Sports Car Championship. It was developed into the GR7 for 1974, and finished fourth at Le Mans.

◁ **Lola-Cosworth T500 1978**

Origin	UK
Engine	2,650 cc, V8
Top speed	210 mph (338 km/h)

Indianapolis racers were faster than contemporary Formula 1 cars, due to the high-speed capacity of the oval track. The T500 turbo won the Indy 500 in 1978 at 161.4 mph (260 km/h).

◁ **Brabham-Cosworth BT44 1974**

Origin	UK
Engine	2,993 cc, V8
Top speed	200 mph (322 km/h)

The BT44 was designed by Gordon Murray with very clean lines incorporating early thoughts on ground-effect aerodynamics. It took several Grand Prix wins in 1974.

▽ **Lotus 72 1970**

Origin	UK
Engine	2,993 cc, V8
Top speed	198 mph (319 km/h)

Colin Chapman and Maurice Philippe achieved a revolutionary design with the 72, using wedge aerodynamics, radiators in side pods, and an overhead air intake.

△ **Lotus 79 1977**

Origin	UK
Engine	2,993 cc, V8
Top speed	205 mph (330 km/h)

The first Formula 1 car to take full advantage of ground-effect aerodynamics, which caused it to suck itself to the road for maximum grip on corners, the 79 was a great success.

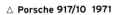

△ Porsche 917/10 1971

Origin Germany
Engine 4,998 cc, flat-twelve
Top speed 213 mph (343 km/h)

The 917 gave Porsche its first Le Mans wins in 1970 and 1971. The 917/10 was turbocharged for the CanAm Challenge; its 850 bhp gave Penske Racing the win in 1972.

▽ Porsche 936/77 1977

Origin Germany
Engine 2,142 cc, flat-six
Top speed 217 mph (349 km/h)

Jacky Ickx almost single-handedly took a superb win at the 1977 Le Mans in the 936; he had won with a 936 in 1976 (also winning the WSC), and would win again in 1981.

△ Matra-Simca MS670B 1972

Origin France
Engine 2,993 cc, V12
Top speed 210 mph (338 km/h)

Matra wanted to be the first French marque since 1950 to win Le Mans: it succeeded when Henri Pescarolo achieved a hat trick with the MS670B in 1972, 1973, and 1974.

△ Surtees-Hart TS10 1972

Origin UK
Engine 1,975 cc, straight-four
Top speed 150 mph (241 km/h)

World Champion John Surtees turned race-car constructor to win the European Formula 2 title, with Mike Hailwood driving the TS10.

△ Alfa Romeo Tipo 33 TT12 1975

Origin Italy
Engine 2,995 cc, flat-twelve
Top speed 200 mph (322 km/h)

Alfa Romeo fitted the ageing T33 with a new 48-valve engine, slab-sided bodywork, and a huge rear spoiler. It won the World Sportscar Championship with ease.

△ McLaren-Offenhauser M16C 1974

Origin UK
Engine 2,650 cc, straight-four
Top speed 205 mph (330 km/h)

McLaren won the Indianapolis 500 three times – the second with Johnny Rutherford driving this M16C in 1974. Almost every car taking part had the 770 bhp "Offy" engine.

◁ Renault RS10 1979

Origin France
Engine 1,496 cc, V6
Top speed 215 mph (346 km/h)

Thanks to gritty determination by Jean-Pierre Jabouille, this was the first turbocharged car to win a Grand Prix, heralding an era of power outputs up to 1,500 bhp.

▷ Chevrolet Nova NASCAR 1979

Origin USA
Engine 5,817 cc, V8
Top speed 200 mph (322 km/h)

North American Stock Car racing used a strict formula of racing chassis clad with silhouette bodies. Dale Earnhardt raced this car in 1979 as a Pontiac and in 1985 as a Chevrolet.

Hatchbacks

Italian designers were the first to introduce rear hatches to compact family saloons, realizing the huge benefits they had in terms of cargo capacity. Previously the style had only been seen on some exotic fastback coupés, but cars such as the Austin A40 Farina showed the way forwards in the 1960s, and as the 1970s progressed, the world's manufacturers increasingly turned to hatchbacks.

▷ **Austin Maxi 1750 1969**

Origin UK

Engine 1,748 cc, straight-four

Top speed 97 mph (156 km/h)

Alec Issigonis's packaging skills were at their best in the transverse-engined, hydrolastic-suspended Maxi. An extremely spacious saloon, it sold well into the 1970s.

▷ **Ford Pinto 1971**

Origin USA

Engine 1,993 cc, straight-four

Top speed 105 mph (169 km/h)

Ford's sub-compact, two-door Pinto of 1970 was joined in six months by the three-door hatchback. It had British 1,600 or German 2,000 cc engines, and four-speed gearboxes.

◁ **Honda Accord 1976**

Origin Japan

Engine 1,599 cc, straight-four

Top speed 94 mph (151 km/h)

Introduced as hatchback only, and joined by saloon versions in 1978, the Accord was a sophisticated car with five-speed manual or optional Hondamatic transmission.

△ **Chevrolet Vega 1970**

Origin USA

Engine 2286 cc, straight-four

Top speed 95 mph (153 km/h)

Chevrolet's all-new sub-compact for the 1970s was conventional, with an aluminium overhead-cam engine and three-speed manual gearbox. It sold 274,699 in its first year.

▷ **Reliant Robin 1973**

Origin UK

Engine 848 cc, four-cylinder

Top speed 80 mph (129 km/h)

This plastic-bodied three-wheeler was popular in the UK during the 1970s fuel crisis. It was thrifty, due to its low weight, and could be driven on a motorbike licence.

△ **AMC Pacer 1975**

Origin USA

Engine 3,802 cc, straight-six

Top speed 92 mph (148 km/h)

Short and wide, the Pacer was a development of AMC's pioneering Gremlin hatchback of 1970. Its rounded form contrasted with the boxy shape of its contemporaries.

▷ **AMC Gremlin 1970**

Origin USA

Engine 3,258 cc, straight-six

Top speed 95 mph (153 km/h)

This first US sub-compact car was cramped in the back and had a column-change three-speed gearbox. It posed little threat to European imports, though the V8 model was popular.

◁ **Volkswagen Passat 1973**

Origin Germany

Engine 1,470 cc, straight-four

Top speed 98 mph (158 km/h)

First of the modern front-wheel-drive VWs, the Passat was based on the Audi 80 and styled by Giugiaro. Fast, modern, and stylish, it sold 1.8 million by 1980.

◁ **Volkswagen Golf GTI 1975**

Origin Germany

Engine 1,588 cc, straight-four

Top speed 112 mph (180 km/h)

The original "hot hatchback" that started a whole new sporting trend was famous for its black trim. It had 110 bhp from its fuel-injected engine and handled beautifully.

△ **Volvo 340 1976**

Origin Netherlands

Engine 1,397 cc, straight-four

Top speed 94 mph (151 km/h)

Volvo's DAF plant in Holland needed a modern small car. Volvo's answer was this long-lived, rear-drive hatch fitted with Renault engines and De Dion rear suspension.

△ **Chrysler Horizon 1977**

Origin France/UK/USA

Engine 1,118 cc, straight-four

Top speed 95 mph (153 km/h)

Chrysler's compact hatchback, intended for sale in Europe and the US, was derived from the Simca 1100, and so had a European style. It had front-wheel drive and all-independent suspension.

△ **Renault 20TS 1975**

Origin France

Engine 1,995 cc, straight-four

Top speed 104 mph (167 km/h)

Renault adopted the hatchback style right across its range, up to the big luxury 20 and 30 saloons, which had 1.6–2.7-litre engines, central locking, and power steering.

▷ **Renault 14 1976**

Origin France

Engine 1,218 cc, straight-four

Top speed 89 mph (143 km/h)

Renault sold almost a million of this bulbous 5-door hatch. It featured a transverse, canted-over Peugeot 104/Citroën Visa-type engine with its transmission in the sump.

▽ **Fiat Strada/Ritmo 1978**

Origin Italy

Engine 1,585 cc, straight-four

Top speed 111 mph (179 km/h)

Fiat were keen to stress that this car was built by robots. Some suggested it had been styled by them too, but the tuned Abarth versions were great fun to drive.

△ **Opel Kadett 1979**

Origin Germany

Engine 1,297 cc, straight-four

Top speed 93 mph (150 km/h)

General Motors' compact hatchback finally adopted front-wheel drive in this version, sold as the Vauxhall Astra in British markets from 1980. It had 1.0–1.8-litre engines.

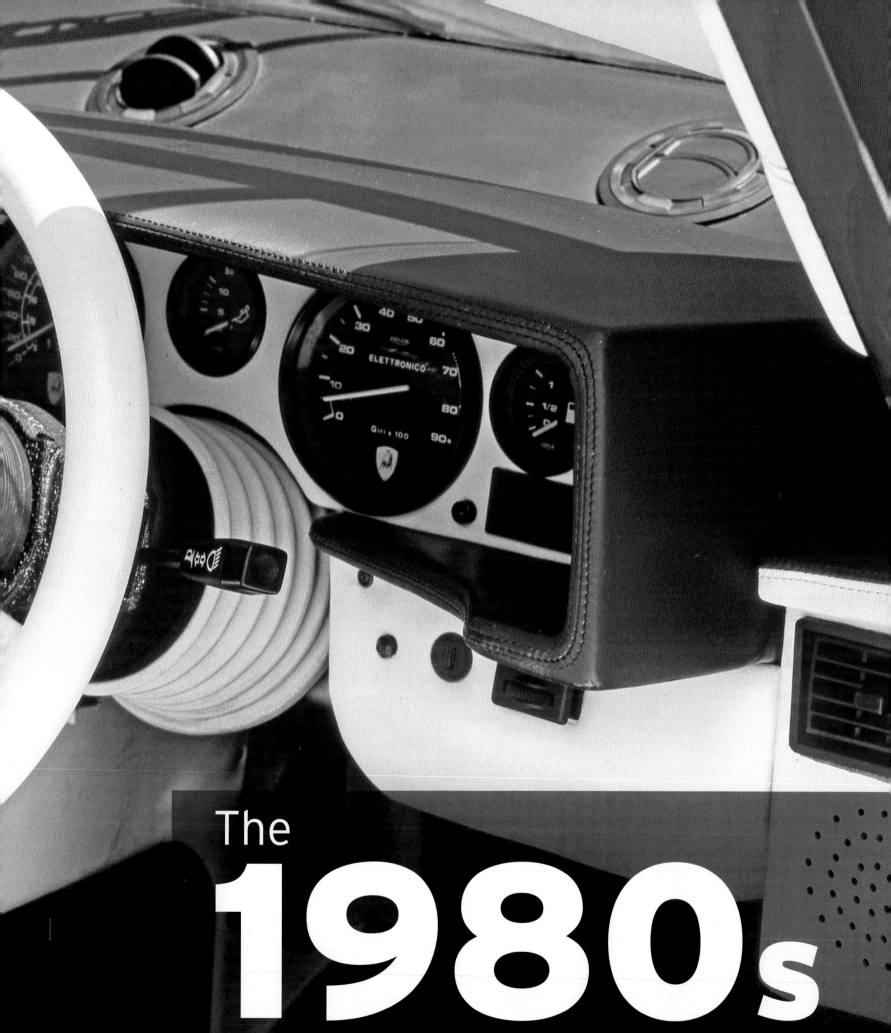

The
1980s

Turbos & tail-spoilers | Yuppies & gullwings | Super-saloons & sports utilities

Boosted Performance

The 1980s was the decade of the turbocharger, transforming the top echelons of motor sport both in racing and rallying: reliability was heavily affected at first by the increased power output, but soon it became impossible to win without one (or more). As technology sent power and speed soaring, legislators struggled to keep up. In the end, turbos became so heavily penalized that normally aspirated engines returned.

△ Ferrari 126C4/M2 1984

Origin Italy

Engine 1,496cc, V6

Top speed 200 mph (322 km/h)

Despite an 850 bhp power output, the 126C4/M2 struggled against the dominant McLaren MP4/2 in 1984, and finished second in the Formula 1 Constructors' Championship.

△ Lancia Beta Monte Carlo 1979

Origin Italy

Engine 1,425cc, straight-four

Top speed 168 mph (270 km/h)

Lancia developed this car to contest the Sports Car Racing World Championship. It dominated the 2-litre class in 1980–81, even beating the Porsche 935s three times.

△ Lancia Rallye 037 Evo 2 1984

Origin Italy

Engine 2,111cc, straight-four

Top speed 150 mph (241 km/h)

Through consistency and great handling on tarmac, the 037 beat Audi's quattro to win the 1983 World Rally Championship. Abarth built lighter Evo 2s with 350 bhp for 1984.

△ Porsche 956 1982

Origin Germany

Engine 2,650cc, flat-six

Top speed 221 mph (356 km/h)

Built for the World Sportscar Championship, the aluminium monocoque 956 was a winner from the start. Jacky Ickx and Derek Bell led the 1982 Le Mans (France) to the finish.

▷ Porsche 911 SCRS 1984

Origin Germany

Engine 2,994cc, flat-six

Top speed 160 mph (257 km/h)

This Group B Porsche lacked four-wheel drive but handled superbly on tarmac, taking Henri Toivonen to second place in the 1984 European Championship.

▷ Porsche 953 4WD 1984

Origin Germany

Engine 3,164cc, flat-six

Top speed 150 mph (241 km/h)

Four 953s (effectively four-wheel-drive 911s) were built for the 1984 Paris–Dakar Rally, and two of them finished 1-2. René Metge and Dominic Lemoyne drove the winning car.

◁ Opel Manta 400 1985

Origin Germany

Engine 2,410cc, straight-four

Top speed 130 mph (209 km/h)

Without four-wheel drive, the Mantas couldn't really compete at World Rally Championship (WRC) level, but both Jimmy McRae and Russell Brookes won British Rally Championships in them.

Audi quattros

Audi revolutionized the world of rallying with its four-wheel drive, four-seat quattro coupé. In its first event, the 1981 Monte Carlo Rally, it failed to finish but Hannu Mikkola was a minute faster than the opposition on almost every stage, demonstrating the car's sensational potential. The competition were forced to go 4x4 too, kicking off the super-fast Group B rally phenomenon.

▷ Audi quattro 1980

Origin Germany

Engine 2,144cc, straight-five

Top speed 138 mph (222 km/h)

Hannu Mikkola and Michèle Mouton were the first quattro works drivers, overcoming teething troubles and showing tremendous pace in 1981.

▷ **Lotus-Renault 97T 1985**

Origin UK

Engine 1,492 cc, V6

Top speed 200 mph (322 km/h)

With Ayrton Senna at the wheel, the 900 bhp Lotus 97T could have won the 1985 Formula 1 World Championship had it been reliable: it took eight pole positions in the season.

◁ **Toyota Celica Twin Cam Turbo 1985**

Origin Japan

Engine 2,090 cc, straight-four

Top speed 135 mph (217 km/h)

It was far from the ultimate in Group B technology, but this Toyota did well in Africa, with Björn Waldegård winning two Safari and two Ivory Coast rallies.

△ **Peugeot 205 T16 Evo 2 1985**

Origin France

Engine 1,775 cc, straight-four

Top speed 155 mph (249 km/h)

With huge turbo, mid-engine, and 4x4, Timo Salonen took the 1985 WRC Drivers' title in the big-wing 500 bhp Evo 2 and won the last Group B event in Europe.

▷ **Peugeot 405 T16 GR 1986**

Origin France

Engine 1,905 cc, straight-four

Top speed 155 mph (249 km/h)

After Group B rallying was cancelled, Peugeot turned to the Paris-Dakar desert endurance rally: Ari Vatanen won in 1989 and 1990 in the mid-engined 405 T16.

△ **McLaren-Honda MP4/4 1988**

Origin UK

Engine 1,496 cc, V6

Top speed 210 mph (338 km/h)

McLaren secured the best engine for 1988 and Gordon Murray designed the best chassis to run it, Ayrton Senna and Alain Prost winning all but one race of the 1988 Formula 1 season.

▷ **MG Metro 6R4 1984**

Origin UK

Engine 2,991 cc, V6

Top speed 155 mph (249 km/h)

Designed by Williams' designer Patrick Head, with a mid-mounted engine later used in the Jaguar XJ220 and four-wheel drive, this was an ultimate Group B rally car.

◁ **Benetton-Ford B188 1988**

Origin UK

Engine 3,493 cc, V8

Top speed 200 mph (322 km/h)

The Italian-sponsored Benetton Formula 1 team turned to Ford Cosworth DFV non-turbo power for 1988. With Alessandro Nannini and Thierry Boutsen driving, they achieved a couple of third places.

△ **Audi Sport quattro 1983**

Origin Germany

Engine 2,133 cc, straight-five

Top speed 154 mph (248 km/h)

Audi chopped 32 cm (12.6 in) out of the centre of the quattro to keep it competitive against purpose-built Group B opposition. It had 306 bhp in road form, and double that for rallying.

△ **Audi Sport quattro S1 E2 1985**

Origin Germany

Engine 2,133 cc, straight-five

Top speed 154 mph (248 km/h)

In a last-ditch fight with the purpose-built Group B cars, Audi added wings and spoilers to make the Evo 2, with 550 bhp. Walter Röhrl won the Sanremo Rally in 1985 with it.

US Compacts

It took a long time for US manufacturers to take much notice of the world trend towards small, fuel-efficient cars. Plentiful inexpensive fuel, wide open roads, and for the most part low traffic densities, encouraged the use of large cruising cars. But the 1980s saw Japanese and European cars make increasing headway into the market, forcing US manufacturers to reconsider.

△ **Dodge Aries 1981**

Origin USA

Engine 2,213 cc, straight-four

Top speed 98 mph (158 km/h)

This spacious front-wheel-drive saloon was *Motor Trend's* Car of the Year in 1981. It sold a million in seven years, helping to improve Chrysler's fortunes in the 1980s.

◁ **Dodge Lancer 1985**

Origin USA

Engine 2,213 cc, straight-four

Top speed 111 mph (179 km/h)

Also available as a 125 mph (201 km/h) turbo, the five-door Lancer was a lively performer. It had a five-speed manual or a three-speed automatic gearbox.

△ **Pontiac Phoenix 1980**

Origin USA

Engine 2,838 cc, V6

Top speed 109 mph (175 km/h)

Sold as a two-door coupé or a five-door hatchback, Pontiac's first front-wheel-drive compact was more efficient than its rear-wheel-drive predecessor. It was made until 1984.

◁ **Pontiac Grand Am 1985**

Origin USA

Engine 3,000 cc, straight-four

Top speed 100 mph (161 km/h)

Pontiac brought back an old name for its mid-80s compact saloon. It had front-wheel drive, 2.5-litre 4-cylinder or 3.0-litre V6 engines, and coupé or sedan body styles.

△ **Pontiac Fiero GT 1985**

Origin USA

Engine 2,838 cc, V6

Top speed 124 mph (200 km/h)

General Motors astonished the world with the mid-engined, part-plastic-bodied Fiero two-seater sports car, which sold 370,158 in five years. Base models had a 4-cylinder engine.

▽ **Buick Reatta 1988**

Origin USA

Engine 3,800 cc, V6

Top speed 125 mph (201 km/h)

Buick's first two-seater for 50 years had touch-screen climate control, a radio, and electronic diagnostics. Unfortunately, its gadgets deterred rather than attracted buyers.

△ **Chrysler LeBaron Coupé 1987**

Origin USA

Engine 2,501 cc, straight-four

Top speed 103 mph (166 km/h)

Turbocharged engine options and a radical new look – including sliding covers over the headlights – gave the LeBaron Coupé, and its convertible counterpart, real 80s appeal.

◁ **Ford Escort 1981**

Origin USA

Engine 1,597 cc, straight-four

Top speed 96 mph (154 km/h)

Not until 1981 was the US market ready for as small a car as the European Ford Escort. This US version became the US's best-selling car for some of the decade.

△ **Chevrolet Spectrum 1985**

Origin Japan

Engine 1,471 cc, straight-four

Top speed 100 mph (161 km/h)

GM's Japanese affiliate built this compact hatchback and saloon as the Isuzu Gemini; it was renamed the Chevrolet Spectrum for the US and Canadian markets.

▷ **Ford Probe 1988**

Origin USA

Engine 2,184 cc, straight-four

Top speed 118 mph (190 km/h)

Originally planned to replace the Mustang, but launched as a new model alongside it, the front-wheel-drive Probe was designed by Mazda and built in its new US factory.

△ **AMC Eagle 1979**

Origin USA

Engine 4,228 cc, straight-six

Top speed 88 mph (142 km/h)

In the late 1970s AMC combined its Jeep-derived four-wheel-drive expertise with its saloon car range. The result was this pioneering US four-wheel-drive crossover vehicle.

△ **Cadillac Cimarron 1981**

Origin USA

Engine 1,835 cc, straight-four

Top speed 100 mph (161 km/h)

In a rush to enter the compact car market – and to compete with European imports – General Motors failed to turn its J-car platform into a convincing Cadillac, despite its high-tech equipment.

◁ **Eagle Premier 1987**

Origin USA

Engine 2,464 cc, straight-four

Top speed 117 mph (188 km/h)

Styled by Giugiaro and developed by AMC and Renault, the Premier boasted electronically controlled four-speed automatic transmission, fuel injection, and air conditioning.

▽ **Volkswagen Jetta 16V 1987**

Origin USA/Germany

Engine 1,781 cc, straight-four

Top speed 126 mph (203 km/h)

Adapting to the US market's resistance to hatchbacks, Volkswagen added a boot to its Golf hatchback in 1979. It sold millions, a third going to the US.

Toyota, 1980
By 1980 the Japanese car industry had gained major footholds in the US and European markets. Toyota Corollas, Cressidas, and Hilux pick-up trucks, here awaiting export, proved to be affordable and reliable.

Superminis

Once the British-made Mini had shown how large the market was for compact four-seater cars with small engines, manufacturers worldwide stepped in to satisfy demand. With safety legislation becoming increasingly influential, the minis grew into superminis, which were larger, but still triumphs of packaging. Virtually all manufacturers followed the Mini's example of having a transverse four-cylinder engine and front-wheel drive.

◁ **Austin Mini-Metro 1980**

Origin UK

Engine 998 cc, straight-four

Top speed 84 mph (135 km/h)

Only 21 years after the Mini, in 1980 a new British supermini arrived. The car's engine dated back to 1953, but it was well packaged and had comfortable Hydragas suspension.

▷ **Talbot Samba 1982**

Origin France

Engine 1,360 cc, straight-four

Top speed 87 mph (140 km/h)

Peugeot took over Chrysler's European arm in 1978, so the Samba was no more than a dressed-up Peugeot 104. This meant it was a good car, with 954–1,360 cc options.

△ **Ford Festiva 1986**

Origin Japan/South Korea

Engine 1,138 cc, straight-four

Top speed 93 mph (150 km/h)

The Ford Festiva was designed by Mazda on a Mazda platform for the US, Australasia, and Japan. It was also produced as the Kia Pride by Kia Motors of Korea.

▷ **Peugeot 205 GTi 1984**

Origin France

Engine 1,905 cc, straight-four

Top speed 121 mph (195 km/h)

The sparkling GTi was an impressive derivative of Peugeot's 2.7-million-selling hatchback – even more so when it grew to 1905 cc, 130 bhp, and 121 mph in 1986.

△ **Volkswagen Polo 1981**

Origin Germany

Engine 1,043 cc, straight-four

Top speed 94 mph (151 km/h)

The second-generation Polo sold 4.5 million from 1981 to 1994, the extra space and more powerful engines making it much more competitive. It was restyled in 1990.

▷ **Nissan Cherry Turbo 1983**

Origin Japan

Engine 1,488 cc, straight-four

Top speed 114 mph (183 km/h)

Nissan's Cherry hatchbacks sold an impressive 1,450,300 between 1983 and 1986. Top of the range was this 114 bhp Turbo, but it suffered from poor handling and turbo lag.

◁ **Nissan March/Micra 1983**

Origin Japan

Engine 988 cc, straight-four

Top speed 88 mph (142 km/h)

Nissan's starter car had durable mechanics and 1.0- or 1.2-litre engines. It was not the most elegant supermini, but it was easy to drive and sold two million in nine years.

▷ Opel Corsa/Vauxhall Nova GTE/GSi 1983

Origin Spain

Engine 1,598 cc, straight-four

Top speed 117 mph (188 km/h)

The "hot hatch" GTE joined the Corsa family a bit later than the other 1.0/1.2/1.3/ 1.4-litre models and was by far the best looking. Like Ford's Fiesta, it was built in Spain.

△ Sinclair C5 1985

Origin UK

Engine Electric motor

Top speed 15 mph (24 km/h)

The C5 was a brave attempt to convert the world, starting in the UK, to light electric personal transportation. The converts were few, however, with just 12,000 made.

◁ SEAT Ibiza 1985

Origin Spain

Engine 1,461 cc, straight-four

Top speed 107 mph (172 km/h)

There was some Fiat influence in SEAT's new hatch, although all of its engines were designed by Porsche. Engines ranged from 950 to 1,714 cc.

◁ Fiat Uno 1983

Origin Italy

Engine 1,301 cc, straight-four

Top speed 104 mph (167 km/h)

The 127's successor was a great all-rounder, and sold 6.5 million by 1994. This was thanks to its good packaging, crisp styling by Giugiaro, and nimble handling.

△ Autobianchi Y10 1985

Origin Italy

Engine 999 cc, straight-four

Top speed 88 mph (142 km/h)

Built by Autobianchi and sold in some markets as a Lancia, this compact city car had dramatic styling and good interior space for its size. However, it was a little cramped for long journeys.

△ Renault 5 1984

Origin France

Engine 1,108 cc, straight-four

Top speed 90 mph (145 km/h)

This second-generation Renault 5 had 956–1,721 cc engines turned transverse for more interior space. It was one of the best-selling European cars of the 1980s.

◁ Citroën AX 1987

Origin France

Engine 954 cc, straight-four

Top speed 83 mph (134 km/h)

Available at first as a three-door, then as a five-door model in 1988, the AX shared its running gear with small Peugeots, but had its own chic styling.

△ Honda Civic CRX V-TEC 1987

Origin Japan

Engine 1,590 cc, straight-four

Top speed 129 mph (208 km/h)

Honda's Civic supermini was easily adapted to produce this coupé. With the 150 bhp, V-TEC, variable valve timing, twin-cam engine, it was astonishingly quick.

△ Geo Metro/Suzuki Swift 1989

Origin Japan/USA

Engine 993 cc, straight-three

Top speed 88 mph (142 km/h)

Built by Suzuki as the Cultus, or Swift, and still produced 20 years later in Pakistan, this "world car" was sold by GM in the US and built in seven different countries worldwide.

August Horch driving
a Horch-PKW, 1908

Great marques
The Audi story

Through innovation, technical excellence, and competition-led promotion, Audi has become a giant of the motor industry. Yet this now-famous German name was dormant for around 20 years after World War II. Since finding a home under the Volkswagen umbrella, Audi has come to epitomize Germany's pioneering spirit.

THE MAN BEHIND AUDI was a German engineer and industrialist called August Horch, who began manufacturing cars under the Horch name in 1901. In 1909, following a disagreement between Horch and the other directors of his Zwickau-based firm, Horch left the company. The next year Horch established another business, also in Zwickau, and began building cars under the Audi banner. Horch called it Audi because he was prohibited from using his own surname by the terms of the severance deal with his former firm. Audi is a Latinized version of Horch, which means "hark" or "listen" in German.

Audi badge
(introduced 1964)

The first Audi product was the 2,612 cc Typ A 10/22PS, with other, larger-engined cars following soon after. Recognizing the promotional value of beating his rivals in the public arena of motor sport, the astute August Horch began entering his cars in long-distance races and other events, including Austria's gruelling Alpine Trial from 1911 through to 1914. Audi's aluminium-bodied, 3,560 cc Typ C entries completed the 1913 event without penalties, and Audi took home the competition's team

prize. After this famous victory, the powerful Typ C became known as the Alpensieger (Alpine Victor).

Although still a fledgling concern, Audi was already at the forefront of automotive technology, being one of the first German marques to adopt electric lighting and starter motors for its cars in 1913. After shepherding

> "When I **dropped the clutch** at 4,500 rpm, it was **like an explosion.**"
> RALLY LEGEND WALTER ROHRL ON THE QUATTRO, 2010

Audi through World War I, when it made trucks for the German army, Horch left in 1920 to work for the Ministry of Economics. A consortium of directors subsequently led the company, but its habit of producing over-ambitious, expensive-to-make, and slow-selling products took its toll. In 1928 Jorgen Skafte Rasmussen,

Sensational quattro
With its sharp-edged styling and powerful engine, the quattro was an immediate success. The permanent four-wheel-drive system gave excellent traction and cornering, making the quattro an ideal rally car.

Audi Poster, 1921
This poster showcasing the Typ E Phaeton conveys an image of luxury and power. Relying on such expensive, slow-selling cars eventually took its toll on the company.

100 AVANT

SPORT QUATTRO S1 E2

TT ROADSTER

R8

1910 Audi Automobilwerke is formed.	**1966** Launch of the Audi 80 executive car; it will remain in production until 1996.	**1985** Michèle Mouton wins the Pikes Peak hill-climb race in the Sport quattro S1.
1920 August Horch leaves the company.	**1968** The 100 is launched; the 100 and its later derivative, the A6, will be the core of the range into the new millennium.	**1986** Alleged safety problems lead to the recall of 5,000 US cars; it is later found that parts of the media rigged failures.
1932 Audi, DKW, Horch, and Wanderer form the Auto Union conglomerate.		
1940 Last pre-war Audi made; the name disappears after World War II, when Auto Union factories come under the control of Germany's Eastern Zone.	**1969** Audi is merged with its rival, NSU, to to create Audi NSU Auto Union AG.	**1990** Audi V8 wins the German Touring Championship for first time.
	1977 The 100 saloon is the world's first car with an in-line, five-cylinder engine.	**1994** New A8 saloon features a weight-saving, all-aluminium chassis/body.
1964 Volkswagen rescues the ailing Auto Union/DKW concern.	**1980** The Audi quattro is unveiled.	**1996** Frank Biela wins the British Touring Car Championship driver's title in an A4; the A3 small family car is introduced.
1965 Audi name is revived for new 60 saloon, based on the DKW F102.	**1984** The short wheelbase Sport quattro (developed for rallying) is launched.	

1998 Audi takes over Lamborghini.
2000 Audi returns to the small car market with the three-cylinder A2; it also wins the Le Mans 24-hour race for the first time with the R8 racing car.
2005 The Q7 full-size crossover SUV is launched; the more compact Q5 appears in 2009.
2006 The R10 TDI is the first diesel-powered car to win Le Mans 24-hour race.
2009 Audi reveals plans to develop its new e-tron electric-drive powertrain.

a Danish-born engineer, acquired a controlling stake in Audi. Rasmussen had been making his DKW motorcycles since 1920, and he was already a long way down the road to launching his first "light car". However, he needed a suitable factory for car assembly, and this was his main motivation for taking over Audi. New products were launched, but most lacked originality. The four-cylinder Typ P, for example, combined a Peugeot 201 engine with a chassis and body made by DKW. As the company began to focus on DKW-branded cars, the Audi marque became marginalized: just 77 Audis

Successful slogan
Since the 1980s Audi has used the slogan *Vorsprung durch Technik* (Progress through Technology) to portray itself as an innovative, visionary, go-ahead company.

were made in 1931 and 22 the year after. In the midst of the economic slump of the early 1930s, a deal was brokered between Audi, DKW, Horch, and another marque, Wanderer, to form the Auto Union conglomerate. From mid-1932 this broad-based concern had blanket coverage of the German car market, with bargain-priced DKWs, mid-range Audi and Wanderer models, and prestigious Horch saloons and limousines. Predictably, crossbreeding was rife – but not always profitable. The 1933 Audi Front, for example, had a front-wheel-drive Wanderer engine, DKW running gear, and styling that aped Horch products; it was not a success. From April 1940 production was given over entirely to military vehicles to aid Germany's war effort.

After the division of Germany at the end of World War II, the Auto Union group lay in the Soviet-controlled Eastern Zone, and the names Audi, Horch, and Wanderer

disappeared from the market, although Horch did make a brief comeback as an East German brand in the 1950s. A new company named Auto Union was founded in West Germany, at first supplying spare parts, but later manufacturing cars under the Auto Union and DKW marques. Daimler-Benz bought a majority shareholding in Auto Union in 1958 and centred production on low-cost, two-stroke-engined cars. By the time Volkswagen took control in late 1964, the range was outmoded and unsophisticated. Keen to compete with BMW as an aspirational brand, Volkswagen put its new 1,696 cc, four-cylinder engine into the existing DKW F102 saloon and relaunched it as the Audi 60 – the first Audi of the post-war era.

The Audi renaissance grew steadily, and in 1969 Volkswagen merged it with another of its brands, NSU, to form Audi NSU Auto Union AG. Audi products initially included several rebadged Volkswagens, and its reputation for innovation was only truly established with the launch of the quattro coupé in 1980. This handsome machine featured permanent four-wheel drive (then still quite a novelty for a mainstream manufacturer) and a turbocharged, five-cylinder engine.

The quattro caused a furore, even more so when it began to clean up in rallying. It dominated the sport from 1982 to 1984, with legendary drivers such as Hannu Mikkola, Stig Blomqvist, and Walter Rohrl all winning world drivers' titles. And the victories kept on coming: Audis won in the US at the Pikes Peak International Hill Climb and the TransAm championship, in addition to taking touring-car titles in France, the UK, and Germany.

Audi increasingly took on the role as the harbinger of new technologies and looks within the Volkswagen group, including pioneering the use of aluminium for its large A8 saloon of 1994 and introducing a bold new styling language with products such as the TT of 1998. More recently, Audi has made its mark in endurance racing, claiming its first win at the Le Mans 24-hour race, France, in 2000. Six years later Audi became the first marque to win this classic event with a diesel-powered car, the R10 TDI, in line with its mission statement to showcase new and alternative technologies in competition.

Audi R10 TDI
Winner at Le Mans from 2006-2008, the R10 used a longitudinally mounted, 5,499 cc, V12 aluminium diesel engine with two turbochargers.

Ultimate Sports Saloons

By the 1980s saloons were so refined that open sports cars became the preserve of hardy enthusiasts; speed-seeking drivers bought sports saloons instead. The surge in popularity of touring-car racing led manufacturers to build homologation specials – road models adapted to meet racing regulations – that would put their marque's cars at the front of the race grid. These limited-edition performance cars are highly collectable now.

△ **Aston Martin Lagonda 1976**

Origin UK

Engine 5,340 cc, V8

Top speed 143 mph (230 km/h)

A computerized digital dashboard and harsh wedge styling made the Lagonda seem futuristic in the 1970s. It took until 1979 for the first car to be delivered, the model truly coming of age in the 1980s.

△ **Holden VH Commodore 1981**

Origin Australia

Engine 5,044 cc, V8

Top speed 125 mph (201 km/h)

Holden of Australia built tough saloons with engines from 1.9 litres upwards; its VH Commodores were successful locally in motor sport. The road version was known as the SS.

△ **Rover 3500 Vitesse 1982**

Origin UK

Engine 3,528 cc, V8

Top speed 133 mph (214 km/h)

Simple mechanics, modern lines, and a light V8 engine helped the Rover SD1 become European Car of the Year in 1977; the Vitesse was the ultimate performance version in the 1980s.

▷ **Bentley Turbo R 1985**

Origin UK

Engine 6,750 cc, V8

Top speed 143 mph (230 km/h)

Rolls-Royce transformed Bentley's flagging sales by introducing turbochargers, giving the marque back its sporting credentials: ultimate luxury with a big kick.

△ **Maserati Biturbo 1981**

Origin Italy

Engine 1,996 cc, V6

Top speed 132 mph (212 km/h)

To expand the market for his Maserati marque, Alejandro de Tomaso launched this two- or four-door, turbocharged saloon; it drove well, but its staid looks and poor build let it down.

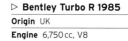

△ **BMW M3 1988**

Origin Germany

Engine 2,302 cc, straight-four

Top speed 143 mph (230 km/h)

In making its E30 3-series fit for racing, BMW produced one of the iconic cars of the 1980s. Terrific performance and handling were matched by luxurious trim.

◁ **Vauxhall Lotus Carlton 1989**

Origin Germany/UK

Engine 3,615 cc, straight-six

Top speed 177 mph (285 km/h)

Sold in mainland Europe as the Opel-Lotus Omega, this was a modified version of the standard Carlton saloon, with an enlarged engine and twin turbochargers to give phenomenal performance.

▽ **Audi V8 DTM 1988**

Origin Germany

Engine 4,172 cc, V8

Top speed 153 mph (246 km/h)

The four-wheel-drive, 4.2-litre V8 brought Audi credibility as a maker of top-league saloon cars. This smaller 3.6-litre won Germany's DTM race series in 1990 and 1991.

△ **Ford Sierra XR4i 1983**

Origin UK/Germany

Engine 2,792 cc, V6

Top speed 129 mph (208 km/h)

This last rear-wheel-drive muscle car from Ford Europe could be exciting in the wet, but refined high-speed cruising was its forte, the bi-plane spoiler keeping it stable.

◁ **Ford Sierra Cosworth RS500 1987**

Origin UK/Germany

Engine 1,993 cc, straight-four

Top speed 149 mph (240 km/h)

With 224-300 bhp, powerful brakes, and huge spoilers, this turbocharged homologation special kept the Sierra at the forefront of touring-car racing; just 500 cars were made.

△ **Ford Taurus SHO 1989**

Origin USA

Engine 2,986 cc, V6

Top speed 143 mph (230 km/h)

Ford ordered Yamaha engines for a planned sports car: when the car was cancelled, the engines were put in the limited-edition SHO. The SHO was so popular it went into full production.

△ **Lancia Thema 8.32 1987**

Origin Italy

Engine 2,927 cc, V8

Top speed 149 mph (240 km/h)

Trimmed to the highest standard and hugely expensive, the Lancia Thema 8.32 was fitted with an engine from the Ferrari 308 sports car, modified to suit the heavier saloon body.

◁ **Volkswagen Golf Rallye G60 1989**

Origin Germany

Engine 1,763 cc, straight-four

Top speed 134 mph (216 km/h)

For those who thought the Golf GTI wasn't quite fast enough, Volkswagen produced the supercharged, four-wheel-drive G60 for just one year, selling 9,780. Rather surprisingly, it was not built for rallying.

Pace-Setting Style from Italian Designers

Producers of ground-breaking car designs since the 1920s, the Italian styling houses were the single most influential styling force in the motoring world by the 1980s. Italian stylists led not just fashion – wedge shapes or rounded – but whole concepts such as the hatchback body style, adding glamour to everything from cheap runabouts to mid-engined supercars.

△ **DeLorean DMC-12 1981**

Origin UK

Engine 2,849 cc, V6

Top speed 121 mph (195 km/h)

Lotus drew up the chassis, Giugiaro styled the body, and it starred in the film *Back to the Future*, but the DeLorean had quality problems that saw it out of production in 1982.

△ **Hyundai Excel/Pony 1985**

Origin South Korea

Engine 1,468 cc, straight-four

Top speed 96 mph (154 km/h)

Hyundai brought in Italdesign to style its first Pony in 1975, replacing it 10 years later with this similar but front-wheel-drive model. It was built up to 1994.

△ **Škoda Favorit 1987**

Origin Czechoslovakia

Engine 1,289 cc, straight-four

Top speed 92 mph (148 km/h)

Škoda's first front-engined, front-wheel-drive model was styled by Bertone and became one of Central Europe's most popular cars. It was simple, with just one engine option.

△ **Lancia Delta Integrale 1987**

Origin Italy

Engine 1,995 cc, straight-four

Top speed 134 mph (216 km/h)

Giugiaro's Delta was very modern for its time, and was European Car of the Year in 1980. This is the 4x4 rally development of what started as a shopping car.

◁ **Chrysler TC by Maserati 1989**

Origin Italy

Engine 2,213 cc, straight-four

Top speed 130 mph (209 km/h)

Though it was built in Italy by Maserati, the TC had a turbocharged Chrysler engine and was styled in the US. Three years in gestation, it took too long to reach the high street and sold poorly.

△ **Citroën BX 1982**

Origin France

Engine 1,905 cc, straight-four

Top speed 106 mph (171 km/h)

Styled by Marcello Gandini of Bertone, 2.3 million BXs were sold in 12 years. They shared the Peugeot 405's floorpan, but with hydropneumatic suspension and 1.1–1.9-litre engines.

▷ **Peugeot 405 1987**

Origin France

Engine 1,905 cc, straight-four

Top speed 116 mph (187 km/h)

Built until 1997 in Europe and still made in Iran, the Pininfarina-styled 405 won European Car of the Year in 1988 and sold 2.5 million worldwide. It has 1.4–2.0-litre engines.

◁ **Volvo 780 1986**

Origin Sweden/Italy

Engine 2,849 cc, V6

Top speed 114 mph (183 km/h)

Built by Bertone, the 780 began life with a live rear axle and an underpowered engine. By 1988 these had been replaced by independent rear suspension and a turbo.

△ **Citroën XM 1989**

Origin France

Engine 2,975 cc, V6

Top speed 143 mph (230 km/h)

Styled by Bertone, and derived from Gandini's Citroën BX, the big, sleek XM had 2.0–3.0-litre engines and electronically controlled hydropneumatic suspension.

△ Fiat Panda 1980

Origin Italy

Engine 1,100 cc, straight-four

Top speed 86 mph (138 km/h)

A Giorgetto Giugiaro-styled classic, this simple, no-frills car set the style for 1980s Fiats. Steadily improved with 650-1,100cc and even a 4x4, it was on sale until 2003.

◁ Fiat Strada/Ritmo Cabriolet 1983

Origin Italy

Engine 1,498 cc, straight-four

Top speed 103 mph (166 km/h)

Bertone gave Fiat the most distinctively styled family hatchback of the 1970s. It was too radical to be popular at first, but by the 1983 Cabriolet launch it had come of age.

◁ Fiat Croma 1985

Origin Italy

Engine 2,500 cc, straight-four

Top speed 121 mph (195 km/h)

Giorgetto Giugiaro styled this big "notchback hatchback" family car with 1.6-2.5-litre engines. It was the world's first passenger car with a direct injection diesel engine.

△ Isuzu Piazza Turbo 1980

Origin Japan

Engine 1,996 cc, straight-four

Top speed 127 mph (204 km/h)

General Motors' Japanese brand had Giugiaro style its new coupé. Sold in the US from 1983 and in Europe from 1985, it was fast, but handled poorly at first.

◁ Ferrari Mondial Cabriolet 1984

Origin Italy

Engine 2,926 cc, V8

Top speed 146 mph (235 km/h)

Pininfarina styled the striking wedge-shaped, mid-engined Mondial, which looked even better with its roof down as it had no rollover bar. Its performance was exhilarating.

△ Lotus Etna 1984

Origin UK/Italy

Engine 3,946 cc, V8

Top speed 180 mph (290 km/h)

Styled by Giugiaro for Italdesign, the Etna was a non-running prototype until 2008 when it finally ran with the intended V8 engine, derived from the Esprit slant-four.

△ Cadillac Allanté 1987

Origin USA/Italy

Engine 4,087 cc, V8

Top speed 119 mph (192 km/h)

Designed and built in Italy, and flown to the US as fully trimmed bodies to be united with the Cadillac chassis, this upmarket roadster was criticized for having front-wheel drive.

▷ Aston Martin V8 Vantage Zagato 1986

Origin UK/Italy

Engine 5,340 cc, V8

Top speed 185 mph (298 km/h)

Echoing the DB4 GT Zagato of the 1960s, just 50 coupés and 25 convertibles of the 1986 V8 Vantage Zagato were built. Though not as elegant, it was brutally fast – and expensive.

DeLorean DMC-12

It is difficult to separate the DeLorean from the financial scandal that engulfed it. Promoted as an "ethical" sports car - safe and durable - it was the brainchild of former General Motors high-flier John Zachary DeLorean, and was bankrolled by the British government, which paid for a brand-new factory in Northern Ireland. Dubious business practices and unbridled extravagance were matched by unrealistic market expectations for the DeLorean. When sales - undermined by poor quality - failed to match the hype, the business crashed.

THE DELOREAN entered production in 1981 retaining the gullwing doors and stainless-steel cladding of the prototype unveiled in 1977. Little else remained, as the car was completely redesigned by Lotus pre-production. Initial plans had been for a mid-mounted Wankel engine, but the final powerplant was a Renault V6 hung behind the rear axle. Despite this tail-heavy configuration, the car handled well. The British sports-car company ditched the DeLorean's plastic bodyshell, which used a sandwich of glassfibre with a foam filling. It substituted this unproven

technology with a traditional Lotus steel-backbone chassis and a two-piece, glassfibre body using its clever vacuum-assisted, injection-moulding process. That the DeLorean made it to production in a new factory within a very short period is essentially due to Lotus; but the rush to launch the car meant that initial quality was atrocious. However, John Z. DeLorean's dream car found an everlasting place in popular culture after it was cast as plutonium-powered, time-travelling transport for Michael J. Fox in *Back To The Future* – the biggest-grossing cinema release of 1985.

SPECIFICATIONS	
Model	DeLorean DMC-12, 1981-82
Assembly	Dunmurry, Northern Ireland
Production	9,000 approx.
Construction	Steel-backbone chassis
Engine	2,849 cc, ohc V6
Power output	130 bhp at 5,500 rpm
Transmission	Five-speed manual
Suspension	All-independent coil
Brakes	All-round discs
Maximum speed	121 mph (195 km/h)

Founder's logo
The symmetrical "DMC" logo was an abbreviation of "DeLorean Motor Company". The model title was always DMC-12. John Z. DeLorean himself was associated with the development of several cars for GM's Pontiac division.

FRONT VIEW WITH OPEN DOORS

FRONT VIEW

REAR VIEW

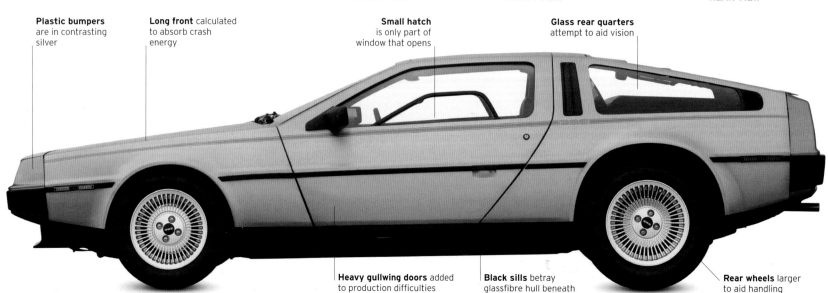

Plastic bumpers are in contrasting silver

Long front calculated to absorb crash energy

Small hatch is only part of window that opens

Glass rear quarters attempt to aid vision

Heavy gullwing doors added to production difficulties

Black sills betray glassfibre hull beneath

Rear wheels larger to aid handling

Style over function

The gullwing doors serve no good purpose – although DeLorean cited the safety benefits of the high sills. However, they look dramatic, as does the brushed stainless-steel body cladding. Both the doors and body cladding were seen as selling points, even though they added weight and complication. The rust-resistant steel cladding was chosen because the original "plastic-sandwich" body could not be painted satisfactorily – and it eliminated the need for paint.

THE EXTERIOR

The DeLorean's appearance is dominated by the attention-grabbing gullwing doors – insisted on by John Z. DeLorean for that very reason. The sharp-edged style is typical of designer Giorgetto Giugiaro's 1970s output, during what has been termed his "folded paper" era. The rear engine facilitates the pencil-thin front end treatment. Whatever one's feelings about the car – and about DeLorean himself – the effectiveness of its styling cannot be denied.

1. "DMC" stands for "DeLorean Motor Company" **2.** Badging graphics typical of 1970s style **3.** Headlights are US-standard rectangular units **4.** Door handles integrated into rubbing strip **5.** Rear vent on right side provides fresh air intake to the engine **6.** Alloy wheels are unique to the DeLorean **7.** Slats are an impediment to rear vision **8.** Tail light style only found on DMC-12

THE INTERIOR

Occupants in the cockpit are snugly sandwiched between the broad centre tunnel – necessitated by the backbone chassis underneath – and the high sills demanded by the gullwing doors. Thick front and rear pillars restrict vision, and early cars with all-black interiors can seem a bit claustrophobic; hence the use of grey trim on later cars. The two-door coupé did not have even token rear seats.

9. Doors held up by torsion bars and gas struts **10.** Cockpit comfortable even for tall drivers **11.** Seats always in leather; note baggage net behind **12.** Despite initial plans, steering-wheel not fitted with airbag **13.** Minor controls are straightforward **14.** Instrumentation is similarly clear yet comprehensive

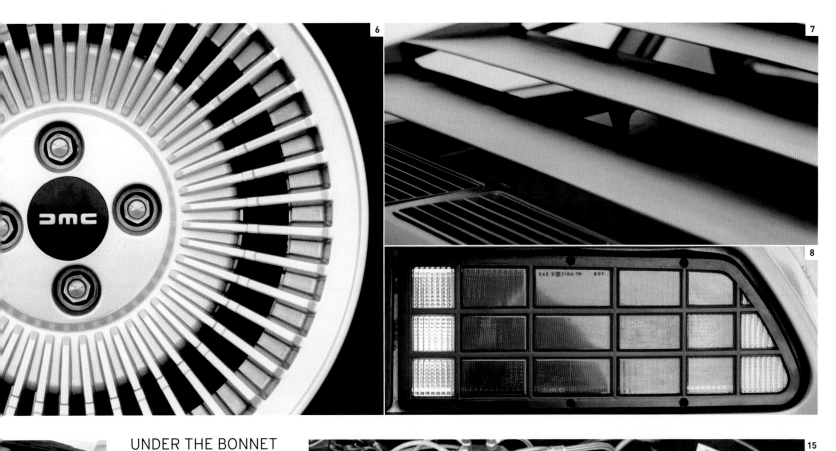

6

7

8

UNDER THE BONNET

The all-alloy V6 comes from France, and was shared with the Renault 30 and Peugeot 604, as well as the Volvo 264. In detuned, US emissions compliant form, power is only 130 bhp, resulting in a 0–60 mph time of 10.5 seconds. This put the DeLorean at a considerable performance disadvantage against its competitor – the Porsche 911SC was barely more expensive, was lighter, and had a power output of 172 bhp. To improve matters, DeLorean planned a twin-turbo version, but this was never made.

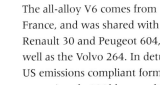

15. Under-bonnet layout untidy by today's standards **16.** Air conditioning is standard equipment **17.** Front fuel tank means filler under bonnet

15

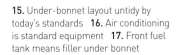

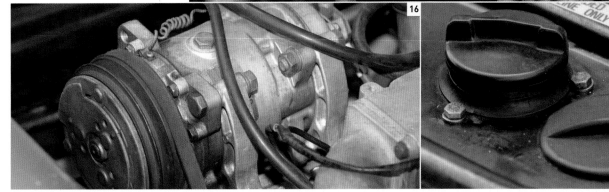

16

17

Porsche 911
flat-six

Porsche's first sports car, the 356, utilized many components from the Volkswagen, including its flat-four engine. When an all-new powerplant was needed for the replacement 911, Porsche kept the horizontally opposed layout and air-cooling but upped the cylinder count to six. The result was one of the most charismatic and enduring high-performance engines of all time.

Six beats four
By the early 1960s the Porsche flat-four engine, used in the 356, had exhausted its development potential. Its flat-six replacement released the extra power the new 911 model would need. The engine's design allowed for progressively increased engine capacity as Porsche further developed the 911.

LASTING SUCCESS

It is a measure of the quality of Porsche's original design that the flat-six remained in production – through numerous variants of increasing capacity, including fearsome turbocharged units – for more than three decades. The 911 refused to die, and its unique engine with it. While the 911 continues, the engine was eventually replaced in 1998 when Porsche retained the flat-six layout but abandoned air cooling for water cooling. One of the benefits was that, for the first time in the 911, Porsche was able to use four valves per cylinder and exploit the improved engine "breathing" (air flow) that resulted.

Low profile
Although the cylinders and crankcase are obscured in this photo of a 1994 flat-six, the engine's low, wide stance is obvious. This helps the engine fit neatly into the tail of the 911, while the lowered centre of gravity aids roadholding.

ENGINE SPECIFICATIONS

Dates produced	1963–1998 (air-cooled version)
Cylinders	Flat-six
Configuration	Rear-mounted, longitudinal
Engine capacities	1,991 cc, progressively increased to 3,746 cc
Power output	128 bhp @ 6,200 rpm (ultimately 402 bhp with twin turbos)
Type	Conventional four-stroke, air-cooled, petrol engine with reciprocating pistons, distributor (later distributorless) ignition, and a wet sump
Head	sohc per bank, chain driven; two valves and (later) twin spark plugs per cylinder
Fuel System	Single carburettor, later fuel injection
Bore and Stroke	80 mm x 66 mm (3.15 in x 2.60 in)
Power	64.3 bhp/litre
Compression Ratio	9.0:1

Silencer

Tailpipe

Ignition components
There are two spark plugs per cylinder in this late version of the air-cooled flat-six, which helps to reduce emissions, increase power, and lower fuel consumption.

▷ **See pp.346-347** How an engine works

Induction system
This is another part of the air inlet system. From 1993 the flat-six was equipped with Porsche's Varioram induction system. The Varioram alters the configuration of the air inlet tracts according to the engine's speed, exploiting resonance effects to force more air into the cylinders and so maximize the engine's output torque.

Idle speed positioner
This device adjusts the flow of air into the engine to maintain the correct idle speed – the speed the engine runs at with the throttle closed (in other words, with the foot off the accelerator pedal).

Multi-blade fan
The fan draws cooling air over the finned cylinder heads and barrels, and helps to create the engine's distinctive sound.

Control flap location
Part of the air inlet system, a flap (missing) that varies the resonance of air in the inlet tracts fits here. It sits alongside a hot-film sensor that measures the mass of air entering the cylinders and sends data to the engine-management computer.

Air filter housing

Air inlet

Air conditioning compressor

Alternator
The engine's alternator (hidden) shares a common axis with the fan – which obscures it in this view – but has its own separate drive belt.

Heat shield

Three-way catalytic converter
Beneath the heat shield, the catalytic converter uses a large-surface-area, precious-metal catalyst to reduce tailpipe emissions of carbon monoxide, hydrocarbons, and oxides of nitrogen.

Silencer

Tailpipe

Lamborghini Countach

The poster boy for the 1970s supercar boom, this rare and exotic road machine was first revealed in prototype form in the spring of 1971. The 25th Anniversary edition, to celebrate Lamborghini's dawn in 1962, was fundamentally the same car but by 1988 it possessed a near-mythical reputation for mid-engined style and excitement. The word *countach* comes from the dialect of the Piedmont region in northern Italy; it is an expression of approval of a beautiful woman from admiring men.

AFTER SEVERAL mid-engined supercar prototypes had stunned visitors at late 1960s motor shows, Lamborghini and design house Bertone were determined to be first to put such a car in customers' hands. Lamborghini's engineers were tasked with designing the tubular spaceframe chassis for "Project 112". Into this, the V12 powerplant earlier seen in the Lamborghini Miura was installed, behind the two seats but ahead of the rear wheels. The engine was longitudinally positioned, with the five-speed gearbox in front, and the driveshaft ran back through the oil sump to the rear differential. Bertone's star designer Marcello Gandini created the aggressive wedge-shaped design, and the car was manufactured with aircraft-grade aluminium. The prototype was called the LP500, and the first production car arrived in 1974 as the Countach LP400 with a 3,929 cc engine.

FRONT VIEW

REAR VIEW

Founder's star sign
Company founder Ferruccio Lamborghini named the Lamborghini Miura after renowned Spanish bullfighter Antonio Miura. But the company emblem of a charging bull signified Ferruccio's own star sign, Taurus. He sold his car-making firm in 1971, three years before the Countach went on sale.

SIDE VIEW

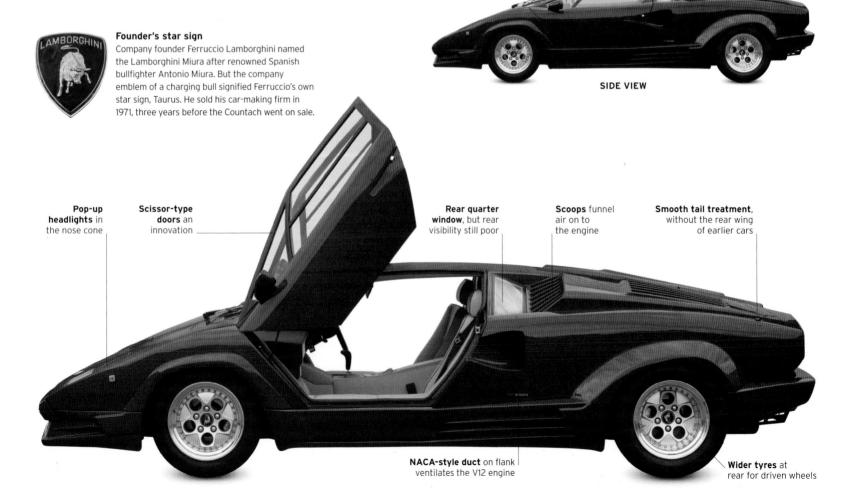

Pop-up headlights in the nose cone

Scissor-type doors an innovation

Rear quarter window, but rear visibility still poor

Scoops funnel air on to the engine

Smooth tail treatment, without the rear wing of earlier cars

NACA-style duct on flank ventilates the V12 engine

Wider tyres at rear for driven wheels

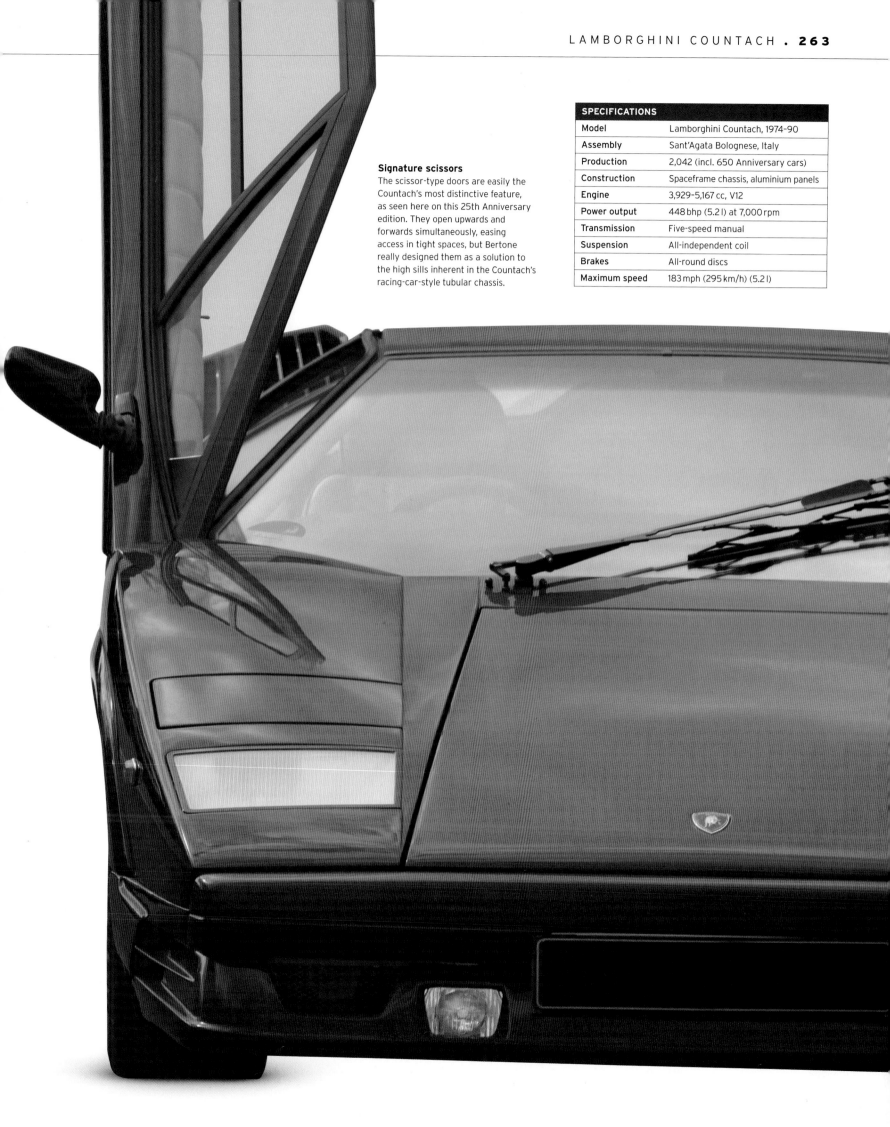

Signature scissors

The scissor-type doors are easily the Countach's most distinctive feature, as seen here on this 25th Anniversary edition. They open upwards and forwards simultaneously, easing access in tight spaces, but Bertone really designed them as a solution to the high sills inherent in the Countach's racing-car-style tubular chassis.

SPECIFICATIONS	
Model	Lamborghini Countach, 1974–90
Assembly	Sant'Agata Bolognese, Italy
Production	2,042 (incl. 650 Anniversary cars)
Construction	Spaceframe chassis, aluminium panels
Engine	3,929–5,167 cc, V12
Power output	448 bhp (5.2 l) at 7,000 rpm
Transmission	Five-speed manual
Suspension	All-independent coil
Brakes	All-round discs
Maximum speed	183 mph (295 km/h) (5.2 l)

THE EXTERIOR

The Countach was the first high-performance road car with an uncompromising wedge shape. It is low and wide, with very little frontal area, and a visual emphasis on the rear, where several intakes feed the high-performance engine with air to keep it cool under hard driving. Rear visibility is always tricky for Countach drivers, made even worse by the huge aerofoils fitted to many cars. This Anniversary model has bespoke wheelarch extensions and side skirts.

1. Lower-case nameplate is characteristically quirky **2.** Charging bull emblem hints at ferocious performance **3.** Pop-up headlights preserve purity of line **4.** Door release in air duct **5.** Lightweight polished alloy wheels **6.** "Designed by Bertone" in Italian **7.** Sculptural air intake **8.** Internal door release **9.** Louvres on tail allow engine heat to disperse **10.** Tail light clusters unique to Anniversary edition

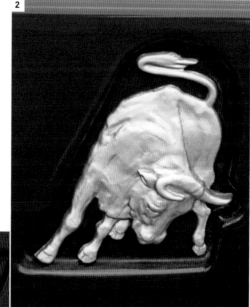

THE INTERIOR

The extremely snug two-seater cockpit is notable for the recumbent angle of the two bucket seats, which give the authentic impression of this being a racing car tamed for road use. Many of the smaller controls and components in specialist Italian cars like this are taken from mass-production models – often Fiats – but the craftsmanship that goes into the leather trim counteracts this and creates a purposeful ambience.

11. Leather-rimmed steering wheel fronts pleasing white-on-black dials **12.** Push-buttons for minor controls, and an Alpine high-tech hi-fi **13.** Air vents skilfully incorporated from another car **14.** Controls for electrically adjusted seats **15.** Leather gear knob and exposed gearchange "gate" **16.** Well-bolstered hump between seats houses gearbox

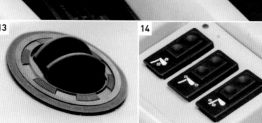

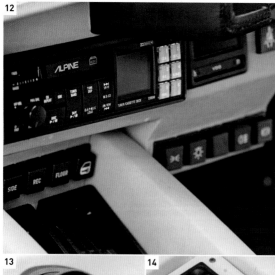

UNDER THE BONNET

At the heart of any Lamborghini is the hand-built masterpiece that is its engine. All Countachs have V12 power units, and the one in the Anniversary car is a 5.2-litre version that was supplied with no less than six Weber carburettors for European markets, or else Bosch K-Jetronic fuel-injection for sale to the US which resulted in a power output drop of 35 bhp as a trade-off for cleaner exhaust emissions. The engine and its ancillaries are tightly packed in, and accessible through an opening engine cover on the tail of the car.

17. The V12 engine designed by Giotto Bizzarrini was unveiled in 1963, and is still made today – with double the capacity

Two-Seater Excitement

The 1980s was the decade of young, upwardly mobile professionals, or "yuppies", whose fun cars gave rise to a rich heritage of roadsters and coupés. Each had its own flavour at a time when, in retrospect, their manufacturers were generally untroubled by the demands of safety legislation. Evergreen classics mixed it with newcomers boasting front- and four-wheel drive; the brute horsepower of the old guard vied with the cutting-edge technology of the new. There was rarely room for the kids.

△ **Aston Martin Bulldog 1980**

Origin UK

Engine 5,340 cc, V8

Top speed 191 mph (307 km/h)

Here was a fantasy Aston Martin: a mid-engined, twin-turbo, gullwing-door concept car that shocked the car world in 1980. The only car built achieved 191 mph in tests.

△ **Alfa Romeo Spider 1982**

Origin Italy

Engine 1,567–1,962 cc, four-cylinder

Top speed 118 mph (190 km/h)

Launched in 1966, the Spider gained a major facelift in 1982. Purists decried the rubber bumpers and tail spoiler, but these crash precautions kept this living classic legally compliant in the US.

△ **Pontiac Firebird Trans Am 1982**

Origin USA

Engine 5,001–5,733 cc, V8

Top speed 140 mph (225 km/h)

The most aerodynamic GM car ever, this third-generation Firebird was a 2+2 coupé. The Trans Ams were all V8s – one starred as KITT in the popular US TV series *Knight Rider*.

▽ **Chevrolet Corvette Convertible 1986**

Origin USA

Engine 5,733 cc, V8

Top speed 142 mph (229 km/h)

The Corvette was fully redesigned in 1983, and three years later a proper convertible option made a return after a gap of 10 years away. A digital dashboard was a notable feature.

△ **TVR 350i 1984**

Origin UK

Engine 3,528 cc, V8

Top speed 143 mph (230 km/h)

TVR's traditional backbone chassis and glassfibre body blended with Rover's superb aluminium V8 engine made for lightning acceleration and entertaining handling.

▷ **Toyota MR2 1984**

Origin Japan

Engine 1,587 cc, four-cylinder

Top speed 120 mph (193 km/h)

The MR2 (Mid-engined Recreational Two-seater) wasn't the first affordable centrally powered sports car, but it was certainly the best yet; responsive and reliable.

△ **Marcos Mantula 1984**

Origin UK

Engine 3,528–3,947 cc, V8

Top speed 150 mph (241 km/h)

The classic Marcos of the 1960s sprang back to life in the 1980s as the Mantula. Features now included a soft-top, a more aerodynamic nose, and a gutsy Rover V8 engine.

▽ **Caterham Seven 1980**

Origin UK

Engine 1,588–1,715 cc, four-cylinder

Top speed 115 mph (185 km/h)

Based on the 1968 version of the 1957 Lotus Seven, the Caterham grew in popularity during the 1980s. It still used Ford engines, and its handling and acceleration excited a new generation.

△ **Porsche 911 Cabriolet 1982**

Origin Germany

Engine 2,687–3,299 cc, flat-six

Top speed 168 mph (270 km/h)

Fans of the 911 who craved fresh air waited until 1982 before Porsche launched a fully convertible bodystyle. It was eventually offered with standard Carrera and Turbo engines.

◁ **Porsche 959 1986**

Origin Germany

Engine 2,994 cc, flat-six

Top speed 190 mph (306 km/h)

Two hundred of these awesome cars were built to qualify the 959 for Group B rallying. It had four-wheel drive, 405 bhp from its twin-turbo engine, and electronic ride height.

△ **BMW Z1 1986**

Origin Germany

Engine 2,494 cc, six-cylinder

Top speed 140 mph (225 km/h)

Originally a prototype to test suspension parts, BMW decided to market the Z1 and sold 8,000. The doors slid down inside the plastic body for access to the cockpit.

△ **Jaguar XJS 1988**

Origin UK

Engine 5,343 cc, V12

Top speed 150 mph (241 km/h)

This fully convertible XJS (previously, there had been a Targa-top cabriolet) came with an electric hood, anti-lock brakes, Jaguar's silken V12 engine, and abundant style.

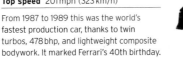

◁ **Ferrari Testarossa 1984**

Origin Italy

Engine 4,942 cc, flat-twelve

Top speed 181 mph (291 km/h)

Featuring in the *Miami Vice* TV series, the Testarossa symbolized 1980s glamour. The all-alloy, 390 bhp engine roared from the back of the widest car on sale at the time.

△ **Lotus Esprit 1987**

Origin UK

Engine 2,174 cc, four-cylinder

Top speed 163 mph (262 km/h)

Amazing performance from the 2.2-litre Esprit Turbo engine made it a genuine Ferrari-baiter; 1987 saw a Lotus restyle of the Giugiaro original as part of a big revamp.

▷ **Ferrari F40 1987**

Origin Italy

Engine 2,936 cc, V8

Top speed 201 mph (323 km/h)

From 1987 to 1989 this was the world's fastest production car, thanks to twin turbos, 478 bhp, and lightweight composite bodywork. It marked Ferrari's 40th birthday.

△ **Lotus Elan 1989**

Origin UK

Engine 1,588 cc, four-cylinder

Top speed 136 mph (219 km/h)

Lotus's only front-wheel-drive sports car, this shortlived Elan was exciting to drive, partly due to clever wishbone front suspension. The Isuzu engine was usually turbocharged.

△ **Lamborghini Countach 1988**

Origin Italy

Engine 5,167 cc, V12

Top speed 180 mph (290 km/h)

The wild-child Countach was cleverly restyled for its final two years, to commemorate the supercar-maker's silver jubilee. It gained the widest tyres then fitted to any car.

Ferrari F40

It was fitting that the F40 was the final model commissioned by Enzo Ferrari before his death in 1988. Launched in 1987 to commemorate the marque's 40th anniversary, this was a supercar that, true to the spirit of *Il Commendatore* himself, incorporated racetrack technology in a road-going car to create a truly exhilarating package. Ferrari's army of devoted fans agreed, with a lengthy waiting list and wealthy customers willing to pay up to a million pounds sterling to get their hands on the fastest street-legal production car in the world.

CONTAINING THE DNA of the similarly jaw-dropping 288 GTO model that it replaced, the F40 was styled by the fabled Pininfarina design house that had shaped many of Ferrari's finest creations for almost as long as the company had been producing cars.

The F40 was a coupé with beauty and brawn in equal measure. Its twin-turbo 478 bhp V8 was capable of transporting a driver and passenger to more than 200 mph (322 mph) for the first time in a standard road car. Originally intended to be manufactured in strictly limited numbers, demand was so high for this sublime yet uncompromising model that Ferrari fulfilled orders until 1992. By this time the F40 was no longer the world's quickest road car, but this was a minor detail for Ferrari aficionados and motoring writers who had run out of superlatives to describe one of the finest automobiles ever made.

FRONT VIEW

REAR VIEW

Made in Modena
Known as the *Cavallino Rampante*, Ferrari's Prancing Horse logo originated from an Italian flying ace, who decorated his aircraft with the horse. The badge also features the colours of the Italian flag, while the yellow background is the colour of Ferrari's home town of Modena.

SIDE VIEW

Forward-lifting bonnet typical of contemporary sport-prototype models

Bonnet-opening hook

Sliding side screens on first 50 models later gave way to wind-ups

Slightly recessed doors emphasize F40's muscular style

Engine cover made of weight-saving Plexiglass

Full-width aerodynamic wing contributes to increased down-force

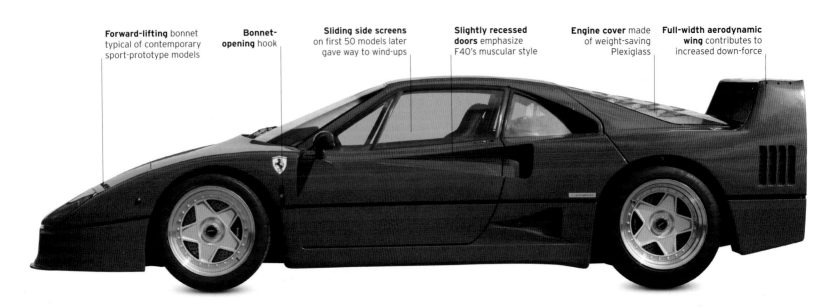

Wind-cheating design

Every aspect of the F40's design was determined by aerodynamics and airflow, from its steeply raked nose to the three air intakes at the front of the car – one large central example for the radiator and two smaller side vents for the brakes – and the conspicuous scoops on the bonnet. Pop-up headlights were supplemented by flush-fitting indicators and foglight assembly.

SPECIFICATIONS			
Model	Ferrari F40, 1987–2002	Power output	478 bhp at 7,000 rpm
Assembly	Maranello, Italy	Transmission	5-speed manual
Production	1,311	Suspension	Front and rear independent
Construction	Oval-section tubular steel and composites	Brakes	Discs front and rear
Engine	2,936 cc, V8	Maximum speed	201 mph (324 km/h)

2260 W 7

THE EXTERIOR

Made up of just 11 panels, the F40's carbon-fibre, Kevlar, and Nomex bodyshell was offered to customers in one colour – *Rosso Corsa*, or Racing Red. The high-tech materials resulted in an exceptionally light kerb weight of just 1,100 kg (2,420 lb) which, combined with the ultra-rigid tubular-steel chassis, contributed to a car with exceptional handling. Unsubtle air vents of varying sizes peppered the bodywork, adding to the sense of menace generated by the F40's aggressive styling.

1. Prancing Horse badge with initials for Scuderia Ferrari, the racing team division   2. Ferrari script positioned above rear numberplate   3. Pop-up headlights replaced by faired lights on some race-modified F40s   4. Air duct for engine cooling   5. Traditional five-spoke wheel design given sporty makeover   6. Locking filler cap for 120-litre (32-gallon) fuel tank   7. F40 logo etched into strut of rear aerofoil   8. Vents in engine cover direct air to wing   9. Cooling air vent on base of wing   10. Ferrari's traditional twin circular tail lights   11. Triple exhaust pipes emerge from centre of rear

THE INTERIOR

The racing character of the F40 was reflected in its bare-bones cockpit, which was functional and spartan in the extreme. There was no place for electric windows, carpets, or even door handles, with the only concession to luxury being the presence of air conditioning. Interior trim was virtually non-existent, and the red cloth-covered Kevlar seats presented the sole splash of colour in what was a predominantly monochrome driving environment.

12. All F40s were produced in left-hand drive   13. Badge doubles as horn   14. Speedometer and rev-counter that red-lines at 8,000 rpm   15. Five-speed gearshift lever in chrome   16. Lightweight drilled pedals

UNDER THE BONNET

Not only did the mighty 90° V8 incorporate twin turbochargers, it also sported two intercoolers to squeeze additional power out of the engine. The unit's performance figures were exceptional, with the engine's record-breaking 478 bhp output equating to a staggering 160 bhp per litre. The absence of power steering or anti-lock braking system provided further proof that this sublime example of automotive engineering really was aimed at those able to drive at the extremes.

17. Engine had a bore (internal cylinder diameter) of 82 mm and a stroke (distance travelled by pistons) of 69.5 mm **18.** Horizontally mounted exhaust muffler **19.** Coil springs and shock absorber, adjustable on later models **20.** Storage area under bonnet

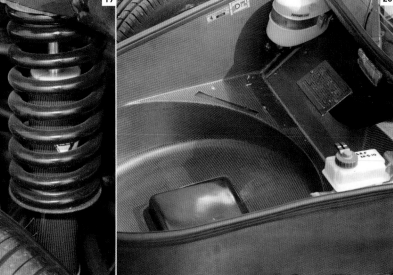

Multi-Purpose Vehicles

The 1980s saw the Sport-Utility Vehicle (SUV) market continue to grow, spawning some powerful 4x4s with exceptional mud-plugging ability, and some comfort-oriented cars with only limited ability on rough terrain. At the same time, a new niche was discovered, for capacious seven-seat Multi-Purpose Vehicles (MPVs), based on car or van platforms and aimed at larger families with a lot to carry.

◁ **Nissan Prairie 1983**

Origin Japan

Engine 1,809 cc, straight-four

Top speed 99 mph (159 km/h)

Boxy and spacious, and with sliding rear doors, the Prairie revealed a new market for van-like road cars and sold over a million in six years. It had 1.5- or 1.8-litre engines.

△ **Land Rover 88 SIII 1971**

Origin UK

Engine 2,286 cc, straight-four

Top speed 68 mph (109 km/h)

The basic Land Rover continued to be among the best off-road vehicles throughout the 1980s. Creature comforts were limited, especially on this ex-army lightweight model.

▷ **Nissan Patrol 1982**

Origin Japan

Engine 3,246 cc, straight-six

Top speed 80 mph (129 km/h)

Rugged and basic compared with more upmarket rivals, the Patrol was an unashamed workhorse with live axles, semi-elliptic springs, and four- and six-cylinder engines.

◁ **Land Rover Discovery 1989**

Origin UK

Engine 2,495 cc, straight-four

Top speed 107 mph (172 km/h)

Bridging the gap between the luxury Range Rover and the basic Land Rover, the Discovery was superb off-road and had a plush Conran-designed interior. It won a British Design Council award.

△ **Mitsubishi Space Wagon 1984**

Origin Japan

Engine 1,725 cc, straight-four

Top speed 97 mph (156 km/h)

Also sold as the Chariot, the Nimbus, and the Expo, this compact five- or seven-seater was one of the first ever MPVs. It had two- and four-wheel-drive models.

▽ **Mercedes-Benz G-Wagen 1979**

Origin Germany/Austria

Engine 2,746 cc, straight-six

Top speed 92 mph (148 km/h)

Coil-sprung live axles gave the G-Wagen a smoother ride than its rival Land Rover, but high price and basic looks limited sales until Mercedes-Benz improved these in 1991.

△ **Plymouth Voyager 1984**

Origin USA

Engine 2,213 cc, straight-four

Top speed 96 mph (154 km/h)

Plymouth's version of Chrysler's all-new Minivan responded to the new MPV craze previously only served by van adaptations like the Volkswagen Microbus.

▷ **Suzuki Vitara 1988**

Origin Japan

Engine 1,590 cc, straight-four

Top speed 87 mph (140 km/h)

Suzuki cleverly mixed its off-road expertise with normal road car comforts in this compact soft-roader, and established a niche market for the comfortable mini 4x4.

△ **Lamborghini LM002 1986**

Origin Italy

Engine 5,167 cc, V12

Top speed 125 mph (201 km/h)

Italian supercar maker Lamborghini gave the LM002 a huge V12 engine feeding from six Weber carburettors. Super-fast on sand, it became a favourite among Arab oil sheikhs.

△ **Renault Espace 1984**

Origin France

Engine 1,995 cc, straight-four

Top speed 105 mph (169 km/h)

Matra's MPV took years to reach production; scheduled to be a Simca, it ended up a Renault. Features included a galvanised inner shell, glassfibre skin, and seven movable seats.

△ **Daihatsu Sportrak 1987**

Origin Japan

Engine 1,589 cc, straight-four

Top speed 89 mph (143 km/h)

Sold as the Rocky or Feroza in some markets, the Sportrak was a compact leisure 4x4. Two- and four-wheel-drive options gave fair on- and off-road performance.

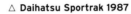

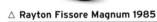

△ **Rayton Fissore Magnum 1985**

Origin Italy

Engine 2,492 cc, V6

Top speed 104 mph (168 km/h)

The Magnum was built by Fissore, using a shortened military Iveco four-wheel-drive chassis. It had Fiat/VM/Alfa 4- or 6-cylinder engines – or a V8 in the US, where it sold as the Laforza.

△ **Pontiac Trans Sport 1989**

Origin USA

Engine 3,135 cc, V6

Top speed 107 mph (172 km/h)

General Motors responded to the Chrysler Minivans with this rakishly styled, long-nosed MPV. It had a galvanized shell and plastic panels like Matra's Espace.

△ **Jeep Cherokee 1984**

Origin USA

Engine 2,838 cc, V6

Top speed 96 mph (154 km/h)

The first Jeep to have its chassis combined into a monocoque welded-steel bodyshell was a much more civilized car than its predecessors. It enjoyed greater sales as a result.

△ **Jeep Wrangler 1987**

Origin USA

Engine 3,956 cc, straight-six

Top speed 105 mph (169 km/h)

Conceived by AMC to rejuvenate the basic Jeep model with overtones of its wartime ancestor, the Wrangler used 2.5-litre 4-cylinder or 4.0-litre 6-cylinder engines.

Armand Peugeot (far left) in his Type 21 Phaeton, 1900

Great marques
The Peugeot story

Peugeot can rightfully claim to be among the oldest car manufacturers still in existence. In business long before the advent of the automobile, Peugeot has been making cars for more than a century. A giant of the industry, it remains one of the world's largest producers, having absorbed several former rivals.

ARMAND PEUGEOT WAS born in 1849 in Hérimoncourt, eastern France. In 1865 he joined the family metalworking business, which made a range of tools and domestic goods. Armand was the main driving force behind the firm's entry into bicycle manufacture in 1882. He was intrigued by the prospect of developing a "horseless carriage", and by the end of the decade he had built a batch of high-wheeled chassis intended for steam propulsion. He abandoned the project after meeting Gottlieb Daimler and Émile Levassor, who persuaded him instead to produce cars based on a Daimler concept. Peugeot's vehicles were powered by petrol-fuelled internal combustion engines made by Panhard et Levassor under licence from Daimler.

The first five cars emerged in 1891, although all were very different in design. Serious manufacture began in earnest two years later, with 24 cars being built. Peugeot was present at the birth of motor sport, taking part in

Peugeot badge
(introduced 2010)

the pioneering 1894 Paris-Rouen Rally. In 1895 Peugeot became the first marque to adopt pneumatic tyres rather than solid rubber ones, along with sliding gear transmission.

The business parted company with Daimler and began designing and building its own engines in-house from 1896. In the same year Armand Peugeot broke free of family ties and set up his own company in Audincourt. By 1900 output was running at 500 cars per year, and three years later the firm was responsible for manufacturing half of all cars produced in France.

Yet as Armand Peugeot's firm grew in stature, his personal wealth began to dwindle. In 1910 he joined forces with his cousin, Eugène, who still ran the family business. Peugeot's Audincourt factory was modernized to aid efficiency, and in 1913 the company unveiled the tiny 6CV Type BP-1, designed by Ettore Bugatti. The production of the popular *Bébé*, as the BP-1 was nicknamed, would exceed

3,000 by the time of its withdrawal in 1916. Rather larger than the *Bébé* was Peugeot's 7.6-litre racer, which claimed the 1912 French Grand Prix and the following year's Indianapolis 500 honours.

During World War I Peugeot's manufacturing facilities were largely given over to the production of armaments and military vehicles. The company emerged from the hostilities with bolstered coffers, enabling it to expand greatly during the 1920s, taking over both the Ballanger and De Dion marques in 1927. A year

Sporty poster
In this poster from around 1918, artist René Vincent uses the colours of the French flag as a swirling backdrop to showcase a Peugeot racing car.

While the move was bold, it was not a commercial success: the French car-buying public proved resistant to their charms, and all three variations on the theme were slow sellers.

As with all other French marques, Peugeot's factories were taken over by the Nazis after France was occupied by German forces in 1940. Post-war

> ## "I cleared the ground for the ... public appreciation of the automobile."
> ARMAND PEUGEOT, c.1900

later it introduced the Peugeot 201, then the cheapest conventional car on sale in France. The 201 was also the first Peugeot model to feature a zero in its model designation.

The 1930s saw Peugeot struggle during the Depression, not helped by the fact that its rapid expansion had saddled it with a vast and incoherent model range and a multitude of inefficient factories. During the second half of the decade it showed great daring by adopting designer Jean Andreau's aerodynamic outlines for the 202, 302, and 402 models.

manufacture restarted in 1945, and three years later Peugeot's first new model, the 203, entered production. Although it borrowed some of its running gear from pre-war models, the 203 had a roomy body that looked very much in tune with the times. The success of the 203 would be long-lived, with nearly 700,000 being made until the end of the model's production in 1960.

An even bigger seller than the 203 was 1955's handsome 403 saloon, styled by the Italian design company Pinin Farina (later called Pininfarina).

402 Éclipse Décapotable
The cabriolet version of Peugeot's 402 family car featured a power-operated retractable hardtop roof – the first of its kind in the world.

BP-1 (BÉBÉ)

403

205 TURBO 16

908 HDI FAP

1810 Peugeot begins commercial life producing steel and hand tools.
1889 Production of automobiles commences under the Peugeot Frères banner.
1890 Armand Peugeot unveils his petrol-powered "Peugeot Type 2" prototype.
1895 Peugeot becomes the first car manufacturer to equip its vehicles with pneumatic tyres.
1912 Peugeot wins the French Grand Prix.
1913 Jules Goux wins the Indianapolis 500 aboard Peugeot's 7.6-litre racing car.

1923 Annual production exceeds 10,000 vehicles for the first time.
1926 The 100,000th Peugeot car is made.
1928 Firm is divided to create Automobiles Peugeot and Cycles Peugeot (also making household appliances).
1934 The 402 Éclipse Décapotable is the world's first cabriolet with an electrically operated retractable hardtop roof.
1955 Arrival of the 403 saloon is the first fruit of a longstanding relationship with Italy's Pinin Farina styling house.

1965 Peugeot's first front-wheel-drive car is the 204; in 1967 it offers the world's smallest-capacity diesel engine.
1969 Total vehicle production passes the 5 million mark.
1974 Peugeot takes major stake in Citröen, increasing it to 90 per cent in 1976.
1978 Peugeot acquires Chrysler's European interests, eventually making the firm Europe's number one producer.
1979 Peugeot offers a turbocharged diesel engine in its 604 – a world first.

1984 Ari Vatanen wins Rally Finland (the "1,000 Lakes Rally") in a 205 Turbo 16 – Peugeot's first major victory of the World Rally Championship era.
1985 Peugeot team wins the World Rally Championship for drivers and manufacturers with the 205 T16.
1987 Peugeot claims the first of four consecutive Dakar Rally victories.
2009 908 HDi FAP diesels finish first and second at Le Mans, breaking Audi's decade-long stranglehold on the class.

Turbo in the snow
Ari Vatanen and his co-driver, Terry Harryman, are seen here in their Peugeot 205 Turbo 16 on their way to first place in the 1985 Swedish Rally. Their victory helped Peugeot win the manufacturers' championship.

This was followed in 1960 by the 404, which used a 1,618cc version of the 403 engine tilted at 45 degrees. The 404 proved rugged enough to win the East African Safari Rally in four of the six competitions between 1963 and 1968. More models followed, many of which were styled by Pininfarina, including the 504 of 1968 – one of Peugeot's most distinctive cars.

Despite the success of its saloons, Peugeot was losing out in the market because its range lacked a small car. The company addressed this with the 204, which, after a protracted gestation period, emerged in 1965. The 204 was the first Peugeot with front-wheel drive – soon to be a standard feature of the marque – and over 1.5 million 204s were made from 1965 to 1976.

In the late 1960s and early 1970s Peugeot embarked on joint ventures with other marques, including Volvo and Renault. In 1974 the company acquired a substantial stake in its arch rival Citroën, which became a 90 per cent shareholding two years later. This effectively doubled Peugeot's turnover and production capacity, but its expansionist aims were not yet satisfied, and in 1978 it also acquired Chrysler's European subsidiaries. The new parent company, Peugeot Société Anonyme (PSA), aimed to maintain separate identities for Peugeot and Citroën while sharing resources. While Citroën models subsequently lost some of their individuality, the Peugeot brand remained strong. In 1983 Peugeot scored a big hit with its 205 hatchback. It used the 205 to re-establish itself as a force in rallying, taking the World Rally Championship title in 1985 and 1986, and the 1992 World Sports Car Championship. More recently, the marque has also returned to the race track, taking the 2009 Le Mans 24-hour title with its diesel-engined 908 HDi FAP.

Future Peugeot plans include developing diesel-hybrid road cars and expanding further into the Chinese and Latin American markets. The Peugeot family still retains a quarter share of the business, itself something of an achievement in such a fickle industry. Despite facing many storms, Peugeot has managed to sustain its position as one of the world's foremost marques.

Premium Luxury

In the 1980s car manufacturers remained convinced that the best way to build a luxury car was with a front engine and rear-wheel drive, plus a good deal of weight. Lightweight construction and materials had yet to influence this sector of the market, and fuel economy was not a priority. The Saab 900 was an exception – a light, front-drive vehicle that opened a new niche in the market for luxury cars.

△ **Aston Martin V8 Vantage 1977**
Origin UK
Engine 5,340 cc, V8
Top speed 168 mph (270 km/h)

The ultimate 1970s Aston Martin became even more potent in 1986 with 432 bhp. The style remained the same, complete with sumptuous leather and walnut veneers.

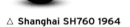

△ **Shanghai SH760 1964**
Origin China
Engine 2,200 cc, straight-six
Top speed 85 mph (137 km/h)

The Shanghai Automotive Industry Corporation built 79,526 of this imposing car almost unaltered from 1964 to 1991. It was inspired by Soviet and Mercedes models.

◁ **Bristol Beaufighter 1980**
Origin UK
Engine 5,900 cc, V8
Top speed 150 mph (241 km/h)

Based on the 412, rather bluntly styled by Zagato, the niche market Beaufighter had the extra appeal of turbocharging for its Chrysler V8 engine and a lift-off roof panel.

▷ **Lincoln Mark VII 1984**
Origin USA
Engine 4,949 cc, V8
Top speed 118 mph (190 km/h)

The Mark VII was a two-door coupé with optional designer interiors. Based on the four-door Continental platform, it had BMW turbodiesel or Ford V8 engine choices.

◁ **BMW 3-series Convertible 1986**
Origin Germany
Engine 2,495 cc, straight-six
Top speed 135 mph (217 km/h)

By engineering rollover protection into the windscreen frame, BMW produced the cleanest-looking convertible of its day. The power hood all but disappeared when it was retracted.

▽ **Rolls-Royce Silver Spirit 1980**
Origin UK
Engine 6,750 cc, V8
Top speed 119 mph (192 km/h)

The Silver Spirit was the ultimate in luxury and quality of build, but its sheer weight, its ageing engine, and its stately styling lost it sales to more modern luxury cars.

△ Cadillac Fleetwood Brougham 1980

Origin USA

Engine 6,037 cc, V8

Top speed 104 mph (167 km/h)

The top of Cadillac's prestige line remained conventional with large dimensions, a large V8 engine and live rear axle. Luxury trim and power steering came as standard.

△ Cadillac Sedan De Ville 1985

Origin USA

Engine 4,087 cc, V8

Top speed 119 mph (191 km/h)

Cadillac gave the world a front-wheel-drive V8. It had the same interior space as before, but in a smaller bodyshell. US buyers still wanted big cars, however, and sales suffered.

△ Jaguar XJ12 1979

Origin UK

Engine 5,343 cc, V12

Top speed 150 mph (241 km/h)

Jaguar's 350 bhp flagship saloon looked more elegant than ever with its makeover by Pininfarina for the 1980s. It continued to make other luxury cars seem overpriced.

◁ Saab 900 Convertible 1986

Origin Sweden

Engine 1,985 cc, straight-four

Top speed 126 mph (203 km/h)

Despite being no more than a progressively developed 1960s front-drive model, the Saab 900 Convertible sold well into the 1990s, and was spoiled only by its turbo lag.

▷ Lexus LS400 1989

Origin Japan

Engine 3,969 cc, V8

Top speed 147 mph (237 km/h)

The Lexus was Toyota's flagship car of 1989. It successfully challenged existing US and European high-end cars on aerodynamics, quietness, top speed, and fuel efficiency.

△ Volvo 760GLE 1982

Origin Sweden

Engine 2,849 cc, straight-four

Top speed 118 mph (190 km/h)

Aimed at the US luxury car market, the 760GLE helped the 700 series sell over a million. In 1984 it became turbocharged and intercooled, which greatly improved its performance.

△ Ferrari 412 1986

Origin Italy

Engine 4,942 cc, V12

Top speed 158 mph (254 km/h)

Ferrari's executive family car came with comfortable seats, leather trim, air conditioning, and anti-lock brakes. Vitally, it was still as exciting to drive as a Ferrari should be.

▷ Mercedes-Benz 190 1982

Origin Germany

Engine 1,997 cc, straight-four

Top speed 117 mph (188 km/h)

Mercedes' entry-level model for the 1980s was very well equipped and extremely durable. It easily ran for 300,000 miles (480,000 km) or so without needing major attention.

◁ Mercedes-Benz 560 SEC 1985

Origin Germany

Engine 5,547 cc, V8

Top speed 156 mph (251 km/h)

The 560 SEC was at the top of Mercedes' quality-laden coupé range. Very expensive when new, it had 300 bhp from its big V8 engine and 6.8-second 0–60 mph acceleration.

The 1990s

Race-tuned & retro | American resurgence & Korean emergence | **Hummers & Hondas**

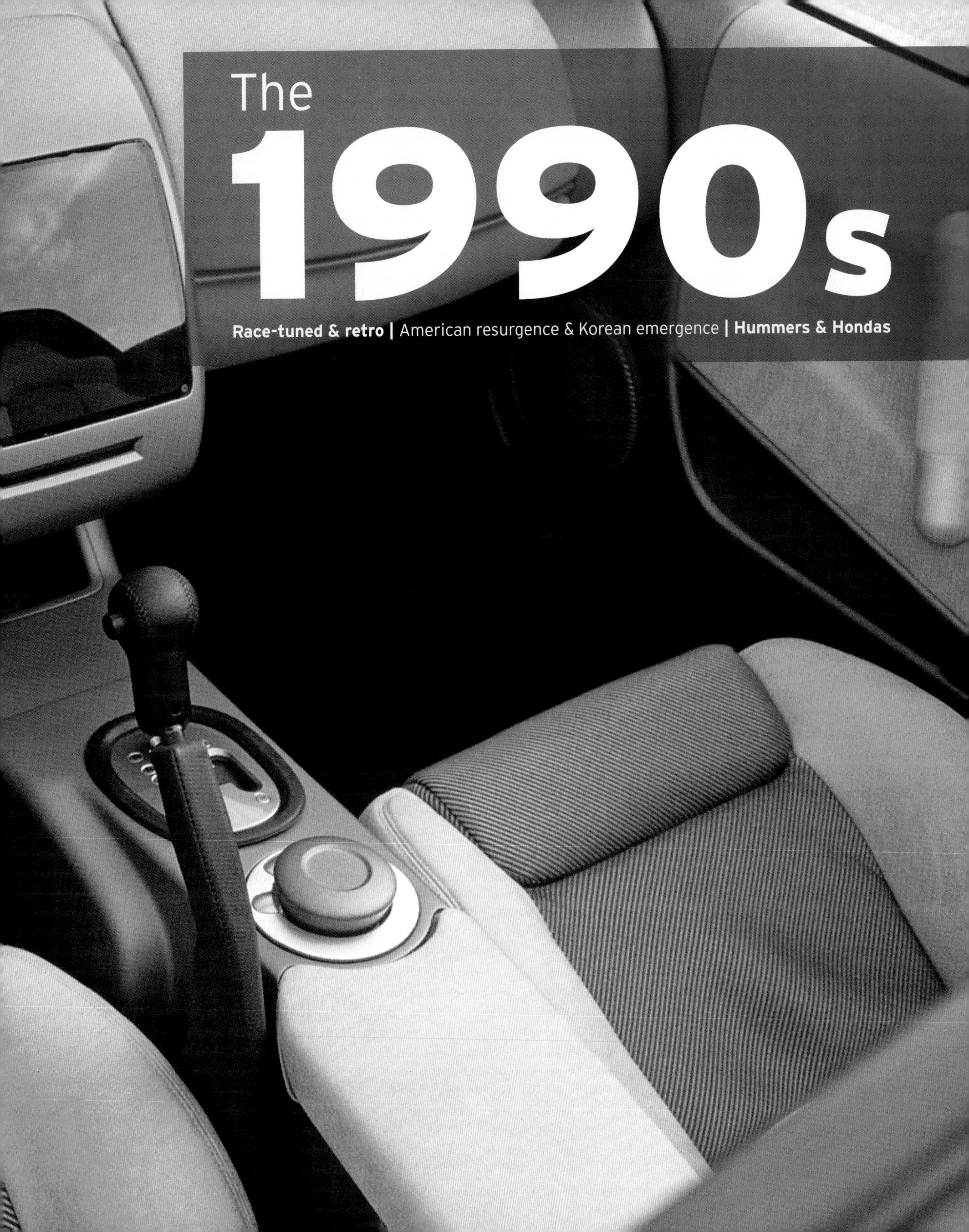

Modern Roadsters

The 1990s saw the resurgence of sports cars, as fears that legislation would ban open cars receded. Manufacturers were divided on whether the best sporting solution was the traditional front-engine rear-drive, mid-engine rear-drive, or front-engine front-drive. Rounded styling returned, along with the arrival of retro – and luxury, including folding hardtop roofs.

△ **Nissan Figaro 1989**

Origin Japan

Engine 987 cc, straight-four

Top speed 106 mph (171 km/h)

Nissan popularized retro styling with this Micra-based two-seater with roll-back sunroof and three-speed automatic transmission. It was fun, but not sporting.

△ **Porsche 944 S2 Cabriolet 1989**

Origin Germany

Engine 2,990 cc, straight-four

Top speed 149 mph (240 km/h)

The final development of the 1976 Porsche 924 was the 944 S2, which was also at last available as a cabriolet – but production ended in 1991.

△ **Porsche Boxster 1996**

Origin Germany

Engine 2,480 cc, flat-six

Top speed 152 mph (245 km/h)

Almost 50 years after its first mid-engined prototype, Porsche finally introduced a mid-engined road sports car, which became its fastest-selling sports car ever.

△ **Mazda MX-5 (MkI) 1989**

Origin Japan

Engine 1,597 cc, straight-four

Top speed 114 mph (183 km/h)

Inspired by the 1960s Lotus Elan, Mazda reintroduced the world to traditional sports-car fun with the twin-cam, front-engined, rear-wheel drive MX-5 (also called Miata/Eunos).

△ **BMW Z3 1996**

Origin Germany

Engine 1,895 cc, straight-four

Top speed 123 mph (198 km/h)

BMW's first ever volume sports car had retro looks, rear-wheel drive, and an uncompromised roadster feel. The Z3 was fitted with 1.8, 1.9, 2.0, 2.2, 2.8, 3.0, or 3.2-litre engines.

◁ **Morgan Plus 8 1990**

Origin UK

Engine 3,946 cc, V8

Top speed 121 mph (195 km/h)

The ultra-traditional Morgan with its wood-framed body and separate chassis started using Rover's 3.5-litre V8 engine in 1968. It got the 3.9-litre version in 1990.

▷ **TVR Griffith 400 1992**

Origin UK

Engine 3,948 cc, V8

Top speed 148 mph (238 km/h)

The best British sports car of the 1990s had stunning lines and effortless Rover V8 power (with the ultimate soundtrack), but reliability issues dogged it, like all TVRs.

△ **Suzuki Cappuccino 1991**

Origin Japan

Engine 657 cc, straight-three

Top speed 85 mph (137 km/h)

Restricted to 85 mph, the Cappuccino was designed to give fun motoring within Japan's *Kei* car tax regulations. Front-engined and rear-driven, it is a proper mini-sports car.

▽ **Renault Sport Spider 1995**

Origin France

Engine 1,998 cc, straight-four

Top speed 131 mph (211 km/h)

Renault wanted to inject some sporty excitement into the brand, so it commissioned this roofless, mid-engine, aluminium-chassis roadster for road and track use.

△ **Alfa Romeo Spider 1995**

Origin Italy

Engine 2,959 cc, V6

Top speed 140 mph (225 km/h)

Available with 2-litre or 3-litre engines, Alfa's Spider for the 1990s was a striking front-wheel-drive sports car designed by Pininfarina, with a high tail but small boot.

◁ **MGF 1995**

Origin UK

Engine 1,796 cc, straight-four

Top speed 130 mph (209 km/h)

The first serious, new MG sports car for over 30 years was a pretty mid-engined two-seater with clever packaging and good handling from its hydragas suspension system.

△ **MG RV8 1992**

Origin UK

Engine 3,946 cc, V8

Top speed 136 mph (219 km/h)

The car MG should have built 25 years earlier finally entered limited production in the 1990s, with a pumped-up MGB bodyshell, Rover V8 engine, and leather trim.

△ **Lotus Elise 1996**

Origin UK

Engine 1,796 cc, straight-four

Top speed 124 mph (200 km/h)

Using a Rover K-series engine in an extruded aluminium chassis with glassfibre body, the Elise weighs just 725 kg (1,599 lb), giving superb handling and performance.

△ **De Tomaso Guarà Spider 1994**

Origin Italy

Engine 3,982 cc, V8

Top speed 170 mph (274 km/h)

More commonly sold as the Coupé or Barchetta (just five Spiders were built), this was the last project of founder Alejandro de Tomaso and used BMW running gear.

◁ **Mercedes SLK 230K 1997**

Origin Germany

Engine 2,295 cc, straight-four

Top speed 148 mph (238 km/h)

Mercedes' answer to the BMW Z3 and Porsche Boxster was a more civilized sports car (almost all those sold were automatics) with an electric hardtop and a supercharger.

▷ **Honda S2000 1999**

Origin Japan

Engine 1,997 cc, straight-four

Top speed 150 mph (241 km/h)

This rear-wheel-drive sports car was built to the highest standards to mark Honda's 50th birthday celebration. It had the world's highest-revving production car engine.

△ **Audi TT Roadster 1999**

Origin Germany

Engine 1,781 cc, straight-four

Top speed 138 mph (222 km/h)

Built in Hungary with either 4X2 or 4X4, Audi's TT uses Volkswagen Golf technology. It suffered bad press due to high speed instability, prompting recall modifications.

◁ **Fiat Barchetta 1995**

Origin Italy

Engine 1,747 cc, straight-four

Top speed 118 mph (190 km/h)

Fiat built the Barchetta on the Punto platform but, with a brand new twin-cam engine and beautiful, in-house-designed body, it's a far better sports car than many expect.

Mazda MX-5

The original MX-5 of 1989 – called Miata in North America – was a smart mix of all that was best in the classic 1960s sports cars. The difference was that it used cutting-edge technology, from its all-wishbone suspension to its fuel-injected, 16-valve, twin-cam engine. The MX-5 was the product of a rigorous design process carried out in both North America and Japan. The result was a car that was delightful to drive and had no obvious failings, and it soon developed an enthusiastic worldwide fanbase.

THE MX-5 was brought to production by a small team of car-loving engineers, and was aimed above all at the US market. Intended to achieve "the ultimate unity of car and driver", the MX-5 was designed around a rear-mounted front engine, to give 50:50 weight distribution. The aluminium backbone chassis helped the car give crisp responses when driven. For an affordable, compact sports car, out-and-out performance was not required, which meant that the car could have a small 1,600 cc engine – although an 1,800 cc unit was later available. It also meant the car could be light in weight. Despite sceptics within Mazda, the MX-5 went on to become a huge success, and in its original form lasted until 1997, by which time over 400,000 had been made. Two subsequent evolutions of the car have stayed true to the character of the original.

FRONT VIEW

REAR VIEW

Oriental symbolism
Mazda has tried various logos over the years. This design was said to represent the sun with a flame within. It was introduced in 1991, but replaced with a new stylized "M" symbol in 1997.

SIDE VIEW WITH CLOSED TOP

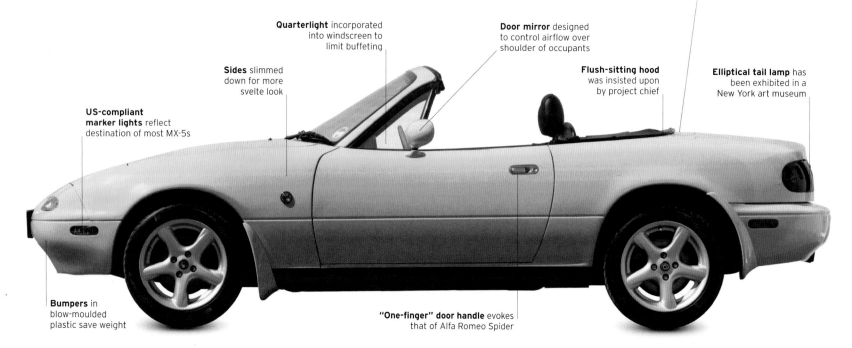

Quarterlight incorporated into windscreen to limit buffeting

Door mirror designed to control airflow over shoulder of occupants

Sides slimmed down for more svelte look

Flush-sitting hood was insisted upon by project chief

Elliptical tail lamp has been exhibited in a New York art museum

US-compliant marker lights reflect destination of most MX-5s

Bumpers in blow-moulded plastic save weight

"One-finger" door handle evokes that of Alfa Romeo Spider

SPECIFICATIONS

Model	Mazda MX-5, 1989–97	Power output	114 bhp at 6,500 rpm (1.6 litre)
Assembly	Hiroshima, Japan	Transmission	Five-speed manual
Production	433,963	Suspension	All-round coil-and-wishbone
Construction	Steel monocoque; aluminium bonnet	Brakes	Discs front and rear
Engine	1,597 cc/1,839 cc, dohc in-line four	Maximum speed	121 mph (195 km/h)

Eclectic influences

Although the low air intake and pop-up headlights can be seen as a reference to the Lotus Elan, Mazda's designers were equally inspired by Japanese culture. The interior allegedly evoked the inviting simplicity of a tea room, and the rounded bonnet and front reflected themes from the carved wooden masks used in *Noh* theatre. This MX-5 California is one of only 300 made in 1995 – all in Sunburst Yellow – to mark the MX-5's fifth anniversary.

THE EXTERIOR

Although the details seem to make reference to past eras, the design of the MX-5 was intended to be timeless. That it still looks fresh is proof of the abilities of its creators, who succeeded in evoking European sports-car heritage without resorting to imitation. Beyond the aesthetics, though, lies intelligent engineering that has resulted in a lightweight, yet strong body.

1. Badge found on later cars, such as this limited-edition MX-5 California **2.** Car called MX-5 in Europe **3.** Pop-up headlights feature only on MkI **4.** Aerodynamics shape mirror design **5.** Alloy wheels, part of California pack **6.** Slick, weatherproof hood **7.** Fuel filler cap located behind hood **8.** Round motif in tail lamps hints at 1960s designs

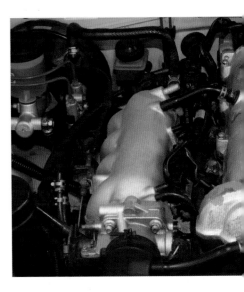

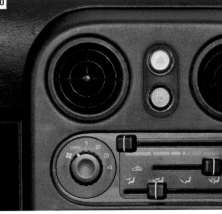

THE INTERIOR

Mazda's designers tried to make the interior as intimate and inviting as possible, while keeping costs low. A controversial decision was made to design a cockpit that would be cosy and comfortable for average-sized people, but too tight for particularly large people – accepting that this would lose the company some buyers. Existing Mazda fittings were used wherever possible, and door trims were kept simple and flat.

9. Tight-fitting interior with Nardi steering wheel **10.** Simple controls and round ventilation grilles have a slightly "retro" flavour **11.** Silver dial rims hint at instrumentation of classic British sports cars **12.** Seat fabric inspired by Japanese tatami mats **13.** Interior door-release echoes external handle

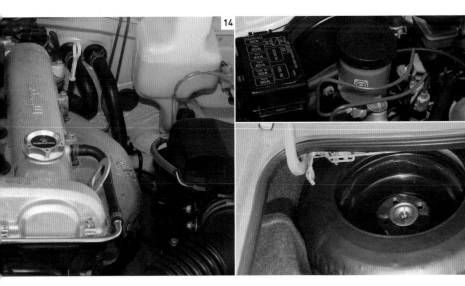

UNDER THE BONNET

The MX-5 uses the same engine as the contemporary Mazda 323, but with retro-look cam covers. The power delivery, however, was changed, and a new silencer system evolved. Recordings of classic exhaust notes were made and their sound waves analysed, to arrive at a suitably sporty burble. The gearbox, borrowed from the bigger 929, was similarly tuned. The flywheel and synchro rings were lightened, the ratios changed, and the throws made shorter.

14. Mazda MX-5 engine has cam covers that echo those of Jaguar, Lotus, and Alfa Romeo power units
15. Fuel injection always standard, rather than carburettors
16. Spare tyre is space saver, in boot with battery

Toyota RH,
1953-1955

Great marques
The Toyota story

With 7.8 million cars and trucks rolling off the production line in 2009, Toyota is the world's largest vehicle producer. A pioneer of hybrid technology, this Japanese marque prides itself on quality and innovation. Its range extends from tiny economy cars through state-of-the-art sports and racing cars to executive limousines.

AFTER GRADUATING in mechanical engineering at Tokyo Imperial University, Kiichiro Toyoda wanted to start building cars in his father Sakichi's factory, which produced automatic weaving looms. In order to learn about the motor trade, Kiichiro visited car manufacturers in Europe and the US. After the sale of one of his father's loom patents to a British company in 1929, he was

Toyota badge
(introduced 1989)

allowed to use the money from this deal to set up the automobile side of the business.

In 1930 Kiichiro built a two-cylinder engine and then a small car to run it, but it was not successful. Starting again from scratch, he then produced a more conventional, American-type car, with a Chevrolet-sourced chassis, flowing Chrysler-like body, and overhead-valve, straight-six, 3,389 cc

engine. Called the Toyoda Model AA, it entered production in 1936. The following year the Toyota Motor Company Limited was formed. The name was changed from Toyoda to Toyota because it was easier to pronounce in English and, crucially, when written in Japanese it had eight strokes – a lucky number in Japan.

At the time, almost all cars sold in Japan were US imports, but that was about to change as the Japanese government struggled with a balance of payments deficit. Japan's Ford and

GM plants were closed, and the government imposed restrictive duties on imports. Toyota was quick to exploit the opportunity, boosting its monthly output of cars, trucks, and buses from 100 to 1,500–2,000 by the end of the 1930s. To bring more of the production process in-house, the company set up the Toyoda Steel Works to supply steel, and the Toyoda Machine Works to make machine tools and auto parts.

During World War II Toyota made trucks for the Japanese army. Post-war production of civilian vehicles began slowly under the economic restrictions imposed by the Allied Occupation Authority. One of Toyota's first vehicles was a 4x4, which in 1951 would be used as the basis for the Land Cruiser – a model that went on to sell over 6 million worldwide by the end of 2008.

Back in 1950, with the company still struggling, wage reductions and

Toyota Tiara
The Tiara saloon was an export version of the Corona. Here, model Diane Chiljan poses for the cameras at a publicity event to mark the car's official US unveiling in New York, 1960.

COROLLA

MR2

LAND CRUISER

IQ

1935 Toyoda G1 truck is launched (20 built).	**1962** Toyota produces its 1-millionth vehicle.	**1989** Toyota Motor Manufacturing UK is formed, producing cars for the European market and beyond – even for export to Japan.	**1999** Toyota produces its 100-millionth vehicle.
1936 The 3,389 cc, six-cylinder Toyoda Model AA is the first production car.	**1966** The Corolla is launched; it soon becomes a worldwide best-seller.		**2002** Toyota's first race in Formula 1.
1937 Toyota Motor Company Limited is formed: all future cars will be known as Toyotas.	**1970** Celica sports coupé is introduced.	**1989** The Lexus brand is launched to target the executive market outside Japan.	**2007** Toyota sells its 1-millionth hybrid vehicle.
	1972 Toyota produces its 10-millionth vehicle.	**1993** Toyota Celica wins the World Rally Championship, and again in 1994.	**2008** The iQ compact car is launched; it is the world's smallest four-seat car.
1947 Toyota's 100,000th vehicle is produced.	**1980** Toyota becomes the world's largest volume producer of private vehicles.	**1994** RAV4 compact leisure off-roader is introduced.	**2010** Toyota recalls over 8 million vehicles to correct faults. It is fined US\$16.375 million for the delayed recall of cars over faulty accelerator pedals; total recall costs are US\$1.93 billion.
1951 The Toyota Land Cruiser is launched.	**1984** The mid-engined MR2 sports car debuts; Toyota reopens a disused GM factory in California, USA.	**1997** The Prius hybrid goes on sale in Japan; it will be sold worldwide from 2001.	
1957 First Toyota Crown exported to the US.	**1986** The 50-millionth Toyota vehicle comes off the production line.		
1961 The Total Quality Control programme is launched in a bid to raise Toyota's production standards.			

layoffs were announced, leading to an eight-week strike by the workforce that caused Kiichiro Toyoda to resign. His nephew, Eiji Toyoda, then took the helm, keeping the family link alive.

Eiji spent three months in the US visiting Ford, and what he saw there would later help him to transform Toyota into one of Japan's most efficient car manufacturers. In the short term, it was a large order for military vehicles from the Allied Occupation Authority during the Korean War of 1950–1953 that saved Toyota from bankruptcy. In an ingenious effort to boost sales, Toyota began teaching people to drive. The scheme was a success, since most new drivers were keen to buy the make of car in which they had learned.

Breakthrough model
The Corolla proved to the world that Toyota could make small, cheap cars without compromising on their quality.

Volkswagen. The family-size Corolla, launched in 1966, rapidly became Japan's best-selling car. Well engineered, well designed, compact, and affordable, it had a universal appeal and proved especially popular in Europe. By 2009 the Toyota Corolla had sold 25 million worldwide.

Under Eiji Toyoda, the company embarked on an aggressive acquisitions policy, taking over Hino in 1966 and Daihatsu in 1967. Expansion was rapid, with Toyota growing from the world's

serious production, but it did earn Toyota respect among sports-car buyers – just what it needed to launch the affordable Celica coupé in 1970. The Celica rapidly became a hit in the US and Europe, winning saloon-car races and rallies around the world.

Shoichiro Toyoda, Kiichiro's son, became president of the Toyota Group in 1982. One of the first all-new cars to be launched under his tenure was an affordable, mid-engined sports model, the MR2. With a 16-valve, double-overhead-cam engine and all-disc brakes, the expertly engineered MR2 was an instant success. Four years later Toyota introduced both a supercharged edition of the MR2 and a T-bar semi-convertible version, turning to turbocharging for the second generation MR2 in 1989. Toyota also launched the Lexus brand in the US in 1989, recognizing that executive-car drivers might be reluctant to buy a brand known for making city cars. Lexus products have since gone global, arriving on the Japanese market in 2005.

For Toyota, motor sport has become an increasingly important marketing tool: the Celica won the World Rally

Championship in 1993, 1994, and 1999, and in 2002 Toyota made its first foray into Formula 1. Toyota has also carved out a name for itself as a leader in the field of hybrid vehicles, which combine conventional engines with electric motors. The Prius, on sale from 1997, was the world's first mass-produced hybrid; by the end of 2010, it had notched up around 2 million sales.

As Toyota grew, it established factories throughout the world. It now has a manufacturing presence in 26 countries, and always endeavours to exploit the opportunities that each presents; one example is the Aygo city car, built in the Czech Republic since 2005 as a joint project with Peugeot.

Akio Toyoda, son of Shoichiro, was made president in 2009 and led Toyota through its most difficult challenge for 60 years: the recall of over 8 million cars due to faulty accelerator pedals. With recall costs of US\$1.93 billion, the crisis resulted in huge losses for Toyota and tarnished its reputation for quality.

"We will **develop ... a car** that can **rival foreign cars** in **performance** and **price.**"

KIICHIRO TOYODA, c.1935

The Crown, one of the marque's best-known models, was launched in 1954, and it spearheaded Toyota's first attempt to break into the American market in 1957. Although it was some time before the US public became receptive to Japanese cars, the firm's production continued to rise as other markets around the world gradually opened up to Toyota. By 1965 Toyota was building 50,000 cars and trucks per month, and by the end of the decade it was exporting more cars to the US than any other manufacturer apart from

fifth-largest car maker in 1969 to the third-largest three years later. Toyota also began moving into sports cars. Its first model, the cute and innovative Sports 800, had a lift-off hardtop. This 790 cc midget was soon joined by the 2000GT, Japan's first serious grand tourer. The 2000GT had beautiful lines, double overhead camshafts, a straight-six engine, a five-speed all-synchromesh gearbox, all-independent suspension, all-disc brakes, and a top speed of 140 mph (225 km/h). The 2000GT never entered

Toyota Prius hybrid powerplant
The Prius has both an electric motor and a petrol engine. The car can start and travel at low speeds on its electric motor; above a certain speed, the petrol engine kicks in.

Competition Machines

This was the decade of technology, as manufacturers strove to achieve more performance than ever before. Restricted by regulations, they designed to reduce speeds and danger. Active suspension, active differentials, traction control, and semi-automatic transmissions were among the developments aimed at helping drivers get the most from cars, while twin turbochargers and their intercoolers helped get the most out of the engines.

△ **Porsche 962 1984**

Origin Germany

Engine 2,995 cc, flat-six

Top speed 200 mph (322 km/h)

A sports prototype designed for races such as Le Mans and the IMSA GTP series, the aluminium-chassis 962 was winning races well into the 1990s.

△ **Benetton-Ford B193 1993**

Origin UK

Engine 3,493 cc, V8

Top speed 200 mph (322 km/h)

Benetton's answer to the high-tech revolution in Formula 1, the B193 had active suspension and traction control. Michael Schumacher used one to win the Portuguese GP in 1993.

◁ **BMW V12 LMR 1998**

Origin Germany

Engine 6,100 cc, V12

Top speed 214 mph (344 km/h)

This striking roadster was built to win the Le Mans 24-hour race in France. It became the first BMW ever to do so in 1999, and won the Sebring 12 Hours in the US that same year.

△ **Leyton House-Judd CG901B 1990**

Origin UK

Engine 3,496 cc, V8

Top speed 205 mph (330 km/h)

Leading Formula 1 designer Adrian Newey tried out some advanced aerodynamic ideas on this Formula 1 racer; it had little success, though it did lead for most of the French GP in 1990.

△ **Sauber-Mercedes C11 1990**

Origin Switzerland

Engine 4,973 cc, V8

Top speed 240 mph (386 km/h)

With 950 bhp from its twin-turbocharged Mercedes V8 engine, the C11 dominated the 1990 World Sportscar Championship and continued winning into 1991.

Subaru

Subaru was a little-known Japanese car maker producing anonymous road cars that happened to have four-wheel drive and "boxer" engines – until it started rallying. After showing potential with the Legacy, Subaru engaged British motorsport company Prodrive to prepare Imprezas for the World Rally Championship. With top drivers such as Colin McRae, Richard Burns, Carlos Sainz, and Juha Kankkunen, their spectacular success made Subaru world famous.

▽ **Subaru Impreza WRC 1993**

Origin Japan

Engine 1,994 cc, flat-four

Top speed 135 mph (217 km/h)

Prodrive began fielding Imprezas in 1993, won its first rally with Carlos Sainz in 1994, and took the World Driver's title with Colin McRae in 1995.

◁ Ferrari F300 1998

Origin Italy

Engine 2,997 cc, V10

Top speed 210 mph (338 km/h)

The F300 was the first Ferrari built under the highly successful pairing of Ross Brawn and Rory Byrne: it gave Michael Schumacher six wins in 1998.

◁ Audi R8R 1999

Origin Germany

Engine 3,596 cc, V8

Top speed 208 mph (335 km/h)

Audi's first Le Mans racer, with twin-turbo 600 bhp V8, proved reliable from the start but needed development to match the pace of rivals Toyota and BMW.

△ Chevrolet Monte Carlo "T-Rex" 1997

Origin USA

Engine 5,850 cc, V8

Top speed 215 mph (346 km/h)

Known by the dinosaur painted on the roof, Jeff Gordon's car won the 1997 NASCAR All Star race so easily that, even though it was legal, officials asked him not to bring it back.

▷ Williams-Renault FW16B 1994

Origin UK

Engine 3,493 cc, V10

Top speed 210 mph (338 km/h)

Damon Hill won six Grands Prix in 1994 in the FW16B; he would have won the World Championship if a brush with Michael Schumacher hadn't taken him out of the last race.

▽ Chevrolet Monte Carlo 2000

Origin USA

Engine 5,850 cc, V8

Top speed 215 mph (346 km/h)

The US's hugely popular NASCAR racing series features composite silhouette bodies resembling road cars, such as this Chevy, mounted on full race chassis with tuned V8s.

▽ Williams-Renault FW18 1996

Origin UK

Engine 3,000 cc, V10

Top speed 210 mph (338 km/h)

The dream team of Patrick Head and Adrian Newey developed another world beater in the FW18, giving Damon Hill a World Championship title in 1996.

△ Subaru Impreza WRC 1999

Origin Japan

Engine 1,994 cc, flat-four

Top speed 140 mph (225 km/h)

The Impreza was steadily redesigned to make full use of rule changes in World Rallying, with active differentials and semi-automatic transmission in place for 1999.

▷ Subaru Impreza WRC 2000

Origin Japan

Engine 1,994 cc, flat-four

Top speed 140 mph (225 km/h)

Richard Burns and Juha Kankkunen led the Subaru comeback in 2000 with the intercooled and turbocharged Impreza, Burns taking four wins in the season.

◁ Subaru Impreza WRX 2000

Origin Japan

Engine 1,994 cc, flat-four

Top speed 137 mph (220 km/h)

From its launch, Subaru included a turbocharged, intercooled version of its new saloon car with racing and rallying in mind: it proved extremely successful in motorsport.

Renault Zoom, 1992
The electric-powered Zoom was a 90s-style, low-emission concept car. A tiny, two-seater city runabout, it had rear wheels that could fold forwards when parked, allowing it to squeeze into the smallest of urban parking spaces.

US Design Reinvigorated

In the 1970s and 80s, other than a few notable exceptions, North American car design seemed to lag behind Europe. US car manufacturers were mildly updating their over-large, slab-like saloons, while smaller Japanese cars picked away at the US's market share. Finally, in the 1990s US designers found new life with retro-inspired models and striking pick-up trucks that all of the US wanted to buy.

△ Buick Park Avenue 1990

Origin USA

Engine 3,791cc, V6

Top speed 108mph (174 km/h)

This big saloon, made until 1996, was the last Buick officially sold in Europe. US customers had the option of a supercharged version capable of close to 130mph (209 km/h).

▷ Cadillac Eldorado 1991

Origin USA

Engine 4,893cc, V8

Top speed 130mph (209 km/h)

This last incarnation of the US's longest-running personal luxury car model ended in 2002 – despite modern styling, large space-wasting cars had become unfashionable.

▷ Chevrolet Camaro 1993

Origin USA

Engine 5,733cc, V8

Top speed 155mph (249 km/h)

The fourth-generation Camaro was built in Canada with V6 or V8 power, a six-speed gearbox being optional on the V8. It was good value against Ford's Mustang.

△ Saturn SL 1990

Origin USA

Engine 1,901cc, straight-four

Top speed 121mph (195 km/h)

GM founded the Saturn brand in 1985 to counter Japanese imports. Stylish and aerodynamic, the S-Series was among the most fuel-efficient cars in the US at the time.

◁ Dodge Neon 1994

Origin USA

Engine 1,996cc, straight-four

Top speed 121mph (195 km/h)

The Neon marked a move by Chrysler to sell worldwide, even in Japan and UK in right-hand-drive form. It was a compact front-wheel-drive saloon with a 2-litre engine.

△ Oldsmobile Aurora 1994

Origin USA

Engine 3,995cc, V8

Top speed 140mph (225 km/h)

GM revitalised the Oldsmobile brand with this striking, new, low-drag sports saloon. Well built, fast, and immensely strong, the Aurora's downfall was its high price.

△ Dodge Intrepid 1993

Origin USA

Engine 3,301cc, V6

Top speed 112mph (180 km/h)

Closely related to the Chrysler New Yorker, the Dodge had more success, as it was built until 1997 and was followed by a second generation. Engines were 3.3 or 3.5 litre.

▷ Dodge Ram 1994

Origin USA

Engine 7,886cc, V10

Top speed 113mph (180 km/h)

Styled to look like a semi-trailer truck, the Ram was unsubtle, with engines from a 3.9-litre V6 to a Viper's 8-litre V10. It was what the US wanted, and sold rapidly.

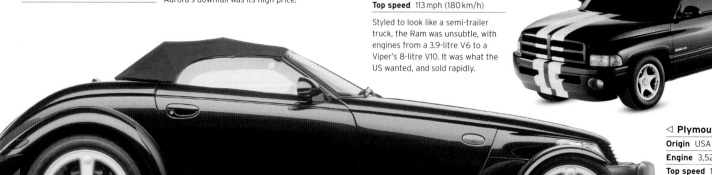

◁ Plymouth Prowler 1997

Origin USA

Engine 3,528cc, V6

Top speed 118mph (190 km/h)

A brave and truly American concept, the Prowler was based on a design by Chip Foose and boasted 5.9-second 0–62mph (0–100 km/h) acceleration to match its exterior.

△ **Ford Mustang GT 1994**

Origin USA

Engine 4,942 cc, V8

Top speed 136 mph (219 km/h)

This successful restyle by Patrick Schiavone retained hints of the original Mustang, and also saw the return of a convertible to the Mustang range. Engines were 3.8-litre V6, or V8 like this model.

△ **Ford Windstar 1994**

Origin USA

Engine 3,797 cc, V6

Top speed 116 mph (187 km/h)

Ford's first front-wheel-drive, seven-seat MPV beat US rivals with its smoother performance and handling. It guaranteed Ford a big slice of the minivan market in the US.

▽ **Ford Taurus 1996**

Origin USA

Engine 2,967 cc, V6

Top speed 130 mph (209 km/h)

Jack Telnack's dramatic 1996 restyle of the Taurus did not prove popular, and it lost its place as the US's best-selling car after the first year, despite its user-friendly interior.

△ **Mercury Villager 1993**

Origin USA

Engine 2,960 cc, V6

Top speed 112 mph (180 km/h)

A joint project with Nissan, which sold it as the Quest, this car could seat seven, with a removable two-seat bench in the middle and a sliding/folding bench for three at the back.

▷ **Mercury/Ford Cougar 1999**

Origin USA

Engine 2,540 cc, V6

Top speed 140 mph (225 km/h)

Ford's second attempt – after the Probe – to emulate the sales success of its 1970s Capri was built in the US, and was too large for most customers in the rest of the world.

◁ **Chrysler New Yorker 1993**

Origin USA

Engine 3,494 cc, V6

Top speed 134 mph (216 km/h)

This final version of Chrysler's flagship model had just a three-year life in which sales tailed off dramatically, despite its high specification and large, airy cabin.

△ **General Motors EV1 1996**

Origin USA

Engine electric motor

Top speed 80 mph (129 km/h)

GM's purpose-built electric two-seater had a 55-150 mile (90-240 km) range; just 1,117 were leased to owners, so GM recalled and crushed them in 2002, due to a lack of consumer interest.

▷ **Chrysler PT Cruiser 1999**

Origin USA/Mexico

Engine 2,429 cc, straight-four

Top speed 121 mph (195 km/h)

Retro-styled and with a resemblance to the Chrysler Airflow, this car sold 1.35 million worldwide in 11 years. The new millennium brought convertible and turbocharged options.

Family-Friendly Cars

By the 1990s the everyday family car had been transformed. Improvements had been made in the unsung areas of car development, such as soundproofing, windproofing, heating, and ventilation. Electronics to make engines start instantly and run smoothly through a wide rev band were also introduced. Almost all cars, from the smallest models up, would now run quietly and comfortably at legal speed limits.

△ **Fiat Cinquecento 1991**

Origin Italy/Poland

Engine 903 cc, straight-four

Top speed 83 mph (134 km/h)

Giugiaro styled Fiat's tiny four-seater for the 1990s, abandoning the rear-engined layout that had served Fiat for almost 40 years. It was neat and efficient and sold well.

◁ **Toyota Previa 1990**

Origin Japan

Engine 2,438 cc, straight-four

Top speed 108 mph (174 km/h)

Toyota made this seven or eight-seater exceptionally spacious for its length by placing the engine near-horizontal under the front seats, behind the line of the front axle. 4x4 was optional.

△ **Fiat Multipla 1998**

Origin Italy

Engine 1,581 cc, straight-four

Top speed 106 mph (171 km/h)

Short and wide compared with rival MPVs, the Multipla has two rows of three seats. It was hailed as one of the most innovative cars of its day, though it was also described as ugly.

△ **Citroën Berlingo Multispace 1996**

Origin France

Engine 1,360 cc, straight-four

Top speed 94 mph (151 km/h)

Related to Peugeot's Partner, the Berlingo (shown here after its 2002 facelift) was offered as a van or an adaptable and inexpensive passenger vehicle, with an electric powered option.

▷ **Peugeot 406 TD 2.1 1995**

Origin France

Engine 2,088 cc, straight-four

Top speed 118 mph (190 km/h)

This large family car proved popular. It had engines from 1.6 to 3.0 litres, and in turbodiesel form it enjoyed a 10-year production life until it was replaced by the 407.

△ **Citroën Xsara Picasso 1999**

Origin France/Spain

Engine 1,749 cc, straight-four

Top speed 118 mph (190 km/h)

Taking over from Renault's Scénic as the best-seller in the compact MPV market in most of Europe, the Picasso offered versatile family transport.

◁ **Peugeot 206 XR 1998**

Origin France

Engine 1,124 cc, straight-four

Top speed 98 mph (158 km/h)

By the end of production in 2010, 6.8 million 206s had been made, making it Peugeot's best-seller. Engines ranged from the 1.0- to 2.0-litre GTi.

△ **Alfa Romeo 156 TS 2.0 1997**
Origin Italy
Engine 1,970 cc, straight-four
Top speed 133 mph (214 km/h)

Alfa achieved class-leading styling with this sporting saloon. Features include concealed rear door handles to give it a coupé look.

◁ **Subaru Forester 1997**
Origin Japan
Engine 1,994 cc, flat-four
Top speed 111 mph (179 km/h)

Subaru's tough 4x4 estate offered comfortable road driving thanks to its low, flat engine. This made it more versatile than its competitors, though its looks were fairly uninspiring.

△ **Rover 25 VVC 1999**
Origin UK
Engine 1,796 cc, straight-four
Top speed 127 mph (204 km/h)

Based on engineering from Honda pre-1994, the 25 was well equipped and good value, with engines from 1.1 to 2.0 litres.

◁ **Volkswagen Sharan 1995**
Origin Germany/Portugal
Engine 1,984 cc, straight-four
Top speed 110 mph (177 km/h)

Also sold as the SEAT Alhambra and produced alongside the similar Ford Galaxy, Volkswagen's people carrier didn't have the best reliability record. Engines ranged from 1.8 to 2.8 litres.

△ **Volkswagen Golf GTI Mk4 1997**
Origin Germany
Engine 1,781 cc, straight-four
Top speed 138 mph (222 km/h)

The perennial hot hatch continued to sell well in its fourth generation with a turbo option. Volkswagen added a 3.2-litre 4x4 model too.

△ **Volvo V70 T5 1997**
Origin Sweden
Engine 2,319 cc, straight-five
Top speed 152 mph (245 km/h)

After the success of the 850 T5, Volvo rounded off the angular style and added a high-pressure turbocharger to create this unassuming, high-spec "Q-car".

△ **Renault Mégane Scénic 1996**
Origin France
Engine 1,598 cc, straight-four
Top speed 106 mph (171 km/h)

Having led the MPV market with the Espace, Renault kickstarted the compact MPV market with the Scénic, based on the small, family-car platform of the Mégane. The Scénic sold far more than expected.

◁ **Renault Kangoo 1997**
Origin France
Engine 1,390 cc, straight-four
Top speed 97 mph (156 km/h)

Renault's adaptable van/MPV (sold as a Nissan in some markets) boasted sliding side doors and a wide range of options, including 4x4. The model shown is with the facelift from 2003.

△ **Volkswagen Beetle 1998**
Origin Germany
Engine 1,984 cc, straight-four
Top speed 115 mph (185 km/h)

A bulky front-wheel-drive hatchback based on the Golf platform seemed an unlikely retro successor to the original Beetle, but the Beetle's long-lasting appeal has kept it selling into 2011.

◁ **Mercedes-Benz A-class 1997**
Origin Germany
Engine 1,598 cc, straight-four
Top speed 113 mph (182 km/h)

Offering a compact hatchback car was a radical step for Mercedes-Benz, forced on it by market trends. Doubts over its roadholding – though challenged by Mercedes-Benz – forced an embarrassing recall.

▷ **Audi A2 2000**
Origin Germany
Engine 1,390 cc, straight-four
Top speed 107 mph (172 km/h)

Audi brought high technology to the supermini with the aluminium, ultra-economical A2. However, Audi discovered that customers were led more by price and looks than quality and pedigree, and sales were somewhat disappointing.

Chrysler/Dodge
Viper V10

With the launch of the Dodge Viper in 1992, Chrysler opened a new chapter in the vibrant history of the US muscle car. Instead of the large-capacity V8 engine that was traditional for the breed, the Viper had an 8-litre V10 – a configuration that had recently been adopted in Formula 1, but at the time was virtually unknown in road cars.

FROM TRUCK TO SPORTS CAR

Despite its mould-breaking layout, the Viper V10 had humble origins, being based on the engine of Chrysler's LA truck. The LA engine's cast-iron construction made it too heavy for a sports car, so Lamborghini was commissioned to design an aluminium-alloy block and heads. The low-tech Viper 10 retained pushrod valve actuation and had only two valves per cylinder, even though some Chrysler personnel had advocated a four-valve head. The result was an unimpressive specific output of only 50 bhp per litre – but all those cubic inches and massive torque still ensured blistering performance.

ENGINE SPECIFICATIONS

Dates produced	1991 to present
Cylinders	10 cylinders in two banks, 90-degree "V"
Configuration	Front-mounted, longitudinal
Engine capacity	488 cu in (7,990 cc), later 505 cu in (8,285 cc) and 510 cu in (8,382 cc)
Power output	400 bhp @ 4,600 rpm, later 415, 450, 500, 600 bhp
Type	Conventional four-stroke, water-cooled petrol engine with reciprocating pistons, distributorless ignition, and a wet sump
Head	ohv actuated by pushrod and hydraulic tappets; two valves per cylinder
Fuel System	Multipoint port fuel injection
Bore and Stroke	4.00 in x 3.88 in (101.6 mm x 98.6 mm)
Specific power	50.1 bhp/litre
Compression Ratio	9.1:1

Throttle body
Inside the throttle body is the butterfly valve, which regulates the flow of air into the engine.

Oil filler

Wiring pipe
This pipe carries electrical wiring to the engine.

Hose connection
A flexible hose that links to the water radiator connects here.

Water pump

Cylinder bank
One of the two cylinder banks lies under the cover and valvegear.

Opening up space
The use of a 90-degree angle between the two banks of cylinders, rather than the natural 72-degree angle for a V10, opens up space between the banks for the inlet components. It also reduces the overall height of the engine, allowing the car to have a lower bonnet line.

Heat shield
This covering protects other components in the engine bay from high exhaust temperatures.

Drive belt
Driven by the crankshaft pulley, this wide, flexible belt powers the water pump and other ancillaries.

Air conditioning compressor

Aluminium-alloy cylinder block

▷ **See pp.346–347** How an engine works

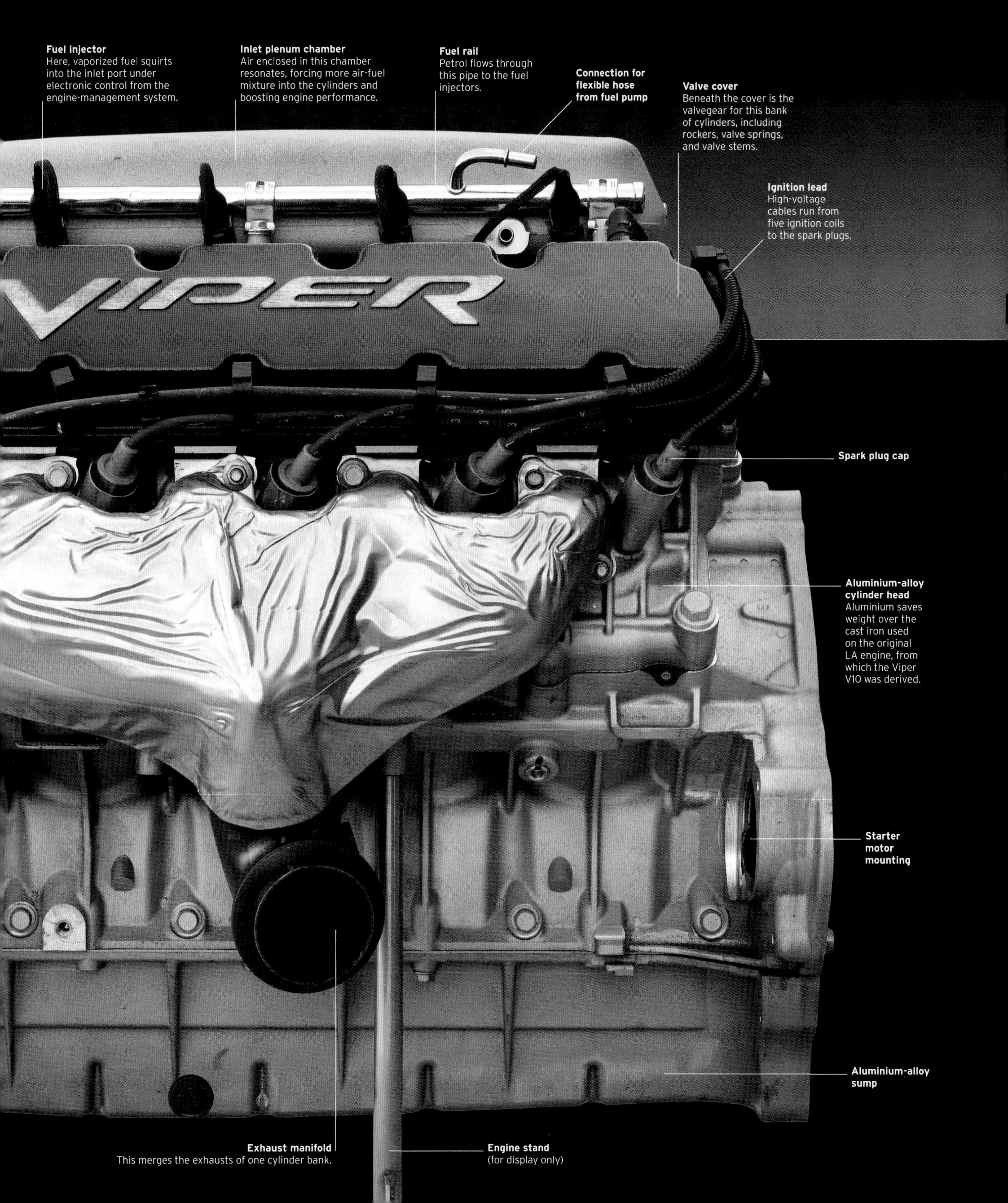

Fuel injector
Here, vaporized fuel squirts into the inlet port under electronic control from the engine-management system.

Inlet plenum chamber
Air enclosed in this chamber resonates, forcing more air-fuel mixture into the cylinders and boosting engine performance.

Fuel rail
Petrol flows through this pipe to the fuel injectors.

Connection for flexible hose from fuel pump

Valve cover
Beneath the cover is the valvegear for this bank of cylinders, including rockers, valve springs, and valve stems.

Ignition lead
High-voltage cables run from five ignition coils to the spark plugs.

Spark plug cap

Aluminium-alloy cylinder head
Aluminium saves weight over the cast iron used on the original LA engine, from which the Viper V10 was derived.

Starter motor mounting

Aluminium-alloy sump

Exhaust manifold
This merges the exhausts of one cylinder bank.

Engine stand
(for display only)

Ferdinand Porsche (far left) in the Löhner-Porsche electric car, 1900

Great marques
The Porsche story

A string of legendary road and race cars has borne the name of Ferdinand Porsche, one of the 20th century's finest automotive engineers. The marque he founded has been synonymous with performance cars since the 1950s and its most famous product, the Porsche 911, has been a sports-car icon for around half a century.

FERDINAND PORSCHE WAS born in 1875 in the town of Maffersdorf in Bohemia, part of Austro-Hungary (now part of the Czech Republic). The son of a plumber, he showed an early interest in all things mechanical and electrical, and went to work for an electrical company in Vienna. There he developed the idea of electric wheel motors to propel a vehicle, a concept that came to fruition in the Löhner-Porsche electric vehicle, displayed at the Paris World Fair in 1900.

Porsche badge
(introduced 1950)

Ferdinand Porsche went on to design cars and aircraft engines for Austro-Daimler and Daimler-Benz, before setting up as a consulting engineer. He was hired to design Auto Union's enormously powerful Grand Prix cars in the 1930s. In complete contrast, Porsche also designed the Volkswagen "people's car", which later became the world's best-selling car when it went into production after World War II.

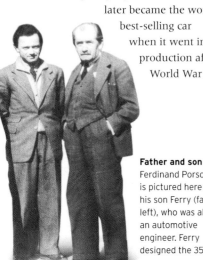

Father and son
Ferdinand Porsche is pictured here with his son Ferry (far left), who was also an automotive engineer. Ferry designed the 356.

Porsche was into his 70s when he went into full-time car manufacture. His Volkswagen design provided the starting point, supplying the engine, suspension, and platform chassis for the one-off Type 64 – a small coupé designed in 1939 for a race that never took place due to the outbreak of World War II. In 1950 Porsche's son Ferry revived and refined the concept into the 356, a road-going sports car that became the Porsche company's first production model.

The 356 was initially built at Porsche's workshops in Gmünd, Austria, but as demand for the car increased, more space was needed to establish a proper assembly line. By 1950 production had relocated to a larger factory in Zuffenhausen, a suburb of Stuttgart in southwest Germany. Ferdinand Porsche died the following year, aged 75.

The 356's flat-four engine was gradually increased in capacity from 1,086 cc to 1,488 cc by using special crankshafts and connecting rods. There were also four-camshaft versions developed for racing, which proved both powerful and temperamental. In 1954 a lightweight version called the 356 Speedster became an instant hit in the US, cementing Porsche's reputation as the maker of the best small sports cars in the world.

In 1963 Porsche replaced the 356 with the 911 – a bigger, more refined, and more powerful car powered by a new 2.0-litre, air-cooled, flat-six

> "It has always been [our] **philosophy** ... that **function** and **beauty** are **inseparable.**"
> FERRY PORSCHE, 1985

engine. Originally called the 901, the car was renamed the 911 to avoid confusion with Peugeot's numbering system. The car's simple styling was designed by Ferry's son Ferdinand Alexander, who was also known as "Butzi". The 911 was reliable and practical enough to use every day, yet it also offered scorching straight-line

performance. The rear-engined design ensured excellent traction, although it also produced oversteer, which could surprise an unwary driver.

The 911 gradually became more powerful and faster, and in 1973 racing demands resulted in the iconic Carrera RS version, with its big-bore, 2.7-litre engine and lightweight body.

Porsche 959 in rally mode
One of the first high-performance cars to use four-wheel drive, the 959 was the most technologically advanced sports car of its day. It proved itself in competition, claiming first and second place in the 1986 Paris–Dakar Rally.

356A

911S

917K

PANAMERA 4S

1930 Ferdinand Porsche establishes his consulting engineering firm in Gmünd, Austria.
1939 Ferdinand Porsche designs the Type 64 racing coupé.
1950 Porsche company introduces its first production car, the 356, which is based on the Type 64.
1951 Ferdinand Porsche dies in Stuttgart, aged 75.
1962 Dan Gurney wins the French Grand Prix, Porsche's first Formula 1 victory.

1963 Porsche unveils its replacement for the 356, called the 901 but soon renamed the 911.
1968 Porsche 911s driven by Vic Elford and Pauli Toivonen finish first and second in the Monte Carlo Rally.
1970 Hans Herrmann and Richard Attwood win Porsche's first Le Mans 24-hour race in a 917K.
1973 Mark Donohue dominates the Can-Am race series in the 1100 bhp Porsche 917-30.

1975 The 930 series – otherwise known as the 911 Turbo – is introduced.
1976 Porsche unveils its first front-engined car with a water-cooled engine, the 924, followed in 1977 by the 928.
1984 Niki Lauda wins the Formula 1 World Championship in a McLaren powered by a Porsche-designed TAG turbo engine.
1986 Launch of the 959, one of the fastest and most technologically sophisticated cars yet built.

1989 The 911 enters a new era with the heavily revised 964-series Carrera 4.
1996 Porsche introduces the entry-level Boxster roadster.
1998 Ferry Porsche dies in Austria, aged 88.
2002 The Cayenne SUV is introduced; it will become Porsche's biggest-selling car.
2009 Launch of the first four-door Porsche production saloon, the Panamera.
2010 After Porsche's failed bid to take over Volkswagen, the two companies agree to merge in 2011.

In the 1960s and 70s the 911 added to Porsche's motor sport success, which already included many class wins in sports-car races and even occasional success at Formula 1 level. The 911 triumphed in such classic events as the Monte Carlo Rally and Sicily's Targa Florio, while the purpose-built 917 racers won the Le Mans 24-hour race in France. Porsche also dominated the North American Can-Am racing series in the early 1970s with its 1,000 bhp, flat-12 turbo cars.

Porsches soon became the cars to beat: the 911-based 934 and 935 were typically the most numerous cars on the grid, while overall race honours were contested by the 936, 956, and

"There is no substitute"
This 1975 Porsche advert promotes the panache, power, and engineering excellence of its 911 and 914 models.

962 models. After nearly two decades away from Formula 1, Porsche made a successful return in 1983 as an engine supplier, designing the TAG turbo engine that powered McLaren's Niki Lauda and Alain Prost to World Championship titles.

Tougher regulations on noise and emissions in the 1970s threatened to spell the end for the 911, and Porsche boss Ernst Fuhrmann was keen to move on to front-engined, water-

cooled cars. However, the V8-engined 928 and the entry-level 924 (later developed into the 944 and 968) failed to win the hearts of Porsche enthusiasts, whereas the 911 continued to do so. The 911 Turbo of 1975 was renowned as one of the fastest-accelerating cars of its era. The ultimate derivative of the original long-running 911 series was the twin-turbo, four-wheel-drive 959, of which just 200 examples were produced between 1986 and 1989.

A new-generation 911 model was introduced in 1989, followed by three further generations over the next two decades – each looking similar to the last, but offering new technology and ever-higher performance levels.

In the early 1990s Porsche was producing good cars, but struggling to make money. As a result, the front-engined cars were dropped, and Porsche developed the Boxster, an entry-level, mid-engined roadster that appealed to a new, younger customer. The Cayenne, a large SUV developed

in partnership with Volkswagen, expanded the line-up in a different direction. To answer criticisms that the Cayenne SUV was unnecessarily extravagant and wasteful, Porsche began to develop electric and hybrid powertrains for use in its future road-car models.

In 2009 a bitter battle for control between Porsche and Volkswagen reached its climax. Porsche had increased its shareholding in Volkswagen to more than 50 per cent, but had built up considerable debts in doing so and could not raise sufficient capital for a full takeover. As Porsche struggled to cope with its debts, Volkswagen secured an agreement for the two companies to merge in 2011, which would see Porsche become the 10th car brand in the Volkswagen Group.

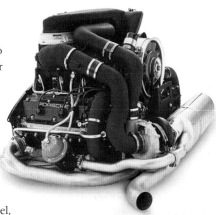

Porsche 911 flat-six turbo
A turbocharged version of Porsche's air-cooled flat-six engine was introduced into the 911 in 1974, giving the car exhilarating acceleration.

Executive Saloons

With the continuing popularity of saloon, or touring car, racing around the world, some executive saloons in the 1990s became much more sporty, but others concentrated on comfort and refinement. All were increasingly fitted with complex electronics, gadgets, and driver aids, while multiple camshafts and valves, as well as light alloy construction, helped keep engine power up and weight down.

△ **Saab 900 Carlsson 1990**

Origin Sweden

Engine 1,985 cc, straight-four

Top speed 135 mph (217 km/h)

Built from 1978 and based on the 1967 Saab 99 floorpan, the 900 was still a surprisingly refined and potent front-wheel-drive saloon in ultimate "Carlsson" version.

◁ **BMW 5-Series 1995**

Origin Germany

Engine 2,793 cc, straight-six

Top speed 142 mph (229 km/h)

The E39 5-series was launched with 2-litre straight-six to 4.4-litre V8 engines and developed with electronic and trim options, retaining the model's strong position in the luxury saloon sector.

△ **Audi A4 Quattro 1994**

Origin Germany

Engine 1,781 cc, straight-four

Top speed 137 mph (220 km/h)

Five valves per cylinder and a turbo gave the four-wheel-drive A4 a reliable 150bhp and made it a success on road and track. This car was Frank Biela's BTCC-winner.

△ **Lincoln Continental 1995**

Origin USA

Engine 4,601 cc, V8

Top speed 120 mph (193 km/h)

Ford's top Lincoln model since 1939, the Continental for 1995 had the Mustang Cobra twin-cam V8 and many luxury fittings, including air-ride suspension.

△ **Holden VR Commodore SS 1993**

Origin Australia

Engine 4,987 cc, V8

Top speed 143 mph (230 km/h)

Australia's native car maker added anti-lock brakes and independent rear suspension to its big saloon's refinements. This is the 1995 Bathurst Great Race winner.

△ **Audi A8 1994**

Origin Germany

Engine 4,172 cc, V8

Top speed 155 mph (249 km/h)

Audi's flagship saloon used the world's first production aluminium monocoque, keeping weight down and performance up. It sold with two- or four-wheel drive and 2.8-litre V6 to 4.2-litre V8 engines.

△ **Mercedes-Benz S-Class 1991**

Origin Germany

Engine 5,987 cc, V12

Top speed 155 mph (249 km/h)

Mercedes' 1990s flagship car was not the most elegant, but it was one of the biggest and was technically magnificent, with double glazing, and engines from 2.8-litre straight-six to 6-litre V12.

△ **Mercedes-Benz C220 1993**

Origin Germany

Engine 2,199 cc, straight-four

Top speed 130 mph (209 km/h)

The C-class was the entry-level saloon from Mercedes for the 1990s. Engines ranged from 1.8-litre four-cylinder to 2.8-litre six-cylinder – or 4.3-litre V8 in the 1998 AMG models.

▷ **Mercedes-Benz S-Class 1999**

Origin Germany

Engine 5,786 cc, V12

Top speed 155 mph (249 km/h)

The new S-class was lighter, smaller, and more elegant than before, with more interior space, but proved to be less well built. Engines ranged from 3.2-litre V6 to 6.3-litre V12.

△ Chrysler LHS 1994

Origin USA

Engine 3,518 cc, V6

Top speed 136 mph (219 km/h)

Eight years in development and via various show cars, the LHS was a radical move for Chrysler, with a large cabin in overall compact dimensions, and a new overhead-cam V6.

△ Lexus GS300 1997

Origin Japan

Engine 2,997 cc, V6

Top speed 143 mph (230 km/h)

High on technology, the GS sports saloon could be ordered with twin turbos, electronic four-wheel steering, and stability control. The US had a 4-litre V8 GS400 option.

△ Bentley Arnage 1998

Origin UK

Engine 4,398 cc, V8

Top speed 150 mph (241 km/h)

Developed under Vickers' ownership of Rolls-Royce/Bentley and visually reminiscent of earlier models, the all-new Arnage featured a Cosworth-tuned BMW engine.

△ Cadillac Seville STS 1998

Origin USA

Engine 4,565 cc, V8

Top speed 150 mph (241 km/h)

The first Cadillac engineered for both left- and right-hand drive was also the most powerful front-wheel-drive car on the market at its launch, with 300bhp in STS form.

△ Jaguar S-type 1999

Origin UK

Engine 3,996 cc, V8

Top speed 149 mph (240 km/h)

For the new millennium Jaguar tried retro styling echoing the 1963 S-type for its executive sporting saloon. Offered with 2.5-litre V6 to 4.2-litre V8 engines, it sold well.

Hyper-Performance Cars

Extreme performance cars came to the fore in the 1990s with models that broke both styling conventions and speed records. Manufacturers used technology and materials from Formula 1 to set new benchmarks for what production models could look like and how they behaved on the road. Some marques created race-tuned models; others added extra horsepower to their existing designs.

△ **Jaguar XK8 1996**

Origin	UK
Engine	3,996 cc, V8
Top speed	155 mph (249 km/h)

Released in 1996 to critical acclaim, Jaguar's all-new XK8 model was available either as a handsome coupé or a stylish convertible.

△ **Jaguar XJS 1991**

Origin	UK
Engine	3,980 cc, straight-six
Top speed	143 mph (230 km/h)

First seen in 1976, the XJ-S was re-engineered and relaunched in 1991 (minus the hyphen). In 1993 it was offered with a 6.0-litre, V12 engine. Production of the XJS ended in 1996.

△ **Jaguar XKR 1998**

Origin	UK
Engine	3,996 cc, V8
Top speed	155 mph (249 km/h)

As a high-performance variant of the XK8, Jaguar's XKR boasted faster acceleration and superior road-handling qualities over the standard model.

△ **Bentley Continental R 1991**

Origin	UK
Engine	6,750 cc, V8
Top speed	150 mph (241 km/h)

This gentleman's express was styled by British designers John Heffernan and Ken Greenley. The turbocharged engine gave about 325 bhp, although no official figure was ever revealed.

△ **Ferrari 456GT 1992**

Origin	Italy
Engine	5,474 cc, V12
Top speed	186 mph (300 km/h)

The Pininfarina styling of the highly popular 456 emphasized refinement and comfort. This exceptionally fast 2+2 coupé remained in production for more than a decade.

△ **McLaren F1 GTR 1995**

Origin	UK
Engine	6,064 cc, V12
Top speed	230 mph (370 km/h)

In 1995 McLaren's F1 road model was developed for competition use. Equipped with a tuned BMW engine, the F1 GTR won the 1995 Le Mans 24-hour race in France.

△ **Aston Martin DB7 Volante 1996**

Origin	UK
Engine	3,228 cc, straight-six
Top speed	165 mph (266 km/h)

The soft-top Volante was launched about three years after the sublime DB7 Coupé. With its supercharged engine giving 335 bhp, it was a firm favourite among Aston Martin fans.

▷ **Ferrari 355 1994**

Origin	Italy
Engine	3,495.5 cc, V8
Top speed	183 mph (295 km/h)

The first Ferrari road model to feature semi-automatic paddle gearshifters, the 355 is one of the most beautiful recent offerings from the famous Italian marque.

◁ **Ferrari 348GTB 1994**

Origin	Italy
Engine	3,405 cc, V8
Top speed	174 mph (280 km/h)

Launched in 1989, the 348 was uprated five years later to GTB specification. Tuned versions were quick enough to compete in top-class race series.

△ **Ferrari F50 1995**

Origin	Italy
Engine	4,698.5 cc, V12
Top speed	202 mph (325 km/h)

The F50, Ferrari's 50th anniversary model, utilized technology and materials derived from the marque's Formula 1 team to create one of the most desirable cars ever produced.

△ Bugatti EB110 1991
Origin Italy
Engine 3,499 cc, V12
Top speed 213 mph (343 km/h)

After an absence of more than 30 years, the fabled Bugatti marque returned in the early 1990s with this 560 bhp supercar, of which just 139 examples were built.

△ Alfa Romeo 155 DTM 1993
Origin Italy
Engine 2,498 cc, V6
Top speed 186 mph (300 km/h)

This highly tuned 155 participated in the German DTM (Deutsche Tourenwagen Meisterschaft) touring-car series, winning the competition in both 1993 and 1996.

△ Lotus Esprit V8 1996
Origin UK
Engine 3,500 cc, V8
Top speed 175 mph (282 km/h)

Thirty years after the Lotus Esprit was unveiled as a concept car, the model was still going strong, with this V8 version boasting scintillating performance figures.

△ Mercedes-Benz C-Class DTM 1994
Origin Germany
Engine 2,500 cc, V6
Top speed 186 mph (300 km/h)

Mercedes-Benz launched its new C-Class compact executive car in 1993. The following year this tuned version of the car secured immediate success by winning the DTM touring-car series in Germany.

△ Lamborghini Diablo 1990
Origin Italy
Engine 5,709 cc, V12
Top speed 202 mph (325 km/h)

Replacing Lamborghini's legendary Countach, the all-new Diablo earned its supercar status by briefly laying claim to being the fastest production car in the world.

△ Lister Storm 1993
Origin UK
Engine 6,996 cc, V12
Top speed 208 mph (335 km/h)

The tuning company Lister Cars' first foray into the supercar market was the impressive Storm, which had one of the largest engines ever fitted to a production car.

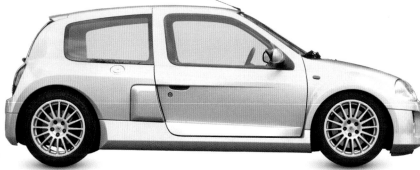

△ Renault Clio V6 2001
Origin France/UK
Engine 2,946 cc, V6
Top speed 146 mph (235 km/h)

To transform the performance of its Clio hatchback, Renault enlisted the help of the British company TWR. The result was this stunningly quick, mid-engined, 230 bhp racer.

◁ Porsche 911 1998
Origin Germany
Engine 3,600 cc, flat-six
Top speed 170 mph (274 km/h)

In 1998 a water-cooled engine was fitted into the Porsche 911, replacing the air-cooled unit that had powered the 911 since the model's inception in 1963.

Bentley Continental R

The Continental R formalized the revival of the Bentley marque, which had degenerated into nothing more than a Rolls-Royce with a different radiator grille, in the years since Rolls-Royce's 1931 takeover of the company. The first Bentley to carry a distinctive body of its own since the 1950s, the R and its sister models combined the muscular performance of a turbocharged V8 engine with an exquisitely trimmed coupé body. The result was one of the very finest grand tourers money could buy.

AT THE BEGINNING of the 1980s Bentley was on the brink of closure. With no models specific to the marque, there was no reason to buy a Bentley other than sentimentalism or a liking for the radiator design. Sales represented about 5 per cent of the parent company's total output of Rolls-Royces and Bentleys. Serious thought was given to discontinuing the marque. Instead, a turbocharged version of the Mulsanne saloon was introduced in 1982, and developed over subsequent years into a magnificent luxury saloon with searing performance.

It was then decided to produce a more sporting coupé badged as a Bentley to replace Rolls-Royce's two-door Camargue. The Continental R emerged in 1991, based on the Mulsanne-derived Turbo R saloon – whose running gear could be traced back to that of the 1965 Rolls-Royce Silver Shadow. A more powerful S model was available in 1994–95, and this led to the high-performance Continental T, which had a 10 cm (4 in) shorter body and uprated brakes and suspension. Other derivatives included a convertible, the Azure.

SPECIFICATIONS	
Model	Bentley Continental R, 1991–2003
Assembly	Crewe, UK
Production	1,854 all types
Construction	Steel monocoque
Engine	6,750 cc, pushrod V8
Power output	385–420 bhp at 4,000 rpm
Transmission	Four-speed automatic
Suspension	Independent by coil; self-levelling
Brakes	Four-wheel discs
Maximum speed	150 mph (241 km/h)

A racing pedigree
Walter Owen Bentley made his name as an aero-engine designer. His first car was announced in 1919, and the company's sports models found fame by winning the Le Mans 24-hour race five times. Since 1998 Bentley has been owned by Volkswagen.

FRONT VIEW

REAR VIEW

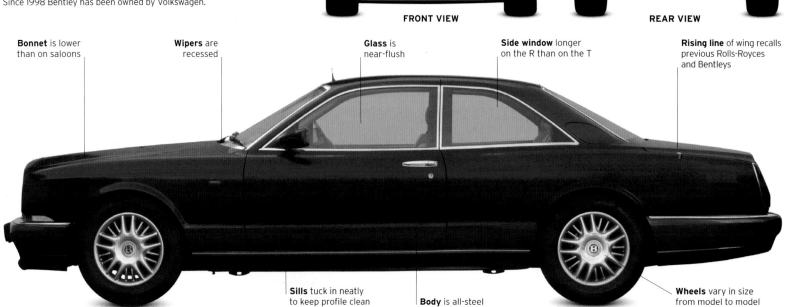

Bonnet is lower than on saloons

Wipers are recessed

Glass is near-flush

Side window longer on the R than on the T

Rising line of wing recalls previous Rolls-Royces and Bentleys

Sills tuck in neatly to keep profile clean

Body is all-steel

Wheels vary in size from model to model

A return to tradition
The Mulsanne series of Bentleys originally featured a
vertical-slat grille and big, rectangular lamp units. But in
1984 a mesh-type grille, evoking Bentleys of the 1920s,
was introduced on the lower-priced Eight, and round
headlights followed on the 1989 Turbo R. Both the
grille and headlights on this Continental R echo
Bentley's traditional design style.

S370 RD

THE EXTERIOR

The starting point for the Continental R was 1985's Bentley "Project 90" styling exercise by British designers John Heffernan and Ken Greenley. The final R design has a lower radiator grille that allows a lower bonnet line, and the kick-up in the line of the rear wing evokes that of Rolls-Royce's Corniche model. The later, shorter-wheelbase T model has flared wheelarches and different bumper and sill treatments.

1. Badge essentially the same since 1919 2. Car revives famous Continental name 3. Twin headlamps first seen on Turbo R 4. Mesh grille is a stainless-steel lattice 5. Slender door mirrors 6. Various designs of alloy wheel used 7. Sleek chrome door handle 8. Retractable radio aerial on rear wing 9. Fuel filler on rear pillar 10. Tail lights unique to Continental and Azure 11. Tail-pipes hint at power

THE INTERIOR

The quality of the Bentley's leather-trimmed interior is unparalleled. The Continental's cockpit has a more sporting flavour than a Bentley saloon, and features a centre console extending into the rear compartment. The R dashboard is in beautifully crafted wood veneer, while on the T it is generally in engine-turned aluminium. A floor-mounted gearshift – as opposed to one on the steering column – was an innovation for a modern-day Bentley.

12. Sophisticated interior with walnut wood finish 13. Steering wheel less elegant than in the past 14. Speedometer bears Bentley logo 15. LCD display for mileage, automatic transmission, and fuel 16. Trademark chrome vents, operated by a small chrome knob 17. Auxiliary dials on console 18. Hefty chrome door "furniture" 19. Seat backs have pleated map pockets 20. Mulliner Park Ward is former in-house Rolls/Bentley coachbuilder 21. One-arm headrest

22

UNDER THE BONNET

The all-aluminium V8, dating back to 1959, has old-fashioned pushrods rather than an overhead camshaft, and still has two valves per cylinder. Use of a turbocharger pushes power to 385 bhp, or to 400 bhp, and latterly 420 bhp in the T model – as also found in the special Continental T Mulliner version. The torque (pulling power) in this ultimate format is 650 lb ft at 2,200 rpm, more than any other car in the world at the time.

22. Modern shrouding hides 1950s engine design **23.** Turbocharger source of Bentley's strong performance **24.** Under-bonnet lamp

23

24

13

14

17

15

16

18

19

21

20

COACHBUILT BY
MULLINER PARK WARD

2000
onwards

Crossovers & off-roaders | City cars & hybrids | **Performance & Economy**

Famous Marques Reinvented

After building cars for more than a century, the motor industry discovered the power of its heritage in public perception. Today, every manufacturer who is able to, draws heavily on its past with evocative model names and styling cues. For other manufacturers, there is a need to create new brands that distance them from any negative associations with the parent brand or its past.

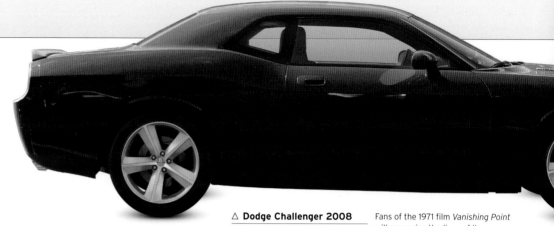

△ **Dodge Challenger 2008**

Origin USA

Engine 6,059 cc, V8

Top speed 145 mph (233 km/h)

Fans of the 1971 film *Vanishing Point* will recognize the lines of its four-wheeled star in this latest version of the model, despite the four-decade gap since the original.

△ **MG ZT 260 2001**

Origin UK

Engine 4,601 cc, V8

Top speed 155 mph (249 km/h)

Based on Rover's 75 saloon, MG put in a Ford V8 and converted it to rear-wheel drive, creating a car with big performance under a subtle exterior.

△ **Maybach 2002**

Origin Germany

Engine 5,980 cc, V12

Top speed 155 mph (249 km/h)

Having not built cars since 1940, this marque had been long dead until it was revived by Daimler-Benz as its hyper-luxury brand in 2002.

△ **Cadillac STS-V 2005**

Origin USA

Engine 4,371 cc, V8

Top speed 155 mph (249 km/h)

Sharp-suited styling and taut handling are at odds with the ungainly, fin-tailed Cadillacs of old. Fitting a supercharger to the Northstar V8 produced 469 bhp for the STS-V.

△ **Mercedes-Benz CLK 320 2002**

Origin Germany

Engine 3,199 cc, V6

Top speed 155 mph (249 km/h)

Based on the company's C-Class models, this car is closer to the E-Class in price. It keeps alive Mercedes-Benz's tradition of offering convertibles.

◁ **Ford Mustang GT convertible 2004**

Origin USA

Engine 4,951 cc, V8

Top speed 149 mph (240 km/h)

The Mustang's design team took styling cues from the very first Mustang for the 2004 model – these included the scallops down the sides and the set-back headlights.

▷ **Maserati Quattroporte 2004**

Origin Italy

Engine 4,691 cc, V8

Top speed 174 mph (280 km/h)

The name simply means "four doors", but it sounds so much more exciting in Italian. The Quattroporte's 434 bhp V8 delivers performance to match.

△ **BMW Alpina B7 Bi-Turbo 2010**

Origin Germany

Engine 4,395 cc, V8

Top speed 188 mph (302 km/h)

Officially registered as a manufacturer, Alpina creates high-performance versions of BMWs, such as this polished 7 Series that delivers 500 bhp.

▷ **Lexus IS-F 2005**

Origin Japan

Engine 4,969 cc, V8

Top speed 155 mph (249 km/h)

Japanese team Gazoo Racing prepared this Lexus to compete in a 24-hour race at the challenging Nürburgring Nordschleife circuit in Germany.

△ **Rolls-Royce Phantom 2003**

Origin UK

Engine 6,750 cc, V12

Top speed 155 mph (249 km/h)

When BMW took control of Rolls-Royce, it built a new factory near Goodwood and created a car that captured the marque's legendary presence.

△ **Rolls-Royce Phantom drophead 2007**

Origin UK

Engine 6,750 cc, V12

Top speed 155 mph (249 km/h)

The drophead's styling remained remarkably faithful to the 100EX, a concept car unveiled to mark the centenary of the company in 2006.

▷ **Infiniti G37 convertible 2009**

Origin Japan

Engine 3,696 cc, V6

Top speed 155 mph (249 km/h)

The Infiniti brand was created by Nissan to overcome resistance in the US market to Japanese cars and is reserved for prestige models.

◁ **Audi A5 Coupé 2007**

Origin Germany

Engine 2,967 cc, V6

Top speed 155 mph (249 km/h)

Reviving Audi's stylish 1970s coupé, the A5's shape was drawn from the Nuvolari quattro concept car exhibited at the 2003 Geneva Motor Show.

△ **Porsche Panamera 4S 2009**

Origin Germany

Engine 4,806 cc, V8

Top speed 175 mph (282 km/h)

Despite putting the engine up front and adding two extra doors, the Panamera manages to retain styling cues that date back to the 911 of the 1960s.

△ **Chevrolet Camaro 2SS 2010**

Origin USA

Engine 6,162 cc, V8

Top speed 155 mph (249 km/h)

Blending 1960s styling with 21st-century film culture, the fifth-generation Chevrolet Camaro is also available in a *Transformers* special edition.

△ **Jaguar XF 2008**

Origin UK

Engine 5,000 cc, V8

Top speed 155 mph (249 km/h)

With this model, Jaguar aimed to re-create the appeal of its mid-sized S-Type model from the 1960s and make Jaguar quality more affordable.

△ **Jaguar XJ 2009**

Origin UK

Engine 5,000 cc, V8

Top speed 155 mph (249 km/h)

The all new XJ has an aerospace-inspired aluminium frame made from 50 per cent recycled material. This is about 150 kg (330 lb) lighter than its steel rivals.

▽ **Aston Martin Rapide 2010**

Origin UK

Engine 5,935 cc, V12

Top speed 184 mph (296 km/h)

Offering four doors in a supercar package, the Rapide takes its name from the 1930s Lagonda model, a famous marque Aston Martin acquired in 1947.

Crossovers and Off-Roaders

For 50 years the trend had been to build cars lower and sleeker, but designers realized that people were increasingly buying four-wheel-drive vehicles because they wanted higher, safer-feeling cars. A surge in production of "crossover" vehicles followed, some with only limited off-road ability.

△ **Land Rover Discovery Series II 1998**

Origin UK

Engine 2,495 cc, straight-five

Top speed 98 mph (158 km/h)

Launched in 1989 for a new market segment where style and comfort were important, the Discovery retained exceptional off-road ability and sold strongly.

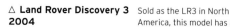

△ **Land Rover Discovery 3 2004**

Origin UK

Engine 4,394 cc, V8

Top speed 121 mph (195 km/h)

Sold as the LR3 in North America, this model has a completely new design with monocoque construction and an all-independent air suspension. It has exceptional off/on-road ability.

△ **Renault Avantime 2001**

Origin France

Engine 2,946 cc, V6

Top speed 137 mph (220 km/h)

Designed and built by Matra, this innovative crossover between a two-door coupé and an MPV failed to find a market niche; just 8,557 were sold in 2001–03.

△ **Honda CR-V 2001**

Origin Japan

Engine 1,998 cc, straight-four

Top speed 110 mph (177 km/h)

The CR-V was one of the first two- or four-wheel-drive option SUVs when launched in 1996. It saw the market niche grow dramatically, and frequent upgrades (this one in 2001) kept it popular.

◁ **Subaru Tribeca 2005**

Origin Japan

Engine 2,999 cc, flat-six

Top speed 121 mph (195 km/h)

Based on the Legacy car platform, the Tribeca benefits from Subaru's long four-wheel-drive and rallying heritage. The lightweight, flat engine gives it a low centre of gravity.

△ **Chevrolet Tahoe 2005**

Origin USA

Engine 5,300 cc, V8

Top speed 123 mph (198 km/h)

A full-size SUV from General Motors, this car is also sold as GMC Yukon and LWB Chevy Suburban. It is available as a two- or four-wheel drive, or as a hybrid.

▷ **Chevrolet HHR 2005**

Origin USA

Engine 2,130 cc, straight-four

Top speed 110 mph (177 km/h)

HHR stands for "Heritage High Roof", referring to styling inspired by the 1949 Chevrolet Suburban. The HHR is also available as a panel van, or turbocharged.

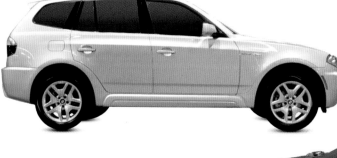

◁ **BMW X3 2004**

Origin Germany/Austria

Engine 2,494 cc, straight-six

Top speed 129 mph (208 km/h)

Designed and built by Magna Steyr of Austria, the X3 was based on the four-wheel-drive 3-Series saloon, and so lacked optimum off-road ability.

▷ **Mazda CX-7 2006**

Origin Japan

Engine 2,260 cc, straight-four

Top speed 130 mph (209 km/h)

Unlike most opposition, Mazda's mid-size crossover SUV is built on an all-new platform. It is clearly primarily a luxury road car, with two- or four-wheel-drive options.

△ Toyota Highlander 2000

Origin Japan

Engine 2,995 cc, V6

Top speed 125 mph (201 km/h)

The first car-based mid-size crossover SUV, based on the Camry platform, this was Toyota's best-selling SUV for the first half of the decade.

▷ Toyota Sienna 2006

Origin Japan

Engine 3,310 cc, V6

Top speed 111 mph (179 km/h)

A family mini van, or MPV, the front-wheel-drive Sienna was launched in 1997. Four-wheel drive became an option in 2004, but this is not an off-road vehicle.

▷ Nissan Qashqai 2006

Origin Japan/UK

Engine 1,997 cc, straight-four

Top speed 119 mph (192 km/h)

The Qashqai sold 100,000 units in its first year. Primarily a road car with two- or four-wheel drive, it has fair off-road ability.

▽ Nissan Rogue 2007

Origin Japan

Engine 2,488 cc, straight-four

Top speed 120 mph (193 km/h)

The North American equivalent of the Qashqai is a compact crossover SUV with constantly variable transmission, and front- or four-wheel drive.

△ Saturn Outlook 2006

Origin USA

Engine 3,600 cc, V6

Top speed 120 mph (193 km/h)

General Motors launched Saturn in 1987 and closed it in 2010. The Outlook was a full-size crossover SUV with eight seats and front- or four-wheel drive.

▷ Volkswagen Touran 2003

Origin Germany

Engine 1,968 cc, straight-four

Top speed 122 mph (196 km/h)

Based on the four-wheel-drive VW Golf, the Touran was a compact SUV that was offered with petrol, diesel, or LPG engines from 1.2 to 2.0 litre, hybrid or battery-only.

△ Ford Kuga 2008

Origin Germany

Engine 2,522 cc, straight-five

Top speed 129 mph (208 km/h)

Based on the Focus platform with front- or four-wheel-drive options, the Kuga is aimed at the on-road premium market with performance engines and a high standard of trim.

△ Jeep Patriot 2007

Origin USA

Engine 1,968 cc, straight-four

Top speed 117 mph (188 km/h)

Jeep's entry into the compact SUV market, the Patriot is sold with completely different choices of engine and drive packages in Europe and in the US.

▷ Ford Escape Hybrid 2009

Origin USA

Engine 2,488 cc, straight-four

Top speed 102 mph (164 km/h)

Launched in 2004, the Escape was the first hybrid (petrol and electric) SUV on the market. It was also the first US-built hybrid from a US manufacturer.

Suzuki Fronte, 1962

Great marques
The Suzuki story

With origins that lie in the Japanese silk industry, Suzuki grew into a world-renowned maker of motorcycles and cars. It has proved expert in producing small, low-cost cars, 4x4s, and commercial vehicles with a global appeal. The marque is now expanding its range into larger, more luxurious passenger cars.

MICHIO SUZUKI, born in Hamamatsu in 1887, founded the Suzuki Loom Works in 1909 to manufacture weaving looms for Japan's extensive silk industry. After many years of success, Suzuki decided to diversify and began working on designs for a compact car in 1937. The prototypes were equipped with a 13 bhp, water-cooled, four-cylinder engine of less than 800 cc, which was notable for its innovative cast-aluminium crankcase. However, the start of World War II halted the project.

It was not until 1951 that Suzuki again attempted to diversify into vehicles, this time beginning with a motor that could be clipped on to a bicycle (just as Honda had done a few years earlier). In 1954 the company changed its name to the Suzuki Motor Co. and built its first complete motorcycle, the Colleda. The first Suzuki production car, the

Suzuki badge
(introduced 1958)

comply with Japanese *kei jidosha* ("light car") regulations. Cars that fall within the limits on vehicle size and engine power specified by these rules qualify for lower tax and insurance.

The first SFs had all-round independent suspension, but they could not cope with the poor roads of the time, so leaf springs were substituted in 1956. From 1958 only van versions of the SF were built, and they were replaced in 1959 by the Suzulight TL van, a more modern design with a side-opening tailgate. A passenger-car version, the Suzuki Fronte, was launched in 1962. A new Fronte 360 was announced in 1965, this time with a more powerful three-cylinder, air-cooled, rear-mounted engine; a larger-engined export model, the Fronte 500, became available in 1969.

In 1970 Suzuki introduced the first of a long-running line of tiny, four-wheel-drive utility vehicles.

the ON360 as the LJ10, installing one of its own two-stroke, two-cylinder engines, restyling the body, and moving the rear-mounted spare wheel into the load area to reduce the overall length. This enabled the LJ10 to qualify for *kei* car status – the first 4x4 to do so. The LJ20 of 1972 switched to a water-cooled engine, and the LJ50 (SJ10 in Japan) of 1974 gained a new 539 cc, three-cylinder engine with 33 bhp. Finally, in 1977 Suzuki unveiled the definitive LJ80 (SJ20 in Japan) with a water-cooled, in-line four-cylinder engine of 797 cc and 41 bhp. The LJ80 became a huge export success. There was also an LJ81 pick-up version, called the Stockman in Australia.

The second-generation of Suzuki 4x4s – the longer, wider SJ-series – was introduced in 1981. Export models were available with larger engines that considerably improved performance. The SJs were sold under a number of different model names, and also as

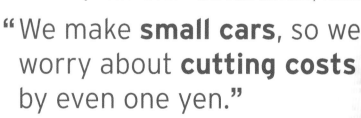

"We make **small cars**, so we worry about **cutting costs** by even one yen."

OSAMU SUZUKI, 1993

Suzulight SF, followed in 1955. Closely modelled on the German Lloyd, the SF was powered by a 360 cc, two-cylinder, two-stroke engine that drove the front wheels. The SF was a *kei* car, built to

The LJ10 was based on the HopeStar ON360 produced by the Hope Motor Company. Only 15 of this Mitsubishi-engined 4x4 were made before Hope ran into financial difficulties. In 1970 Suzuki bought Hope and redeveloped

SC100

VITARA

CAPPUCCINO

KIZASHI

1909 Michio Suzuki opens the Suzuki Loom Works in Hamamatsu.	**1958** Suzuki adopts the "S" logo.	**1982** Suzuki establishes production facilities in India and Pakistan.	**1993** Suzuki signs a joint-venture agreement to produce cars in China.
1937 Work begins on the first Suzuki car, but the project is suspended at the outbreak of World War II.	**1962** The Fronte passenger car is launched.	**1988** The Vitara SUV is introduced to wide acclaim, becoming a major export success.	**2000** Osamu Suzuki steps down as chief executive, but remains chairman.
1951 Suzuki introduces the Power Free bicycle motor.	**1970** Suzuki buys the Hope Motor Company; the HopeStar ON360 compact 4x4 is relaunched as the Suzuki LJ10.	**1989** Total production of Suzuki cars reaches 10 million.	**2008** Now in his 80s, Osamu Suzuki returns to the position of chief executive.
1954 The newly renamed Suzuki Motor Co. produces its first motorcycle, called the Colleda.	**1977** The Cervo, introduced in 1977, the SC100 coupé of 1978, and the Alto of 1979 all help to boost export sales.	**1990** Suzuki establishes a factory in Hungary, and changes its name to Suzuki Motor Corporation.	**2009** The Kizashi saloon takes Suzuki into a new market sector.
1955 The first Suzuki production car, the Suzulight SF, is unveiled.	**1978** Osamu Suzuki becomes chief executive.	**1991** Cappuccino roadster launched; Suzuki begins building cars in South Korea.	**2009** Volkswagen and Suzuki form a strategic partnership; Volkswagen takes a 20 per cent stake in Suzuki, giving Suzuki greater stability.
	1981 General Motors buys a 5.3 per cent stake in Suzuki, later raising it to 20 per cent.		

Chevrolets in the US and Holdens in Australia. They were manufactured under licence by Santana in Spain and by Maruti in India.

Alongside these small but capable off-roaders, Suzuki continued to produce passenger cars. The Fronte Coupé, launched in 1971, offered a unique combination of *kei*-car size, 2+2 seating, styling by the Italian designer Giorgetto Giugiaro, and up to 37 bhp – giving it excellent performance for its size. The Fronte was joined in the 1970s by the Cervo and Alto, and a restyled Cervo coupé called the SC100, all of which increased Suzuki's export sales.

General Motors (GM) bought a 5.3 per cent stake in Suzuki in 1981, which it later increased to 20 per cent. From then on, all Suzuki passenger cars sold in the US went out under GM's Chevrolet brand name. A new compact SUV, known as the Vitara in some markets and the Escudo or Sidekick in others, was introduced in 1988. The three-door Vitara's handy size, neat styling, and good blend of

Ignis S1600 at Rally Finland
A supermini-hatchback, the Ignis was produced from 2000 to 2008. Per-Gunnar Andersson and his co-driver Jonas Andersson took a competition S1600 model to victory in the Junior Class of the 2004 Rally Finland.

Creating a stir
The stylish, two-seater Cappuccino was the embodiment of Suzuki's desire for a model that would give the marque a sporting image.

on- and off-road performance made it a huge success, and its appeal was enhanced when a five-door version was added to the range in 1990.

The next year Suzuki unveiled the Cappuccino, one of its best-loved cars. This roadster *kei* car came with a turbocharged, 657cc, twin-cam engine mounted at the front, and rear-wheel drive. The two-seat Cappuccino had removable roof panels that could be stowed in the luggage area. It continued in production until 1997, outliving rivals such as the Honda Beat, Daihatsu Leeza Spyder, and Autozam (Mazda) AZ-1.

Under the leadership of Osamu Suzuki, the company expanded into Pakistan and India in the 1980s, and in the 1990s it signed agreements to establish factories in Hungary and South Korea. The tiny Wagon R+, jointly developed by Suzuki and

GM, went into production in Hungary in 2000. The company also expanded its range of full-size cars, adding the seven-seat Grand Vitara SUV, new versions of its Swift and Alto hatchbacks, plus the "crossover" SX4 – a car with 4x4 looks but the on-road performance and running costs of a conventional car.

In 2009 Volkswagen bought almost 20 per cent of Suzuki, and the two companies entered into a long-term partnership. With the stability afforded by Volkswagen's investment, the launch of the Kizashi model (taking Suzuki into the important mid-size saloon market), and with Osamu Suzuki back as chief executive, the future for the company looks bright.

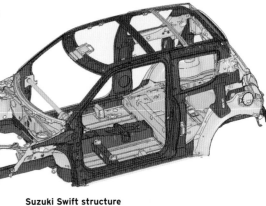

Suzuki Swift structure
To stiffen the frame of 2009's Swift Sport, Suzuki made some sections of hyper-tensile steel (in red). This greater rigidity boosted road-handling and also improved safety.

City Cars

As manufacturers worldwide strove to meet legislation that demanded reduced emissions and greater fuel efficiency, interest turned again to tiny city cars with two, or at most four, seats. Some manufacturers produced tiny, sub-1,000cc, two- or three-cylinder cars designed for city use. Others made small cars that could still be comfortable on motorways, and had efficient-running, lightly stressed, four-cylinder engines.

◁ REVA/G-Wiz i 2001

Origin India

Engine Electric motor

Top speed 50 mph (80 km/h)

The world's best-selling electric car of the decade was this 2+2 Indian model with a 75-mile (120-km) range. A larger and safer model was planned for the next decade.

▷ Ligier Ambra 2000

Origin France

Engine 505 cc, straight-two

Top speed 65 mph (105 km/h)

Former F1 racing-car maker Ligier has long catered for the two-seat "quadricycle" market. The car has tax and regulatory advantages, but is limited to 550 kg (1,212 lb) and 20 bhp.

△ Smart City-Coupé 1998

Origin Germany/France

Engine 599 cc, straight-three

Top speed 84 mph (135 km/h)

The most popular two-seat city car yet was the vision of Swatch creator Nicolas Hayek. Features included rear-wheel drive, electronic stability control, and anti-lock braking.

△ Fiat Panda 2003

Origin Italy/Poland

Engine 1,108 cc, straight-four

Top speed 93 mph (150 km/h)

The Panda of 2003 proved a worthy successor to the name. It was voted European Car of the Year in 2004 and sold 1.5 million in its first six years. It had 1.1–1.4-litre engines.

▷ Subaru R1 2005

Origin Japan

Engine 658 cc, straight-four

Top speed 85 mph (137 km/h)

Not widely marketed outside Japan, the R1 was a short, 2+2, upmarket sporty model in the Japanese *kei car* cheap tax bracket. The R1 had leather trim and optional supercharger.

◁ Opel/Vauxhall Agila 2000

Origin Poland

Engine 973 cc, straight-three

Top speed 88 mph (142 km/h)

Badged as a Vauxhall in the UK, the Opel was a version of Suzuki's Wagon-R or Splash. It had five doors and good interior space.

▷ Kia Picanto 2005

Origin South Korea

Engine 999 cc, straight-four

Top speed 93 mph (150 km/h)

Built on a Hyundai Getz platform, the Picanto had 1.0- or 1.1-litre petrol engines, or a 3-cylinder direct-injection turbodiesel engine. In Europe it sold as a budget car.

△ Peugeot 1007 2004
Origin France
Engine 1,360 cc, straight-four
Top speed 107 mph (172 km/h)

This was a brave attempt to market an unconventional city car with powered sliding doors and semi-automatic gears. Sales were poor, however, due to its high price.

▷ Toyota Yaris/Vitz 2005
Origin France
Engine 1,364 cc, straight-four
Top speed 109 mph (175 km/h)

Designed in Toyota's European studios and sold worldwide with engines from 1.0- to 1.8-litre, this second generation Yaris was the first in its class to have nine airbags.

◁ Toyota iQ 2008
Origin Japan
Engine 1,329 cc, straight-four
Top speed 106 mph (171 km/h)

The ultra-compact iQ had four seats, good performance, and a five-star European crash safety rating. Stability control, anti-lock brakes, and brake assist were all standard.

△ Fiat 500 2007
Origin Italy/ Poland
Engine 1,242 cc, straight-four
Top speed 99 mph (159 km/h)

Retro-styling gave Fiat a new best-seller with this well-engineered four-seater. It had 1.2–1.4-litre engines at its launch; more options were added later.

△ Toyota Aygo 2005
Origin Japan/Czech Republic
Engine 998 cc, straight-three
Top speed 98 mph (158 km/h)

Built alongside the identical Peugeot 107 and Citroën C1, the Aygo had three- or five-door options and a 1.0-litre petrol or 1.4-litre diesel engine.

△ Tata Nano 2009
Origin India
Engine 624 cc, straight-two
Top speed 65 mph (105 km/h)

This home-market Indian car has attracted worldwide interest due to its price (under $3,000). Stripped of all extras, it is potentially the Ford Model T of the 21st century.

◁ Secma F16 Sport 2008
Origin France
Engine 1,598 cc, four-cylinder
Top speed 110 mph (177 km/h)

Weighing just half a tonne, the F16 promises fun but little practicality, even with its optional gullwing doors. It has a rear-mounted, fuel-injected 16-valve Renault engine.

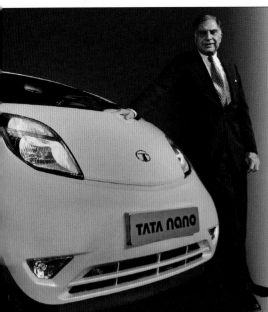

Tata Nano

The Nano is one of the boldest and most fascinating back-to-basics small cars since the original Mini. Designed to lure India's burgeoning middle classes away from two-wheelers, it received much publicity because of its suggested price of 100,000 rupees – roughly £1,250. When the car went on sale in 2009, the price was closer to £1,500, including taxes and delivery, or £2,300 for the most expensive version. That still made the Nano the world's cheapest car, even if the price represented roughly 80 per cent of the average annual salary in India.

THE NANO goes back to first principles in its quest for lightness, simplicity, and low manufacturing costs. It has a rear engine, which is cheaper than a front engine, as there are fewer, simpler parts needed. The engine is also a light and cost-efficient twin-cylinder unit, while the brakes are dependable drums. Thanks to the rear engine, the steering is light enough not to need assistance. The body does not have an opening boot, trim levels are kept to a minimum, and sound insulation is used sparingly. Even the fuel tank is reduced in size, having a mere 15-litre (4-gallon) capacity.

As a result of all this, the Nano has a kerb weight of only 600 kg (1,323 lb). In spite of this lightness, the body is sufficiently strong, thanks to clever touches such as front seat frames that reinforce the body and an exposed bracing bar across the rear compartment.

FRONT VIEW

REAR VIEW

From trucks to cars
Indian conglomerate Tata, led by Ratan Tata, made its name in the automotive field with trucks. In 1998 it introduced the Indica, India's first indigenous design of a private car. Tata now owns Jaguar and Land Rover, as well as Tetley's Tea and what remains of British Steel.

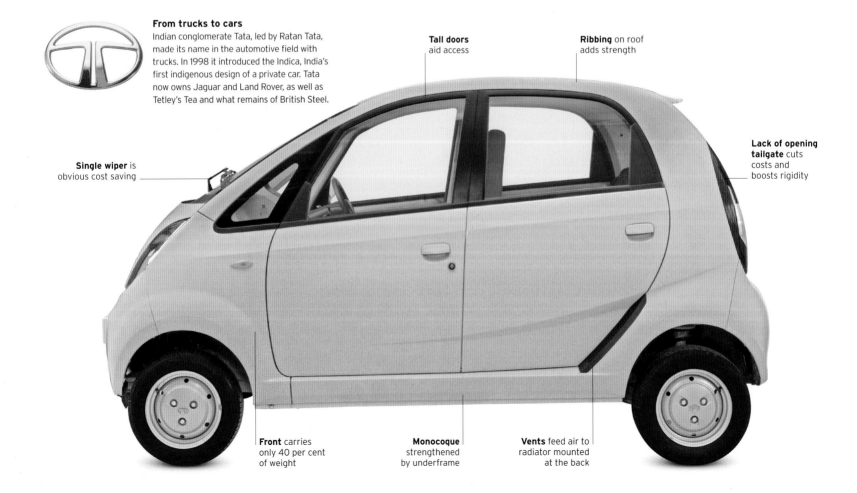

Tall doors aid access

Ribbing on roof adds strength

Lack of opening tailgate cuts costs and boosts rigidity

Single wiper is obvious cost saving

Front carries only 40 per cent of weight

Monocoque strengthened by underframe

Vents feed air to radiator mounted at the back

SPECIFICATIONS

Model	Tata Nano, 2009 onwards
Assembly	Pantnagar and Sanand, India
Production	n/a
Construction	Steel monocoque body
Engine	624 cc, straight-two
Power output	35 bhp at 5,250 rpm
Transmission	Four-speed manual
Suspension	Independent coil; strut front
Brakes	Drum
Maximum speed	65 mph (105 km/h)

A small car like no other

Tata threw out the rule book for the Nano, making a tall, narrow car when Western manufacturers were moving towards lower and ever-wider vehicles. But for Indian traffic conditions, narrowness is a virtue, while the Nano can comfortably tackle uneven roads thanks to its generous ground clearance.

THE EXTERIOR

The one-box design creates maximum interior space for the small size – a claimed 22 per cent more than the yardstick Indian mini-car, the Maruti 800. The 12-inch wheels (fatter at the rear) prevent the wheelarches from eating into the interior, as does their position right at the corners. The wide track and long wheelbase also aid stability – important in a rear-engined car.

1. Chrome badging is one of few extravagances **2.** Tata name is well respected in India **3.** Bumper houses auxiliary lights **4.** Bold headlamps **5.** Single door mirror **6.** One door lock cuts costs **7.** Three-stud fitting for wheels saves money and weight **8.** Scoops feed air to rear radiator **9.** Vertical tail lamps **10.** Mechanicals visible under the car

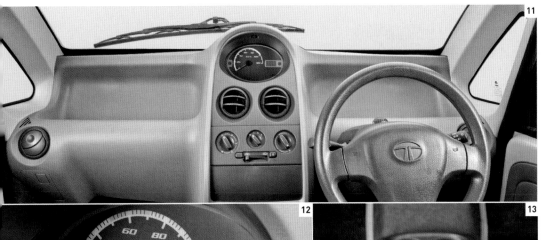

THE INTERIOR

Despite being roughly the length of a BMC Mini – 3.1 m (10 ft 2 in) against the Mini's 3 m (10 ft) – the Nano is impressively roomy. A long wheelbase and thin, upright seating are aids to spaciousness, as is the tall roofline. The extra height also brings with it packaging advantages. The base model has a bare minimum of trim in a low-cost jute-based fabric.

11. Simple dashboard with two troughs   12. Speedometer and digital fuel gauge   13. Gearbox is four-speed unit
14. Room for two in back   15. Battery under driver's seat helps weight distribution   16. Jack stows under front seat

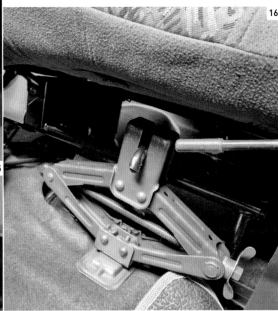

UNDER THE BONNET

The Nano is powered by a water-cooled, all-alloy, two cylinder of just 624 cc, which is simple, economical, and weight-saving. With a single overhead camshaft, power is nevertheless a respectable 35 bhp. A balancer shaft dampens the inevitable vibrations of this engine format, and fuelling is looked after by a Bosch management system that is wonderfully simple thanks to the use of only two cylinders.

17. Rear seat folds forward for access to boot   18. Fixings such as this wing nut are simple
19. Water-cooled two cylinder sits at rear   20. Spare wheel and ancillaries under front bonnet; also fuel filler   21. Brakes are drum all round; no servomechanism on base model

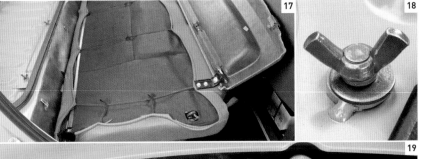

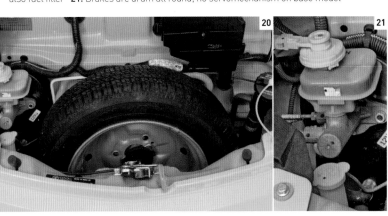

Towards 200 mph

After the Ferrari F40 road car passed the 200 mph mark in 1987, this figure became the badge of honour for any supercar to aspire to. Some machines, German ones especially, had factory-fitted speed limiters to bridle owners' enthusiasm. The 250 mph Bugatti Veyron went a step further in 2005 with its technical magnificence.

△ **Lamborghini Murcièlago Roadster 2004**

Origin Italy

Engine 6,496 cc, V12

Top speed 200 mph (322 km/h)

Fighter aircraft, Spanish architecture, and mega-yachts were among the things that inspired the styling of this awesome, soft-top Lamborghini, with its low-tech manually-operated roof.

△ **Pagani Zonda 1999**

Origin Italy

Engine 7,291 cc, V12

Top speed 220 mph (354 km/h)

Some early development was done on the Zonda by five-time Formula 1 champion Juan Manuel Fangio. With just 10 cars built each year, it is a rare delicacy.

◁ **Lamborghini Murcièlago 2001**

Origin Italy

Engine 6,496 cc, V12

Top speed 213 mph (343 km/h)

The first new model under Volkswagen ownership, the Murcièlago was named after a famous fighting bull that survived 28 sword strokes in Spain in 1879.

◁ **Bentley Continental Supersport 2003**

Origin UK

Engine 5,998 cc, W12

Top speed 204 mph (328 km/h)

An attempt to unleash the performance potential of this luxury coupé, cued a stripped-out interior, no rear seat, pumped-up suspension, and 630 bhp.

△ **Aston Martin V12 Vantage 2009**

Origin UK

Engine 5,935 cc, V12

Top speed 190 mph (306 km/h)

The V12 engine shoehorned into the V8 Vantage and pumped up to give more than 500 bhp produces an irresistible combination of performance and agility.

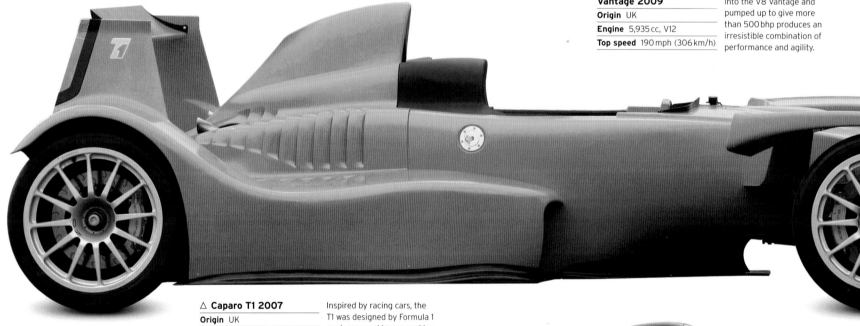

△ **Caparo T1 2007**

Origin UK

Engine 3,496 cc, V8

Top speed 205 mph (330 km/h)

Inspired by racing cars, the T1 was designed by Formula 1 engineers and is powered by an engine descended from Indianapolis racers.

◁ **Ferrari Enzo 2002**

Origin Italy

Engine 5,998 cc, V12

Top speed 226 mph (363 km/h)

The ultimate Ferrari road car when it was released, just 400 models were produced for the most wealthy and discerning customers.

△ **Ferrari 599 GTB Fiorano 2006**

Origin Italy

Engine 5,999 cc, V12

Top speed 205 mph (330 km/h)

The archetypal Ferrari for the modern age, this civilized coupé with the classic V12 engine up front is blisteringly quick.

△ Bristol Fighter 2004

Origin UK

Engine 7,996 cc, V10

Top speed 225 mph (362 km/h)

Produced in very small numbers, strictly to order, the top-of-the-range Fighter T extracts more than 1,000 bhp from its Chrysler Viper engine.

▷ Bugatti Veyron Grand Sport 2005

Origin France

Engine 7,993 cc, W16

Top speed 253 mph (407 km/h)

Rumour has it that the company loses money on every car it builds, but the prestige and technology benefits to the parent company Volkswagen are worth it.

▷ Koenigsegg CCX-R 2006

Origin Sweden

Engine 4,719 cc, V8

Top speed 250 mph (402 km/h)

This car's engine is based on Ford's V8, but with almost every component, including the block, modified or re-manufactured to give 800 bhp.

△ Mercedes-McLaren SLR 722S 2003

Origin UK

Engine 5,439 cc, V8

Top speed 209 mph (336 km/h)

The 722 in the name is a tribute to the race number of the Mille Miglia-winning Mercedes driven by Sir Stirling Moss in 1955.

▷ Nissan GT-R Spec V 2007

Origin Japan

Engine 3,799 cc, V6, twin-turbo

Top speed 193 mph (311 km/h)

A stripped-out version of the standard GT-R, the Spec V features racing front seats, no rear seat, and carbon-fibre, aerodynamic bodywork trim.

△ Mercedes-Benz SLS AMG 2010

Origin Germany

Engine 6,208 cc, V8

Top speed 197 mph (317 km/h)

An attempt to recapture the spirit of the 1950s 300SL Gullwing, the SLS was designed in-house by AMG and saw action as Formula 1's safety car.

△ Mercedes-Benz SL65 Black 2008

Origin Germany

Engine 5,980 cc, V12

Top speed 155 mph (249 km/h)

Produced in limited numbers, this ultimate version of the SL roadster would exceed 200 mph (322 km/h) if there was no electronic speed limiter fitted in it.

△ RUF Porsche CTR3 2007

Origin Germany

Engine 3,746 cc, flat-six

Top speed 233 mph (375 km/h)

The highly respected German tuner RUF is famous for its uncompromising versions of Porsches. This one features weight-saving, carbon-fibre bodywork, and a 691 bhp engine.

◁ Lexus LFA 2010

Origin Japan

Engine 4,805 cc, V10

Top speed 203 mph (327 km/h)

The pearl in this oyster is the 1LR-GUE V10 engine that is smaller than most V8s and will rev from tickover to 9,500 rpm in just 0.6 seconds.

△ Noble M600 2009

Origin UK

Engine 4,439 cc, V8

Top speed 225 mph (362 km/h)

From the company founded by the highly respected maverick car designer Lee Noble, the M600 is thought by some to be one of the finest-handling current supercars.

Motor Sports Contenders

At the start of the 21st century the biggest impact on the design and manufacture of racing cars was created by computers. Their influence was so great that they had to be severely limited within the car to stop them from taking over the driving. Now the typical racing car has fewer computer systems than the average road car, but they still have a huge impact on the way these machines are designed and operated.

△ Aston Martin DBR9 2005

Origin UK

Engine 6,000 cc, V12

Top speed 186 mph (299 km/h)

Winning on its debut at Sebring in the US in 2005, the future looked bright for the DBR9, and it bagged a Le Mans class win in France in 2007.

▷ Lola Aston Martin LMP1 2009

Origin UK

Engine 6,000 cc, V12

Top speed 209 mph (336 km/h)

Having conquered GT racing with its DBR9, Aston Martin transferred its V12 engine into a Lola chassis to tackle the GT1 Prototype class.

△ Bentley Speed 8 2001

Origin UK

Engine 4,000 cc, V8

Top speed 205 mph (330 km/h)

Returning to Le Mans 73 years after its glory days in the 1920s, it took Bentley three attempts before winning once again in 2003.

◁ BAR Honda 2004

Origin UK

Engine 3,000 cc, V10

Top speed 200 mph (322 km/h)

Engine supplier Honda bought the BAR team, but only managed one win before pulling out at the end of 2008. The team then became Brawn.

△ Mercedes-Benz CLK DTM 2003

Origin Germany

Engine 4,000 cc, V8

Top speed 180 mph (290 km/h)

Based on a tubular-steel chassis and powered by V8 engines, German Touring Cars have only a passing resemblance to the production models they represent.

△ McLaren-Mercedes MP4/23 2008

Origin UK

Engine 2,400 cc, V8

Top speed 200 mph (322 km/h)

In only his second season of Formula 1 Grand Prix racing, Lewis Hamilton became the youngest world champion ever at the wheel of this car.

◁ Chevrolet Monte Carlo 2001

Origin USA

Engine 5,860 cc, V8

Top speed 190 mph (306 km/h)

Prepared for North American Stock Car racing, this one was raced by the late NASCAR legend Dale Earnhardt, known to his fans as the "Intimidator".

△ Dodge Charger 2005

Origin USA

Engine 5,860 cc, V8

Top speed 190 mph (306 km/h)

Although branded a Charger, very little of the road car is used in NASCAR; just the engine within a purpose-built tubular chassis and sheet metal body.

Audi R Series

The Le Mans 24-hour race in France is one of the three biggest races in the world and renowned for being one of the toughest challenges in motor sport. For the first decade of this century the race has been dominated by Audi, which won 9 times out of 11 races between 2000 and 2010; a remarkable achievement.

△ Audi R8 2000

Origin Germany

Engine 3,600 cc, V8

Top speed 211 mph (339 km/h)

One of the most successful endurance racing cars ever, the R8 won Le Mans five times over six years, only losing out to Audi-owned Bentley in 2003.

▷ Red Bull-Cosworth STR1 2006

Origin UK

Engine 3,000 cc, V10

Top speed 200 mph (322 km/h)

In 2004 when Red Bull was sponsoring the Sauber team, it bought Jaguar Racing from Ford for a symbolic $1 and is now a front runner in Formula 1.

▽ Toyota TF108 2008

Origin Germany

Engine 2,400 cc, V8

Top speed 200 mph (322 km/h)

Entering Formula 1 in 2002, Toyota had moments of promise but never won a race. It eventually pulled out after the 2009 season.

△ Ferrari F2008 2008

Origin Italy

Engine 2,400 cc, V8

Top speed 200 mph (322 km/h)

Having impressed in the F2007, Kimi Räikkönen, in the heavier F2008, helped Felipe Massa deliver F1 team championship honours for the 2008 season.

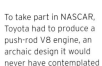

△ Toyota Camry, NASCAR Nextel Cup 2007

Origin Japan

Engine 5,860 cc, V8

Top speed 190 mph (306 km/h)

To take part in NASCAR, Toyota had to produce a push-rod V8 engine, an archaic design it would never have contemplated otherwise.

◁ BMW M3 GT2 2008

Origin Germany

Engine 3,999 cc, V8

Top speed 180 mph (290 km/h)

Introduced for the American Le Mans series in 2009, this car raced at Le Mans in 2010 and was the cover car for the racing game *Need for Speed*.

△ Peugeot 908 HDI FAP 2009

Origin France

Engine 5,500 cc, V12

Top speed 212 mph (341 km/h)

Peugeot entered Le Mans in France with the diesel 908 in 2009 and won the race – breaking Audi's dominance in the process.

◁ Audi R10 TDI 2006

Origin Germany

Engine 5,500 cc, V12

Top speed 211 mph (339 km/h)

Following on from a string of successes with the petrol-engined R8, the R10 became the first diesel-engined car to win Le Mans.

△ Audi R15 TDI 2009

Origin Germany

Engine 5,500 cc, V10

Top speed 205 mph (330 km/h)

Although the R10 was fast, its handling was compromised by a heavy V12 engine. Changing to a V10 design made the engine lighter and the car faster.

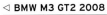

Ferrari 250 GTO driven by Graham Hill at Goodwood, 1960s.

Great marques
The Ferrari story

Enzo Ferrari forged his reputation on the race track before setting up as a car manufacturer in 1940, so it is no surprise that the marque founded by the fiery Italian has the most successful record in Formula 1. As well as being a major name in motor sport, Ferrari has made many of the world's fastest, most desirable road cars..

ENZO FERRARI was born in 1898 near Modena, northern Italy. As a boy, Enzo went to motor races with his father and brother. He quickly fell in love with the sport and decided that when he grew up he would emulate his hero, Felice Nazarro, and become a racing driver. Enzo made his competitive debut in 1919, and the following year he became a works driver for Alfa Romeo. During his racing career Enzo Ferrari recorded many victories and was awarded the honorary titles of *Cavaliere* and *Commendatore* by the Italian state for his achievements.

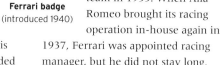

Ferrari badge
(introduced 1940)

In 1929 Enzo founded the Scuderia Ferrari racing team, using the *cavallino rampante* (prancing horse) as its logo. The Scuderia took over the running of Alfa Romeo's racing team in 1933. When Alfa Romeo brought its racing operation in-house again in 1937, Ferrari was appointed racing manager, but he did not stay long.

The terms of Enzo Ferrari's departure prevented him from using his own name in motor racing, so he called the company he founded in 1940 Auto Avio Costruzione. This new company manufactured parts for the aircraft industry, but Enzo Ferrari continued to follow his interest in motor racing, and he was soon building competition cars based on Fiat chassis. In 1943 the company moved to Maranello, just outside Modena, where it is still based today.

The first Ferrari car, the 125S, was announced in 1946 and went on sale the following year. Success soon followed, initially in sports-car racing, with Ferrari winning Italy's Mille Miglia and Targa Florio in 1948, and France's Le Mans 24-hour race in 1949. Ferrari's first victory in Grand Prix racing came in 1951, and Alberto Ascari won the Formula 1 World Championship for Ferrari in 1952 and 1953. During the next six decades of competition, Ferrari won almost every trophy in motor racing. Maranello cars won Le Mans nine times, the US Sebring 12-hour race nine times, the Mille Miglia eight times, and the Targa Florio six times. In Formula 1, Ferrari was an almost constant presence right from the start of the World Championship era in 1950, winning the constructors' title 16 times and taking nine drivers to

Chinese Grand Prix, Shanghai, 2007
Ferrari has had an unparalleled record in Formula 1 in recent years. Here, mechanics push driver Felipe Massa to the starting grid at the 2007 Chinese Grand Prix.

125 SPIDER

1898 Enzo Ferrari is born on 18 February.
1920 Ferrari becomes a driver in the Alfa Romeo works team.
1929 Scuderia Ferrari is founded.
1940 Ferrari starts Auto Avio Costruzione.
1943 Auto Avio Costruzione moves to Maranello, near Modena, northern Italy.
1946 The first Ferrari road car, the 125S, is unveiled.
1951 Argentinian driver José Froilán González wins the British Grand Prix, Ferrari's first Formula 1 race win.

250GT SWB

1956 Enzo Ferrari's son, Alfredo, known as Dino, dies of muscular dystrophy.
1966 A Ferrari-designed V6 engine is used in the Fiat Dino road car, and adapted for Formula 2 competition.
1968 Ferrari's own version of the V6 is used in road cars under the Dino brand.
1969 Fiat buys 50 per cent of Ferrari.
1976 Reigning world champion Niki Lauda crashes his Ferrari in the German Grand Prix; despite serious injuries, he returns to racing just six weeks later.

F40

1977 Niki Lauda wins the Formula 1 World Championship again in a Ferrari.
1982 Ferrari driver Gilles Villeneuve is killed while practising for the Belgian Grand Prix.
1987 Launch of the F40, the last Ferrari road car to be produced during Enzo Ferrari's lifetime; it is the world's fastest production car at this time.
1988 Enzo Ferrari dies at the age of 90 on 14 August; Fiat raises its shareholding in Ferrari to 90 per cent.

ENZO

2002 Ferrari unveils the Enzo, a V12 supercar with a top speed in excess of 226mph (363km/h).
2004 Michael Schumacher and Ferrari crown a spectacular period of success in Formula 1, taking Ferrari's sixth constructor's title and Schumacher's fifth driver's title with Ferrari.
2010 At the Geneva Motor Show, Ferrari displays the 599 HY-KERS, a hybrid fitted with an electric motor powered by lithium ion batteries.

Ferrari stamps
These stamps were issued by the Republic of San Marino in 1998 to celebrate both the 100th anniversary of Enzo Ferrari's birth and Ferrari's 50 years of racing triumphs. They show eight famous Ferrari Grand Prix models.

15 individual world titles. Along the way it won over 200 Formula 1 races, more than any other team in the World Championship's history.

Ferrari's success in motor racing was built on focused effort from the best engineers and drivers, inspired by the determination of the man in whose name they were racing. Failure was not tolerated and lost races were followed by a post-mortem meeting in the company boardroom, which was nicknamed the "museum of mistakes". Enzo Ferrari would hurl broken car parts across the table at startled engineers, and he often set two teams of engineers working independently on rival projects to drive development harder and faster. Relationships between Ferrari and his team members were often frosty. Paying customers were sometimes treated with similar disdain. The successful industrialist Ferruccio Lamborghini

was so incensed at his treatment when he complained about the quality of the Ferrari he had just bought that he started his own car company in 1963, which became one of Ferrari's biggest road-car rivals. Such incidents added to the mystique of Ferrari and the man behind the company.

Meanwhile, the amazing performance and superb looks (styled by Italian design company Pininfarina) of Ferrari's road models, including the V12-engined 275GTB/4 and 365GTB/4 Daytona, and the V6 Dino 206 and 246, were matched by few other cars.

Ferrari was too small to survive indefinitely as a wholly independent company. In the 1960s an approach

from the US giant Ford very nearly led to investment in Ferrari and the formation of two new companies: Ford-Ferrari, which would build road cars, and Ferrari-Ford, which would concentrate on racing. Enzo Ferrari put a stop to the deal at the last minute. The Ford management, feeling slighted by Ferrari's rebuttal, vowed to beat him

at his own game and instituted the GT40 sports-car racing programme. The GT40 trounced Ferrari at Le Mans, winning the race from 1966 to 1969.

Ferrari did later join up with the major Italian manufacturer Fiat, which took a 50 per cent shareholding in 1969. The financial stability this gave Ferrari led to further great exploits on the race track, including success in sports-car racing and two World Championship wins in Formula 1 for Niki Lauda in the mid-1970s. It also allowed Ferrari to develop a series of breathtaking supercars, including the 1970s' 365BB and 512BB, the Testarossa and F40 of the 1980s, the 1990s' F50, and the 2002 Enzo, named after the company founder.

After Enzo Ferrari's death in 1988, Fiat raised its shareholding to 90 per cent, enabling Ferrari to produce more cars than ever and improve quality. In Formula 1, Ferrari had suffered a relatively barren period since Jody Scheckter's world title win in 1979, but its fortunes were boosted when driver Michael Schumacher and engineer Ross Brawn joined the team in 1996. Ferrari and Schumacher together secured an unprecedented five driver's titles and six constructor's championships between 1999 and 2004. Kimi Räikkönen added another driver's title in 2007, and Felipe Massa was nearly victorious in 2008.

Today, Ferrari's range of cars is more extensive than ever, encompassing two- and four-seater front-engined V12s (the 599 and 612 models) and a pair of V8-engined cars (the mid-engined 458 Italia and the front-engined California). For Ferrari, the challenge will be to remain relevant in an age of concern over CO_2 emissions and energy consumption, without compromising a long history of very fast, very beautiful, motor cars.

"**Ferrari** demanded a lot. He was **a racer** - he was just interested in **winning**"

GIAN PAOLO DALLARA, FERRARI ENGINEER 1959-1961

Ferrari 330LMB V12 engine
Ferrrari has based its track success on mighty V12 engines. This 3,967 cc V12 powered Ferrari's 330LMB in the Le Mans 24-hour race of 1963.

Compact Genius

Ever-shrinking microchip technology has allowed more and more functionality to be added to cars, putting paid to the idea that the smallest vehicles must be stripped of all extra features. Engineers know that lighter cars are the most fuel-efficient, but legislators – and the driving public – insist on the latest safety systems, and these naturally add weight. Designers wrestle with these requirements as they create the latest models, ensuring that size is no barrier to safety, comfort, and efficiency.

▷ Honda Fit/Jazz Mkl 2001

Origin Japan

Engine 1,497 cc, four-cylinder

Top speed 106 mph (171 km/h)

As the Civic became larger, Honda attacked the supermini sector anew with the Honda Fit (or Jazz in Europe). It became an instant class benchmark.

◁ Mercedes-Benz A-Class MkII 2004

Origin Germany

Engine 2,034 cc, four-cylinder

Top speed 114 mph (183 km/h)

◁ BMW 1 series 2004

Origin Germany

Engine 1,599 cc, four-cylinder

Top speed 138 mph (222 km/h)

BMW's 1 Series reworked the 3 Series in a tighter package. As well as this five-door model, there was a three-door version, a coupé, and a convertible.

The 1997 Mercedes-Benz A-Class was a small car designed so that its engine diverted below the cabin in the event of a crash. This is the more mature, second-generation model.

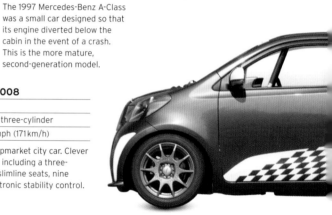

▷ Toyota Prius MkII 2004

Origin Japan

Engine 1,496 cc, four-cylinder

Top speed 104 mph (167 km/h)

With a 76 bhp petrol engine augmented by a 68 bhp electric motor – plus on-the-move battery recharging – the Prius MkII offered minimal fuel consumption.

▷ Toyota iQ 2008

Origin Japan

Engine 1,329 cc, three-cylinder

Top speed 106 mph (171 km/h)

This is Toyota's upmarket city car. Clever features abound, including a three-cylinder engine, slimline seats, nine airbags, and electronic stability control.

▽ MCC Smart Crossblade 2002

Origin France

Engine 599 cc, three-cylinder

Top speed 84 mph (135 km/h)

The Smart City-Cabrio was a tiny car, but the Crossblade (of which 2,000 were built) was pared down even further. It had no doors, no windscreen, and no roof.

◁ MCC Smart Roadster 2003

Origin France

Engine 698 cc, three-cylinder

Top speed 109 mph (175 km/h)

This tiny two-seater extended the Smart city car philosophy to create a latterday Frogeye Sprite. It was fun to drive, and economical.

▷ Renault Megane MkII 2002

Origin France
Engine 1,998 cc, four-cylinder
Top speed 149 mph (240 km/h)

Designers at Renault caused a stir with the upright rear window of this second-generation Megane. As before, the five-door family car was only one of many Megane incarnations.

△ Citroën DS3 2009

Origin France
Engine 1,598 cc, four-cylinder
Top speed 133 mph (214 km/h)

There is nothing retro about the neat DS3 – nothing links it to the famous DS of old – but the short length and massive cabin make it an intriguing Mini alternative.

▷ Opel/Vauxhall Astra 2004

Origin Germany/UK
Engine 1,998 cc, four-cylinder
Top speed 152 mph (245 km/h)

The Astra, from General Motors Europe, took a quantum leap forwards in its design in 2004. This three-door car, called the GTC, introduced a panoramic windscreen stretching into the roof panel.

▽ Peugeot RCZ THP 200 2010

Origin France/Austria
Engine 1,997cc, four-cylinder
Top speed 146 mph (235 km/h)

This coupé, which is similar in size to Audi's TT, began life as a motor show concept car, but huge public demand pushed it into showrooms. It has two small seats in the back.

▷ Ford Streetka 2003

Origin Spain/Italy
Engine 1,597 cc, four-cylinder
Top speed 108 mph (174 km/h)

Ford based this tiny two-seat roadster on its Ka hatchback. Designed and built in Italy, it was given a traditional fabric hood, and launched by diminutive pop star Kylie Minogue.

△ Volvo C70 MkII 2006

Origin Sweden
Engine 2,521 cc, five-cylinder
Top speed 130 mph (209 km/h)

This four-seater is not small, but the all-steel, three-part roof mechanism that converts it from snug saloon to open convertible is a masterpiece of space-efficiency.

◁ Ford Focus Mk2 RS 2009

Origin Germany
Engine 2,522 cc, five-cylinder
Top speed 163 mph (262 km/h)

With over 300 bhp of power going through the front wheels of what is essentially a family hatchback, the Mk2 has bespoke limited-slip differential and front suspension.

◁ Alfa Romeo MiTo 2008

Origin Italy
Engine 1,593 cc, four-cylinder
Top speed 136 mph (219 km/h)

Sharing its underpinnings with the Fiat Grande Punto, this was the first ever really small Alfa. MiTo stands for Milan, where it was designed, and Turin, where it is built.

▽ Cadillac CTS-V coupé 2010

Origin USA
Engine 6,162 cc, V8
Top speed 191 mph (307 km/h)

The stocky CTS-V saloon holds the production car record for lapping Germany's Nürburgring, at 7min 59.3sec. This coupé shares its 556 bhp power unit.

△ Scion xB 2007

Origin Japan
Engine 2,362 cc, four-cylinder
Top speed 109 mph (175 km/h)

To target younger US buyers, Toyota introduced its Scion sub-brand in 2004. The chunky xB, now in its second incarnation, is the mainstay.

▷ Mini Clubman 2008

Origin UK
Engine 1,598 cc, four-cylinder
Top speed 125 mph (201 km/h)

BMW's reinvention of the Mini saw the production of this estate car. It has twin, van-style doors at the rear, and a small "clubdoor" on the driver's side.

High-Performance Sports Cars

In the last couple of decades, a whole new tier of cars has emerged that bridges the gap between sports cars and supercars. They range from hot versions of affordable coupés and roadsters to entry-level models from prestige manufacturers. Stylish and exciting, their existence proves that demand for performance has never been stronger – and the choice has never been wider.

△ **Ferrari F430 2004**

Origin Italy

Engine 4,308 cc, V8

Top speed 196 mph (315 km/h)

The first Ferrari road car to use an electronically-controlled differential, derived directly from the company's F1 traction, the F430 was aerodynamically designed underneath as well as on top.

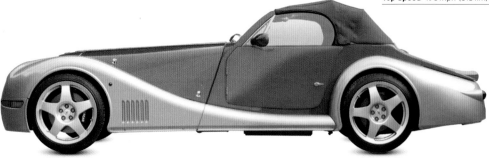

△ **Morgan Aero 8 2001**

Origin UK

Engine 4,398 cc, V8

Top speed 150 mph (241 km/h)

The overall profile may have been familiar, but the Aero 8 was a radical car for Morgan, the first with an aluminium chassis and a BMW V8 engine.

△ **Ferrari California 2008**

Origin Italy

Engine 4,297 cc, V8

Top speed 193 mph (311 km/h)

This is the first time Ferrari has put a V8 engine in the front of one of its road cars; the shape is the result of 1,000 hours in the wind tunnel.

◁ **Aston Martin Vanquish 2001**

Origin UK

Engine 5,935 cc, V12

Top speed 196 mph (315 km/h)

This car re-created the link with James Bond when Pierce Brosnan was issued with one in the film *Die Another Day*.

▷ **Aston Martin DB9 2003**

Origin UK

Engine 5,935 cc, V12

Top speed 190 mph (306 km/h)

Sporting the company's new V12 engine, the DB9 was the car that ushered in a new era of Aston Martin under Ford ownership.

△ **Ferrari 458 Italia 2009**

Origin Italy

Engine 4,499 cc, V8

Top speed 202 mph (325 km/h)

This car received input from former world champion Michael Schumacher, and it features winglets that drop at speed to reduce drag.

◁ **Aston Martin V8 Vantage convertible 2005**

Origin UK

Engine 4,735 cc, V8

Top speed 180 mph (290 km/h)

With a V8 from Ford-owned Jaguar, it may be a smaller car than the DB9, but there is plenty of performance and nimble handling.

△ **Mercedes-Benz SL 2008**

Origin Germany

Engine 5,513 cc, V12

Top speed 155 mph (249 km/h)

Back in 1954 the 300SL Gullwing was a genuine supercar. The latest version retains that tradition with more than 500 bhp on tap.

▷ **Audi R8 2006**

Origin Germany

Engine 5,204 cc, V10

Top speed 196 mph (315 km/h)

Inspired by the company's multiple Le Mans-winning car of the same name, this is a fully fledged, Porsche-rivalling supercar with performance to match.

△ Spyker C8 Aileron 2000

Origin Holland

Engine 4,163 cc, V8

Top speed 186 mph (299 km/h)

The Aileron's design draws heavily from the company's aviation past, and even the spokes of the steering wheel are ex-propeller blades.

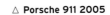

△ Porsche 911 2005

Origin Germany

Engine 3,800 cc, flat-six

Top speed 180 mph (290 km/h)

Unofficially referred to as the 997, this is the spiritual descendant of the original 911 and still has its engine hanging out the back.

△ Chevrolet Corvette C6 2005

Origin USA

Engine 5,967 cc, V8

Top speed 198 mph (319 km/h)

Originally known as a car that had looks and power but little else, this Corvette can also boast of handling to match.

◁ Nissan 350Z 2008

Origin Japan

Engine 3,498 cc, V6

Top speed 156 mph (251 km/h)

Following an online contest in the computer game *Gran Turismo*, the quickest drivers competed for the prize of a real race drive with the Nissan team.

△ Artega GT 2009

Origin Germany

Engine 3,597 cc, V6

Top speed 170 mph (274 km/h)

Styled by Henrik Fisker, also responsible for the Aston Martin Vantage, the Artega is focused on low weight. At just 1,100 kg (2,205 lb), it is light for a supercar.

◁ Maserati 4200 2002

Origin Italy

Engine 4,244 cc, V8

Top speed 177 mph (285 km/h)

Being part of the Fiat stable alongside Ferrari, Maserati concentrates on grand tourers rather than outright sports cars.

△ Alfa Romeo 8C Competizione 2007

Origin Italy

Engine 4,691 cc, V8

Top speed 181 mph (292 km/h)

Few believed that the design study exhibited at the 2003 Frankfurt Motor Show would ever make it into production, but Alfa built 500 coupés.

▷ Maserati Granturismo S 2007

Origin Italy

Engine 4,691 cc, V8

Top speed 183 mph (295 km/h)

Although based on the floorpan of the Quattroporte saloon, the Granturismo S is a very fast GT with the bonus of two extra rear seats.

△ Jaguar XKR 75 2010

Origin UK

Engine 5,000 cc, V8

Top speed 174 mph (280 km/h)

To celebrate the company's 75th anniversary, Jaguar built 75 of these special edition XKRs with improved handling and engines updated to 530 bhp.

Morgan Aero 8

The first all-new offering from Morgan since 1936, the Aero 8 combined modern mechanicals and advanced construction with traditional looks. Its structure was based on a bonded and riveted aluminium chassis tub, attached to a wood frame for the body. In 2008-09 a hundred of a closed coupé version, the AeroMax, were built, and in 2010 the Aero SuperSports, with lift-off roof sections, replaced the original drophead Aero 8.

WHEN MORGAN announced the Aero 8 in 2000, the shock was considerable. The cars of the small family-run British company had been largely unchanged since the 1930s. They had a separate chassis, a body with a wooden frame, and board-hard suspension, independent only at the front. The Aero 8, developed from a Morgan racing car, changed all that. The aluminium panels on the body were heat-formed rather than painstakingly shaped by hand. But the lightweight aluminium tub was only the start; underneath was supple, racing-type, all-independent suspension with inboard springs and dampers, and the steering was power-assisted. The car also featured electric wind-up windows in place of a regular Morgan's lift-off sliding sidescreens. At launch, the price was twice that of the cheapest traditional models still in production.

From three wheels to four
H.F.S. Morgan unveiled his first car in 1910 – a three-wheeler with a single rear wheel. "Trikes" were made until 1952, but in 1936 Morgan introduced a four-wheel sports car, the 4/4. The firm is currently run by the grandson of "HFS".

FRONT VIEW

REAR VIEW

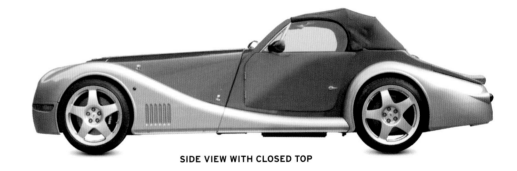

SIDE VIEW WITH CLOSED TOP

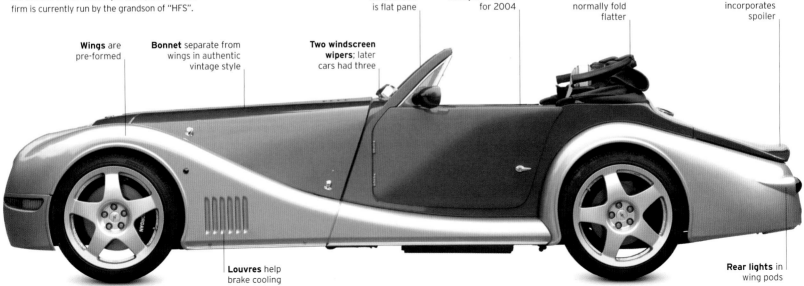

Windscreen is flat pane

Cockpit widened for 2004

Hood would normally fold flatter

Bootlid incorporates spoiler

Wings are pre-formed

Bonnet separate from wings in authentic vintage style

Two windscreen wipers; later cars had three

Louvres help brake cooling

Rear lights in wing pods

The cross-eyed look

The Aero 8 front is dominated by its headlights. The original model, as seen here, used Volkswagen "New Beetle" units. However, their inward-pointing position gave the car a cross-eyed look that was widely criticized. From 2006 new headlights from a BMW Mini were used. Another prominent feature, the traditional Morgan radiator grille, is a dummy. Air is fed to the engine through the splitter below the number plate.

SPECIFICATIONS			
Model	Morgan Aero 8, 2001-09	Power output	286-367 bhp at 6,300 rpm (4.8 litre)
Assembly	Malvern, UK	Transmission	Six-speed manual; optional automatic
Production	Approx. 1,000	Suspension	Independent by inboard coil
Construction	Aluminium hull; ash body frame	Brakes	Four-wheel discs
Engine	4,398 cc/4,799 cc, dohc V8	Maximum speed	150-170 mph (241-274 km/h)

BRANDS HATCH MORGANS · www.morgan-cars.com

THE EXTERIOR

The Aero 8 was styled by company managing director Charles Morgan. An updating of traditional Morgan lines, the body features a "splitter" in the front apron – a shaped spoiler that aids stability at speed. The apron also incorporates the air intake for the radiator. At the rear, the opening boot – a first for Morgan – has a lip forming an aerofoil. The aerodynamics are a considerable improvement on those of earlier Morgans.

1. Traditional Morgan badge 2. Aero name first used on Morgan three-wheeler 3. Front indicators built into lower wing 4. Inward pointing headlights 5. Towing eye (early cars only) 6. Main grille is dummy 7. Louvres on bonnet top 8. Internally-adjustable mirror 9. 18 in alloy wheels have run-flat tyres 10. Round rear lights recall those of earlier models 11. Hood has heated glass window 12. Filler cap same as on traditional Morgans 13. Rear light pod has an elegant curve 14. Boot spoiler helps Aero achieve a drag coefficient of 0.39

THE INTERIOR

The well-equipped interior marks a departure from traditional Morgan style. It has an engine-turned aluminium dashboard in place of the wood, leather, or simulated leather that was previously used. A modern echo of past practice is the beautifully crafted wooden dashboard top rail. On all but the last cars the handbrake is fly-off: pull back and press the top to lock, pull back again and it disengages.

15. Steering column and its controls come from the BMW 7-series 16. Bespoke switches add quality feel 17. Chrome gear knob is a non-standard feature 18. Pouch pocket 19. Chrome interior light on the left side of the front seats 20. Seats have good side support

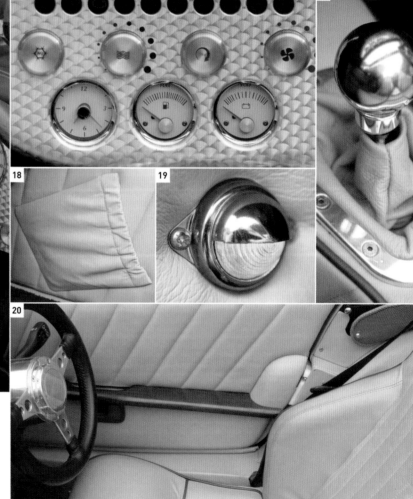

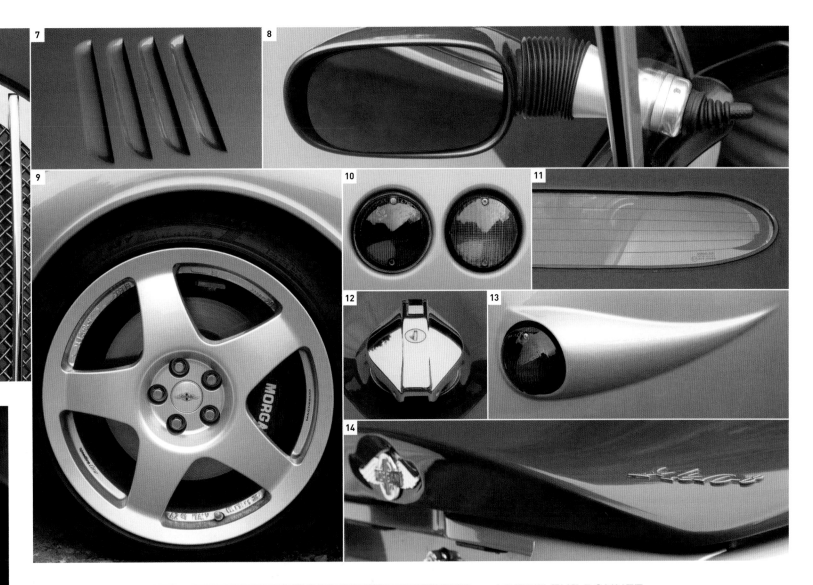

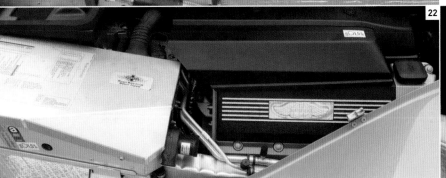

UNDER THE BONNET

The BMW V8 engine is a state-of-the-art, all-aluminium unit with two camshafts per bank of cylinders, and four valves per cylinder. The original 4,398 cc engine develops a power output of 286 bhp, with a maximum torque of 324 lb ft at 3,600 rpm. It gives the Morgan a top speed of over 150 mph (241 km/h), with a 0–60 mph time of under 5 seconds. Power was upgraded to 330 bhp for 2004 and the engine enlarged to 4,799 cc in 2007.

21. Battery located under the bonnet **22.** The powerful V8 engine is a tight fit within the Aero 8's aluminium structure **23.** Wiper motor is exposed to view

Lotus Racing T127, Formula 1, 2010
Lotus Racing's Jarno Trulli receives lightning
service from his pit crew during the 2010 World
Championship. Servicing can take as little as
seven seconds, proving that racing is still about
human skill as well as technology.

Sports Cars

In the 1980s many thought the sports car could become extinct, but they are now back with a vengeance. Every major car manufacturer today has its own interpretation of the sports car, and legions of small specialists build nothing else. Ranging from cutting-edge concepts to shameless attempts at evoking the past, the golden rule is that they should always be fun.

△ **Ariel Atom 1996**

Origin UK

Engine 1,998 cc, straight-four

Top speed 140 mph (225 km/h)

This is as stripped down as a car gets: a steel frame hung with the bare essentials, and bodywork positively prohibited. The Atom is still in production.

▷ **Vauxhall VX220 2000**

Origin UK

Engine 1,998 cc, straight-four

Top speed 150 mph (241 km/h)

Also branded as an Opel and a Daewoo, the VX220 was developed by Lotus Cars and based on the Elise chassis, but with a GM engine.

△ **Lotus Elise 340R 2000**

Origin UK

Engine 1,795 cc, straight-four

Top speed 130 mph (209 km/h)

The car was designed in collaboration with *Autocar* magazine and developed from the Elise. Just 340 examples of this were produced, all finished in black and silver.

△ **Lotus Elise 2000**

Origin UK

Engine 1,792 cc, straight-four

Top speed 145 mph (233 km/h)

Praised for its extreme light weight and wonderful handling, the Elise exceeded all expectations. In 2000 Lotus introduced a restyled version of its Elise to meet European crash regulations.

▷ **Lotus Evora 2009**

Origin UK

Engine 3,456 cc, V6

Top speed 162 mph (261 km/h)

With legendary Lotus handling and 2+2 accommodation, Lotus hoped this car would find fans among performance-loving drivers with young families.

◁ **Ginetta/Farbio F400 2002**

Origin UK

Engine 2,967 cc, V6

Top speed 185 mph (298 km/h)

From Farboud to Farbio to Ginetta, this car had a difficult birth but has always been impressive. With its carbon-fibre chassis, it weighs just 1,046 kg (2,205 lb).

△ **Ginetta G50 EV 2009**

Origin UK

Engine Electric motor

Top speed 120 mph (193 km/h)

Shattering the illusion that electric power is for milk floats, the G50 EV is a low-carbon vehicle that also delivers a thrilling drive.

▽ **MG TF 2002**

Origin UK

Engine 1,795 cc, straight-four

Top speed 127 mph (204 km/h)

Re-engineered to improve its stiffness and crash protection, and then relaunched in 2002, the MG F was renamed the TF in tribute to the 1950s MG.

△ **BMW Z4 2002**

Origin Germany

Engine 2,996 cc, straight-six

Top speed 155 mph (249 km/h)

With a straight-six engine up front and rear-wheel drive, this is a rare chance to experience the thrill of a classic 1950s-style sports car.

△ **Mercedes-Benz SLK 2004**

Origin Germany

Engine 5,439 cc, V8

Top speed 155 mph (249 km/h)

The SLK was revised in 2004 to update its styling and improve its performance. This Mark II R171 version was named one of the "Ten Best" by a US car magazine.

▷ **Mazda MX-5 2005**

Origin Japan

Engine 1,999 cc, straight-four

Top speed 131 mph (211 km/h)

This Mark III MX-5 is perhaps the most perfect mass-production sports car ever conceived; even beyond its 20th birthday it still sells well.

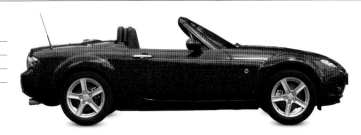

▷ **Pontiac Solstice 2005**

Origin USA

Engine 2,376 cc, straight-four

Top speed 120 mph (193 km/h)

This European-style roadster from General Motors was a hit when launched but production ended just four years later when the Wilmington factory closed.

△ **Porsche Cayman 2006**

Origin Germany

Engine 3,436 cc, flat-six

Top speed 171 mph (275 km/h)

More than just a Boxster with a roof, the Cayman captures the spirit of the original 911 and arguably offers all the performance you could need.

△ **Audi TT 2006**

Origin Germany

Engine 2,480 cc, straight-five

Top speed 155 mph (249 km/h)

In its original form, the TT captured attention with its striking retro look and the latest version remains faithful to that classic coupé style.

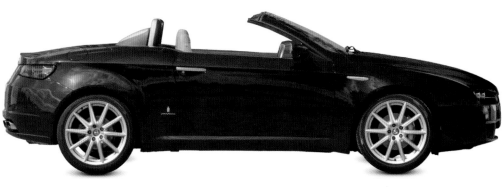

△ **Alfa Romeo Spider 2006**

Origin Italy

Engine 3,195 cc, V6

Top speed 144 mph (232 km/h)

With a direct lineage going back to the 1950s, the Spider is an icon, even though the latest version has given in to front-wheel drive.

◁ **Caterham Superlight 300 2007**

Origin UK

Engine 1,999 cc, straight-four

Top speed 140 mph (225 km/h)

Descended from the 1950s Lotus Seven that inspired a legion of imitators, the Caterham is the rightful heir to the original. It had the fastest 0–60 mph acceleration when launched.

▽ **Tramontana 2007**

Origin Spain

Engine 5,513 cc, V12, twin-turbo

Top speed 202 mph (325 km/h)

A monster in all respects, the passenger seat is an optional extra and is mounted directly behind the driver. Just 12 cars are built each year.

△ **KTM X-Bow 2008**

Origin Austria

Engine 1,984 cc, straight-four

Top speed 136 mph (219 km/h)

The first car to be produced by this motorcycle manufacturer offers little more comfort than a two-wheeler, but it provides just as much of a thrill.

Off-Road Luxury and Power

The 1990s trend for using big 4x4s as road cars developed into large-scale production of big, fast, luxuriously equipped vehicles with four-wheel drive. Some of these "crossover" cars were still good off-road, though many were not. Criticism of "gas-guzzling" sport-utility vehicles (SUVs) eventually led manufacturers to produce hybrid powertrains.

△ **Volvo XC90 2002**

Origin Sweden

Engine 2,922 cc, straight-six

Top speed 130 mph (209 km/h)

Volvo's best-selling car in 2005 with 85,994 sold worldwide in that year alone, is a mid-size SUV with turbo engines (or a 4.4 Ford V8), and either front or four-wheel drive.

△ **Audi Q7 2005**

Origin Germany/Slovakia

Engine 4,163 cc, V8

Top speed 154 mph (248 km/h)

The Q7 combines good performance with spacious comfort. It has four-wheel drive, not for driving across ploughed fields but for superb road grip.

△ **Toyota Sequoia 2007**

Origin Japan/USA

Engine 5,670 cc, V8

Top speed 120 mph (193 km/h)

Toyota's full-size SUV for the US market is based on the Tundra pick-up but with independent rear suspension, two- or four-wheel drive, and 4.6–5.7 V8 engines.

▷ **Mercedes-Benz GLK 2008**

Origin Germany

Engine 3,498 cc, V6

Top speed 143 mph (230 km/h)

A compact and luxurious road car that retains useful off-road ability, the GLK is more upright than its rivals but moves well, aided by a seven-speed automatic gearbox.

◁ **Lexus RX 400h 2005**

Origin Japan/USA

Engine 3,311 cc, V6, two electric motors

Top speed 124 mph (200 km/h)

Since its introduction in 1997, the RX has been the best-selling luxury crossover car in the US. The 400h was the world's first luxury hybrid – successful despite its still-heavy fuel economy.

▷ **Range Rover 2002**

Origin UK

Engine 4,398 cc, V8

Top speed 130 mph (209 km/h)

Fitted with BMW V8 engines (more recently Jaguar/Ford units) the Range Rover has come a long way from its luxury off-roader origins, but it still does both jobs well.

◁ **Range Rover Sport 2005**

Origin UK

Engine 4,197 cc, V8

Top speed 140 mph (225 km/h)

Using a supercharged Jaguar engine on the Discovery 3 platform with added adjustable air suspension, the Sport has good off-road and excellent on-road performance.

▷ **Chrysler Pacifica 2004**

Origin USA

Engine 3,518 cc, V6

Top speed 131 mph (211 km/h)

A two/four-wheel-drive crossover marketed as a "sports tourer", the Pacifica was engineered with Daimler-Benz. However, its sales were poor and it was discontinued in 2008.

◁ **Lincoln Mk LT 2005**

Origin USA

Engine 5,408 cc, V8

Top speed 110 mph (177 km/h)

Lincoln's luxury pick-up with optional four-wheel drive is based on the Ford F-150. It had to be heavily discounted to achieve good sales figures, and production ended in 2008.

◁ Nissan Armada 2004
Origin Japan/USA
Engine 5,552 cc, V8
Top speed 120 mph (193 km/h)

Nissan's full-size SUV shared its platform with the Titan pick-up and was built only in Canton, Mississippi, for the US market. Rear- or four-wheel drive was produced.

▷ Cadillac Escalade EXT 2002
Origin USA/Mexico
Engine 5,327 cc, V8
Top speed 108 mph (174 km/h)

Cadillac's first Sport Utility Vehicle appeared in 1998, and by 2002 offered eight seats, except for the five-seat EXT pick-up. A 345 bhp, 6-litre V8 engine was optional.

▽ BMW X6 2008
Origin Germany/USA
Engine 4,395 cc, V8
Top speed 155 mph (249 km/h)

Marketed as a "sports activity coupé", the X6 combined high ground clearance, all-wheel drive, and large wheels, with coupé styling and a twin-turbocharged six or V8 engine.

△ Jeep Grand Cherokee 2004
Origin USA
Engine 6,059 cc, V8
Top speed 152 mph (245 km/h)

The all-new WK-series Grand Cherokee used Jeep's sophisticated Quadra-drive II system for excellent off-road performance. It came with 3.1-litre V6 to 6.1-litre V8 engines.

△ Jeep Commander 2006
Origin USA
Engine 3,701 cc, V6
Top speed 113 mph (182 km/h)

The Commander was a mid-size SUV based on the Grand Cherokee but was more like earlier Jeeps, with its angular, rugged lines. There was also a high performance V8 version.

◁ Porsche Cayenne Hybrid 2010
Origin Germany
Engine 2,995 cc, V6 + electric motor
Top speed 145 mph (233 km/h)

Sports-car builder Porsche scored remarkable success with its 4x4 Cayenne soft-roader. A 325 bhp petrol engine was joined by a token 47 bhp electric motor on the Hybrid.

△ Infiniti FX50 2008
Origin Japan
Engine 5026 cc, V8
Top speed 155 mph (249 km/h)

Nissan's premium brand Infiniti, which is unknown in Japan, appeared in the US in 1989, then in Europe in 2008. This top performance SUV is very fast and well equipped.

▷ Hummer H3 2005
Origin USA
Engine 3653 cc, straight-five
Top speed 113 mph (182 km/h)

Derived from the US army vehicle called a Hummer, this large 4x4 is great off-road but compared with purpose-built road 4x4s, it is rather crude and cramped.

Honda Insight
petrol/electric hybrid

Opinion is divided about whether hybrid cars – which combine an internal combustion engine with electric traction motors – are really the best way to improve fuel economy and reduce exhaust emissions. But while the jury has been deliberating, two major Japanese car makers, Honda and Toyota, have forged ahead and put hybrid cars on the market.

HYBRID VIGOUR

Hybrids are divided into two categories, series and parallel. In a series hybrid the heat engine – usually a small piston engine, but possibly a gas turbine – acts purely as a generator of electric power for the battery pack and electric motors; it is not connected to the driven wheels. In a parallel hybrid the heat engine and electric motors can both provide tractive force. In Toyota's Prius these two modes are cleverly combined; in Honda's simpler Insight (shown here) the small petrol engine and integral electric motor operate in parallel to enhance performance and fuel economy.

ENGINE SPECIFICATIONS	
Dates produced	2010 to present
Cylinders	Straight-four (originally straight-three)
Configuration	Front-mounted, transverse
Engine capacities	1,339 cc (81.7 cu in)
Power output	98 bhp @ 5,800 rpm with electric motor
Type	Conventional four-stroke, water-cooled petrol engine with reciprocating pistons; 13 hp electric motor and drive-by-wire throttle
Head	sohc with i-VTEC variable valve timing and lift; two valves per cylinder operated by rockers
Fuel System	Multipoint port fuel injection
Bore and Stroke	73 mm x 80 mm (2.87 in x 3.15 in)
Power	73.2 bhp/litre
Compression Ratio	10.8:1

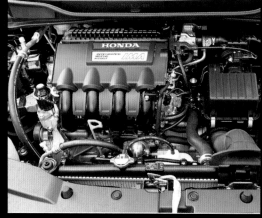

▷ **See pp.346-347** How an engine works

Engine mounting

Exhaust gas recirculation valve
A controlled amount of exhaust is returned to the cylinders via this valve to aid emissions control.

Cylinder block
Within the cast-aluminium-alloy cylinder block, ion plating of the piston rings and plateau-honing of the cylinder bores reduce friction, improving fuel economy.

Water temperature sensor

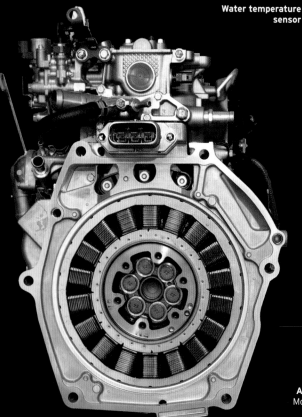

Crankshaft pulley

Water pump

Air conditioning compressor
Mounted here, the compressor can be driven either by the engine or, when the engine is deactivated, by a dedicated electric motor.

Electric motor
Copper coils form part of the Honda Insight's electric motor, which performs three functions: it starts the engine, boosts torque, and provides regenerative braking to recharge the battery pack.

Fuel injector

Dipstick

Fuel rail

Water galleries
These cavities carry coolant around the engine.

Solenoid valves for i-VTEC variable valve actuation system
Controlled by these solenoid valves, the actuation system uses five rocker arms per cylinder to provide three modes of operation. The modes are determined by driving conditions: low-load, high-load, and one mode that shuts down and closes off the cylinders during deceleration.

Inlet port

Flexible water hose

Water hose connector

Electric power connector
This delivers current to the brushless DC electric motor when required and returns current to the battery pack under regenerative braking.

Water thermostat housing

Electric motor housing
The gearbox (not shown) attaches here.

Oil level sensor
This measures both the level and condition of the engine oil, and alerts the car owner when a service is necessary.

Economy, economy, economy
Although the latest Insight has the more powerful four-cylinder engine shown here, not the smaller three-cylinder of its predecessor, it still offers impressive fuel economy of 64.2 mpg (3.66 litres per 100 km) in the combined European test cycle, and carbon dioxide emissions of only 101 g/km

Water pipe

Oil filter

Oil pressure sensor

Cars of the Future

Exotic materials and hybrid powertrains are the hallmarks of today's pioneering car designs. The challenge is to produce a car that is environmentally friendly, but can travel further than a battery-only vehicle, which is usually limited to a range of under 300 miles (480 km). The current solution is a car with both lithium-ion batteries and an on-board engine. The engine engages at a certain speed and charges the batteries as it powers the car.

▷ Ford Start 2010

Origin USA

Engine 1,000 cc, straight-three

Top speed 110 mph (177 km/h)

Unveiled at the 2010 Beijing Auto Show, the turbocharged Start concept car has an aluminium/steel structure and an LCD dashboard. It could replace Ford's Ka in emerging markets from 2014.

△ Tesla Roadster 2007

Origin USA/UK

Engine Electric motor

Top speed 125 mph (201 km/h)

A huge step forward in electric vehicle manufacture, the Roadster entered production in 2008. It has batteries with a 300-mile (480-km) range and a Lotus Elise shell.

▷ Land Rover LRX 2008

Origin UK

Engine 2,179 cc, straight-four

Top speed unknown

Land Rover unveiled its LRX concept car in 2008, then in 2010 announced it would be built in 2011 as the Range Rover Evoque; in that form it would offer two- or four-wheel drive and a 58 mpg (4.9 litres per 100 km) capability.

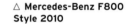

△ Mercedes-Benz F800 Style 2010

Origin Germany

Engine 3,498 cc, V6/electric motor

Top speed 155 mph (249 km/h)

Mercedes showcased its new technology in the front-wheel-drive F800. It has sliding rear doors, state-of-the-art electronics, and hybrid or fuel cell power options.

◁ Rinspeed UC? 2010

Origin Switzerland

Engine Electric motor

Top speed 75 mph (120 km/h)

This two-seat commuter car has a range of 65 miles (105 km). It can be loaded onto trains with special wagons – and the latter can be booked on the car's computer.

△ Audi e-tron 2009

Origin Germany

Engine Four electric motors

Top speed 124 mph (200 km/h)

Unveiled at the 2009 Frankfurt Show, this R8-based electric supercar has four-wheel drive, using a motor for each wheel. Limited production is promised.

▷ **Frazer Nash Namir 2009**

Origin UK/Italy

Engine 814 cc, rotary/four electric motors

Top speed 187 mph (301 km/h)

The reborn Frazer Nash company worked with Italdesign to produce this striking concept car to showcase its hybrid rotary and electric powertrains.

△ **Honda P-NUT 2009**

Origin Japan/USA

Engine Petrol/hybrid/electric options

Top speed Undetermined

Designed in Honda's US Advanced Design Studio, the Personal-Neo Urban Transport concept car has a central driving seat with two rear seats and a rear power unit.

△ **Stile Bertone Mantide 2009**

Origin Italy

Engine 6,162 cc, V8

Top speed 217 mph (349 km/h)

Styled by Jason Castriota, the Mantide is intended to be the ultimate luxury supercar. It is built to order for $2 million, using Chevrolet Corvette ZR1 running gear.

△ **Hyundai i-flow 2010**

Origin South Korea

Engine 1,700 cc, turbodiesel /electric motor

Top speed 120 mph (193 km/h)

The i-flow is a fully working concept car with complex rear-hinged doors, hybrid drivetrain, and futuristic interior. Its air conditioning is powered by solar panels.

△ **Renault Twizy ZE 2009**

Origin France

Engine Electric motor

Top speed 47 mph (76 km/h)

Planned for production in 2011, the Twizy Zero Emission has two seats in tandem. It is just over 1 m (3 ft) wide, 2.3 m (7.5 ft) long, and is designed to make electric travel look fun.

△ **Opel/Vauxhall Ampera 2010**

Origin USA

Engine Hybrid

Top speed 100 mph (161 km/h)

General Motors' electric car will be sold as the Chevrolet Volt, or the Opel/ Vauxhall Ampera. It has a 1.4-litre petrol engine, which drives a generator to boost electric charge.

◁ **Dodge Demon 2007**

Origin USA

Engine 2,400 cc, straight-four

Top speed 125 mph (201 km/h)

This affordable, rear-wheel-drive sports car – with aggressive mini-Viper looks – was shown by Dodge in 2007. Unfortunately, Chrysler's financial crisis made production impossible.

△ **Opel Flextreme GT/E 2010**

Origin Germany/USA

Engine Hybrid

Top speed 124 mph (200 km/h)

Derived from General Motors' Volt hybrid, the Flextreme is powered by an electric motor. Its battery lasts for 37 miles (60 km) before a 1.4-litre diesel engine starts to charge it.

◁ **Alfa Romeo/Bertone Pandion 2010**

Origin Italy

Engine 4,691 cc, V8

Top speed 199 mph (320 km/h)

Mike Robinson at Stile Bertone was principally responsible for the Pandion, a tribute to Alfa Romeo's centenary. Its doors pivot up from the rear wheelarch.

△ **Peugeot bb1 2009**

Origin France

Engine Two electric motors

Top speed 80 mph (129 km/h)

Powered by lithium-ion batteries, the bb1 is a city car with bike-style handlebars, double-bubble roof, and a 75-mile (120-km) range.

How an engine works

The powerhouse under the bonnet of nearly every modern car is an internal combustion engine, just as it was in the first car made by Karl Benz in Germany more than a century ago. Today's engines are more compact, powerful, fuel-efficient, and clean than their forerunners, yet they operate on the same principle: they burn fuel (usually a mixture of petrol and air or diesel and air) inside a number of closed cylinders, and harness the energy released by this combustion to drive the wheels of the vehicle. Petrol and air form a highly flammable mixture that burns even more readily when compressed. Inside the cylinders, the mixture of vaporized petrol and air is squeezed by drum-shaped pistons and then ignited. The burning fuel-air mixture expands, forcing down the pistons so that they push on pivoting connecting rods that turn the crankshaft. The rotation of the crankshaft is transmitted via the gears to the car's wheels.

EXPOSED ENGINE

The engine block and sump of this modern four-cylinder engine are cutaway to reveal the principal components within. For clarity, all the moving parts are chrome-plated and the engine block is enamelled.

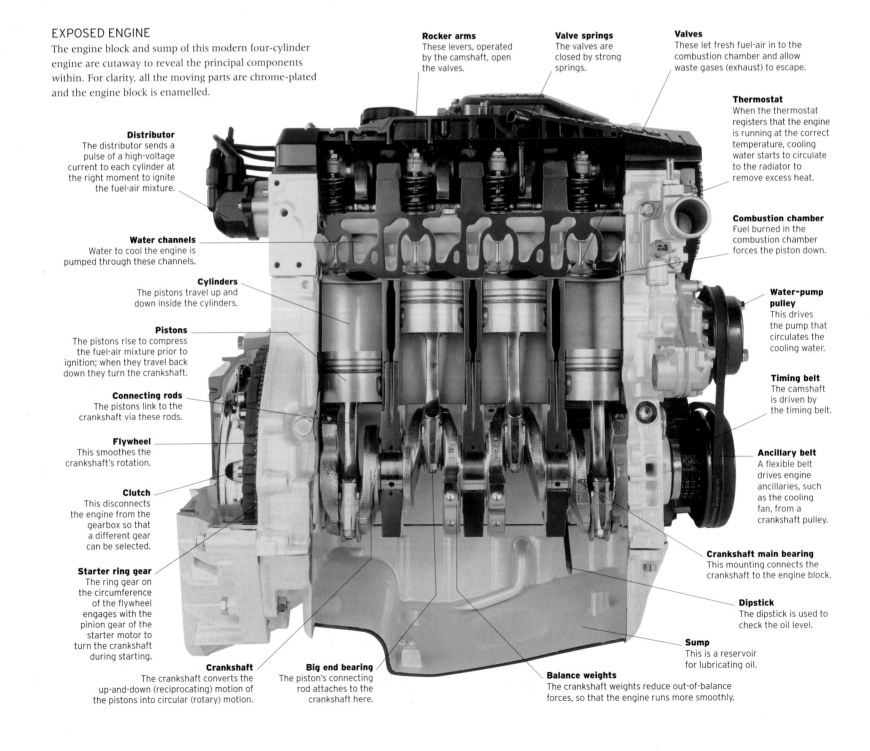

Rocker arms
These levers, operated by the camshaft, open the valves.

Valve springs
The valves are closed by strong springs.

Valves
These let fresh fuel-air in to the combustion chamber and allow waste gases (exhaust) to escape.

Distributor
The distributor sends a pulse of a high-voltage current to each cylinder at the right moment to ignite the fuel-air mixture.

Thermostat
When the thermostat registers that the engine is running at the correct temperature, cooling water starts to circulate to the radiator to remove excess heat.

Water channels
Water to cool the engine is pumped through these channels.

Combustion chamber
Fuel burned in the combustion chamber forces the piston down.

Cylinders
The pistons travel up and down inside the cylinders.

Water-pump pulley
This drives the pump that circulates the cooling water.

Pistons
The pistons rise to compress the fuel-air mixture prior to ignition; when they travel back down they turn the crankshaft.

Timing belt
The camshaft is driven by the timing belt.

Connecting rods
The pistons link to the crankshaft via these rods.

Flywheel
This smoothes the crankshaft's rotation.

Ancillary belt
A flexible belt drives engine ancillaries, such as the cooling fan, from a crankshaft pulley.

Clutch
This disconnects the engine from the gearbox so that a different gear can be selected.

Crankshaft main bearing
This mounting connects the crankshaft to the engine block.

Starter ring gear
The ring gear on the circumference of the flywheel engages with the pinion gear of the starter motor to turn the crankshaft during starting.

Dipstick
The dipstick is used to check the oil level.

Sump
This is a reservoir for lubricating oil.

Crankshaft
The crankshaft converts the up-and-down (reciprocating) motion of the pistons into circular (rotary) motion.

Big end bearing
The piston's connecting rod attaches to the crankshaft here.

Balance weights
The crankshaft weights reduce out-of-balance forces, so that the engine runs more smoothly.

ENGINE LAYOUTS

The majority of modern car engines have four or more cylinders set out in a row. This arrangement – called a straight, or in-line, layout – has the benefit of being relatively easy and inexpensive to manufacture. Yet this is by no means the only possible disposition of the cylinders, or necessarily the best when taking into account factors such as power output, smoothness of running, centre of gravity height, and the ease with which the engine will fit, or "package", into its allotted space. The straight layout and some alternatives are shown here.

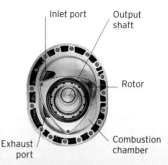

Inlet port **Output shaft**
Rotor
Exhaust port **Combustion chamber**

STRAIGHT-FOUR
Straight, or in-line, layouts dominate today's four-cylinder engines. In-line engines with six or more cylinders run very smoothly, but they are long, and that makes them difficult to fit into a small engine bay.

V6
Big-capacity in-line engines are too long and tall to fit into low sports cars, and their long crankshafts can flex ("whip") under stress. Many sports cars have compact engines with two cylinder banks arranged in a "V".

FLAT-FOUR
In this layout the cylinders are in two horizontally opposed banks. The result is a wide engine with a low centre of gravity, which aids roadholding. The balanced motion of the pistons reduces vibration and gives smooth running.

ROTARY (CUTAWAY)
Instead of pistons moving up and down in cylinders, the Wankel rotary engine uses one or more three-cornered rotors turning inside a specially shaped housing to generate rotary motion directly – and very smoothly.

CYLINDER CUTAWAY

This cross-section of a cylinder was made by slicing across an engine, as shown at the foot of the page. The engine has double overhead camshafts – that, is two camshafts at the top of the engine above the cylinder, one for the inlet valves and one for the exhaust valves.

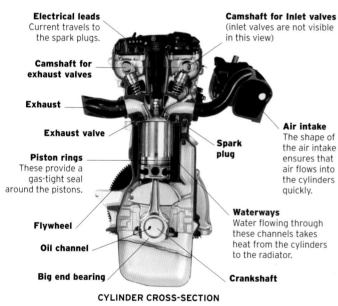

Electrical leads
Current travels to the spark plugs.

Camshaft for Inlet valves
(inlet valves are not visible in this view)

Camshaft for exhaust valves

Exhaust

Exhaust valve

Piston rings
These provide a gas-tight seal around the pistons.

Air intake
The shape of the air intake ensures that air flows into the cylinders quickly.

Spark plug

Waterways
Water flowing through these channels takes heat from the cylinders to the radiator.

Flywheel

Oil channel

Big end bearing

Crankshaft

CYLINDER CROSS-SECTION

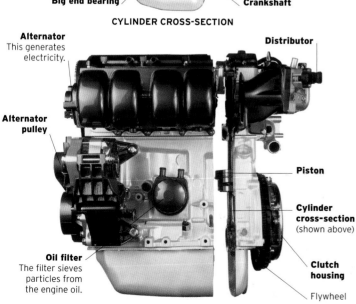

Alternator
This generates electricity.

Distributor

Alternator pulley

Piston

Cylinder cross-section
(shown above)

Oil filter
The filter sieves particles from the engine oil.

Clutch housing

Flywheel

EXTERNAL VIEW OF FOUR-CYLINDER ENGINE

FOUR-STROKE CYCLE

While the engine is running, every cylinder goes through the same series of events – called the four-stroke cycle – dozens of times each second. The four stages, or "strokes", are: intake, compression, combustion, and exhaust. Only the combustion stroke generates power, and in each cylinder it occurs only once for every two crankshaft turns. In a four-cylinder engine the spark plugs fire in sequence, so there is always a power stroke in at least one cylinder.

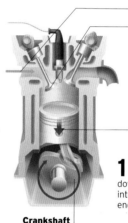

Air and fuel

Inlet valve
Air and fuel are drawn into the cylinder via this valve.

Descending piston
Turned by the crankshaft, the piston descends to its lowest position, called "bottom dead centre" (BDC).

Crankshaft

1 Intake stroke The inlet valve opens and the piston moves down, drawing fuel-air mixture into the cylinder through the engine's inlet and fuelling system.

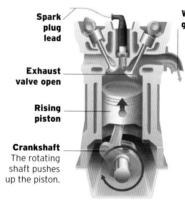

Spark plug lead

Waste gases

Exhaust valve open

Rising piston

Crankshaft
The rotating shaft pushes up the piston.

4 Exhaust stroke As the piston reaches the bottom, the exhaust valve opens. As it rises again, the piston forces waste gases out into the exhaust.

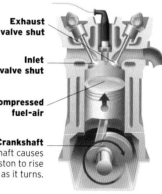

Exhaust valve shut

Inlet valve shut

Compressed fuel-air

Crankshaft
The shaft causes the piston to rise as it turns.

2 Compression stroke The piston moves back up the cylinder. This increases the pressure inside the cylinder, heating the fuel-air mixture.

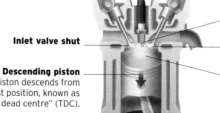

Inlet valve shut

Descending piston
The piston descends from highest position, known as "top dead centre" (TDC).

Spark plug

Exhaust valve shut

Ignition
The spark plug ignites the fuel-air mixture.

Crankshaft
The descending piston turns the crankshaft.

3 Combustion stroke When the piston is near the top of its stroke, a spark plug fires. The burning gas expands, forcing the piston down the cylinder again.

Glossary

2+2
Shorthand for cabin accommodation with two full-size front seats and two small rear seats. The rear seats are suitable for young children, or for adults on short journeys.

4x4
Shorthand for four-by-four, or four-wheel drive (FWD). A four-wheel-drive vehicle is one that has power transmitted to each wheel.

ABS (Anti-lock Braking System)
A braking system that stops the wheels from locking during braking, so the car can be steered away from danger in an emergency.

air filter
A felt or paper component that cleans air of particles before it enters the engine.

air-cooled engine
An engine that circulates air externally to cool its hot components. Internal water-cooling is the favoured cooling system in modern engines.

air-ride suspension
A suspension system that uses gas or pumped air to help keep the car level on rough roads.

alternator
A small generator that converts mechanical energy produced by the engine into electrical current. The electricity it produces charges the battery and powers circuits for equipment such as lights, electric windows, and radio.

anti-surge baffle
A plate that stops liquids from shifting position inside a reservoir, particularly an oil sump, as a result of the car's movements.

automatic
A clutchless transmission that automatically selects the appropriate gear for the driver.

autotest
A competitive motor sport that tests precision driving skills at low speed.

backbone chassis
A longitudinal, central structure supporting a car's body, drivetrain, and suspension.

BDA engine (Belt-Drive A-type)
A Ford-based engine designed by Cosworth.

beam front axle
A single suspension beam with a wheel on either end, attached to the car's frame by coil or leaf springs.

bearing
A device that provides a support between the fixed and moving parts of a machine.

Bertone
An Italian coachbuilder and design consultancy. The company was founded in 1921 and is still in business.

bhp (brake horsepower)
Horsepower originally gave a measure of the energy output of steam engines in terms of the equivalent amount of pulling power provided by a draft horse. In relation to cars, "gross" bhp is a measurement of the power output of a standalone engine. "Net" bhp is an engine's output after power has been sapped by ancillary equipment, such as the alternator. Bhp is measured by applying a special brake to the crankshaft.

big end bearing
The larger, lower bearing of the connecting rod that links the pistons to the crankshaft.

block
See cylinder block.

blown (engine)
A general term for an engine that has its power boosted by a turbocharger or a supercharger.

bonnet
A hinged covering for a car's engine.

bore
The usually cylindrical hole within which an engine's piston moves. The bore is also the diameter of this cavity.

Brooklands
The world's first purpose-built race circuit, near Weybridge, Surrey, UK. It was in use from 1909 to 1939.

bubble-top
A term for the roof of a car that is notably rounded, made from glass, Perspex, or metal.

butterfly valve
A disc that pivots along its diameter within a duct, forming a valve that can be opened and closed to regulate the flow of air into an engine component, such as a carburettor.

cabriolet
A two-door car, although usually not a sports car, with a fabric-covered removable or folding roof.

camshaft
A rotating shaft featuring cam lobes that open and close the engine's inlet and exhaust valves. It can operate the valves indirectly by pushrod (usually in an overhead-valve engine) or directly (in an overhead-cam engine). Two camshafts per cylinder are used in double-overhead-camshaft engines – one for the inlet valves, and one for the exhaust valves.

carburettor
A device on older engines in which fuel and air are combined to produce a combustible mixture. The mixture is then ignited in the cylinder.

Carlsson tuned
A level of engine power offered in a special-edition Saab, named in honour of Swedish rally driver Erik Carlsson.

catalytic converter
A device fitted to the exhaust of cars running on unleaded petrol. It uses a chemical catalyst to stimulate reactions that convert harmful gases into harmless ones.

cc (cubic centimetres)
The standard volumetric measurement of cylinder capacity – and therefore engine size – for engines in Europe and Japan.

chassis
A load-bearing frame on wheels, which, in all early cars, carried the mechanical parts and to which the body was attached. Most of today's models are of monocoque design, and so have no chassis, but the word survives to denote the drivetrain package.

choke
A carburettor valve that temporarily restricts air flow so that the fuel-air mixture is petrol-rich and therefore easier to ignite when the engine is cold.

classic
A car built after 1 January 1930, and more than 25 years old.

close-coupled
A body style of a two-door compact car that places the rear two seats within the wheelbase.

clutch
A device that disconnects the engine from the transmission so that a different gear can be selected.

coachwork
A car's outer, painted body panels – traditionally the work of a coachbuilder.

column gearchange
A gear-selector lever mounted on the steering column instead of on the floor. It is no longer found on modern cars.

combustion chamber
The space at the top of an engine's cylinder into which the fuel-air mixture is compressed by the piston when at its high point, and where the spark plug is located to initiate combustion.

compression ratio
The ratio between the volume of one cylinder and the combustion chamber when the piston is at the bottom of its stroke, and the volume of the combustion chamber alone when the piston is at the top of its stroke.

compression ring
See piston ring.

compressor
A device that increases the pressure of a gas by reducing its volume by compression. It is used in turbochargers and superchargers to increase the performance of the engine.

connecting rod
A mechanism that connects an engine's piston to the crankshaft.

Cosworth-tuned
An engine tuned by Cosworth, a UK-based designer, builder, and modifier of engines for road and race cars.

coupé
From the French verb *couper*, meaning "to cut", the word originally described a two-door closed car with a lower or abbreviated roof-line. Coupés today generally have a roofline that tapers away at the rear.

courtesy light
A small light that is activated when a car door is opened. It illuminates the interior of the car, the door sill, or the ground beneath the car.

crank pulley
The main pulley at the end of an engine's crankshaft. It is used to drive ancillary devices such as the alternator and the water pump.

crankcase
The lower part of the cylinder block that houses the crankshaft.

crankshaft
The main engine shaft that converts the reciprocating (up and down) motion of the pistons into the rotary motion needed to turn the wheels.

crossover
Any type of car that mixes elements of two distinct types of car. The term mostly applies to cars that are conventional hatchbacks or saloons above the body waistline and SUV/4x4 vehicles below.

cu in (cubic inches)
A former volumetric measurement of cylinder capacity – and therefore engine size – for engines in the US. It was replaced by the litre from the 1970s onwards.

cylinder
The usually cylindrical bore within which an engine's pistons move up and down.

cylinder block
The body, of usually cast metal, into which cylinders are bored to carry the pistons in an internal combustion engine, and to which the cylinder head or heads attach.

cylinder head
The upper part of an engine, attached to the top of the cylinder block. It contains the spark plugs that ignite the fuel in the cylinders and usually the valves.

desmodromic valve
An engine valve that is closed mechanically by a leverage system, rather than by a spring. It gives more exact control of valve motion but is costly to manufacture and so tends to be reserved for racing engines.

dickey seat
A passenger seat that hinges up from the rear deck of a pre-World War II car. In the US it is called a "rumble seat".

differential
A gearset in the drive system of a car that allows an outer wheel to rotate faster than an inner wheel, which is necessary when turning a corner.

DIN figures
A measure of engine power output defined by Germany's Deutsches Institut für Normung.

direct injection
See fuel injection.

disc brakes
A braking system in which each wheel hub contains a disc that rotates with the wheel and is gripped by brake pads to slow the car.

distributor
A device that routes high voltage from the ignition coil to the spark plugs in the correct firing order.

dohc (double-overhead camshaft)
See camshaft.

downdraught carburettor
A carburettor in which fuel is fed into a downward current of air.

drag coefficient
A number that provides a measure of how aerodynamic a car is. "Drag" is the resistance caused by air as an object passes through it.

drag-racing
A motor sport in which cars compete to see which can cover a set distance fastest in a straight line from a standing start.

drivebelt
A belt that drives various devices in or attached to a car's engine, including the alternator.

drive-by-wire throttle
A new type of engine throttle that is controlled electronically, rather than by mechanical linkage to the accelerator pedal.

driveshaft
A revolving shaft that takes power from the engine to the wheels.

drivetrain
The group of mechanical assemblies – engine, transmission, driveshafts, and differentials – that generate and harness power in a car. Today these are collectively know as the "chassis", and can be transplanted into several different models to save on development costs. Sometimes "drivetrain" can mean just the engine and the transmission.

drophead
A body style featuring a convertible top that folds flat.

drum brake
A braking system, largely supplanted by disc brakes, in which braking shoes are pressed against the inner surface of a drum that is attached to the car's wheel.

dual-circuit brakes
A braking system that has two independent hydraulic circuits, to retain braking capability if one circuit fails.

dynamo
An engine-driven generator of electric power in early cars. It has largely been replaced by the alternator.

entry-level
A car model that is the lowest-priced or has the lowest specifications in a range.

estate
A square-backed car adapted to carry cargo, with a load bay accessed by a fifth door or tailgate. The term was originally coined for a utility vehicle used for running errands on large country estates. In the US it is called a station wagon.

exhaust manifold
A piping system that carries waste exhaust gases from the cylinders to the exhaust pipe.

exhaust port
A passageway in the cylinder head leading from the exhaust valve(s) to the exhaust manifold.

exhaust valve
A valve in the cylinder head that opens at the start of the exhaust stroke, allowing the piston to push the exhaust gases out of the cylinder.

factory team
A racing team funded by a car manufacturer.

fairing
Any cover or cowling designed to make components that stand proud (of an engine, for example) more aerodynamic.

fastback
A rear roofline profile that tapers to the end of the car's tail.

flat-twin, flat-four, flat-six, flat-twelve
Any engine that has its cylinders and pistons positioned horizontally in two opposed banks. These are sometimes called "boxer" engines because the pistons in opposing pairs of cylinders move towards and away from each other alternately, as if trading punches.

floorpan
A shallow, pressed-metal tray that forms the underside of the car and carries suspension and other drivetrain elements. Clever design allows the same floorpan to be shared by several different models.

fluid flywheel
A now-redundant transmission device that allowed the driver to change gear without the use of a clutch.

flywheel
A heavy circular plate attached to the crankshaft that stores the rotational energy produced by the engine's torque impulses. By releasing this energy between the impulses, it smoothes engine operation.

Formula 1
More formally known as the FIA (Federation Internationale de l'Automobile) Formula One World Championship, this is the premier world series of single-seater motor races. It was inaugurated in 1950.

Formula Libre
A form of automobile racing in which different types of racing cars compete head-to-head.

four-stroke engine
This is the predominant type of car engine today. There are four stages in the power cycle, which occupies two crankshaft rotations: intake, compression, combustion, and exhaust. Each of these is governed by the upward or downward movements, or "strokes", of the piston.

four-wheel drive (FWD)
See 4x4.

front-wheel drive
Power transmitted to the two front wheels of a vehicle only. This lightens the car, which needs no transmission to its rear wheels.

fuel injection
A fuel supply system, universal to new cars, that dispenses with a carburettor. Fuel is pumped from the petrol tank and sprayed by injectors straight into the engine's inlet ports, where it mixes with air before being burned in the cylinder. In diesel and direct-injection petrol engines, fuel is injected straight into the cylinder, rather than the inlet port.

Futuramic
A term used by the Oldsmobile division of General Motors to describe the styling of its 1948–50 car range.

gas turbine
A jet-type rotary engine that draws its energy from the continuous burning of a flow of fuel-air mixture, which drives a turbine. It has been used experimentally in cars, but is too slow-reacting to directly replace the reciprocating engine.

gate gearchange
An abbreviation of "open-gate gearchange" – a style of gearbox in which the slots into which the gear selector lever must be pushed are visible. It is usually found in sports or racing cars; other types of car tend to cover it up with a rubber or stitched-leather gaiter.

Gear
A toothed or cogged machine part that meshes and rotates with other such parts to transmit torque.

Giugiaro
This can refer to the Italian car stylist Giorgio Giugiaro, or to the design consultancy he started in 1968, which is more formally called Italdesign-Giugiaro. The consultancy was acquired by Volkswagen in 2010.

grand routier
An informal name, more common in English than French, which translates as "grand road traveller". It is often applied to elegant and fast European touring cars.

GT
From the Italian *gran turismo*, meaning "grand touring", these initials refer to high-performance closed cars.

gullwing doors
Doors that open upwards. They are a key feature of the Mercedes-Benz 300SL and the DeLorean DMC-12.

hardtop
A sports, or sporty, car with a rigid roof that is either fixed or removable. A car with a fabric roof is called a soft-top.

hatchback
The tailgate, sometimes called the third or fifth door, on any non-estate car with a sloped, instead of vertical, tail. It is also a style of car exemplified in five-door form by the Renault 16 of 1965, and in three-door form by the Renault 5 of 1972.

head
See cylinder head.

heat shield
Rigid or flexible layers of heat-resistant material that protect a car's components or bodywork from excessive engine- or exhaust-generated heat.

hood
The folding, canvas-covered top of any convertible car. It is also the US word for "bonnet".

homologation
A rigorous testing programme that new cars must undergo to ensure they meet construction and usage rules in a territory; only then can they be legally driven on the road. The term is also applied to the rules governing individual motor sport categories. An "homologation special" is, in general, a roadgoing version of a racing car; a minimum number of these must be constructed for it to qualify as a production model.

horizontally opposed layout
The full technical term for an engine whose cylinders are mounted flat on either side of the crankshaft.

hot hatch
The British nickname for a high-performance version of a compact three-door (sometimes five-door) car, exemplified by the Renault 5 Alpine and Volkswagen Golf GTi of 1976.

hot rod
Short for "hot roadster", a US term that originated in the 1930s to describe any standard car whose engine had been modified for higher performance. After World War II hot rods were modified production cars used in straight-line speed trials.

hp (horsepower)
See bhp (brake horsepower).

hybrid
A car-propulsion technology that combines the use of both electric and petrol/diesel power. Electric power slashes emissions in urban driving, while fossil fuel gives enough sustained power for motorway cruising and recharges the battery.

Hydramatic transmission
General Motors' own brand of automatic transmission.

hydraulic damper
A damper is the proper name for a shock absorber, which dissipates the energy of a car's suspension movement and converts it hydraulically, via internal oil, into quickly dissipated heat.

Hydrolastic suspension
A brand of suspension system featuring fluid-filled rubber displacement units. It was used in cars made by the British Motor Corporation in the 1960s.

Hydropneumatic
Citroën's own brand name for its self-levelling suspension system. Hydraulic fluid from an engine-driven pressure pump transmits the movement of the suspension arms to metal gas springs containing pressurized nitrogen, which absorb bumps and maintain constant ride height. The system has pre-set ride heights to cope with differing driving conditions. Complex and eccentric, it never became popular.

idle-speed positioner
A device that optimizes the rate at which the engine runs at idle, when the throttle is closed, to maximize fuel efficiency.

ignition coil
An ignition system component that converts the car battery's 12-volt power into the thousands of volts required to ignite the spark plugs.

independent suspension
A suspension system that allows every wheel to move up and down independently of the others. Its advantages are better handling and a more comfortable ride.

Indianapolis 500
An iconic US motor race for single-seater cars, staged annually since 1911 at the oval Indianapolis Motor Speedway.

induction system
The apparatus through which air passes as it enters the engine.

inlet plenum chamber
An air chamber between an engine's throttle body and inlet manifold that beneficially affects the operation of the induction system.

inlet port
The route within a cylinder head through which the fuel-air mixture passes to the inlet valve.

inlet trumpet
A trumpet-shaped engine air intake designed to exploit the effects of wave motion to force more air into the cylinders.

inlet valve
The valve through which fuel is drawn into the engine cylinder.

in-line engine
An engine that has its cylinders arranged in a straight line.

intercooler
A radiator that cools the compressed air from a turbocharger or supercharger before it enters the engine. This increases power and enhances reliability.

IRS (Independent Rear Suspension)
A suspension system in which the rear two wheels are free to move up and down independently of each other.

kei **car**
A Japanese taxation class for very small cars, which, currently, may be no longer than 3.4 m (11.15 ft) and have an engine of no more than 660cc to qualify.

Le Mans 24-Hours
A 24-hour endurance motor race, staged annually at Le Mans, France, since 1923. It uses a circuit consisting of public roads cordoned off for the event.

leaf spring
Also known as a "cart spring", this is a basic means of suspension noted for its toughness, though not for its supple ride quality. The spring comprises overlaid arcs (or leaves) of steel that are fixed to the underside of the car, forming a shock-absorbing cushion on which the car's axle presses. The heavier the car, the more leaves must be added to the spring.

limited-slip differential
A differential that counteracts the tendency of wheelspin if one driven wheel hits ice or another slippery surface.

limousine
A luxury saloon car, usually with a long wheelbase, with an emphasis on rear-seat comfort. Limousines are sometimes fitted with a division between driver and rear passengers.

live axle
A beam-type axle that contains the shafts that drive the wheels.

LPG
Liquified-petroleum gas, a fuel that can be used in largely unmodified petrol engines, and gives reduced noxious emissions.

MacPherson strut
Named after its inventor, Ford engineer Earl MacPherson, this is a suspension upright comprising a hydraulic damper with a coaxial coil spring. Most often used for front suspensions, it has the advantage of causing little intrusion into the engine bay.

magneto
An electro-magnetic generator used in early cars to produce high voltage for the spark plugs.

Mille Miglia
A 1,000-mile (1,609-km) road race around Italy on public roads, held 24 times between 1927 and 1957. In 1977 the name was revived for an annual parade of historic cars.

monobloc
An engine design in which the cylinders are cast together as a single unit. This improves the mechanical rigidity of the engine and the reliability of the sealing.

monocoque
A car structure, now almost universal, in which the car body bears all the structural loads. It is, effectively, the chassis and the body combined in one strong unit.

MPV
Shorthand for Multi-Purpose Vehicle or Multi-Passenger Vehicle. The term applies to tall, spacious cars that can carry at least five passengers, and often as many as nine, or versatile combinations of people and cargo as a people carrier.

muscle car
A US standard production car, usually with two doors, featuring a large-capacity, high-performance engine. The first muscle car was the Pontiac GTO in 1964.

NACA duct
America's National Advisory Committee for Aeronautics created this distinctively shaped air intake, which can be used to ventilate internal components such as brakes while causing minimal disturbance to external aerodynamics.

NASCAR
The National Association for Stock Car Auto Racing – a US organization that oversees motor racing series and events.

ohc (overhead-camshaft)
See camshaft.

ohv (overhead valve)
See overhead-valve engine.

overdrive
A gear ratio for fast cruising that causes the gearbox output shaft to turn faster than the input shaft. This lowers the engine revs for a given vehicle speed, which cuts fuel consumption, but also torque, which restricts overtaking power.

overhead-camshaft
See camshaft.

overhead-valve engine
An engine in which the inlet and exhaust valves are contained within the cylinder head, and not beside the cylinder, as they are in a side-valve engine.

overlapping four-door
A style of body in which the front set of doors overlap the rear set when closed.

overrider
A metal or rubber-faced metal upright fitted to a bumper to protect against the bumpers of other cars in a collision.

oversquare engine
An engine in which the cylinder bore measurement is greater than the stroke.

people carrier
A popular term to describe an MPV, particularly one that has at least seven seats.

Pinin Farina/Pininfarina
An Italian coachbuilder and design consultancy founded as Pinin Farina in 1930 by Battista "Pinin" Farina. The company adopted the Pininfarina title in 1961.

piston
The component that moves up and down inside the engine cylinder and which, on the combustion stroke, transfers force from the expanding gas to the crankshaft via a connecting rod.

piston ring
An open-ended ring that fits into a groove in the outer surface of an engine's piston, sealing the combustion chamber. Piston rings also act to cool the piston by transferring heat to the cylinder wall, and regulate oil consumption.

planetary gearset
The US term for an epicyclic gearbox, in which small pinions revolve around a central "sun" gear and mesh with an outer ring gear.

platform
The concealed, but elemental and expensive, basic structure of a modern car. It is the task of contemporary car designers to achieve maximum aesthetic diversity from a single platform.

pony car
A genre of car informally named after the Ford Mustang, which was one of the first compact sporty coupés, aimed at the US "baby boomers" of the 1960s. It could be ordered with several high-performance engines options.

powertrain
See drivetrain.

propshaft
A contraction of "propeller-shaft"; a long shaft that conveys engine torque to the rear axle of a rear-wheel-drive or four-wheel-drive car.

pushrod engine
An engine in which the valves are not operated directly via the camshaft but via intermediate rods. This allows the valves and camshaft to be widely separated.

Q-car
A car with a performance that belies its mundane appearance. The name derives from the heavily armoured but innocuous-looking Q-ships in Britain's Royal Navy in World War I. A Q-car is often called a "wolf in sheep's clothing".

rack-and-pinion steering
A rack and pinion consists of two gears that together convert rotational motion into linear motion. It is the favoured system for car steering because it provides good feedback to the driver about the behaviour of the wheels.

radiator
A heat-exchanger used to cool liquids by presenting a large surface area to a flow of air.

razor-edge styling
A car styling trend towards sharp-edged lines that emerged in the UK coachbuilding industry in the late 1930s. It was a reaction to the prevailing preference for rounded, streamlined forms.

rear-wheel drive
Power transmitted to the two rear wheels of a vehicle only.

reciprocating engine
Also known as a piston engine, which converts the up and down (or "reciprocating") motion of pistons to the rotary motion needed by the wheels.

redline
The maximum speed at which an engine is designed to operate without incurring damage. It is usually indicated by a red line on the rev counter dial.

regenerative braking
A system found in electric and hybrid cars in which electric traction motors are operated as generators during braking, thereby providing braking force while generating current to recharge the battery pack.

rev
Short for revolutions-per-minute, a measure of engine speed.

roadster
A term that originally described an open car with a single seat to accommodate two or three abreast, but which now applies to any kind of two-seater open sports car.

rocker arm
A pivoted lever, one end of which is raised and lowered by the camshaft, either directly or via a pushrod, while the other end acts on the stem of the engine valve.

rolling chassis
The frame of an older, separate-chassis car, with all drivetrain components fitted.

rollover bar
A strong metal hoop incorporated into the structure of a car with a folding roof. It is designed to protect the heads and upper torsos of driver and passengers should the vehicle overturn.

rotary engine
Any type of power unit that dispenses with the reciprocal motion of pistons, producing rotary motion directly. The only type ever fitted to production cars was one designed by Dr Felix Wankel, and the last car to feature one was the Mazda RX-8, which appeared in 2001.

running gear
The wheels, suspension, steering, and drivetrain of a car.

saloon
Any type of car with a fixed metal roof. The equivalent US term is "sedan".

scavenge oil pump
In a dry sump engine this additional pump evacuates oil that collects at the bottom of the engine, sending it to a separate oil tank.

scuttle
The bodywork sections that form a barrier between the engine and the passenger compartments and that support the windscreen.

sedan
See saloon.

semi-automatic paddle gearshift
A clutchless gearchange mechanism that enables the driver to change gear using levers (or "paddles") attached to the steering wheel.

semi-elliptic springs
Another term for leaf springs.

semi-trailing suspension
An independent suspension assembly for the rear wheels of a car in which each wheel hub is linked to the chassis by a lower triangular arm that pivots at an acute angle to the vehicle centreline.

servo assisted braking
A braking system that uses a stored vacuum (or "vacuum servo") to magnify the force the driver applies to the brake pedal.

shaft drive
Power delivered from the engine to the wheels by means of rotating shafts.

side-valve engine
A form of engine design in which the valves are placed at the side of the cylinder, rather than within the cylinder head. In an L-head engine the inlet and exhaust valves are placed together on one side of the cylinder; on a T-head engine they are located on opposite sides.

silencer
A chamber placed along the route of the exhaust pipe and designed to reduce exhaust noise.

six-pot
"Pot" is slang for "cylinder"; a "six-pot" engine is a six-cylinder unit.

sleeve-valve engine
An engine that has a metal sleeve placed between the piston and cylinder wall. The sleeve oscillates with the motion of the piston and has holes that align with the cylinder's inlet and exhaust ports, facilitating the entry and exit of gases.

slide throttle
A type of throttle featuring a perforated plate that slides across the air inlet to allow more or less air to enter the engine.

sliding gear transmission
An old-fashioned manual gearbox. When in neutral, nothing inside the transmission revolves apart from the main drive gear (attached to the crankshaft) and cluster gear (attached to the wheels). To mesh the gears and apply engine power for motion, the driver presses the clutch and moves the shift handle to slide a gear along the mainshaft mounted above the cluster.

The clutch is then released and the engine power transmitted to the driven wheels. This system has been superseded by constant-mesh, or "synchromesh", gears.

small-block
The smallest V8 engines from Chevrolet and Ford, first produced in the 1950s.

soft-roader
A four-wheel-drive car designed for occasional off-road leisure use, rather than for heavy-duty activities on farms or construction sites.

sohc (single overhead-camshaft)
See camshaft.

solenoid switch
An electronically controlled switch, more properly known as a relay, which allows a low-current electric circuit to control a high-current one. A car's starter motor, for example, requires a high-current circuit.

Spa 24 Hours
An annual endurance motor race held in Spa, Belgium, since 1924.

spark plug
An electrical device, screwed into the engine cylinder head of a petrol engine, that ignites the fuel in the cylinder.

sports car
A two-seater with a convertible top, low or rakish lines, good roadholding, and above-average speed and acceleration.

spider
A "spider-phaeton" was originally a light horse-drawn cart with two seats and large wheels. Alfa Romeo adopted the name for its two-seater sports cars in 1954, and it is now the standard name for cars of that type, particularly ones that are compact and low.

spyder
The German equivalent of a "spider", and most commonly associated with Porsche.

stovebolt
A nickname for a Chevrolet straight-six-cylinder engine, coined because the fastener securing the valve cover, lifter cover, and timing cover resembles the bolt found on wood-burning stoves.

straight engine
See in-line engine.

sub-compact
A North American term that originated in the 1970s to describe domestically produced rivals to the Volkswagen Beetle, such as the Ford Pinto and the Chevrolet Vega. The latter were smaller than the Ford Falcon and the Chevrolet Corvair, which at the time were "compact" by Detroit manufacturing standards.

sump
An oil reservoir at the bottom of an engine. A "dry sump" is usually fitted to a racing-car or sports-car engine that is likely to be subjected to high cornering, braking, and acceleration forces. In a conventional "wet sump" these forces can cause oil to surge, uncovering the oil pick-up pipe, which can result in engine damage. In a dry sump system a scavenge pump removes oil as it falls into the sump, pumping it to a separate oil tank.

supercar
A very expensive, high-performance sports car. The first supercar is widely recognized to have been the Mercedes-Benz 300SL of 1954, but the term quickly came to describe a mid-engined two-seater as exemplified by the Lamborghini Miura.

supercharger
An engine-driven compressor that forces air into the inlet system, thereby increasing the amount of fuel-air mixture entering the cylinders, and hence the torque and power.

supermini
A market term for a small hatchback car with a four-cylinder engine, as exemplified by the Renault 5 of 1972.

suspension
A system that cushions the car's structure (and occupants) from motion of the wheels as they traverse uneven road surfaces.

SUV
Sport-Utility Vehicle.

swash plate
A plate attached at an angle to a rotating shaft that is used to convert the shaft's rotational motion into reciprocal motion at push rods lying parallel to the shaft axis.

synchromesh gearbox
A gearbox in which gear wheels are in constant mesh. All-synchromesh gearboxes are universal in modern road cars.

tappet
A valvetrain component that makes sliding contact with the camshaft lobe, converting the cam's profile into the reciprocating motion of the valve.

Targa Florio
An open-road race through the mountains of Sicily, staged between 1906 and 1973, and since revived as a classic car event.

throttle
A device that controls the amount of air flowing into the engine.

torque
The twisting force produced by the engine.

torsion-bar
A suspension part that acts as a spring when twisted by the wheel's movements.

transaxle
The term for an assembly that combines the gearbox and differential components in a single casing.

transmission
All the components of a car's drivetrain, though often the gearbox alone.

transmission tunnel
The raised section running lengthways along the centreline of the cabin of a car with a front engine and rear- or four-wheel drive. It houses the propshaft.

transverse engine
An engine that is mounted with its crankshaft axis across the car, rather than parallel to its centreline.

tuned
A term to describe an engine that has been modified for extra performance.

turbocharger
A device fitted between an engine's inlet and exhaust systems that uses the exhaust gases to drive a turbine. This in turn drives a compressor that forces air into the inlet system.

turning circle
The diameter of the circle described by a car's outer front wheel when turning with its steering at full-lock.

twin-cam
See camshaft.

two-stroke engine
An engine with pistons that move up once and down once (performing two "strokes") in the combustion cycle.

two-wheel drive
Transmission to the front two or rear two wheels only, in contrast to four-wheel drive.

unitary construction
See monocoque.

unblown
An engine without a supercharger or turbocharger, properly termed "normally aspirated".

V4, V6, V8, V10, V12, V16
The designations for engines designed with their cylinders arranged in a V-formation for compactness. The numbers relate to the number of cylinders in each engine.

vacuum advance
A mechanism that enables the distributor to adjust spark timing according to engine load.

valvetrain
The parts of the engine that control the operation of the valves.

water-cooling
A system that uses circulating water to cool engine components. It is the predominant cooling system in modern engines, though some use an air-cooling system.

wet-liner
A cylinder liner that is in direct contact with the engine's liquid coolant.

wheelbase
The exact distance between the axes of the front and rear wheels.

whitewall tyres
Tyres featuring a decorative ring of white rubber on their sidewalls. It was a popular styling, particularly in the US, from the late 1930s to the early 1960s.

wishbone suspension
An independent suspension system that uses two wishbone-shaped arms to link each wheel hub to the chassis.

works driver
A racing driver employed by a car manufacturer to drive for its team, as opposed to an independent "privateer".

Index

Page numbers in **bold** indicate
main entries.

Acknowledgments

Dorling Kindersley would like to thank the following for their kind permission to reproduce their photographs:

(Key: a-above; b-below/bottom; c-centre; f-far; l-left; r-right; t-top)

8 Getty Images: Car Culture (c). 10 Giles Chapman Library: (cla). 11 Louwman Museum. Corbis: The Bettmann Archive (cl). Getty Images: Ed Clark / Time Life Pictures (tl). Malcolm McKay: (cr, bl). TopFoto.co.uk: Topham Picturepoint (tr). 13 Louwman Museum. Motoring Picture Library/ National Motor Museum. 14 Corbis: The Bettmann Archive (tl). Giles Chapman Library: (cra, bl). courtesy Mercedes-Benz Cars, Daimler AG: (cla). 15 Giles Chapman Library: (br). 17 Louwman Museum: (crb, cr). Giles Chapman Library: (clb). 18 Giles Chapman Library: (tl). 24 Corbis: The Gallery Collection. 26 Louwman Museum. 27 Art Tech Picture Agency: (tr). Louwman Museum: (cr). Corbis: Car Culture (cl). 28 Giles Chapman Library: (bc). Used with permission, GM Media Archives. 29 Giles Chapman Library: (br). Used with permission, GM Media Archives.: (cla). 30 Louwman Museum: (tc, ca, cla, bl, br, cr, cra). TopFoto.co.uk: National Motor Museum/HIP (clb). 31 Louwman Museum. Giles Chapman Library: (bl). TopFoto.co.uk: Alinari (clb). 32 Giles Chapman Library: (tl). 38 Alamy Images: pbpgalleries (tc). Art Tech Picture Agency: (cl). Louwman Museum: (cra). Motoring Picture Library / National Motor Museum: (cb). 39 Motoring Picture Library / National Motor Museum. Rex Features: Gary Hawkins (tr). 40 Motoring Picture Library/ National Motor Museum: (tl). 44 Used with permission, GM Media Archives.: (c). 45 Alamy Images: culture-images GmbH (br). 46 Louwman Museum. Getty Images: Car Culture (tl). 47 Louwman Museum. Giles Chapman Library: (cla). James Mann. TopFoto.co.uk: (cb). 48 Giles Chapman Library: (c). 50 Art Tech Picture Agency: (cl). Louwman Museum: (bc). James Mann: (cra). TopFoto.co.uk: 2006 (tr). 51 Louwman Museum: (tl). James Mann: (crb). Motoring Picture Library / National Motor Museum. TopFoto.co.uk: 2005 (cb). Ullstein Bild: (cl). 56 Motoring Picture Library/ National Motor Museum: (tl, cr). 57 Louwman Museum: (cra, c). James Mann: (tr). Motoring Picture Library/ National Motor Museum: (cl). 58 Alamy Images: Mary Evans Picture Library (bl). Giles Chapman Library: (tl). Rolls-Royce Motor Cars Ltd: Rolls-Royce Enthusiasts Club (cra); (cla). 59 Alamy Images: Pictorial Press Ltd (cb). Art Tech Picture Agency: (tr). 60 Alamy Images: Motoring Picture Library (cl). Louwman Museum: (tc, clb). Motoring Picture Library / National Motor Museum: (cr). 61 Giles Chapman Library: (cra). Motoring Picture Library / National Motor Museum: (tc, cl). 62 akg-images: Erich Lessing (bl). Lebrecht Music and Arts: Rue des archives (br). Giles Chapman

Library: (tl). Renault Communication: (cl). 63 akg-images: (br). Art Tech Picture Agency: (tc). 64 Alamy Images: Interfoto (ca). Louwman Museum. Magic Car Pics: (tr). Motoring Picture Library / National Motor Museum: (crb). 65 Alamy Images: Prisma Bildagentur AG (bc). Corbis: Car Culture (cla). 66 TopFoto. co.uk: (tl). 70 Corbis: The Bettmann Archive (c). 72 Corbis: Car Culture (c). 74 Giles Chapman Library. Motoring Picture Library / National Motor Museum: (tr). Reinhard Lintelmann Photography (Germany): (bl); (clb). 75 Art Tech Picture Agency: (bc). The Car Photo Library: (cb). Giles Chapman Library. TopFoto.co.uk: ullstein bild / Paul Mai (tl). 76 Louwman Museum: (cra). 78 Alamy Images: Esa Hiltula (cla). Corbis: The Bettmann Archive (cr). TopFoto.co.uk: (tl). 79 The Advertising Archives: (cla). Corbis: Transtock Inc. (crb). Orphan Work: (ftl). 82 Getty Images: Fox Photos (c). 84 Flickr.com: Ludek Mornstejn (tc). 85 Flickr.com: Stefan Koschminder (br). Motoring Picture Library / National Motor Museum: (cra). Oldtimergalerie Rosenau. : (clb). 86 Alamy Images: Autos (bc). 87 Giles Chapman Library: (clb). Reinhard Lintelmann Photography (Germany): (tr). 90 Alamy Images: Lordprice Collection (c). 92 Louwman Museum: (cl). Giles Chapman Library: (cra). Malcolm McKay: (cr). Motoring Picture Library / National Motor Museum: (bl). TopFoto.co.uk: (tl). 93 Louwman Museum. Motoring Picture Library / National Motor Museum: (tr). 94 Corbis: The Bettmann Archive (tl). 98 Louwman Museum: (bc). Giles Chapman Library: (cb). James Mann: (ca). Motoring Picture Library / National Motor Museum: (cl). TopFoto.co.uk: (tc). 99 Art Tech Picture Agency: (tr, br, cr, cra). Louwman Museum: (cla). Giles Chapman Library: (bl, br). 100 Alamy Images: Motoring Picture Library (tl). BMW AG: (cla). Corbis: Tatiana Markow/Sygma (bl). Giles Chapman Library: (cra). 101 Alamy Images: Alfred Schauhuber/ imagebroker (tl). Corbis: Martyn Goddard (bc). 102 Giles Chapman Library: (cl). Malcolm McKay. 103 Alamy Images: Tom Wood (br). Magic Car Pics: (tl). Malcolm McKay: (tc). Motoring Picture Library/ National Motor Museum. 104 Corbis: Car Culture (c). 106 Louwman Museum: (cb). Image created by Simon GP Geoghegan: (cr). Giles Chapman Library: (tr). Motoring Picture Library / National Motor Museum: (ca). Reinhard Lintelmann Photography (Germany): (c). 107 Art Tech Picture Agency: (br). Giles Chapman Library: (cra). Magic Car Pics. James Mann: (tl). 108 Magic Car Pics: (tr). 110 Corbis: The Bettmann Archive (c). 112 Alamy Images: Transtock Inc. (bl). Louwman Museum: (bc). Cody Images: (ca). 113 Giles Chapman Library: (cla). James Mann: (crb). Malcolm McKay: (crb). Motoring Picture Library / National Motor Museum: (bc). 114 Giles Chapman

Library: (tl). 118 Art Tech Picture Agency: (tl). James Mann: (bc). 119 Louwman Museum: (tr). James Mann: (bl, br). 122 Giles Chapman Library. Tata Limited: (cla). 123 Motoring Picture Library / National Motor Museum: (bc). 124 Giles Chapman Library: (clb, crb). Magic Car Pics: (tc). Motoring Picture Library / National Motor Museum. 125 Louwman Museum: (tr). Giles Chapman Library: (tl, br). Motoring Picture Library / National Motor Museum: (crb). Reinhard Lintelmann Photography (Germany): (clb). 126 Giles Chapman Library: (tl). 130 Alamy Images: Marka (tl). Citroën Communication: (cla, bl). 131 Alamy Images: Noel Yates (bc). Art Tech Picture Agency: (tr). Giles Chapman Library: (cra). 132 The Car Photo Library: (fclb). Magic Car Pics. 133 Alamy Images: culture-images GmbH (br). Fiat Group: (cb). Giles Chapman Library. Magic Car Pics: Paul Deverill (clb); (cl). James Mann: (tl). Motoring Picture Library/ National Motor Museum: (tc). TopFoto.co.uk: Roger-Viollet (cra). 134 Getty Images: Car Culture (c). 136 Art Tech Picture Agency: (clb). Giles Chapman Library: (bl). 137 Art Tech Picture Agency: (cr). Giles Chapman Library: (br). Malcolm McKay: (cl). 138 Corbis: Minnesota Historical Society (c). 140 Corbis: Car Culture (c). 143 Art Tech Picture Agency: (cra). 144 Corbis: Car Culture (bc); Eric Thayer/Reuters (cl). TopFoto.co.uk: Topham Picturepoint (tl). 145 Alamy Images: Iain Masterton (br). Giles Chapman Library: (cla). 150 Giles Chapman Library: (tl). 156 Louwman Museum: (tc). Magic Car Pics: (tr). Malcolm McKay: (cla, bc). 157 Alamy Images: Coyote-Photography.co.uk (tl). Louwman Museum: (cb, fcla). Giles Chapman Library: (cra). Malcolm McKay. Reinhard Lintelmann Photography (Germany): (clb). 158 Giles Chapman Library: (tl). 162 Fiat Group: (c). 164 Giles Chapman Library: (clb). 165 Getty Images: Bloomberg (cb). Giles Chapman Library. 166 Archivio Storico Alfa Romeo: (cla). Art Tech Picture Agency: (cr). Giles Chapman Library: (cb). Volvo Group: (tr). 167 Art Tech Picture Agency: (cla). The Car Photo Library: (crb). 168 The Advertising Archives: (cr). Corbis: Andrea Jemolo (bl). Courtesy of Chrysler Group LLC: (cl). Giles Chapman Library: (tl). 169 Corbis: DaZo Vintage Stock Photos/Images.com (bc). 172 Giles Chapman Library: (tl). 178 Giles Chapman Library. 179 Art Tech Picture Agency: (fcra). Louwman Museum: (clb, bc). The Car Photo Library: (c). Giles Chapman Library. 182 Motoring Picture Library/ National Motor Museum: (fcr). 183 Alamy Images: Stanley Hare (fbr); Martin Berry (bc). Rudolf Kozdon : (clb). 184 Alamy Images: Antiques & Collectables (fbl). Aston Martin Lagonda Limited: (ftl). Corbis: Bruce Benedict / Transtock (fcl). 185 Alamy Images: Photos 12 (fbr). Giles

Chapman Library: (fcr). 190 Giles Chapman Library. 191 Art Tech Picture Agency: (fbr). Giles Chapman Library: (fcl). 192 Getty Images: Bentley Archive/Popperfoto (c). 194 Getty Images: Nat Farbman / Time Life Pictures (fbl). Giles Chapman Library: (ftl). Motoring Picture Library / National Motor Museum: (fcl). 195 Giles Chapman Library. 200 Giles Chapman Library: (c). 204 Giles Chapman Library: (ftl). 208 Alamy Images: Phil Talbot (c). 210 Alamy Images: Tom Wood (clb). 212 Giles Chapman Library: (ftl). 216 Art Tech Picture Agency: (clb). LAT Photographic: (fbl). Giles Chapman Library. 217 Art Tech Picture Agency: (fcr, fbl). LAT Photographic: (clb, ftr). Giles Chapman Library. 218 Art Tech Picture Agency: (ca, c). Ford Motor Company Limited: (fcla). The Car Photo Library: (fbr). LAT Photographic: (cl). Giles Chapman Library: (ftr). Suzuki Motor Corporation: (clb). 219 Alamy Images: Trinity Mirror / Mirrorpix (bc). Art Tech Picture Agency: (fbl). Courtesy of Chrysler Group LLC: (tr). Giles Chapman Library. Magic Car Pics: (fbr). James Mann: (cl). Wisconsin Historical Society. : Image ID 25823 (ftl). 220 LAT Photographic: (ftl). Giles Chapman Library: (cl, bc). 221 Art Tech Picture Agency: (ftr). Giles Chapman Library. 222 Art Tech Picture Agency: (c). 223 BMW AG: (fcla). Magic Car Pics: (ca). 225 Art Tech Picture Agency: (cla). Greig Dalgleish: (fcl). Giles Chapman Library: (fcl). Reinhard Lintelmann Photography (Germany): (cb). 226 Giles Chapman Library: (fbl). 228 Art Tech Picture Agency: (cra, ftl, clb). 229 Art Tech Picture Agency: (ca, cb). 230 NASA: (c). 232 Alamy Images: Phil Talbot (fcl); Eddie Linssen (fbr). Giles Chapman Library: (ftl). 233 The Advertising Archives: (ca). Art Tech Picture Agency: (tr, ftr). LAT Photographic: (fbr). 234 Louwman Museum: (ftr). Motoring Picture Library / National Motor Museum: (clb). 235 Motoring Picture Library / National Motor Museum: (cra). 236 Art Tech Picture Agency: (ftl). LAT Photographic: (clb, crb). James Mann: (fbl). 237 TopFoto.co.uk: Phipps/Sutton/HIP (clb). 238 Giles Chapman Library. Magic Car Pics: (fcla). 239 LAT Photographic: (cla). Giles Chapman Library. 240 The Car Photo Library. 241 The Car Photo Library: (c). 243 James Mann (afl). 244 Art Tech Picture Agency: (c). Giles Chapman Library. 245 Giles Chapman Library. Wikipedia, The Free Encyclopedia: (tc). 246-247 Corbis: JP Laffont/ Sygma. 248 Art Tech Picture Agency: (c). Giles Chapman Library. 249 Art Tech Picture Agency: (fbl). Giles Chapman Library. Malcolm McKay: (clb). 250 akg-images: (fbl). Alamy Images: Niall McDiarmid (cl). Bundesarchiv: Bild 183-1983-0107-307 / Zimmermann (ftl). Dennis Images: (fbr). 251 The Advertising Archives: (ca). Alamy Images: Hans Dieter Seufert / culture-images GmbH (fbr). Reinhard Lintelmann

Photography (Germany): (ftl). 252 Art Tech Picture Agency. Giles Chapman Library: (fbl). James Mann: (ftr). 253 Art Tech Picture Agency. Giles Chapman Library: (fcr). 254 Art Tech Picture Agency: (fcl). (c): Aventure Peugeot: (cb). Citroën Communication: (crb, fbr). LAT Photographic. Giles Chapman Library: (clb). 255 Art Tech Picture Agency: (cra, cr). Magic Car Pics. 256 Corbis: Tony Korody / Sygma (ftl). Dorling Kindersley: DeLorean Motor Company (fcl). 260 Porsche AG: (fbl). 266 Art Tech Picture Agency: (cb). Giles Chapman Library: (cra). 267 Art Tech Picture Agency: (cla, cra). 268 Alamy Images: Motoring Picture Library / National Motor Museum (ftl). 272 Giles Chapman Library. 273 Art Tech Picture Agency. Giles Chapman Library. 274 The Bridgeman Art Library: Vincent, Rene (1871-1936) / Private Collection / Archives Charmet / The Bridgeman Art Library (cra). (c): Aventure Peugeot. Giles Chapman Library: (fbl). 275 LAT Photographic: (c). Giles Chapman Library: (tl, ftl). 276 Art Tech Picture Agency. Louwman Museum: (cla). 277 Art Tech Picture Agency: (c, bc). Giles Chapman Library. 278 Corbis: Ron Perry / Transtock (c). 279 Corbis: Ron Perry / Transtock (bl). 282 Getty Images: Pete Seaward (ftl). 286 Corbis: The Bettmann Archive (fbl). Getty Images: Peter Macdiarmid (cl). Giles Chapman Library: (ftl). 287 Art Tech Picture Agency. Louwman Museum: (ftl). Giles Chapman Library: (fbr). Motoring Picture Library / National Motor Museum: (c). 288 Art Tech Picture Agency: (tc). 290 Renault Communication: (c). 292 Art Tech Picture Agency: (fbl). Giles Chapman Library. 293 Art Tech Picture Agency: (ca, ftl, fcra, fcr). Giles Chapman Library: (tc, fcl, bl, cb). 294 LAT Photographic: (fcla). Giles Chapman Library: (cra, c, fbl). 295 Alamy Images: Phil Talbot (ftl). Art Tech Picture Agency. Giles Chapman Library. 296 Giles Chapman Library: (fbl). 298 Corbis: Raymond Reuter / Sygma (cl). Giles Chapman Library. 299 The Advertising Archives: (c). Giles Chapman Library: (fbr). 300 Art Tech Picture Agency: (cr). Giles Chapman Library: (c, fcla). Orphan Work: (fcl). 301 Art Tech Picture Agency: (cra, fcl, ftr). Giles

Chapman Library: (ftl). 304 Giles Chapman Library: (ftl). 308 Motoring Picture Library / National Motor Museum: James Mann (c). 312 Alamy Images: Transtock Inc. (fclb); Motoring Picture Library (fcra); izmostock (c). Giles Chapman Library: (fbr). 313 Alamy Images: Robert Steinbarth (ftr). Giles Chapman Library: (fcrb). 314 Corbis: Suzuki Motor Corporation / Frank Rumpenhorst / epa (cl). Giles Chapman Library: (br, ftl). 315 Giles Chapman Library. Suzuki Motor Corporation. 316 Giles Chapman Library. Magic Car Pics: (fcra). courtesy Mahindra Reva: (tc). 317 Giles Chapman Library. Malcolm McKay: (fcl). 318 PA Photos: Gautam Singh / AP (ftl). 326 Corbis: Car Culture (cl); Schlegelmilch (fbl). Motoring Picture Library / National Motor Museum: (ftl). 327 Alamy Images: Phil Talbot (ftl, fbr). Corbis: Staff / epa (fcl). 328 Art Tech Picture Agency: (ftr). 329 LAT Photographic: (fcr) Giles Chapman Library: (ftl, fclb). 331 Giles Chapman Library: (frca). 332 Giles Chapman Library: (ftl). 336 LAT Photographic: Steven Tee (c). 340 Alamy Images: Transtock Inc. (fcrb); Drive Images (fbl). Ford Motor Company Limited: (bc). Giles Chapman Library: (ca, fclb). Motoring Picture Library / National Motor Museum: (fcla). 341 Alamy Images: Drive Images (fcra). Corbis: Car Culture (cla). LAT Photographic: (ca). Giles Chapman Library. Nissan Motor Company: (tr). 344 Bertone: (bc). Ford Motor Company Limited: (flca). Giles Chapman Library: (c, cra). 345 Giles Chapman Library. 347 Mazda Motors UK Ltd: (ftr)

All other images © Dorling Kindersley For further information see: www.dkimages.com

Chapter Opener images:
8-9 Napier 7-passenger Touring
36-37 Bugatti T35B
72-73 Wanderer W25K
104-105 Chrysler Town and Country
134-135 Oldsmobile F-88 Concept
176-177 Ford Mustang
208-209 Citroën DS21 Convertible
240-241 Lamborghini Countach 25th Anniversary
278-279 Mitsubishi SST
308-309 Mini Cooper

The publisher would like to thank the following people for their assistance with this book:

Steve Crozier and Nicola Erdpresser for design assistance; Catherine Thomas for editorial assistance; Jyoti Sachdev, Sakshi Saluja, and Malavika Talukder for arranging the India photoshoot; Caroline Hunt for proofreading; and Helen Peters for the index.

The publisher would also like to thank the following companies and individuals for their generosity in allowing Dorling Kindersley access to their vehicles and engines for photography:

Alex Pilkington
Audi UK: www.audi.co.uk
Beaulieu National Motor Museum, Brockenhurst, Hampshire: www.beaulieu.co.uk
Brands Hatch Morgans, Borough Green, Kent: www.morgan-cars.com
Chris Williams, The DeLorean Owners Club UK: www.deloreans.co.uk
Chrysler UK, Slough, Berkshire: www.chrysler.co.uk
Claremont Corvette, Snodland, Kent: www.corvette.co.uk
Colin Spong
DK Engineering, Chorleywood, Hertfordshire: www.dkeng.co.uk
Eagle E-Types, East Sussex: www.eaglegb.com
Gilbert and Anna East
Haynes International Motor Museum, Yeovil, Somerset: www.haynesmotormuseum.com
Heritage Motoring Club of India (HMCI), New Delhi, India: Mr. HW Bhatnagar, Mr. Avinash Grehwal, Mr. SB Jatti, Mr. Ashok Kaicker, Mr. Sandeep Katari, Mr. Ranjit Malik, Mr. Bahadur Singh, Mr. Navinder Singh, Mr. Harshpati Singhania, Mr. Diljeet Titus www.hmci.org
Honda Institute, Slough, Berkshire: www.honda.co.uk
Jaguar Daimler Heritage Trust, Coventry, Warwickshire: www.jdht.com
John Mould
P & A Wood, Rolls Royce and Bentley Heritage Dealers, Dunmow, Essex: www.pa-wood.co.uk
Peter Harris

Philip Jones, Byron International, Tadworth, Surrey: www.allastonmartin.com
Porsche Cars (Great Britain) Ltd, Reading, Berkshire: www.porsche.com/uk/
Roger Dudding
Roger Florio
Silver Arrows Automobiles, Classic Mercedes-Benz, London: www.silverarrows.co.uk
Silver Lady Services Ltd, Rolls Royce and Bentley Car Services, Bournemouth, Dorset: www.silverladyservices.co.uk
Tata Motors, Mumbai, India: www.tatamotors.com
Tim Colbert
Timothy Dutton, Ivan Dutton Ltd, Aylesbury, Buckinghamshire: www.duttonbugatti.co.uk
Tuckett Brothers, North Marston, Buckinghamshire: www.tuckettbrothers.co.uk

Dorling Kindersley would also like to thank Editor-in-chief Giles Chapman for his unstinting support throughout the making of this book.

Giles Chapman is an award-winning writer and commentator on the industry, history, and culture of cars. A former editor of Classic & Sports Car, the world's best-selling classic car magazine, he has written over 15 books, including Chapman's Car Compendium and DK's Illustrated Encyclopedia of Extraordinary Automobiles, and has edited or contributed to many more besides.